Armenia and Azerbaijan

If the Homeland is small, one dreams it large.

Rubén Darío, *Retorno*

Armenia and Azerbaijan
Anatomy of a Rivalry

Laurence Broers

EDINBURGH
University Press

Edinburgh University Press is one of the leading university presses in the UK. We publish academic books and journals in our selected subject areas across the humanities and social sciences, combining cutting-edge scholarship with high editorial and production values to produce academic works of lasting importance. For more information visit our website: edinburghuniversitypress.com

© Laurence Broers, 2019, 2021

Edinburgh University Press Ltd
The Tun – Holyrood Road, 12(2f) Jackson's Entry, Edinburgh EH8 8PJ

First published in hardback by Edinburgh University Press 2019

Typeset in 11/14 Sabon by
Servis Filmsetting Ltd, Stockport, Cheshire

A CIP record for this book is available from the British Library

ISBN 978 1 4744 5052 2 (hardback)
ISBN 978 1 4744 5053 9 (paperback)
ISBN 978 1 4744 5054 6 (webready PDF)
ISBN 978 1 4744 5055 3 (epub)

The right of Laurence Broers to be identified as the author of this work has been asserted in accordance with the Copyright, Designs and Patents Act 1988, and the Copyright and Related Rights Regulations 2003 (SI No. 2498).

Contents

Acknowledgements	vi
Maps, Figures and Tables	x
Terminology	xii
Introduction: Beyond 'Frozen Conflict'	1
1. A Violent Unravelling	17
2. Questionable Borders	48
3. Borderland into Cornerstone	84
4. Displacements	121
5. Regime Politics and Rivalry	152
6. Truncated Asymmetry	185
7. An Exception in Eurasia	213
8. Unrecognised Reality	249
9. 'Land for Peace'	276
Afterword: Rivalry Unending?	308
Notes	317
Index	385

Acknowledgements

For authors writing on conflict acknowledgements are always fraught. Many of the dozens of people who helped me on the path to this book may disagree vehemently with the argument herein. I can only emphasise its provisional and contestable nature, and underline that responsibility for its flaws remains mine alone.

This book came out of my work at Conciliation Resources (CR), a London-based peacebuilding organisation (www.c-r.org). I am greatly indebted to the vision and counsel of CR's executive director, Jonathan Cohen, conversations with whom led to the germination of this project. I am grateful to Andy Carl, Rachel Clogg, Rhona Miller, Mira Sovakar and Juliet Williams for their moral support. It has also been a privilege to work with Marc Behrendt, Jenny Norton and Siegfried Woeber, to whom I give thanks. In surviving to book stage, the project owes a great deal to the inspiration, advice and support at critical junctures of the following individuals: Bhavna Dave, Thomas de Waal, Salpi Ghazarian, Tabib Huseynov and Gerard Toal. I am deeply grateful to each of them.

In Armenia, I would like to thank Konstantin Geodakyan, Natalie and Hakop Harutyunyan, Levon Kalantar, and Harutyun Mansuryan of the Media Initiatives Center, with special thanks to Nune Sargsyan for advice, perspective and hospitality. For a generous supply of analytical insight and for sharing office space I am grateful to Richard Giragosian. I am likewise greatly indebted to the Caucasus Institute and the insights of its director Alexander Iskandaryan and former deputy director Sergey Minasyan. My thanks also go to Tatul Hakobyan of Civilitas for sharing his encyclopaedic knowledge. I would also like to thank the

Acknowledgements

following individuals who helped me in myriad ways while in the field in Armenia: Lara Aharonyan, Jonathan Aves, Artak Ayunts, Laura Baghdasarian, Judith Farnworth, Mark Grigorian, Nina Iskandaryan, Edgar Khachatrian, Hranush Kharatyan, Kathy Leach, Charles Lonsdale, Roubina Margossian, Ashot Melyan, Tigran Mkrtchyan, Oksana Musaelyan, Artur Sakunts, Alex Sardar, David Shahnazaryan, Araik Shirinyan, Timothy Straight, Naira Sultanyan, Gevorg Ter-Gabrielyan and Maria Titizian. (In spelling Armenian surnames I have tried to be consistent with personal preferences, common usage or original sources, hence I use both -ian and -yan.)

In Azerbaijan, I give special thanks to Avaz Hasanov and Mehriban Mammadova for sharing wisdom and hospitality. I am greatly indebted to Arif Yunusov and Leyla Yunus for their generosity in sharing their knowledge, intellect and insight over many years. My thanks go too to Ilham Safarov and his colleagues: Myrsadyg Agayev, Naila Babayeva, Rahman Badalov, Aliya Haqverdi, Toghrul Jufarli, Shahin Rzayev and Ayaz Salayev. I would also like to thank the following individuals for assistance in the field in Azerbaijan: Arzu Abdullayeva, Shamkhal Abilov, Leila Alieva, Sevinc Aliyeva, Zardusht Alizade, Bakhtiyar Aslanov, Akram Aylisli, Rauf Garagozov, Ilgar Gasimov, Maryam Haji-Ismayilova, Jamil Hasanli, Novella Jafaroglu-Appelbaum, Kerim Kerimli, Ceyhun Mahmudlu, Kamal Makili-Aliyev, Polad Mammadov, Xamis Masimov, Tofig Musayev, Eldar Namazov, Atakhan Pashayev, Gulshan Pashayeva, Akif Nagi Qazakh, and Irfan Siddiq. I am particularly grateful to Adalet Tahirzade for his kind permission to feature the cover of his 2003 book *The Path to Liberation and Unity* as an illustration, and to Turgut Gambar for helping me with translation.

In Nagorny Karabakh I would like to thank Gegham Baghdasarian and his colleagues at the Stepanakert Press Club, with special thanks to Anahit Danielyan for hosting me in September 2014. I am very grateful to the following individuals for their unfailing assistance over many years: Svetlana Danielyan, Masis Mayilian, Karen Ohanjanian, Karine Ohanyan and Albert Voskanyan. I also thank Iosif and Karine Adamian, Armine Aleksanyan, Artak Beglaryan, Vera Grigorian, Naira

Hayrumyan, Margarita Karamyan, Tigran Kyureghyan and Saro Saroyan.

For conversations and exchanges that have enriched my thinking about the issues dealt with in this book I would like to thank the following individuals: Caner Alper, Karena Avedissian, Günther Bächler, Donnacha Ó Beacháin, Mehmet Binay, Carey Cavanaugh, Roxana Cristescu, Jacques Faure, Martha Freeman, Magdalena Frichova Grono, Phil Gamaghelyan, Arzu Geybulla, Sevil Huseynova, Sossie Kasbarian, Arsen Kharatyan, Sergey Markedonov, Cigdem Mater, Anna Matveeva, Marina Nagai, Murad Nasibbeyli, Craig Oliphant, Kevork Oskanian, Amanda Paul, Dennis Sammut, Arsène Saparov, Gwendolyn Sasse, Silvia Serrano, Anahit Shirinyan, Zaur Shiriyev, Jale Sultanli, Ronald Grigor Suny, Olesya Vartanyan, Cory Welt, Ulrike Ziemer, Mikayel Zolyan and Christoph Zürcher. I am greatly appreciative of the scholarly collaborations I have been fortunate to enjoy with Ceyhun Mahmudlu, Anna Ohanyan, Jean-François Ratelle, Mairbek Vatchagaev and Galina Yemelianova: thank you for broadening my horizons.

I also thank all those in public office who facilitated research they had no reason to believe would support their positions on the conflict. I wish to acknowledge the openness to my enquiries of the Armenian and Azerbaijani embassies in London, and the Ministries of Foreign Affairs in both states. The representatives of the de facto Nagorno-Karabakh Republic in Stepanakert, and Robert Avetisyan of its representation in Washington, have been similarly helpful.

Those who read and generously commented on draft chapters helped me to clarify my thinking. I am very grateful to Nina Caspersen, Thomas de Waal, Tabib Huseynov, Armine Ishkanian, Famil Ismayilov, Harrison King, Jo Laycock, David Lewis, Elene Melikishvili, Emil Sanamyan, Licínia Simão, Gerard Toal, Bettina Vaughan, Siegfried Woeber and Eliza Wright. At Edinburgh University Press I thank Jen Daly, Joannah Duncan, Sarah Foyle and Adela Rauchova for their enthusiasm for this project and support in seeing it to fruition. I am grateful to Glory Hall for designing the maps and Alfonso and María-Paola Rizo for advice on the epigraph. Lastly and most of all, I would like to

Acknowledgements

express my profound gratitude to my parents Robert and Patricia for their considerable forbearance and steadfast support of this and many other endeavours. I dedicate this book to the memory of my sister, Anita.

Maps, Figures and Tables

Maps

1	The South Caucasus	xiv
2	Nagorny Karabakh	xv

Figures

2.1 Visualising 'Greater Azerbaijan': President Elchibey stares out from an expansive Azerbaijani homeland on the cover of this 2003 book, whose title reads *The Path to Liberation and Unity*   61

2.2 A 2015 wall calendar commemorating 'Wilsonian Armenia'   70

3.1A and B Policing 'augmented Armenia': graffiti at bus stops in Yerevan, 2015   103

3.2 Visualising Azerbaijanism: poster board of Heydar Aliyev, Sheki, 2011   113

5.1 Armenia and Azerbaijan Freedom House Ratings, 1991–2018   156

5.2 World Bank Governance Indicators: Voice and Accountability in Armenia and Azerbaijan, 1996–2016   157

7.1 Russia's pivotal deterrence between Armenia and Azerbaijan   246

8.1 Rejecting 'compliant Armenia': school classroom wall, Lachin, 2014   271

9.1 Poster-board, Meghri, Armenia, 2015. The legend reads: 'Armenians, Meghri is the door to your home!' 290

Tables

2.1 Traditions and territorialisations in Azerbaijani geopolitical culture 78
2.2 Traditions and territorialisations in Armenian geopolitical culture 79
3.1 Territorial visions and conceptions of Nagorny Karabakh in post-Soviet Armenian geopolitical culture 91
3.2 Territorial visions and conceptions of Nagorny Karabakh in post-Soviet Azerbaijani geopolitical culture 105
4.1 General development indicators in early Soviet Armenia and Azerbaijan (%) 128
4.2 Armenian (ArmCP) and Azerbaijani (AzCP) Communist Party membership by nationality (%) in major census years 131
4.3 Azerbaijani population growth in regions of the ArmSSR, 1959–79 136
6.1 Armenian and Azerbaijani demographic indicators compared, 1990–2015 194
7.1 Schemas of Russian policy towards the Armenian–Azerbaijani rivalry 240
8.1 Domestic income, expenditure and interstate credits in the de facto Nagorno-Karabakh Republic, 2007–16 (in current US dollars) 259
8.2 Traditions and territorialisations of Nagorny Karabakh, 1991–present 270
9.1 Armenian–Azerbaijani peace proposals discussed by the Minsk Group, 1997–present 286

Terminology

In my earlier work, I used the term 'Nagorny Karabakh conflict' because it avoided embroilment in the naming and numbering of the belligerents, and because it underscored that the conflict is, in essence, territorial. However, the space and scope of the conflict have never been limited to Nagorny Karabakh itself, and as I argue in this book, it is the interstate dimension that has become dominant since the 1994 ceasefire. In this work, I therefore refer to the Armenian–Azerbaijani conflict, while being aware that this term conflates distinct inter-communal, intra-state, and interstate layers.

The terminology describing the territory at the heart of the conflict is confusingly diverse and politically fraught. I prefer Nagorny Karabakh as – from a Russian point of view – linguistically more correct, although it is more widely referred to as Nagorno-Karabakh. This is an adaptation into English from the Russian adjectival form *Nagorno-Karabakhskaya Avtonomnaya Oblast'*, literally meaning the 'autonomous region of mountainous Karabakh' and describing the Soviet-era autonomous region that existed from 1923 to 1991. Nagorny Karabakh denotes a smaller territory than a pre-twentieth-century understanding of Karabakh encompassing both highland and lowland areas. However, in order to avoid laborious repetition of the word 'Nagorny', I use the terms 'Karabakh' and 'Nagorny Karabakh' interchangeably.

I use the 'Nagorno-Karabakh' form only when it is part of an official name or title, for example when referring to the unrecognised republic that exists in the area today, the Nagorno-Karabakh Republic. This entity changed its name in 2017 to the Republic of Artsakh, evoking an ancient Armenian province, although both terms were and remain official. I retain the earlier term in this book as the still more widely used name at the time of writing. I do not use the qualifiers 'de facto' or 'unrecognised' at every mention of the republic and its institutions, but underscore here that no United Nations member-state – including Armenia – recognises it.

Since the ceasefire of 1994 place-names in and around Nagorny Karabakh have become intensely politicised, as Armenians and Azerbaijanis have developed rival topographies for the same space. Armenian and Azerbaijani maps today depict cartographies that are distinct in every way, from district boundaries to the names of settlements. Outsiders have few palatable options, other than to continue using the place-names in most popular use at the beginning of the conflict in 1988. I therefore refer to the capital of Nagorny Karabakh by its Armenian name, Stepanakert, and not its Azerbaijani variant, Khankendi. I refer to what was the territory's second city by its Azerbaijani name, Shusha, and not its Armenian variant, Shushi. Place-name choices were not always so zero-sum. Before the conflict some settlements in Karabakh were widely known by two names, such as the village of Dashalty/Karintak. Duality in place-naming can thus also be read as a local tradition reflecting distinct but compatible geographies.

This is not the case, however, in the occupied territories within the de facto jurisdiction of the Nagorno-Karabakh Republic, where the effacing of what were Azerbaijani settlements has been ongoing for twenty-five years. Previously overwhelmingly Azerbaijani-populated towns, such as Lachin and Kelbajar, are now known to their settler inhabitants by Armenian names (Berdzor and Karvajar respectively). In this work I use the Azerbaijani nomenclature for these areas, and indicate at first usage their current Armenian equivalent in brackets. I acknowledge that this will be objectionable to more partisan readers, as either the imposition of a retrograde geography that no longer meaningfully exists, or the legitimation of an occupational regime. My intent is neither, but to juxtapose place-names that are currently experienced in complete isolation from each other. The imagined worlds of Lachin and Berdzor, for example, could not be further apart today, and this distance is set only to grow for the foreseeable future. Resolution of this conflict, however, requires that one day these worlds become more aware of one another, and eventually meet.

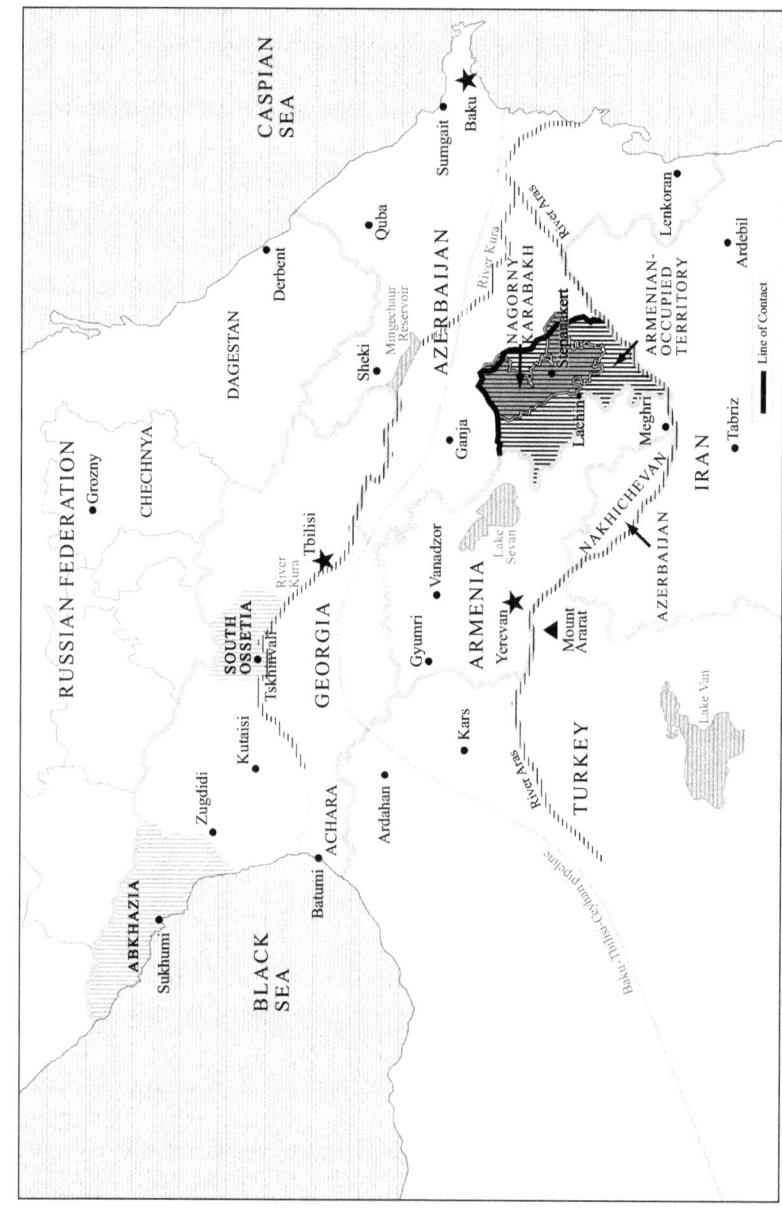

Map 1 The South Caucasus. (Place-names in contested areas follow popular pre-conflict usage.)

Map 2 Nagorny Karabakh.

Introduction: Beyond 'Frozen Conflict'

In the early hours of 2 April 2016, while President Ilham Aliyev of Azerbaijan and President Serzh Sargsyan of Armenia were returning from a nuclear security summit in Washington, fighting broke out in Nagorny Karabakh, the territory disputed between the two states. As the presidents' aircraft wound their ways home, Azerbaijani forces penetrated Armenian positions at three locations along the approximately 200-kilometre Line of Contact forming the frontline. For Armenians, the line was a defensive perimeter and border – even if internationally unrecognised – of a fledgling, self-determined republic. For Azerbaijanis, it was the frontline of occupying forces far inside the homeland, a violation of international law and a deep psychological scar. It had held fast without moving for twenty-two years, longer than many of the conscripts manning the fortifications had been alive.

Dozens of servicemen were killed in the opening hours of the attack, as Armenian positions were pushed back in several areas. For the next four days Armenian and Azerbaijani forces pounded each other in intensive fighting, some of it showcasing new high-tech weaponry. Azerbaijan deployed state-of-the-art, Israeli-manufactured kamikaze drones; one hit a bus bringing volunteers from the town of Sisian in Armenia, killing seven. Armenian counter-attacks recouped most of the positions initially lost, inflicting heavy losses, but – for the first time since 1994 – Azerbaijan recaptured slivers of territory. Some 200 people lost their lives before Russia brokered a ceasefire.[1] For a few days a rarely remembered conflict flashed across the world's newsrooms. Yet although pundits warned plausibly of contagion, April's outbreak subsided quickly. After a short-lived flurry of diplomacy, Armenian–Azerbaijani tensions rapidly disappeared from the international news roll amid violence in Syria and 2016's political earthquakes, Brexit and the election of US President Donald Trump.

Obscurity and danger vied in the competing analyses of what had happened. Was this still a 'frozen conflict', a regrettable but ultimately low-priority hangover from the collapse of the Soviet Union? Or did Armenian–Azerbaijani fighting signify a new front – another 'Russian land grab' – in the new geopolitics of confrontation between the West and President Vladimir Putin?[2] Did any outside actor have the key to solving the conflict? Or was another war – a fourth conflagration in more than a century of Armenian–Azerbaijani contestation – likely or even inevitable, pointing to the existence of long-term hatred between Armenians and Azerbaijanis? These competing storylines served notice of deeper policy and analytical challenges. Where should this long-forgotten conflict be placed on the spectrum between justifiable neglect and the risk of a small but dangerous war? Why does the Armenian–Azerbaijani conflict still continue? How can its resilience be understood in terms of dynamic action and local agency – rather than as a conveniently 'frozen conflict' or an outgrowth of geopolitics? What are the obstacles to peace?

Both obscure and dangerous, the Armenian–Azerbaijani conflict for control of Nagorny Karabakh, an area smaller than Palestine or Corsica, has lingered on the very edge of Europe for more than three decades. It is the longest-running conflict in post-Soviet Eurasia, outliving the Soviet Union, the false dawn of Russian–Western rapprochement in the 1990s, and more recent Russian–Western confrontations. A perennial second-order priority for outside powers, it has been repeatedly eclipsed by conflicts in nearby Chechnya, Georgia, Ukraine and the Middle East. Yet the Armenian–Azerbaijani Line of Contact is one of only three such heavily militarised frontlines in the world, alongside the Line of Control between Indian and Pakistani forces in Kashmir, and the Military Demarcation Line between North and South Korea. What the Armenian–Azerbaijani confrontation lacks in nuclear weapons, it compensates for in geopolitical sensitivity. Tangled patterns of geopolitical alliance and enmity in the volatile South Caucasus mean that in the event of all-out war, spillover could be difficult to contain.

The positions of the parties present themselves as deceptively simple. For Azerbaijanis, the conflict is the unfinished business of the collapse of the Soviet Union and the re-emergence of an independent Azerbaijani republic in 1991. Regaining jurisdiction over Nagorny Karabakh is Azerbaijan's foundational mission, without which Azerbaijani statehood and identity will remain incomplete. Azerbaijan defines the conflict as irredentist in nature and its quarrel is with Armenia – not the Armenians of Karabakh. The latter are parsed in Azerbaijani thinking as one of two equal communities, alongside Karabakh Azerbaijanis forcibly exiled from the territory. Azerbaijan pledges autonomy to Karabakh Armenians within a reintegrated Azerbaijani state as the only appropriate resolution of the conflict. It has borne the cost of a massive humanitarian disaster in the form of hundreds of thousands of internally displaced persons, as well as Azerbaijani refugees from Armenia. Under a constant stream of criticism for its human rights record, restoring territorial integrity is a rare and emblematic moment where international legal opinion – symbolised in four United Nations Security Council resolutions dating from 1993 – and the claims of Azerbaijan's ruling elite appear as one.

For Armenians the self-determination of Nagorny Karabakh in 1991 as an Armenian entity separate from Azerbaijan is a question of historical justice. It finally rectified – through popular will – the decision by Soviet totalitarians to give the territory to Azerbaijan in the early 1920s. Armenians see the campaign that emerged in 1987 to unify Karabakh and Armenia as peaceful, yet met with organised pogroms killing dozens of Armenians in the Azerbaijani cities of Sumgait, Kirovabad (today's Ganja) and Baku in 1988–90. They believe that the restoration of Azerbaijani jurisdiction over Nagorny Karabakh would risk another annihilation of an Armenian population in their historical homeland, triggering memories of genocide in Ottoman Turkey. Few signs of once vibrant Armenian communities remain elsewhere in sovereign Azerbaijan. For the Armenians of Karabakh the war of 1992–4 was a war of independence. Since 1991 they have pursued a separate political identity in an unrecognised republic, the Nagorno-Karabakh Republic (NKR). A position hardening over time sees the return of any territories won in a war of self-defence to Azerbaijani jurisdiction as unacceptable.

Understanding Territorial Conflicts in the Former USSR

The Armenian–Azerbaijani conflict is one of several that emerged in the Soviet Union's twilight years, alongside others in Abkhazia and South Ossetia, two territories that seceded from Georgia in 1992–3; Transdniestria, which seceded from Moldova in 1992; and Chechnya, which inflicted defeat on Russia in the First Chechen War of 1994–6, to later succumb in the Second Chechen War of 1999–2009. As a cluster of conflicts with broadly proximate geographic, historical and institutional settings, they have often been grouped and thought about together. Two traditions have shaped understandings of these conflicts since their emergence in the early 1990s.

A comparative tradition among scholars has found in the Caucasus – a region also rich in interethnic relations that remained peaceful – a treasure trove for the analysis of factors mediating outcomes of war or peace. With the exception of Chechnya, the conflicts emerging in the 1990s have attracted more attention as a set than any single one of them has on its own.[3] Comparative studies have rejected explanations of Caucasus conflicts based on economic disparities or mountainous terrain, to stress instead what Christoph Zürcher calls the common 'script of post-Soviet wars'.[4] This script emphasises the common origins of these conflicts in causal factors at work in the Caucasus in the late 1980s–90s: the ethnic demography institutionalised by the Soviet state, the security vacuum following its collapse, the weakness of successor states and incompatible nationalist ideologies.

A second tradition also finds similarity in the conflicts of the former USSR, but as prisms of geopolitical forces competing for its south-western peripheries, where all extant territorial conflicts are located. Since the mid-2000s this shared neighbourhood has emerged as the epicentre of a revived competitive geopolitics between Russia, regarding the former Soviet republics as a 'near abroad' subject to its privileged interests, and the Euro-Atlantic powers, seeking to extend a European security community.[5] In 2014 the addition of conflict in eastern Ukraine with open Russian involvement and Russia's annexation of Crimea have solidified understandings of 'frozen conflict' – aggregated into 'Putin's frozen conflicts' – as part of a wider repertoire of coercive diplomacy in a higher-order geopolitical contest.[6] Styling itself as commonsense realism, this tradition suffuses media commentary and is popular in policy and some scholarly analysis.[7]

The rationale for this book is that neither perspective serves us well in understanding the Armenian–Azerbaijani conflict today. In terms of the balance of power between the belligerents, the scale of forces deployed and the sustainability of real destructive potential, the Armenian–Azerbaijani conflict presents an entirely different picture to other Eurasian conflicts dating from the 1990s. New dynamics are at work that are no longer meaningfully 'post-Soviet', but rather thoroughly contemporary. Yet the Armenian–Azerbaijani conflict is also a significant exception to the competitive geopolitics of post-Soviet Eurasia today. While the conflict is certainly not free of competitive influence-seeking by outside powers, reading across from conflicts in Georgia and Ukraine involves problematic conflations of history, politics and geography. Rather than folding the Armenian–Azerbaijani conflict into interpretive routines charting a single arc of conflict from the Dniester to the Caspian, this study argues for contextual difference, local logic and endogenous causalities. All conflicts of course have their unique aspects, none of which make them immune to comparison. Yet Armenian–Azerbaijani exceptionality is a surprisingly consistent observation across comparative studies of post-Soviet conflicts.[8] I summarise this exceptionality here in terms of six distinguishing features marking the Armenian–Azerbaijani conflict as an outlier among conflicts in post-Soviet Eurasia today. Teasing out their implications forms the research agenda addressed in this book.

A first distinction is that the Armenian–Azerbaijani conflict was the first territorial dispute to appear in the Soviet Union's twilight years. It appeared already at the beginning of 1988, before the collapse of the Soviet Union had become imaginable. This chronology poses challenges for theories emphasising the momentum of systemic collapse, and the security vacuum that followed, as a cause of conflict.

Second, through its early stages violence was not contained to the area disputed between Armenians and Azerbaijanis, Nagorny Karabakh, but encompassed a multitude of locations across Armenia and Azerbaijan. This in turn questions the overwhelming focus on Soviet institutions of territorial autonomy in Nagorny Karabakh itself as the source of conflict.

A third distinguishing feature is that no other post-Soviet war spilled beyond the territory originally under dispute to such disastrous effect for the losing party, Azerbaijan. In 1992–4 Armenian forces carved out and occupied a belt of territories surrounding Nagorny Karabakh, doubling its size, and expelled their Azerbaijani inhabitants. This means, on the one hand, that humiliation marks this conflict like no other in Eurasia. On the other, it has generated a dynamic post-war interaction of differing territorial regimes. Self-determination, the clarion call of the 1990s, became increasingly blurred with occupation.

A fourth distinctive aspect is the conflict's atypical structure. Post-Soviet territorial conflicts in the 1990s usually ended in a standoff between a secessionist entity and the internationally recognised state from which it had seceded – referred to here as the 'parent state'. While an unrecognised republic, the NKR, was also founded in 1991, the Armenian–Azerbaijani conflict became embedded at the interstate level between Armenia and Azerbaijan. Both are members of the United Nations, Organization for Security and Co-operation in Europe (OSCE) and Council of Europe, and participants in the Eastern Partnership of the European Union (EU) and NATO's Partnership for Peace. This has diffused the conflict across a wide scope of international theatres and issues, made it difficult for international organisations to take sides between two member-states, and alleviated the pressures on the NKR as an unrecognised entity.

Structural distinction ties into a fifth distinguishing attribute in Russia's atypical role. While Russia brokered the

Armenian–Azerbaijani ceasefire in May 1994, it did not manage – as it did in Abkhazia, South Ossetia and Transdniestria – to insert Russian-led peacekeeping forces into the post-war context. Neither does it have 'compatriots' in the form of ethnic Russian or Russian-speaking populations in Nagorny Karabakh deprived of alternative citizenship. While present in Armenia, Russia has no forces directly engaged in the conflict area. The Armenian–Azerbaijani ceasefire is uniquely self-regulating, and Russia pursues friendly relations with both parties.

A final distinctive feature is the idiosyncratic nature of the conflict's mediation structure. Beginning in 1992 the OSCE's Minsk Group, led since 1997 by a permanent troika of France, Russia and the United States, has brokered talks. It consequently brings together three permanent members of the United Nations Security Council, who also happen to be locked in geopolitical competition in Georgia, Ukraine and the Middle East, into a mediation structure predicated on cooperation. Despite constant domestic criticism, the continuation of this multilateral structure, which does not leave them alone with Russia, generates what is perhaps the sole moment of consensus between Armenia and Azerbaijan today. Outside of this consensus are the de facto authorities of the NKR, who since the late 1990s have had no seat at the negotiating table. Although they are briefed by the Minsk Group, the negotiations about the political status of the Karabakh Armenians – the issue that lies at the heart of the conflict – take place without their participation. By the same token, they bear no responsibility for either the effectiveness or outcomes of the Minsk Group negotiations.

These features distinguish the Armenian–Azerbaijani conflict from others emerging in the last years of the Soviet Union. In seeking to understand their impact, this book does not provide a new chronicle or history of the Armenian–Azerbaijani conflict. Rather, its aims are interpretive. It takes seriously the conflict's outlier status through two methodological perspectives. The first relates to the understanding of geopolitics.

A Critical Geopolitical Analysis

All observers agree on the importance of geopolitics to the Armenian–Azerbaijani conflict. Lying along the troubled fault-line between Russia's contested 'near abroad', the EU's Eastern Partnership, and the interests of regional powers Turkey and Iran, the conflict is framed as a 'major pressure point' in Eurasia's competitive geopolitics by one account.[9] Credible scenarios depict how the resumption of war between Armenia and Azerbaijan could drag outside powers into a wider conflagration. A constant flow of policy research refracts the conflict through a quintet of metropolitan gazes emanating from Moscow, Washington, Brussels, Ankara and Tehran, emphasising opportunities and risks for their respective foreign policies. This is a strategy also pursued by the belligerents, as they seek to embed their respective causes within the agendas of powerful outsiders. This continual framing of the Armenian–Azerbaijani antagonism as an object of external interest often threatens to overwhelm understandings of the conflict on its own terms.

This study takes a different approach, drawing on the conceptual foundations of *critical geopolitics*. A traditional view of geopolitics sees it as an approach to the world 'as it really is': a rational-scientific articulation of geography to power that explains the rise, fall and relations of states. Contemporary realist perspectives see geopolitics as a form of statecraft, circumscribed by the objective realpolitik of material and military endowments, geography, proximity and alliance options. Emerging in the 1990s at the meeting point of geography, critical theory and international relations, critical geopolitics is a scholarly tradition that rejects assumptions of inherent realism. This tradition does not see geopolitics as a neutral reflection of realities 'out there' or an innocent body of knowledge, but as a self-selecting assemblage of actors and practices competing to define spaces in the service of power.[10] Scholars in this tradition reject the detached objectivism of conventional geopolitical discourse and strive to avoid the seamless reproduction of categories of practice as categories of analysis in academic writing. A critical geopolitics lens emphasises instead the situated origins of geopolitical knowledge and discourse, in order to expose the power relations behind portrayals of putatively objective geographic, historical and ethno-demographic factors. It interrogates visual cultures and strategies of representation, such as maps, that naturalise spatial imaginaries as geographic facts.

A fundamental premise of this study is that critical geopolitical analysis can give us invaluable purchase on the reified categories of long-running conflicts. I use a critical geopolitics lens to examine three sets of categories in the Armenian–Azerbaijani conflict. The first are the categories of 'Armenia' and 'Azerbaijan', neither of which has been territorially stable or immobile in modern history. Neither republic had existed in their Soviet borders prior to 1920, while other 'Armenias' and 'Azerbaijans' continued to exist – whether in physical or mental landscapes – beyond Soviet borders after that time. I explore these fractures through the prism of what critical geopolitics calls *geopolitical culture*: the collected myths and narratives through which elites and the wider populace conceptualise their state's place, origins, ideals and allegiances in a world of states.[11] Different geopolitical traditions tell different stories – and make different sense – of the state's spatial identity, and compete to define its geopolitical culture.[12] This study disaggregates Armenian and Azerbaijani geopolitical cultures, in order to expose the historical origins of differing and incompatible commitments to borders.

The second set of categories analysed here are those used to connote the contested territory of Nagorny Karabakh. Over the quarter-century since the ceasefire of 12 May 1994, military lines of control may have remained stable – at least until 2016 – but the spatial and cognitive boundaries of the territory originally under dispute have been anything but still. On the Armenian side the contested Soviet delimitation of Nagorny Karabakh became submerged within a wider wartime space incorporating territorial conquests. In Azerbaijan, Nagorny Karabakh was expunged from the national map, yet mediascapes, political rhetoric and the teaching of history increasingly embedded a central role for Armenians in defining Azerbaijan's historical, political and spatial coordinates. Karabakh is consequently a moving object, creeping from the geographic margins to the conceptual core of Armenian and Azerbaijani geopolitical cultures and transforming both in the process. I chart these movements and the plural and evolving meanings ascribed to the contested space at the heart of the conflict.

The third set of categories relates to forced displacement. The Armenian–Azerbaijani conflict entailed the mass forced displacement of more than a million people, dwarfing similar movements in other post-Soviet theatres of the 1990s. The scope of displacement was exceptional: people of both (and other) nationalities were forced out of a wide variety of different settings and socio-cultural milieus spanning the entirety of Soviet Armenian and Azerbaijani homelands. This has implications that have not been sufficiently explored. One is that the contested space of Nagorny Karabakh was only one thread in a broader canvas of demographic unravelling and remaking. Another is that the motivations driving forced expulsion were not necessarily the same, but varied according to local configurations of group relations. This study argues for a differentiated view of forced displacement as a geopolitical practice grounded in variable motives and conceptions of space. This is important not only for a retrospective understanding of displacement but for the trajectories of communities living in displacement today and perspectives on their eventual return.

Reframing Conflict as Rivalry

An understanding of the Armenian–Azerbaijani antagonism today requires more than an unpacking of the territorial issues at stake, complex and dynamic though they are. In order to analyse the superstructure that has built up around these issues over the last quarter-century, this study draws on a second conceptual framework to reframe the conflict as an *enduring rivalry*. The language of rivalry is of course commonly used as a figure of speech to describe Armenian–Azerbaijani relations. But I use it here in a more specific sense associated with a scholarly tradition emerging in international relations theory in the 1990s addressing repeated conflict between the same two states.

An enduring rivalry is a conflict between two states that lasts at least two decades and is punctuated by recursive episodes of violence.[13] Another definition describes the phenomenon as 'a *persistent, fundamental* and *long-term* incompatibility of goals between two states'.[14] The concept comes from the finding that rather than an equal or random distribution of wars among states over the last 200 years, the same small minority of states have fought a wildly disproportionate number of wars – largely, of course, against each other. These are, as Paul Diehl puts it, the 'career criminals' of the world of interstate war.[15] Diehl and Gary Goertz found that if only 5 per cent of interstate rivalries became 'enduring', these accounted for an astonishing 49 per cent of all wars between 1816 and 1992.[16] Enduring rivalries are often caused by geopolitical shocks, such as major wars, dramatic shifts in the distribution of regional or global power, and the emergence of new states. Prominent examples count among them some of the most notorious of militarised competitions, including the Cold War, Arab states and Israel, and India–Pakistan. These cases lend credence to the claim that enduring rivalries are 'the most dangerous form of interstate interaction'.[17]

I use the enduring rivalry concept loosely, according with the needs of a single case study rather than the multivariate statistical analysis of the international relations theorists who conceived the idea. Applied to the Armenian–Azerbaijani conflict today, the enduring rivalry framework offers a number of analytical dividends. First, by substituting *conflict* with *rivalry* as the framework of analysis, it avoids the dichotomies of 'war/peace' and 'hot/cold conflict' and shifts the analysis from an event-centred focus on war to a process-driven focus on the sustainability of rivalry. This replaces the false image of stasis conjured by the term 'frozen conflict' with the dynamism of strategic rivalry. This move also allows me to shift the question from why the Armenian–Azerbaijani conflict broke out to why the rivalry between the two states has not ended or abated, inviting interpretation of long-term institutional, strategic and international processes beyond the scope of unresolved territorial issues.

Second, unlike the proximate term 'protracted conflict', enduring rivalry refers exclusively to conflict between two states. While the number and agency of the belligerents continues to be disputed by Armenians and Azerbaijanis, it is the interstate dynamic between Armenia and Azerbaijan that is the most strategically salient today. The existence of an unrecognised republic in Nagorny Karabakh – if largely invisible at the policy level – nevertheless retains a vital causal role as the keystone of Armenian commitments to maintaining the rivalry and is included in this analysis. In what follows I refer to the Armenian–Azerbaijani conflict when speaking about the core set of territorial issues and their violent contestation in 1988–94. When referring to broader competitive dynamics building up between Armenia and Azerbaijan since then, I refer to the Armenian–Azerbaijani rivalry.

A third dividend is the opening up of new comparative horizons through similarities not with post-Soviet conflicts but the wider category of enduring rivalries. Of course, comparison needs to avoid crude transpositions and 'apples and oranges' problems, but there are a number of instructive parallels with other rivalries.

Finally, the idea of an enduring rivalry – or 'dangerous dyad', to use another term in the literature – explicitly acknowledges the danger inherent in rivalries of this kind.[18] This challenges the complacency embedded in the terminology of 'frozen conflict' without, however, pre-determining future violence since enduring rivalries can end without war.

The indivisibility of territory as the symbolic and non-fungible property of ethnic groups provides one explanation of why land disputes are more intractable than those over other issues – especially between neighbours. By one account contested territorial issues appear in 81 per cent of all enduring rivalries.[19] Few enduring rivalries develop without some impetus from militarised territorial confrontation, and the more territorial the rivalry, the more severe on average it will be.[20] The Armenian–Azerbaijani rivalry is in this sense a typical one. But while enduring rivalries are often correlated with territorial disputes, not all rivalries revolve around contested territorial issues, such as the Cold War. Not even all rivalries with a strong territorial component remain impervious to termination or abeyance, such as the Greek–Turkish rivalry; in others, such as the Sino-Indian rivalry, territorial issues ebb and flow.[21] It is therefore crucial to extend analysis beyond the territorial factor in order to account for the Armenian–Azerbaijani rivalry's salience and longevity.

To open up these wider perspectives, it is useful to reverse the causal pathway and begin by asking how rivalries end. Simply stated, there are three ways that this can happen. First, domestic attitudinal change, motivated by policy innovation or the arrival on the political scene of new policy entrepreneurs, can challenge prior strategies and public expectations surrounding the rivalry. Second, one rival coerces the other into submission. Third, an external shock, or more gradual change in the surrounding international environment, alters the structural context supporting the status quo. These are not of course mutually exclusive. Domestic policy innovation needs a supportive international environment to be viable; geopolitical shocks may offer windows for coercion. The fundamental question posed by the Armenian–Azerbaijani rivalry today is: why has none of these three routes to rivalry de-escalation been open? This study finds answers in a triadic dynamic between the resilience of authoritarian regimes in both states, Armenia's reduction of a significant power asymmetry with Azerbaijan, and the rivalry's diffusion across multiple, cross-cutting international linkages.

Reframing the Armenian–Azerbaijani conflict as an enduring rivalry allows us – finally – to move on from the stale metaphor of 'frozen conflict'. In realist perspectives and the grand narrative of Russian–Western competition, this term conveniently flattens post-Soviet spaces old and new and affirms a classical geopolitical vision of great powers, spheres of influence and local proxies.[22] This book offers a different view, finding explanations for the durability of the Armenian–Azerbaijani rivalry in the historical legacies and geopolitical cultures of the rivals, the normative preferences of their regimes, the power strategies they pursue and the equilibrium among outside powers that the rivalry between them sustains. These factors have made the Armenian–Azerbaijani rivalry a surprisingly, if imperfectly, stable configuration that has outlived a succession of distinct global and regional geopolitical conjunctures. This book attributes this stability not to impersonal historical forces or the connivance of great powers, but first and foremost to the political strategies pursued by local actors. In doing so, it hopes to overcome the 'altitude problem' of geopolitical analysis from afar, and to situate the agency driving rivalry nearer the ground. This in turn has implications for understanding how the rivalry may end peacefully, by emphasising that it is domestic actors – enabled and supported by outside forces – who must ultimately lead this process.

A critical perspective invites reflexive consideration of the researcher's own experiences and influences. I am an outsider to the Caucasus with no family or religious ties. I speak neither Armenian nor Azerbaijani, and have been able to utilise only a very small number of Azerbaijani and Armenian sources with the help of translation. For printed materials I rely mainly on Russian and English sources, which inevitably introduces questions of perspective and emphasis. I hope that these limitations are balanced by prolonged exposure to the field. For over a decade from 2005 to 2015 I was a frequent visitor to Armenia and Azerbaijan, and in most years to Nagorny Karabakh as well. Most of these visits were conducted while managing civil society-level confidence-building programmes for the London-based peacebuilding organisation Conciliation Resources. All political authorities, de jure and de facto, consensually approved of these programmes. British and European governments funded but did not direct or determine the content of this work – a fact not always appreciated or believed in the South Caucasus. In 2006–8 I worked as the researcher for Armenia and Azerbaijan at the International Secretariat of Amnesty International in London, researching and writing a number of reports on human rights concerns in both states.

This study draws liberally on field notes from my years as a practitioner, as they cover a wide range of interlocutors from across fragmented and often inaccessible social and political settings over a prolonged period of time. In most cases I have preserved the principle of anonymity when referring to what were notes taken during meetings or personal conversations, and not interviews. Occasionally, where a political office-holder was expressing an officially held position I have indicated their identity. Six months of fieldwork and around 100 semi-structured interviews (conducted in Russian or English) in Azerbaijan and Nagorny Karabakh in 2014 and Armenia in 2015 supplemented this experience. I have also drawn on interviews with eyewitnesses of events in 1988–94, conducted in 2012–15 by Conciliation Resources' local partners (Media Initiatives Center, Internews Azerbaijan and the Stepanakert Press Club) for a documentary film series about the conflict, *Parts of a Circle*, supported by the EU.[23]

My experience as a peacebuilding practitioner among Armenian and Azerbaijani media professionals, analysts, youth and others has shaped my outlook. I do not identify with any of the parties to the Armenian–Azerbaijani conflict, however defined. But I am not detached from endeavours by citizens of either nationality to reach across the fundamental divides described in this book. Over more than a decade of engagement, I have been convinced of the many additional factors flowing from the context of militarised competition that threaten Armenians and Azerbaijanis with dangers other than war. This book engages with the many unheard voices in Armenian and Azerbaijani societies who express concern at the rivalry's negative long-term effects on values, political cultures and basic freedoms.

With that said, it is important to emphasise that this study does not attempt to balance or symmetrically juxtapose Armenian and Azerbaijani narratives. External writing on conflict is often charged with false moral equivalence preserving what critics maintain is an artificial but politically expedient balance. I make no claim in this book to be inclusive or representative with regard to the entirety of perspectives that exist on the Armenian–Azerbaijani rivalry today. This aims to be an analytical work informed by social science theories privileging certain kinds of causality and explanatory framework over others. It also approaches the Armenian–Azerbaijani rivalry as it is, and not as we might wish it to become. Given the contentious state of affairs in Armenian–Azerbaijani relations today, it is inevitable that some readers will not find my choices of inclusion and emphasis to their taste. But I hope that readers will judge this book on the relevance of the questions that it poses and the efficacy of its arguments, rather than the completeness of its narrative.

The chapters that follow are part-narrative, part-argumentative essays tackling the unresolved territorial issues left after the

1988–94 conflict period, and the multifaceted dynamics to the enduring Armenian–Azerbaijani rivalry since then. Chapter 1 provides a systematic overview of prominent explanations for the outbreak of Armenian–Azerbaijani conflict and violence in 1988–94. Chapter 2 examines the historical trajectories of different traditions of homeland in twentieth-century Armenian and Azerbaijani geopolitical cultures. It develops an argument on the different importance and weight accorded to boundaries in each geopolitical culture. Chapter 3 homes in on the contested territory of Nagorny Karabakh and traces its trajectory through Armenian and Azerbaijani geopolitical visions from 1988 to the present. Chapter 4 explores the multiple types, theatres and motives of forced displacement in the late 1980s and during the 1992–4 war. Chapter 5 traces the relationship between the rivalry and the regime types in Armenia and Azerbaijan, and how the rivalry has provided a resource 'demobilising' democracy. Chapter 6 addresses the peculiar configuration of the power relations between Armenia and Azerbaijan, and how the power asymmetry between them has been truncated. Chapter 7 examines the international diffusion of the Armenian–Azerbaijani rivalry and its implications for the rivalry's stability and longevity. Chapter 8 examines the evolution of the unrecognised republic in Nagorny Karabakh, and Chapter 9 discusses the OSCE-mediated peace process between Armenia and Azerbaijan.

1 A Violent Unravelling

Understanding the Armenian–Azerbaijani rivalry today requires an appreciation of the conflict engulfing the societies in which Armenians and Azerbaijanis lived between 1988 and 1994. This is no easy task, as Armenian–Azerbaijani conflict in this period is both over-determined and under-documented. One complication is that the dispute is both inseparable from the wider unravelling of the Soviet Union, which was surprisingly peaceful overall, yet exceptional as an example where conflict became violent. Another complication is that unlike the Balkan wars of the 1990s, on which there is an extensive and theoretically sophisticated literature, Armenian–Azerbaijani conflict remains 'live'. Scholarship must navigate rival epistemologies of blame that are still inseparable from contemporary identity and regime politics. Ideologically consistent but causally incoherent, mirroring narratives swing between the inevitability and spontaneity of violence – premeditated 'genocide' by outsiders and circumstantial 'hooliganism' by insiders. The rapid and dispersed succession of events and lack of media reporting during the early phases of the conflict fuel factual disagreements over what actually happened. Meanwhile, conspiracy theories have circulated since the beginning of the conflict, explaining violence as the work of foreign sponsors, 'hidden hands' and their local *agents provocateurs*. These theories linger on, unchallenged by either strong traditions of independent local scholarship or the investigative work of external bodies such as the International Criminal Tribunal for the former Yugoslavia.

A more easily treatable encumbrance to understanding is conflation of the relevant questions. There are in the end two fundamental questions, rarely distinguished, that need answering. First, why did a border dispute emerge among the Armenians and Azerbaijanis of the Soviet Union in 1988? Second, why did violence erupt between Armenians and Azerbaijanis in the late 1980s? Put differently to emphasise the conflation, why did Armenian and Azerbaijani communities across a wide range of different geographic, social and institutional settings, *including many far from the disputed border*, turn violently against one another? Comparative macro-scalar models developed to explain all of the post-Soviet conflicts isolate and focus on the elements they share. This approach does little justice to the plurality of theatres and motives driving Armenian–Azerbaijani violence in 1988–94 beyond the immediate context of secessionism in Nagorny Karabakh. Moreover, the geographic dispersal and rapid succession of violent episodes indicate that different causal mechanisms were at play, requiring different kinds of answers.

This chapter explores answers to these questions through four clusters of explanatory category: structure, transitional factors, leadership and culture. Caricatures of each of these explanations are common, especially when isolated from the others with the political purpose of portraying Armenian–Azerbaijani conflict as either artificial or inevitable. I argue instead that only a multifactor framework can answer the questions posed above. A single chapter cannot, of course, aim at more than the most general outlines of a comprehensive approach. The empirical gaps in the record are many, and several await a different political conjuncture in order to be adequately researched. The more limited goal here is to provide sufficient context for the chapters to follow.

Structural Vulnerabilities: Geography, Imperial Legacies and Institutions

The Soviet Union was a 'communal apartment', an 'Affirmative Action Empire', an 'empire of nations'.[1] The flaws inherent in the Soviet Union's nationalities policy have received more attention than any other single feature of its collapse. Its ethno-federal structure contrived a pervasive coupling of ethnicity and territory, bestowing all the trappings but none of the content of sovereignty upon fifteen major nationalities in eponymous union republics. Within the union republics myriad smaller autonomous units were founded, usually also named for 'titular' ethnic groups.[2] In the 1920s pervasive Soviet policies sought to institutionalise national cultures within these territorial frames. Ascribed nationality (*natsional'nost'*), fixed in identity documents from the 1930s, came to play a central role in the education, social mobility and lifeways of all Soviet citizens. But unlike Yugoslavia – where citizens could from 1961 identify as 'Yugoslavs' – a supra-national Soviet nationality was never created in the USSR.[3] Soviet nationalities were induced to learn Russian, but could neither assimilate nor exercise the right to self-determination that their constitutions formally accorded them. This maintained an enduring tension between Russian domination and the USSR's multinational composition. The Soviet project consequently never quelled a reading of its structure, and its problems, as being 'imperial' in nature, and remediable through national self-determination. It fell victim, in the end, to ethno-federal institutions that incubated the very nationalism that they were designed to contain.

As the Soviet centre weakened and collapsed, numerous minority groups in the Caucasus rebelled against the union republics of which they formed part. A popular analysis argues that institutions of territorial autonomy provided the symbols, coordination, leadership and capacity for minority group revolt in Abkhazia, South Ossetia and Nagorny Karabakh.[4] In the Armenian–Azerbaijani case, the territorial arrangement appeared especially conflict-prone, with an autonomous island within one union republic, Azerbaijan, culturally associated with a neighbouring one, Armenia. It was a peculiar, if not unique, situation: Crimea had been a Russian-majority island within Ukraine, but this was 'rectified' with Crimea's transfer to Ukraine in 1954. Moscow steadfastly refused a similar manoeuvre to transfer Nagorny Karabakh to Armenia. Yet to attribute conflict to Soviet institutions is mechanical and loses explanatory power outside of the Caucasus. A historical perspective further suggests that territorial autonomies in the region were as much responses *to* pre-existing fractures as potential incubators of future conflict.

An examination of how structural vulnerabilities contributed to Armenian–Azerbaijani conflict can perhaps most usefully begin with geography. The Armenian–Azerbaijani space comprises a highly diverse set of terrains, climatic zones and micro-geographies, ranging from the Caspian littoral through the arid plains of central Azerbaijan, to the highlands of Nagorny Karabakh and southern Armenia and the dry Ararat plain beyond. Mountainous terrain, as elsewhere in the Caucasus, is not in itself a source of fracture, but a long-term factor qualifying both the penetration of external control and the emergence of centralised indigenous polities. Diverse terrains supported distinct socio-cultural niches often marked, in peacetime, by loose hierarchies. This variable geography was overlaid with shifting tides of projects of imperial control. It is a cliché that empires have contested the Caucasus, yet imperial confrontations, furthest lines of advance, and final boundaries of conquest and capitulation have been constitutive of Armenian and Azerbaijani spaces in the most fundamental, physical way. The European conquest of a Middle Eastern frontier, Russia's penetration of regions south of the Caucasus Mountains in the early nineteenth century supplanted a prior modus vivendi between the Ottoman Empire and Iran.[5] To the south-west, territories would continue to change hands as Russian and Ottoman armies fought repeatedly up to World War I. To the south-east Iran was more decisively ousted: a stable new frontier along the River Aras (Araxes) established in the treaties of Gulistan (1813) and Turkmanchay (1828) delineates the southern borders of Azerbaijan and Armenia to this day. Secluded from central Russia by the Caucasus Mountains, what became known as Russian Transcaucasia emerged as a fissiparous shatterbelt never fully integrated with a distant metropole in Moscow and forever connected to lands and communities on the other side of recent and, in the south-west, still shifting borders.[6]

Russian rule gradually streamlined the numerous small Muslim polities – khanates and sultanates – inherited from a loose Iranian suzerainty into a unified administrative system of *guberniyas* (provinces). Demographically and developmentally, however, Transcaucasia became more heterogeneous. Russian conquest and subsequent wars with the Ottoman Empire resulted in recurrent population movements, involving varying degrees of coercion. Major population movements were not new to the region: in 1603–29 Shah Abbas I of Persia deported as many as 60,000 Armenian families, or 300,000 individuals, from the prosperous city of Julfa, the Ararat valley and the wider Caucasus to his capital at Isfahan and other locations in Persia.[7] But from the nineteenth century mass displacements increasingly connoted imperial spaces as Christian Armenians moved into the Russian Empire from Persia after Gulistan and Turkmanchay or from the Ottoman Empire after Russian military campaigns, and Muslims moved in the opposite direction. These movements transformed the Armenian population from marginal urban minorities into a third major nationality in Transcaucasia alongside Georgians and Azerbaijani Muslims, or 'Tatars' as today's Azerbaijanis were then known.

Ethnic heterogeneity increasingly intersected with developmental disparities. A salient divide emerged between industrialising, multi-ethnic cities and more homogenous rural hinterlands, yet Transcaucasia's cities were not melting pots. Baku's oil industry dominated the region's industrialisation, attracting labour from across the region and Iran, but was ethnically stratified in terms of both ownership – in which Russian, Armenian and foreign capital competed fiercely with the local Azerbaijani bourgeoisie – and management and skilled labour, dominated by Russians and Armenians.[8] These tensions erupted in 1905 in the 'Armeno-Tatar war', a wave of communal violence spreading over several months from Baku westwards to Yerevan and killing thousands.[9] Communal violence accelerated the development of local nationalism over socialist, liberal and transnational cultural ideologies. But typically for multinational empires of the time, all nationalisms in Transcaucasia confronted, if from different angles, what was to a nationalist worldview an awkward geography of intermingled populations, cosmopolitan–industrial enclaves dominated by 'aliens', cultural communities as riven by class as united by ethnicity, and an absence of historically proximate territorial templates for statehood.

In the period immediately following World War I this geography was cleft into two new geopolitical spaces claimed as

Armenian and Azerbaijani homelands. This process was so violent yet inconclusive that the legacies of this era can be considered a second structural vulnerability. The toppling of the Romanov dynasty in 1917, Bolshevik seizure of power and the Russian civil war cut Transcaucasia adrift in 1918 against the backdrop of the collapse of the Caucasian front with Ottoman Turkey. Transcaucasia became a periphery without a centre, precipitating two years of many-sided interstate, civil and partisan wars, insurgencies, Ottoman invasions and finally annexation by Soviet power. A forced experiment in federation, the Transcaucasian Democratic Federative Republic, collapsed after a month in May 1918, giving rise, alongside the Democratic Republic of Georgia, to two short-lived republics, the Azerbaijan Democratic Republic (ADR) and the first Republic of Armenia (RA). Neither had defined or controlled borders; indeed, neither state declared independence in its presumptive capital city, Baku and Yerevan respectively. The struggle to define their common border was only one of multiple struggles by their ruling parties, the Armenian Revolutionary Federation (ARF, or Dashnaktsutyun) and the Azerbaijani Musavat ('Equality'), and not necessarily the most important at the time. Both republics faced other, more immediate threats, for the RA from Ottoman Turkey and for the ADR from the Bolsheviks' sole foothold in Transcaucasia, the Baku Commune.[10]

Armenian–Azerbaijani border disputes focused on the mountainous southern marchlands of Nagorny Karabakh, Zangezur and Nakhichevan. Violence devastated communities across all three regions. Reliable numbers are elusive, but Ottoman Turkish–Azerbaijani forces killed or drove out many thousands of Armenians from Nakhichevan, while Armenian militias visited a similar fate upon Azerbaijani Muslims in Zangezur. In Karabakh Azerbaijani control was initially secured with Ottoman support and subsequently mandated by a British expeditionary force under the command of General William Thomson. Under duress the Armenian population came to a provisional agreement on semi-autonomous status within Azerbaijan, but Baku revoked the accord after six months in February 1920. An Armenian rebellion followed in March, crushed by an Azerbaijani army and ending in the destruction of the Armenian quarter in the region's capital, Shusha. Elsewhere civil strife between Bolsheviks and Armenian paramilitary forces on the one hand and Azerbaijani nationalist forces on the other intersected with communal reprisals to result in pogroms across Azerbaijan, claiming many thousands of lives among both Azerbaijani Muslim and Armenian communities. In the capital Baku two large-scale massacres bracketed the struggle for the city between the Bolsheviks, locally supported by Dashnaktsutyun (Dashnak) paramilitary forces, and Azerbaijani forces supported by Ottoman Turkey.[11] In the context of a Muslim rebellion against the Bolshevik city leadership (the latter led by Marxist and ethnic Armenian Stepan Shahumyan), Dashnak forces massacred thousands of Azerbaijani Muslims in the 'March Days' of 31 March–2 April 1918.[12] When Baku fell on 15 September, Azerbaijani and Ottoman forces massacred some 10,000 Armenians. The legacies of this horrific violence were never addressed in the Soviet era, which subsumed them in an enforced meta-narrative of heroic communists overcoming reactionary nationalists, leaving them ripe for rediscovery after the violence of 1988.[13]

By incorporating the ADR and the RA in April and December 1920 respectively, the Soviet state inherited a highly fragmented ethno-social terrain featuring identities both sharpened by the preceding interlude of sovereignty and traumatised by mass violence, and contiguous with a strategically significant neighbour, Turkey. This was a context to stretch even the most capable governors, let alone a revolutionary Marxist regime with a limited local support base and few resources. Strategic – and often Machiavellian – motives have been ascribed to the young Soviet state's deployment of territorial autonomy in the Caucasus. Particularly in Georgia and Azerbaijan, territorial autonomies founded in the early 1920s have been interpreted as Bolshevik artifice seeking to 'divide and rule'.[14] An alternative view is that the Bolsheviks were consummate tacticians, treading the path of least resistance by leaving contested territories in the hands of those holding them at the time of sovietisation. The resulting Soviet delimitation of territory was certainly complex, and constitutes a third structural vulnerability.

The Armenian–Azerbaijani space was organised according to the principles of Soviet ethno-federalism. This system territorialised ethnic groups according to a hierarchy of units from union republics to autonomous republics, autonomous regions (*oblasts* in Russian, hereafter oblast), and autonomous areas (*okrugs*). Each tier possessed corresponding attributes of statehood in descending order, with union republics possessing a formal right of self-determination and all the symbolic attributes of statehood (such as flags, anthems, a full range of formal executive and representative institutions, and so on). What had been Russian Transcaucasia now became the Transcaucasian Socialist Federal Soviet Republic (usually referred to by its Russian acronym, ZSFSR). Within the ZSFSR, Armenians and Azerbaijanis were both recognised as nations (*natsiya*), the highest category of ethnic group in the Soviet Union, and territorialised across four distinct units. Two union republics were founded in the Azerbaijani Soviet Socialist Republic (AzSSR) on 28 April 1920, and the Armenian Soviet Socialist Republic (ArmSSR) on 29 November 1920. Even after the violent purges of 1918–20, each republic's largest minority belonged to the other's nationality.[15] Within the AzSSR, two autonomous units were subsequently founded. An autonomous republic was founded in Nakhichevan (Nakhichevan Autonomous Soviet Socialist Republic, NASSR), dividing the AzSSR into mainland and exclave. Nakhichevan had been contested by the early Soviets with Kemalist Turkey; Soviet control was agreed in the 16 March 1921 Treaty of Moscow on condition of autonomy being granted. On 7 July 1923 an autonomous oblast was founded in Nagorny Karabakh (AONK; this acronym was later reversed to NKAO, *Nagorno-Karabakhskaya Avtonomnaya Oblast'*), establishing an Armenian-majority territorial autonomy in the mountainous part of Karabakh. In the 1930s four small exclaves were added to this complicated map. (The NKAO itself is mistakenly referred to as an enclave *sensu stricto*; it was never a part of one sovereign state-political entity surrounded by the territory of another.)

The single most consequential decision in the history of Armenian–Azerbaijani relations is the 5 July 1921 vote by the Bolsheviks' Caucasus Bureau (*Kavburo*), the body entrusted with the conquest of Transcaucasia in 1918–21, to leave Karabakh to Azerbaijan, reversing a decision the previous day to allocate it to Armenia. The *Kavburo*'s dramatic reversal has long been associated with Stalin's nefarious presence – although he did not vote – and the logic of 'divide and rule'. With hindsight the establishment of an Armenian-majority island within an Azerbaijani-majority republic certainly appears replete with conflict potential. In the most thorough study yet published of this episode, historian Arsène Saparov has instead convincingly argued that tactical contingencies lay behind the *Kavburo*'s decision.[16] He points out that communist officials had made differing public commitments with regard to the final allocation of Nagorny Karabakh in the preceding months. Rather than sincere statements of intent, these were effectively a weathervane on the uneven process of sovietising Armenia and Azerbaijan, two republics with recent experience of violent conflict and narrow Bolshevik support bases. Pledges to allocate Karabakh to Armenia reflected the later and contested sovietisation of that republic. Nationalist rebels associated with the RA's former ruling party, the Dashnaktsutyun, were still actively opposing the Soviet regime in the southern region of Zangezur through the summer of 1921. Rather than a strategic logic of 'divide and rule', short-term tactical prerogatives drove the Bolshevik decision-making process:

> The Kavburo considered [Karabakh] a part of Azerbaijan when it needed to strengthen its position there in the period between the summer and fall of 1920, but was prepared to grant it to Armenia to help with the establishment of Soviet power there in December 1920, or as a way of undermining the [Armenian nationalist] rebels in Zangezur in the summer of 1921.[17]

While the NKAO was a new institutional formation, it expressed – and attempted to provide a resolution for – a pre-existing reality: Armenians formed a demographic majority in a highland area more easily accessible from the neighbouring lowlands of Azerbaijan than from Armenia across the Karabakh mountain range.[18] There was no passable road connecting Yerevan to Karabakh (accessible only via Nakhichevan at the time), while the Turkic pastoralists of the eastern plains below traditionally passed the summer in Karabakh's rich highland pastures. To alleviate conflict, the NKAO's borders were designed in such a way as to maximise the separation of the two groups, accounting for its intricate boundaries especially in more populated areas. These resulted in an entity with an Armenian majority of 89.1 per cent, according to the 1926 census, covering 5.1 per cent of the AzSSR's territory.

That the local legitimacy of the delimitation was doubtful was clear from the regularity with which this question was raised whenever the Soviet regime went through periods of relative liberalisation.[19] While the obligatory Marxist gloss had to be given to petitions and letter-writing campaigns, perhaps the single most important aspect in the process of forming the NKAO was the public image of prevarication in its allocation. Subsequent efforts to naturalise Azerbaijani ownership of the NKAO never shook off the apparent contingency of the decision made on 5 July 1921. Even if it can be plausibly argued that the Bolsheviks never really intended to grant Karabakh to Armenia, from the public record it appeared as a decision that *could* have gone either way. Lodged in the very earliest days of the Soviet project, the decision was a visible reference point for any assessment of the Soviet Union's subsequent trajectory. This gave the questioning of the 1921 decision a specific nuance in the late 1980s: it enabled Armenian contestation of Karabakh's allocation to be framed as a corrective to early Soviet mishandling, but not the founding principles of the Soviet state itself. This made for a striking congruence with Mikhail Gorbachev's programme to reform the Soviet Union, perestroika ('restructuring') after 1986.[20]

Rather than any over-arching principle or long-term strategy, then, it is the contingency of the Soviet territorial delimitation that is striking. Although cloaked in the formal templates of Soviet ethno-federalism, a mixture of different logics and goals mediated the distribution of Armenians and Azerbaijanis across an uneven institutional terrain: the regulation of foreign policy, the resolution of recent conflict, and the facilitation of sovietisation. In effect, two conceptually distinct but in the event empirically inseparable processes merged: the Armenian–Azerbaijani delimitation and sovietisation. Institutional pluralism did not translate into political pluralism, however. Diverse territorial units were all subordinated to the unitary power structure of the Communist Party of the Soviet Union (CPSU) and its local affiliates, the Azerbaijani Communist Party (AzCP) and Armenian Communist Party (ArmCP). This combination of unitary authoritarianism with the cultural and institutional diversity of Armenian and Azerbaijani spaces constituted a fourth structural vulnerability.

A fifth and final structural vulnerability was what I call the ambiguity of autonomy in the NKAO. Of course, all autonomies in the Soviet authoritarian system were ambiguous in the sense that they did not delegate any real representative functions to their beneficiaries. To Armenians near-contiguity with a co-ethnic union republic also looked like contiguity denied. But the NKAO was ambiguous in other ways too. Designating a geographic concept, it lacked the usual Soviet designation as the homeland of a primordial national community. Again, this was unusual but not unique in the Soviet Union.[21] Indeed, elsewhere in the AzSSR the autonomous republic in Nakhichevan was a concession to an important foreign policy relationship rather than a minority group interest. But although the NKAO manifestly *was* established to represent such an interest, official documentation consistently avoided attaching any ethnic character to the autonomy.[22] The sole indication of ethnic difference in the 1924 statute on the formation of the NKAO was a stipulation that the 'native language' of the population was to be used in official correspondence, court proceedings and primary education. Nearly sixty years later a statute regulating the NKAO produced by the AzSSR's Supreme Soviet in 1981 made no reference to ethnic affiliation, with just one provision in Article 64 stipulating that court proceedings be enacted in 'the language of the autonomous region or Azerbaijani'.[23]

This silence on the NKAO's ethnic character undermined its putative raison d'être for both Azerbaijanis and Armenians. For Azerbaijanis, it validated perceptions of the NKAO as an artificial creation, not essentially different from any other region of the AzSSR. By its formal title, the NKAO did not affirm an Armenian claim to legitimately dominate the ethnic hierarchy in the oblast. For Armenians, this silence fuelled suspicions that the NKAO was inadequate even in the cultural realm where Soviet territorial autonomies did confer some symbolic rights. The comparatively very low level of cultural production in the NKAO seemingly corroborated the silence on its 'proper' ownership. Between 1938 and 1967 a total of just nine book titles were printed in the NKAO, compared with dozens yearly in the territorial autonomies of Abkhazia and South Ossetia in neighbouring Georgia.[24] Instead, cultural production for the NKAO's Armenians was in effect 'outsourced' to the ArmSSR, building a de facto irredentist attraction into the relationship between the NKAO and the ArmSSR; many Karabakh Armenians studied and pursued careers in Yerevan (and Moscow). The Armenians of the NKAO were also in the unusual position of constituting only part of a wider co-ethnic minority within the same union republic. This created the potential for a rival ethnic Armenian elite originating in the large community of Armenians living in Baku and other cities in the AzSSR to emerge over time. From the late 1960s metropolitan appointees from this community who had risen up through AzCP patronage circles were posted as leaders in the NKAO.[25] Career bureaucrats with russified surnames, poor knowledge of Armenian and loyal to patrons in Baku, these 'middle-men' constituted in their own way a third silence. They were disparagingly referred to by local Armenians as 'seasonal labour'.[26]

There were, then, numerous structural vulnerabilities to the Soviet context in which Armenians and Azerbaijanis lived. Perhaps no other two groups in the Soviet Union interacted with each other across such a varied array of theatres nested within one another, yet simultaneously crosshatched by competing claims to entitlement and uneven patterns of development. Viewed through the prism of Soviet ideology, this diversity of intermingled communities validated ideals of internationalism. Internationalist gloss nevertheless obscured a more complex reality of several distinct but contiguous theatres, in all of which by the 1980s Armenians and Azerbaijanis were for each other the largest proximate group. This could, under certain conditions, be a situation vulnerable to spillover, collapsing diverse localities – each different in character and circumstance – into the perception of a single, over-arching ethnic confrontation.

Transitional Factors: Failed Liberalisation, Mass Movements and the Security Dilemma

From 1988 to 1991 the Armenian–Azerbaijani conflict unfolded against the backdrop of Mikhail Gorbachev's ill-fated attempt to reform the Soviet Union, the emergence of mass movements and the transition to national independence. Systemic crisis affected all Soviet populations, weakening the CPSU's power vertical, exposing the bankruptcy and legitimation failure of Soviet internationalism, and leading to waves of nationalist mobilisation sweeping across the stricken Soviet state.[27] Against this dynamic background, Armenian–Azerbaijani violence has a distinctive place as an 'early riser'. It was the first instance of interethnic violence occurring after Gorbachev had begun to introduce the policies of glasnost and perestroika in 1986. Transitional factors cannot explain the early appearance of Armenian–Azerbaijani violence, to which we will return below. Where transitional factors are most relevant to our questions is in how they narrowed the field for non-violent options and their advocates, to the point where these options were no longer seen as feasible or credible, and only violence remained.

On 20 February 1988, the local soviet (regional assembly) in the NKAO passed a resolution calling for the oblast's unification with the ArmSSR. It was an unprecedented act for a lower-level unit in the Soviet ethno-federal hierarchy. Violence was almost immediate, first on 22 February when two Azerbaijanis were killed as Azerbaijanis protesting the resolution clashed with local Armenians on the road between Askeran and Agdam, an Azerbaijani city just outside of the NKAO.[28] More seriously, a three-day pogrom in the industrial suburb of Sumgait outside Baku a week later claimed the lives of twenty-six Armenians and six Azerbaijanis and profoundly shocked Soviet society. Moscow's early responses to these unprecedented developments revealed a policy void in the centre's toolkit for addressing interethnic conflict. An initial economic investment programme betrayed a fundamental misunderstanding of the nature of the problem. After reaffirming the status quo for several months, Moscow's main policy initiative in July 1988 was to remove the NKAO from the AzSSR's jurisdiction, placing it under direct rule. Industrialist Arkady Volsky was installed as a local prefect, governing the province through a Special Administration Committee (*Komitet Osobogo Upravleniya*, KOU).[29] The KOU was a manoeuvre straight out of Moscow's 1970s playbook, defusing political conflict with an offer of economic regeneration that satisfied neither side. Communal violence gathered momentum in both the ArmSSR and AzSSR through autumn 1988, incited in part by the failure of the criminal justice system to investigate and prosecute those arrested after the February pogrom in Sumgait. Hesitant authorities – fearing widely publicised and politically inflammatory trials – parcelled out the process across courts in the AzSSR and Russia.[30] Across both the ArmSSR and AzSSR gangs terrorised minorities of the other nationality, leading to a near-complete mutual expulsion of populations between the two republics outside of the NKAO by the end of 1989. Within the NKAO, populations were violently exchanged between the oblast's two largest towns, Stepanakert and Shusha, in September 1988.

The inadequacy of the centre's policy toolkit was quickly overtaken by another consequence of systemic liberalisation. The ceding of the CPSU's political monopoly generated new constellations of political actors in the form of civic associations (*neformaly*), movements and eventually political parties. Oppositional activity evolved quickly from small circles of intellectuals to mass movements.[31] These new forces obviated Moscow's traditional toolkit by linking the resolution of conflict to groundswells of popular support, precluding intra-elite deals behind closed doors and leveraging the symbolic politics of mass mobilisation. They drew on these groundswells for a new kind of popular legitimacy, coming for the first time from outside of the party's unitary structure. This process was most advanced in the ArmSSR, where the consolidation of the Pan-Armenian National Movement (PANM) in June 1989 culminated in victory in the republic's first multiparty elections in May 1990. Armenia declared independence on 23 August of that year. In the AzSSR, the Azerbaijani Popular Front was founded in July 1989; it would not enter power until 1992, after a more tortuous struggle with the AzCP. But in both republics nationalist mobilisation was institutionalised, either in the form of a new elite in the ArmSSR, or a weakened communist leadership pressured into co-opting the nationalist opposition's agenda in the AzSSR. Liberalisation of the unitary Soviet state thus allowed for the diffusion of nationalist agendas across weakened, newly democratising institutions.

Two crucial shifts followed the emergence of these new political actors. First, policy initiative increasingly shifted from the centre to national movements that were being institutionalised in the union republics. As embryonic successor states to the Soviet Union, however, these were extremely weak. They lacked armies, party structures or funds, leading to a dual power vacuum at Soviet centre and periphery. Moreover, in their pursuit of conflicting goals, emerging Armenian and Azerbaijani national movements had no bilateral institutional channels through which to influence one another. This created the opening for the entry into politics of paramilitary organisations and what Christoph Zürcher calls 'patriot-businessmen'.[32] Patriot-businessmen capitalised on various sources of social capital to establish volunteer units capable of pursuing security objectives, while also profiting from insecurity. They founded uneasy coalitions with nationalist intellectuals at the head of fragile new states.

Second, the centre lost its adjudicatory authority to become instead a player in local conflicts, increasingly seeing trade-offs in territorial conflicts as part of the higher-order game of preserving the Soviet state. The AzSSR regained control over the NKAO in November 1989 after the abolition of the KOU, and participated in the referendum for – and approved – the preservation of the USSR on 17 March 1991. This set the stage for a tactical alliance between the AzCP and Moscow. From April to July 1991 the Soviet Army combined with Azerbaijani special paramilitary forces to implement 'Operation Ring', flushing out Armenian guerrillas in several villages mainly around the NKAO and then deporting their inhabitants.[33] Essentially directed by Moscow's man in Azerbaijan, AzCP Second Secretary Viktor Polyanichko, Operation Ring resulted in large-scale if unequal fighting. It appeared to yield results in a series of Armenian delegations from the NKAO seeking dialogue in Moscow and Baku. But in August 1991 the failed putsch in Moscow laid to rest a Soviet frame of reference for resolving the conflict.

The rapid dissolution of the Soviet state over the following six months resulted in what scholars term a 'security dilemma'.[34] The security dilemma holds that when 'sovereigns' (such as the former Soviet or Yugoslav states) disappear, proximate groups are suddenly required to provide for their own security in conditions of emerging anarchy. As communities reidentify neighbours as enemies, defensive actions are read as threatening and worst-case scenarios assumed. Particularly for intermingled groups in strategically indefensible situations, such as was the case for Armenians and Azerbaijanis in the NKAO, a threat perception spiral is difficult to control. On 30 August 1991 Azerbaijan declared its independence from the stricken Soviet Union. Three days later the Karabakh Armenians declared the foundation of a Nagorno-Karabakh Republic (NKR), comprising the NKAO plus an Armenian-majority area to the immediate north, Shahumyan. Nearly three months later on 26 November 1991 the AzSSR abolished the NKAO.[35] Simultaneous to the emergence of the security dilemma was the appearance of an ostensible solution to it: opportunities to procure substantial quantities of modern weaponry from the fragmenting Soviet military. A conflict that had begun with stones and hunting rifles assumed the technological and destructive scope of a modern war. When the Soviet Union finally dissolved at the end of December 1991, Armenia and Azerbaijan were reborn as sovereign states already at war.

Yet as Stuart Kaufman observes, if a security dilemma is clearly evident in and around the NKAO by 1990, it provides little traction in explaining the early onset of Armenian–Azerbaijani violence.[36] When the first pogrom broke out in Sumgait in February 1988 there were few signs of the 'emerging anarchy' to which the reflexes powering the security dilemma are a response. The failure of local police to intervene to protect ethnic minority citizens, Moscow's ambivalence and inability to manage interethnic conflict, and institutionalised impunity for perpetrators were all still in the future. The only recent precedent of public unrest had been rioting in Alma-Ata in Kazakhstan in 1986. Indeed, Soviet security officials witnessing the aftermath of pogroms in Sumgait drew on examples from outside of the Soviet Union to make sense of what they had seen. Russian general Aleksandr Lebed' arrived shortly after the violence in Sumgait:

> There, for the first time after Afghanistan, in what I still thought of as my own country I saw burnt out trucks and buses, buildings that had burnt down, people whose dark hair had turned white from the horror they had lived through, and the eyes, the eyes . . .[37]

Armenian–Azerbaijani tensions were for Lebed' the beginning of the Soviet Union's death throes (*nachalo agonii*).[38] Likewise, a recurring motif in the testimony of eyewitnesses to Sumgait was incredulity that such a thing could happen in the Soviet Union.[39] Early Armenian–Azerbaijani violence was consequently a prism through which the decay of the Soviet state, and emerging conditions of anarchy, became widely perceived. It was more a contributory factor *to* a security dilemma than the product of one. What, then, was the role of local leadership in the unfolding violence?

The Leadership Factor: Elite Fusion and Fracture

Armenian–Azerbaijani violence in the late 1980s and early 1990s poses challenges for theories of ethnic mobilisation focusing on leadership and manipulative elites. Unlike the Balkans, although massacres and ethnic cleansing are as much a part of the story, outside of nationalist narratives there is no clear host of villains. No Armenians or Azerbaijanis have ever been tried for war crimes, and no single individual has ever come to personify the tragedies visited upon hundreds of thousands of people of both (and other) nationalities between 1988 and 1994 in the manner of Slobodan Milošević. It is instead imagery of mass protest, of people standing in the Caucasian winter cold in their thousands and of crowds with raised fists, which provides some of the most iconic images of the conflict. The Armenian word *hraparak* and Azerbaijani word *meydan*, both literally meaning 'square', figuratively capture the sense of crowd power that leaders found so compelling in 1988–90.

The evidence of organisation in the communal violence of 1988–90 is patchy. To the extent that there was leadership, it was at the local levels of city (*gorispolkom*) and district (*raispolkom*) Communist Party executive committees and it was not consistent. Some local party bosses tried to stem violence, some appeared to cave in to it, others fled it and some actively enabled it by sharing public platforms with advocates of violence or perpetrating it themselves.[40] Other agencies of the state, such as electricity and gas boards and housing authorities, facilitated violence by organising power cuts and providing perpetrators with the addresses of target populations. Law enforcement agencies looked the other way as violence was ongoing. Patterns are not necessarily consistent, however. Some rioters in the AzSSR were provided with weapons – steel bars – and addresses, but others did not know where Armenians lived and relied on their Azerbaijani neighbours to give them away (which they did not always do).

The elusiveness of leadership – sometimes literal as in the case of Kirovabad, where *gorispolkom* First Secretary Bagirli fled the November 1988 pogrom in that city[41] – is one source of the enduring popularity of conspiracy theories. Such evocations of backstage master-manipulators need rebuttal. As Thomas de Waal writes, 'local leaders in Armenia and Azerbaijan discovered with alarm that the "decorative nationalism" they had encouraged had real destructive power—and it destroyed most of them'.[42] Stuart Kaufman concurs on the 'relative unimportance of the national leadership in mobilising people on either side'.[43] Far from reflecting the machinations of a small coterie of master-manipulators, the Armenian–Azerbaijani conflict created a political graveyard out of leaders unable to control, contain or outlast developments on the ground, even, in some cases, those that they had played a central role in creating. The long succession of dismissed officials and toppled presidents between 1988 and 1993 shows that until the end of the war violence did not secure elites' hold on power but imperilled it. Yet the absence of personalised explanations is dissatisfying, as the desire to attribute responsibility is one of the most natural reactions to violence. Without leaders, ethnic violence becomes ascribable only to anonymous historical forces or to the cultural differences of masses, risking crude essentialism. Appreciating the roles of leadership – why certain kinds of leader came to the fore, and how leadership struggles interacted with popular politics – is therefore important.

In the 1990s the nested Russian doll, or *matryoshka*, was a popular metaphor for the nested nationalisms of the Soviet ethno-federal system. What the *matryoshka* metaphor missed, however, was the struggle *between* conservatives and reformers within every layer of the *matryoshka*. Reformers were themselves a diverse group, varying in their commitments to nationalism and democracy. Multi-sided leadership contests at each layer of the Soviet hierarchy ensued, between and among conservatives, nationalists and democrats. The dynamics differed at each layer. In the NKAO, the oblast regional assembly's resolution for unification with the ArmSSR symbolised the fusion of conservative and reformer elements. This was what made the Karabakh issue so congruent with perestroika. But at the union republican level a leadership vacuum followed the breaking of the Karabakh crisis in February 1988. Republican-level party leaders were dismissed and outsiders without roots in local party patronage circles brought in, and, as we have seen, Moscow assumed direct control over the oblast.

Outside of official power structures new clubs and associations sprang up in accordance with Gorbachev's perestroika ideals. The ArmSSR and AzSSR took different paths out of this fragmentation. In the ArmSSR a process of fusion reassembled fragmented elites into a broad-based movement. Emanating concentrically outwards from the Karabakh Committee, an eleven-person collective of activists from outside of the political establishment, this process eventually established the PANM and led to victory in the ArmSSR's first multiparty elections in May 1990. In August of that year Karabakh Committee member Levon Ter-Petrossian, a scholar of Semitic languages with Syrian Armenian roots, became Armenia's first post-Soviet leader. A well-defined popular consensus on the Karabakh issue served as the political adhesive enabling elites otherwise torn by allegiance to the Soviet state to cede power to the movement.

In the AzSSR elite politics would be severely fractured from the onset of the conflict in early 1988 until 1993. At one level, Azerbaijan's party elite, under the new leadership of Abdurahman Vezirov after May 1988, would be fiercely challenged by the nationalist opposition in the Popular Front, led by scholar and former dissident Abulfaz Elchibey. Staged against the backdrop of the NKAO's removal from Azerbaijani jurisdiction – and the AzCP leadership's powerlessness to rectify this situation – the Popular Front leveraged appeals to ethno-nationalism to consistently attack the party at its weakest point. This dynamic culminated in the twin tragedies of 'Black January': the massacre of some ninety Armenians and deportation of Baku's remaining Armenian population on 13–15 January 1990, and the Soviet Interior Ministry's late intervention – by invading the city with tanks and troops – in which more than 130 Azerbaijanis died and hundreds more were injured on 19–20 January. After 'Black January', the republic was increasingly run by AzCP Second Secretary Polyanichko, who effectively co-opted the nationalist agenda with a more violent counter-insurgency strategy in the NKAO. Increasing violence thus flowed from the meeting point of intense elite competition and an isolated Soviet centre desperate for demonstrations of loyalty in its recalcitrant periphery. The Soviet intervention allowed the AzCP to cling to power under the new leadership of Ayaz Mutalibov, and was reciprocated with Azerbaijan's vote to preserve the Soviet Union in the March 1991 referendum. In September Mutalibov, a charismatic but strategically inept technocrat, became Azerbaijan's first post-Soviet president, with 98.5 per cent of the vote in a non-competitive election.[44]

Although the evidence is murky, the contest between communist and nationalist elites intersected with a second, *intra*-elite dynamic following the replacement of the AzCP leadership in May 1988. Several conservative figures associated with the patronage network of Heydar Aliyev, former AzCP first secretary 1969–82 and later Soviet Politburo member until his dismissal by Gorbachev in October 1987, were dismissed at that time.[45]

This created an economically and politically well-connected elite faction seeking re-entry into power. It would be too much to suggest that this faction 'controlled' the Popular Front, but the latter's populist challenge to the AzCP certainly intersected with the agenda of conservatives who had lost office as a result of perestroika and the Karabakh crisis, and were seeking to regain it.[46] The Popular Front's opportunity came in the wake of the devastating impacts of Azerbaijan's early losses on the battlefield.

Full-scale war in Nagorny Karabakh followed the final collapse of the Soviet Union at the end of December 1991. Over the early weeks of 1992, Azerbaijani forces held the tactical advantage, surrounding the former oblast's capital, Stepanakert, and holding adjacent high ground in its second city (and largest Azerbaijani settlement), Shusha. Shusha's indiscriminate shelling of Stepanakert remains a low point in the Armenian narrative of the war. To the north-east, another Azerbaijani town, Khojaly, had been a regular trouble-spot and a site where Azerbaijani refugees from the ArmSSR were being resettled. Breaking out of their besieged capital in February 1992, Karabakh Armenian forces surrounded Khojaly and on the night of 25–6 February killed several hundred Azerbaijani civilians in a hail of gunfire as they tried to escape to Agdam accompanied by militiamen. While death counts vary, there is no doubt that the Khojaly massacre was by a large margin the worst single atrocity of the Armenian–Azerbaijani war.[47] Footage of the slain was shown in the Azerbaijani parliament, forcing Mutalibov's resignation.[48] Vicious village-by-village fighting followed, with Azerbaijanis reciprocating the atrocity at Khojaly with the massacre of some fifty Armenian civilians at Maragha on 10 April. But political chaos in Baku continued to debilitate the Azerbaijani war effort. On 8–10 May Azerbaijan suffered the comparatively less deadly but even greater symbolic loss of Shusha, ceding strategic high ground and the last Azerbaijani demographic presence in the former oblast. The Armenians consolidated their gains on 18 May by occupying the Azerbaijani district of Lachin neighbouring the former oblast to the west. They had broken the Azerbaijani siege and now had control of a corridor to supplies from Armenia.

In days of high drama and chaos following the fall of Shusha, the Popular Front blocked an attempted return to power by Mutalibov. In presidential elections on 7 June 1992, Popular Front leader Abulfaz Elchibey became Azerbaijan's first president elected in a competitive election with nearly 60 per cent of the vote. Elchibey initially fared better on the battlefield, presiding over a large-scale Azerbaijani counter-offensive beginning in June that by September had retaken control of almost half of the former oblast. Yet within a year of his election, Elchibey was overthrown by his own lieutenants. Confronted with the insurrection of Ganja-based army commander Suret Huseynov, Elchibey resigned in June 1993, and in desperation invited Heydar Aliyev back to Baku to take power.[49]

Leaving the exile of his home region Nakhichevan, Aliyev resumed control but not until after Armenian forces had taken advantage of Azerbaijani disarray to recapture northern Karabakh and then occupy, in addition to Lachin, another five surrounding regions, Kelbajar, Agdam, Fizuli, Jebrayil and Qubatly, in as many months in April–August 1993. Despite a major offensive under Aliyev's leadership and intensive fighting over the winter of 1993–4, Armenian forces ended the war in control of these and another Azerbaijani province, Zangelan, and expelled their Azerbaijani populations in their entirety.[50] With the belligerents exhausted, hostilities ended with a Russian-brokered ceasefire. Armenian and Azerbaijani leaders were reluctant to sign a ceasefire document.[51] What became known as the 'Bishkek Protocol' was initially drawn up in the Kyrgyz capital on 5 May 1994, then signed separately by the Armenian and Azerbaijani speakers of parliament. Three ministers of defence in Armenia, Azerbaijan and the NKR then assented to the protocol, which finally came into force on 12 May. Over the nearly two-and-a-half-year war more than 25,000 had been killed or were missing in action.[52]

The dynamics of fusion and fracture in Armenian and Azerbaijani elite politics qualify the idea that leadership was irrelevant, by showing that inter-elite competition, conducive to ethnicising 'bidding wars' and violent radicalisation, was present but only partially so. Consensus on the Karabakh issue, solidified by Moscow's prevarication, mitigated domestic power struggles in the ArmSSR and enabled a pacted transition from communist to nationalist elite. By contrast, domestic power struggles in Azerbaijan foregrounded the Karabakh issue as 'the most suitable playing field on which to score political points off opponents'.[53] Put differently, under variable conditions of elite fracture, charismatic appeals to ethno-nationalism served to legitimate a new regime in Armenia, but to delegitimate an existing one in Azerbaijan. The fusion versus fracture dynamic also provides one compelling explanation of why Armenians won the war.

The Armenian–Azerbaijani case challenges the notion that ethnic war is a 'myth' conjured by manipulative leaders in pursuit of power.[54] The sheer number of leaders transiting through office over the course of the 1988–94 period indicates that most of them were not in control of events. But even if we agree that this is a case of mass-led mobilisation, this does not make leadership irrelevant. Quiescence in the face of pogroms – especially among local authorities through active sanction, passive neglect or flight – signalled complicity in the violent creation of new, segregated ethno-territorial orders and impunity for those enacting it. Ethnic antagonism was leveraged in centre-republican and inter-elite struggles in ways that broadened its scope, cutting further ground from under already narrow institutional alternatives to violence, and empowering political entrepreneurs willing to use it. Weak state-political leaders entered into unholy alliances with patriot-businessmen, who waged ethnic war for private profit. But we are still left with the question of why the cultural templates of Armenian–Azerbaijani antagonism were so resonant for large swathes of the population that leaders followed them.

Hardening 'Culture': Constructing Ethnic Ownership, Existential Mobilisation and an Eventful Perspective

More peripheral to a European consciousness than the Balkans, modern caricature of the South Caucasus as a cauldron of either 'ancient hatreds' or 'clashes of civilisations' is mercifully less prominent, if certainly not absent. Although neophytes in policy-making and media reporting reached for these tropes in the

1990s, no book premised on the incompatibility of its nations has achieved the same notoriety, for example, as Robert Kaplan's *Balkan Ghosts*.[55] Rather, 'ancient hatreds' loom larger as a straw man in academic arguments than they do on the ground, so obviously refuted by the historical intermingling of Caucasian nationalities. These collective memories are being lost in today's younger generations, revealing enmity as a product rather than a cause of conflict. The 'clash of civilisations' – especially if understood in religious terms – is even less useful. Neither the patterning of conflict among groups of different religions, nor the relevance of religion to structuring salient grievances supports such a view. The frequent bookending of references to a dispute between 'mainly Christian Armenia' and 'mostly Muslim Azerbaijan' in Western media reporting serves more to locate an obscure conflict than to accurately convey its nature.

Rather than any intrinsic hardness to Armenian–Azerbaijani cultural difference, more important are the cumulative effects of political strategies to solidify difference among populations that remained obstinately intermingled. The impacts of culture can perhaps best be appreciated in terms of the collision of three sources of identity at the end of the 1980s. The first was the formal sphere of cultural production, institutionalised as part of the Soviet ethno-federal order and tasked with legitimating that order through 'orthodox nationalism' compatible with socialism. Each union republic had its own educational system, cultural intelligentsia, school textbooks, newspapers and TV, scholarly journals, and an academy of sciences responsible for publishing scholarship about that republic, to a variable extent in the titular language. Production of ethnographic or historical knowledge about any given republic became the fief of its titular nationality, to which political loyalty to the Soviet state was the essential gateway. From the 1950s archaeologists, medievalists and cultural historians in each republic served at the ideological frontline, producing theories of origin (in Russian: *etnogenez*, or 'ethno-genesis') that rationalised the Soviet ethno-territorial order and the hierarchies of groups within it.[56] Although largely limited to specialist publications, these debates carried profound implications in their construction of titular majority claims to be 'first nations'. Others were, by more or less explicit inference, the demographic residue of migration.

No attempt to create a supranational Soviet nationality ever challenged the status of titular nations: the friendship of peoples *was* the Soviet Union's imagined community.[57] But as class lost meaning as an organising metaphor of Soviet life, the friendship of proletarians was gradually and imperceptibly displaced by the ambivalence of nations. In Soviet Transcaucasia repeated attempts to write a unified history of the region failed in the 1950s, 1970s and 1980s owing to incompatible historical narratives among the region's constituent nationalities.[58] Scholarship embedded everywhere hierarchies between indigenes and 'newcomers'. In the late 1980s only a change of literary register was needed for these pseudo-scholarly nationalist narratives to reach mass audiences. Couched in bilious language, previously arcane disputes flooded the mass media in a methodological free fall and free-for-all. Ethno-historical categories were publicly reloaded with ominous political meanings: non-indigenes became 'ungrateful guests', titular groups long-suffering 'hosts'. Cultural elites long indulged by the Soviet state thus played central roles in providing the raw materials and scholarly imprimatur to exclusive nationalist visions. It would be satisfying to draw a straight line from the hierarchies elaborated by Soviet cultural elites and the leaders of the Armenian and Azerbaijani national movements that had emerged by 1990. This would give us some clear leadership figures to whom responsibility for the violent turn of events could be attributed. Some individuals, such as Armenian publicist Zori Balayan and Azerbaijani academician Ziya Buniyatov, appear as key point-men linking the two.[59] But the violent, mass segregation of Armenians and Azerbaijanis based on hardened, incompatible identities largely preceded the emergence of organised political movements and new nationalist elites. Two other sources of hardened collective identity are critical to understanding how mutually exclusive identities were mobilised so quickly.

Using the Armenian–Azerbaijani conflict as a case study, Stuart Kaufman's theory of 'symbolic politics' argues that while hatreds indeed cannot be 'ancient', they can be renewed in each generation. The 'myth–symbol complex' is central to his account:

'What determines a group's response to its situation is its mythology—which determines its expectations—more than the situation itself.'[60] Symbols and myths rationalising and justifying hostility towards other groups combine, in Kaufman's theory, with conflicts of interest and opportunities to act on them. In a deservedly influential account, Thomas de Waal likewise ascribes central importance to mirroring 'hate narratives'. He contends that Armenians and Azerbaijanis frame each other as threatening by upscaling to the great power threat that each is said to 'represent' – Russia and Turkey respectively.[61] Kaufman's and de Waal's accounts both point to an important difference between the Armenian–Azerbaijani context and many others in the Soviet Union: the intersection of Soviet codes of inclusion and exclusion with a local symbolic fund of traumatic collective memories inherited from early twentieth-century violence. The former arranged the multi-ethnicity of the Armenian–Azerbaijani space into invidious hierarchies; the latter charged these hierarchies with danger. Folk remembrances and informal lore, inter-generational family memories, popular stereotypes, linguistic colloquialisms and the off-stage lionising of national heroes from the pre-Soviet past all contributed to hidden transcripts of collective violence from the late Ottoman and Russian imperial periods, and independence in 1918–20.[62] Victimhood was the touchstone of these threads of collective memory. These melded with Soviet categories to construe 'indigenes' as victim-nations surrounded by hostile powers, and 'non-indigenes' as treacherous fifth columns.

Behind the mass mobilisation that brought Armenians onto the streets in their hundreds of thousands in February 1988 lay the popular memory of genocide at the hands of Turks in the Ottoman Empire in 1915–16. By then genocide had become a pervasive interpretive routine that was no longer meaningfully 'hidden', being expressed in forms as diverse as official commemorations conceded by the Soviet state since the 1960s, the art and architecture of the ArmSSR, everyday proverbs warning against naive friendship with Turks, and popular songs celebrating World War I-era *fedayi* (Armenian guerrillas fighting Ottoman forces).[63] As a narrative of victimisation this routine legitimated violence as resistance. This combined with the revision of the rescue fantasy underpinning the social contract between the Armenian people and the Soviet Union, as the Soviet state failed to secure the lives of Armenians in the AzSSR from 1988 or to pursue accountability for those that killed them. In early 1991, with Soviet Army units supporting AzSSR forces to deport Armenians from villages around the NKAO, Armenians saw armed struggle as the sole route to salvation and the avoidance of another historical catastrophe.

A prior, consensual schema of victimisation is more difficult to identify for Azerbaijanis (in Chapter 4 I suggest an alternative reading of symbolic politics in the AzSSR).[64] Under conditions of leadership paralysis, intellectual ferment, and the flow of refugees from the ArmSSR, however, one quickly appeared. Azerbaijanis became gripped by disturbing perceptions of a well-organised Armenian conspiracy to seize territory. This conspiracy had already captured powerful and influential advocates, such as Russian liberals and the perestroika press, international media outlets including the *Voice of America*, *Radio Free Europe* and the BBC, Soviet 'first lady' Raisa Gorbacheva, and funders in the Armenian diaspora.[65] Orators at mass rallies from late 1988 told Azerbaijani crowds that they were victims of a plot reaching, as the visibility of Armenians in high Soviet office showed, right to the top. The trope of 'Greater Armenia' became ubiquitous as the driving ethos of Armenian nationalism and the real reason – not local grievance – for the Karabakh Armenian campaign. That this threat could be violent was evident in the consistent stream of refugees from the ArmSSR beginning in the winter of 1987–8. In Sumgait in February 1988, public recitals of horrifying atrocities allegedly perpetrated against Azerbaijanis in the southern Armenian province of Kapan from late 1987, on a platform shared with local party officials, preceded anti-Armenian communal violence. Such recitals drew plausibility from hidden transcripts of massacres and terror perpetrated against Azerbaijanis by Armenians – Dashnak units in Baku, *fedayi* in Zangezur – in 1918–20. The message was that Azerbaijanis had been, and could again become, victims of Armenian land hunger.

These incitements led to what Gerard Toal and Carl Dahlman call 'existential mobilisation': 'the enrolment of people into stark scenarios of existential threat through unbounded fear'.[66] Fear and uncertainty were magnified by an inchoate information environment, in which Soviet practices of censorship, oblique reporting and adhering to party lines were weakened but still operative. Confusion over what had happened in Sumgait, and who had killed whom, predominated, for example, among the Armenians in the AzSSR's second city, Kirovabad (today's Ganja).[67] Rumour, conspiracy theories and dangerous talk filled the resulting vacuum. *Raispolkom* and *gorispolkom* bosses surrendered to, or endorsed, an escalatory symmetry whereby reported displacements and atrocities in the other republic justified the same fate for that republic's nationality living within their jurisdictions. A poisonous levelling of contextual, situational and power differentials ensued, as perpetrators 'there' were conflated with their co-ethnics 'here', mandating the pre-emptive ethnic cleansing of defenceless minorities.

Yet even given these conditions, it is important to ask why existential mobilisation was compelling for large numbers of people. Myth–symbol complexes are emphatically both pluralistic and unstable, and can support differing interpretations of the past. For Armenians, other stereotypes of Azerbaijanis existed: as industrious, humorous and 'civilised' Turks – and even as 'our Turks', in contrast to those in Turkey. There likewise existed positive stereotypes of Armenians among Azerbaijanis as hard-working, clean, educated and intelligent.[68] As communal violence unfolded in the AzSSR many individuals did not follow the roles accorded them in symbolic schemas, but protected and defended Armenians. Even in the aftermath of violence elsewhere, local ties survived. Grisha Oganezov, an Armenian in Kirovabad, tells of his encounter with Azerbaijani colleagues, discussing whether they would kill Armenians in the aftermath of a rally. Asked if they would kill him, they told Oganezov he was beyond reproach as their teacher and mentor.[69] Why did scripts of mass murder eclipse these stereotypes and local bonds?

A third source of hardened cultural identities lies in the transformative effects of events themselves. Advocates of an event-centred perspective in studies of nationalism have criticised as overly deterministic views of collective identity as flowing directly from structurally positioned interests or culturally elaborated schemas. They argue for an 'eventful' study of nationalism, focusing on collective action during periods of contested politics that forge new identities for both participants and observers.[70] The analogy with sport makes this clear: ever increasing numbers of fans will identify themselves with a team that continually wins, while one that consistently loses haemorrhages support. In the context of ethnic violence, participation in the social interactions of violence – whether as perpetrator or victim – consolidates 'groupness' and hardens communal over other kinds of identity positioning.[71] Writing on the November 1988 pogrom in Kirovabad, Harrison King argues that the 'demographic and spatial transformations that accompanied the pogroms also facilitated a more intangible process of ethnonational consolidation . . . local actors, either by committing or enduring violence, reified, manipulated, and absorbed "essentialized ethnic categories" that far outlived the pogroms themselves'.[72] This perspective stresses the constitutive role of collective violence in hardening and homogenising what had previously been, to be sure, segmented yet still meaningfully hybrid identities.

The resulting image is the opposite of 'ancient hatreds': in many contexts (although by no means all) Armenians and Azerbaijanis were sufficiently integrated into supra- or non-national modes of identification that extreme violence was needed to destroy them. The collective violence of 1988–90 changed the meaning of being Armenian or Azerbaijani, reifying homogenised, existentially threatening and totalising scripts of ethnic violence which had previously lingered in the illicit, off-stage recitals of the nationalist margins. Violence made ethnic homelands out of multi-scalar Soviet spatialities, in which hybridity between Armenian and Azerbaijani identities on the one hand, and nationally unmarked or ambiguous identities – Soviet, local, city, regional, class and cosmopolitan – on the other, was no longer possible. One could no longer be intermittently Armenian or Azerbaijani, or to situationally regulate how 'Armenian' or 'Azerbaijani' one wanted to be with regard to a specific question or milieu.[73] The extent of the violence is indeed testament to the commitments to such flexible bonds among many whose lives it irrevocably changed in 1988–90.

The origins of the Armenian–Azerbaijani conflict are an immensely complex subject and there is much that we still do not know. Within a single chapter it is possible only to give the broadest of outlines. But it is now possible to revisit the questions posed at the outset. In answering the question of why a border dispute broke out, it is structural factors that need to be kept central. Interrupted sovereignty in 1920 created a fundamental tension between the Soviet ethno-territorial order within which Armenia and Azerbaijan would be encased, and prior conceptions of homeland. The contorted Soviet delimitation improvised numerous symbolic accommodations to resolve conflict inherited from the 1918–20 period. These made sense in the context of a unitary, authoritarian state, and accorded with the state-building imperative of the early Soviet leadership. In this sense, the NKAO was a solution to another problem, sovietisation, and not ethnic conflict. This solution satisfied neither side, however, and subsumed both within a coercive state-building project. Even under ideal political conditions, tensions could have been expected to accompany simultaneous centre-to-periphery devolution and transition from authoritarian rule. But conditions were far from ideal, as the questioning of the border coincided with institutional and ideological bankruptcy of the framework within which the problem could be peacefully solved, and was almost immediately overrun by communal violence.

In answering the question of why violence erupted, a combination of the insecurity proceeding from systemic collapse, leadership dynamics and factors converging to harden cultural identities explains the escalation of organised violence from 1990 to 1991. The institutionalisation of nationalist mobilisation, the popularisation of cultures of victimhood and the collusion of weak republican leaderships with entrepreneurs of violence combined to displace the centre's adjudicatory authority and coercive monopoly. This engendered a security dilemma, focused on the contested territory of Nagorny Karabakh. These arguments take us a long way towards an understanding of the causes of Armenian–Azerbaijani violence, and reflect wider causalities driving violence elsewhere in the South Caucasus. Yet the early emergence of communal violence in February 1988, right at the beginning of the cycle of nationalist mobilisation and before the constituent elements of the security dilemma had come into play, remains an Armenian–Azerbaijani peculiarity. Systemic factors transformed the actors and means by which territory could be contested in 1990–1, yet in its communal variant Armenian–Azerbaijani violence had been part of the story from the beginning, pursuing its own causal logic. We still lack a micro-theory of what made ordinary people participate in or condone the murder and expulsion of defenceless minorities in areas far from contested borders and before the consolidation of new national movements. Chapter 4 returns to this crucial question.

First, however, it is necessary to look in greater depth at the evolving conceptions of space framing and driving conflict in 1988–94. Both Armenia and Azerbaijan experienced unsettled territorial politics throughout their period of incorporation into the Soviet state. In their Soviet templates, the borders of both republics were subject to continual questioning by cultural and political elites. To understand this dynamic a deeper engagement with the trajectories of Armenian and Azerbaijani homelands over the twentieth century is necessary, both of which transcend a Soviet frame of reference in their plurality.

2 Questionable Borders

> Today, on April 24, 2016, I would like to publicly declare that there will be no purging or deportation of Armenians in Artsakh. We will not allow another Armenian Genocide. We means the Armenian nation, all of its parts, the unity of all Armenians.
>
> *President Serzh Sargsyan, 2016*[1]

> We are different. [Ethnic Azerbaijanis in Iran] do not look at us as a symbolic point of attraction, they see 'us' as part of 'them'. But Azerbaijan does not need a return to the ideas of Elchibey, that is not in its interests.
>
> *Deputy Foreign Minister Araz Azimov, 2015*[2]

There have been many Armenias and Azerbaijans, and the ones existing today are smaller than others might have been. Like Poland, Serbia or Macedonia, both nations have plural and convoluted territorial genealogies. Separately from their mutual contestation, this plurality has also been contested within Armenian and Azerbaijani communities. Older and wider than a Soviet frame of reference, these negotiations of boundaries generated different conceptions of Armenian and Azerbaijani homelands. These were intermittently realised over the twentieth century as politically sovereign – but always territorially diminished – state traditions. Of course, few nations – if any – comply with Ernest Gellner's definition of nationalism as the principle that political and national boundaries should be congruent.[3] Yet the Armenian and Azerbaijani republics emerging from the Soviet Union in 1991 were perhaps particularly imperfect approximations of Gellner's definition. Their predecessors in the Armenian and Azerbaijani republics that briefly emerged from the collapse of the Russian Empire in 1918–20 faced similar issues. All had ambivalent relationships with expansive co-ethnic spaces beyond their borders. Their claims to embody an integral national tradition – to balance in sufficient and legitimate equilibrium the two components of 'nation-state' – were ambiguous. As a result, the perception of truncation as a legacy to be accepted and rationalised, or as a wound to be sutured and healed, is a highly consequential variable in the geopolitical cultures of both nations.

A historically sensitive understanding of this variable, and the territorial issues at stake in the Armenian–Azerbaijani rivalry today, requires more than reference to territorial integrity and self-determination, or to Nagorny Karabakh's enclave geography. This chapter develops an argument that contemporary reluctance to contemplate territorial compromises is inseparable from the *intra*-ethnic contestation of truncation within both national communities. This resulted in differing commitments to borders that are foundational to contemporary Armenian and Azerbaijani national identities. These supply the content and boundaries defining the different meanings of the collective 'we' referred to in the quotes above. Put differently, Armenian and Azerbaijani geopolitical cultures came up with different solutions to territorial homelands perceived as partial, fractional or incomplete. Understanding these solutions is in turn critical to understanding why sovereignty over Karabakh today elicits a zero-sum test of both Armenian and Azerbaijani nation-state traditions.

Mental maps of the nation's outline are sites of accumulated public affect and consistent, instantly recognisable icons in the lives of citizens from their earliest days in the classroom, to myriad visualisations across media, national rituals and cartography. Thongchai Winichakul's concept of the *geo-body* captures this process of mental mapping. The geo-body refers not only to physical territory as the most literal characteristic of nationhood, but also to the subjective association with the outline of the nation's borders and consequent preoccupations with its shape and size as 'a source of pride, loyalty, love, passion, bias, hatred, reason, unreason'.[4] I use the idea of the geo-body here in a simplified way to denote spaces deemed to be Armenian or Azerbaijani national homelands in each nation's geopolitical culture. Against a historical backdrop of persistent territorial flux, I trace a disjuncture between actual, physical and sovereign spaces that have constituted Armenian and Azerbaijani states on the one hand, and cultural, cartographic and spiritually imagined homelands on the other. Whether to accept and rationalise a truncated geo-body, or mobilise against it, has been a key axis of contention within both Armenian and Azerbaijani geopolitical cultures. The chapter proceeds by considering ebbs and flows in the Azerbaijani geo-body, before examining those of its Armenian counterpart, before reflecting on how the two geo-bodies that eventually emerged came to 'see' one another.

Borders and the Azerbaijani Geo-body

Whereas Georgians and Armenians had enjoyed medieval traditions of separate statehood, the Turkic ancestors of the Azerbaijanis played a leading role in ruling an empire, Safavid Iran. Azerbaijan was the name of the Safavid state's north-western province (*iyalat*), incorporated in 1501 and initially home to the royal court at Tabriz. Turkic groups founded and sustained ruling Safavid dynasties, and Azerbaijani Turkic was used as a literary medium at court and in the army. Weakening Safavid power from the 1730s precipitated the assertion of local dynasts in the Azerbaijani periphery. In the mid-eighteenth century an agglomeration of more than two dozen khanates and smaller sultanates appeared, stretching from Derbent in the North Caucasus to Urmia in the south. Around half of these north of the River Aras fell to Russian conquest in the early nineteenth century; those south of the Aras remained under the suzerainty of the (Turkic) Qajars, to follow a separate history as Iranian Azerbaijan. This historical legacy consequently juxtaposed Turco-Persian synthesis across the wider imperial space of the Safavid state with the micro-geographies of local khanates in the aftermath of its collapse. This complicated the later imagining of a modern Azerbaijani homeland.

Against this backdrop, the modern history of the Azerbaijani geo-body is a cyclical story of the embrace, then containment, of cross-border cultural continuity with Turkic spaces and groups beyond the Caucasus. Repeatedly in the twentieth century, resolutions to this pattern were found in a limited territorial referent – *Azerbaijan* – and the articulation of a national identity defined more by borders than by culture. Recurrence testified to the effectiveness of this strategy, but it also brought complications of its own. As a geographic concept Azerbaijan had plural traditions and had moved around. As the basis for a territorialised national identity, the term was in perennial tension with the wider ethno-space out of which it appeared.

Muslims, Tatars, Turks

At the nexus of wider Shia, Sunni, Iranian, Turkic and Russian secular worlds, the national identity of the Muslim population in Russian Transcaucasia was intensely but inconclusively debated until World War I.[5] Imperial Russian classificatory schemas were haphazard and inconsistent, conflating Turkic-speakers in the Caucasus with Tatars in the Urals and Crimea, yielding 'Caucasian Tatars'. Since Caucasian Tatars spoke the same language as the Turkic population living in Iran's north-west *iyalat* of Azerbaijan, they were also referred to as 'Persian', 'Azerbaijani' or 'Aderbaijani' Tatars. Most often Russian documentation referred simply to 'Muslims'. Moving freely between Russia, the Ottoman Empire and Iran, Transcaucasian Muslim intellectuals such as Ali bey Huseynzade (1864–1940), Ahmad bey Aghayev (Ağaoğlu) (1869–1939) and Ali Mardan-bey Topchibashev (1863–1934) played leading roles in the elaboration of ideologies oriented toward co-religionist or co-ethnic communities beyond Transcaucasia.[6] These luminaries did not initially propose the founding of a distinct, local national identity. Rather, they envisioned Muslim Transcaucasia as a hinterland to reforming metropolitan centres elsewhere, whether cultural, secular or religious. To simplify, a turcophile project was oriented towards a reformed Ottoman Empire, a liberal project towards a unified Muslim community within a reformed Russian Empire, and an Islamist project towards a modernised but global Islamic community (*umma*).

These projects ultimately failed to speak to local concerns of the political and economic marginality of Muslims in Russian Transcaucasia. By the early twentieth century, they had ceded ground to a localising tradition that for the first time confined itself to a limited territorial referent. The union of the Musavat ('Equality') and Turkish Federalist parties on 20 June 1917 symbolised the fundamental commitments of this tradition: the liberation of socially oppressed Muslims, identified as ethnic Turks, within a national homeland – Azerbaijan.[7] In the Russian Empire this term had become increasingly popular, although its meaning was far from consistent, as shorthand for Muslim Transcaucasia. In Russian usage Azerbaijan 'moved' north from Persia to Transcaucasia because the 'Tatars' in each were the same. Under the tactically chameleonic leadership of Mamed Emin Rasulzade (1884–1955) the 'Azerbaijani Turk' tradition crystallised as a defensive construction of Transcaucasian Muslim nationality.[8]

As a national identity project the Azerbaijani Turk tradition achieved several things. First, it provided a new term for the modernising, secular Muslim identity that had emerged under Russian rule and finally named the nationality of the Transcaucasian Muslim ('Turks'), while also insulating this identity from the assimilatory potential of Ottoman Turkey ('not *Ottoman* Turks'). Second, it detached Azerbaijani Turks from the deterritorialised, cultural autonomy agenda of Tatars and other Muslims in Russia's inner provinces, which assumed an increasingly implausible reform of the Russian Empire. Third, it staked a Muslim majority claim within the territorial referent Azerbaijan, undercutting Russian and Armenian dominance in Baku commerce and municipal politics. Finally, it assuaged local fears of sectarian Sunni–Shia divisions by its commitment to secularism and an inclusive, culturally conceived Muslim identity. Azerbaijan's pivot from a geographical to a cultural category made sense of ethno-linguistic and kinship links across the Aras that local Muslims wished to maintain. It also created a new identity reflecting the socialist, secular and communal agendas distinct to the Muslim community in Russian Transcaucasia, while establishing a border with a potentially oppressive Ottomanism.[9]

Questionable Borders

As the signifier of an ethnic identity Azerbaijan was a neologism north of the Aras, but the term offered solutions to contemporary threats of both new overlords and internal schisms.

Defining the borders of an Azerbaijani Turk homeland remained a submerged problem for as long as it was imagined as part of a wider state. It was in 1918, in the unexpected and inauspicious circumstances of a global and several regional wars, that the Azerbaijani Turk tradition was territorialised as the Azerbaijan Democratic Republic (ADR). Several problems accompanied the ADR's precipitous territorialisation. First there was the problem of territorial control. Cartographically the ADR emerged as an integral nation-state composed of five provinces (Baku, Ganja, Karabakh, Nakhichevan and Zaqatala). On the ground, however, the ADR's sovereignty was challenged in three locations. The Bolsheviks' Baku Commune held control over the capital, forcing the new state to temporarily establish its capital at Ganja until the fall of Baku in September 1918. In the south-west, Armenian militias and local assemblies disputed sovereignty over the city of Shusha and its environs in Nagorny Karabakh. Armenian militias also resisted control over the south-west regions of Zangezur and Nakhichevan. Although Turkey and then Britain affirmed Azerbaijani sovereignty over its south-western periphery, in practice sovereignty on the ground remained contested through to the end of the ADR's short existence.

A second problem was ethno-demographic. There were substantial numbers of non-Muslims in the territories claimed by the ADR, and substantial numbers of Muslims in territories claimed by Armenians. South-east Russian Transcaucasia had been divided into three large provinces: the *guberniyas* of Baku, Yelizavetpol' and Yerevan. These were in turn subdivided at district (*uezd*) level. Russian rule had consolidated Muslim majorities in Baku and Yelizavetpol' *guberniyas*, but both featured substantial Armenian minorities. Azerbaijani Turks were a minority in their presumed capital city of Baku, and nearly a third of Yelizavetpol' *guberniya*'s population was Armenian; Armenians also comprised a local majority in Shusha *uezd* in Karabakh. Conversely, in Yerevan *guberniya* Muslims were a substantial minority comprising more than a third of the population. They comprised local majorities in Yerevan itself, and three other districts constituting the eastern and southern territories claimed by Armenians for their state (Nakhichevan, Surmalinsk and Sharur-Daralagaz). These demographic settlement patterns confronted national delimitations with few easy options. Applying an ethnographic principle denied coherence and continuity to future nation-states. But basing new states on inherited Russian administrative borders made substantial minorities inevitable.

A third problem lay in the inchoate category of 'Azerbaijani Turk', which was still ill-defined by World War I. In determining the borders of the new state, the ADR delegation to the Paris Peace Conference in 1919 presented a medley of linguistic, confessional and strategic claims 'aimed at establishing a unified state of all the Muslims of Transcaucasia regardless of geographic contiguity, with its capital in Baku'.[10] Significantly, the ADR's proposed geo-body did not include Turkic-speaking areas in Iran, for whom the very idea of a sovereign republic named Azerbaijan was controversial. Tehran adhered to what it saw as an older and more authentic meaning of Azerbaijan as the geographic term for its north-west *iyalat*, with its capital at Tabriz and its 'proper' northern border along the River Aras. The appearance of a sovereign entity named Azerbaijan north of the Aras conjured the spectres of Iranian territorial losses to Russia in 1813 and 1828 and the prospect of new claims in the future. The ADR deferred to Iranian sensitivities by naming itself Caucasian Azerbaijan in official correspondence.[11]

Incorporation by the Soviet state in April 1920 brought an end to the short-lived sovereign politics of Azerbaijani Turkic nation-building. But sovietisation did not spell the end of the Azerbaijani Turk tradition *tout court*. For the first seventeen years of Soviet rule the majority nationality in the Azerbaijani Soviet Socialist Republic (AzSSR) continued to be known in Russian by the term *tyurki* and their language as *tyurkskiy*. These terms are distinct in the Russian language from *turok* ('Turk') and *turetskiy* ('Turkish'). While *tyurkskiy* can be parsed as 'Turkic' (as in Germanic, Gallic, Nordic, and so on), there is no obvious translation in English for *tyurk*. Used inconsistently by early Soviet officials, this term referred loosely to Turkic peoples in the

Soviet Union, and especially to the Turkic majority in Azerbaijan: the Azerbaijani Turks.

The Soviet Union's nominal preservation of the Azerbaijani Turk tradition obscured several important disjunctures. First, retaining the Azerbaijani Turk category conspicuously maintained a relational framework to Turkic identities beyond Soviet borders, but inverted the defensive emphasis on *Azerbaijani* Turk identity into an offensive emphasis on Azerbaijani *Turks* as a 'red beacon' showcasing the Soviet model to the Middle East.[12] The AzSSR became 'the bridge to Soviet politics in the East'[13] and an emblematic venue for events symbolising cross-border connectivity, such as the Congress of the Peoples of the East in 1920 and an inaugural Turcological Congress in February–March 1926.[14] Second, the closely proximate borders of the AzSSR submerged the unfinished and internally contested nature of bordering the ADR. Continuity obscured local Armenian resistance to the ADR's sovereignty over the south-western periphery of the republic, neither completely pacified nor resolved through negotiation.[15] This allowed the ADR to be subsequently remembered as a more solidly sovereign space than it actually was: an integral cartographic image of a continuous and sovereign Azerbaijani Turk geo-body. Third, though close, the borders of the ADR and AzSSR were not identical. Through Moscow's allocation of Zangezur to Armenia, the creation of an exclave in Nakhichevan and the establishment of a territorial autonomy in the Nagorno-Karabakh Autonomous Oblast (NKAO), the AzSSR was a truncated, ruptured and ethnically stratified version of the Azerbaijani Turk tradition.[16]

Finally, unlike almost everywhere else in the Soviet Union, the Azerbaijani Turks were not the eponymous titular nation of their republic. As Azerbaijani *Turks*, their titular claim to Azerbaijan – still conceived in geographic terms – remained implicit and adjectivally qualified. The same was true for the new republic's two autonomies: both Nakhichevan and Nagorny Karabakh designated geographic, rather than ethnographic, spaces. The AzSSR and its constituent parts were thus sovietised ambiguously as *shared space*, and not the primordial homelands of designated titular nations. For Azerbaijani Turks this was underscored by the fact that *tyurki* accounted for just 63 per cent of the overall population in 1926, a proportion that further declined until World War II. By institutionalising the AzSSR as a shared space without an explicit, eponymous titular nationality, sovietisation established a geo-body with defined borders, but remained ambivalent on the question of whose geo-body it was.

From 'Lighthouse' to 'Fortress'

In 1937, as if someone had flipped a switch, 'Azerbaijani Turks' (*tyurki*) became just 'Azerbaijanis' (*azerbaydzhantsy*), and 'Azerbaijani Turkic' (*tyurkskiy*) became the 'Azerbaijani' (*azerbaydzhanskiy*) language. The change followed the 1936 dissolution of the Transcaucasian Socialist Federal Soviet Republic, the bureaucratic structure comprised of Armenia, Azerbaijan and Georgia, and the AzSSR's formalisation as a separate unit of the Soviet Union. But there was more than bureaucratic expedience involved. The change also coincided with the Great Terror, and assumed its modalities. Accusations of pan-Turkism claimed thousands of lives.[17] Historian Harun Yilmaz writes: 'When the carnage came to an end in 1938, there were no experienced historians left . . . Baku, an important center of Turkology before 1937, was deprived of Turkologists.'[18]

The AzSSR was one of several borderland units in the Soviet Union conceived in terms of a 'Piedmont principle' projecting Soviet values beyond its borders.[19] This kind of 'lighthouse policy' emphasising cross-border commonality was vulnerable, however, to developments in the external identities to which such lighthouses were vectored and could reverse to a 'fortress policy' emphasising difference. The raw materials of nationhood – ethnonyms, scripts and theories of origin – could change with regional and international winds. This was the case with the AzSSR. Through the 1920s and early 1930s its majority Turkic identity was seen as an asset in influencing neighbouring Turkic communities in the Middle East. But unlike similar 'lighthouses' in Moldova or Karelia, for example, Azerbaijan's intended audiences were not small and relatively marginal states like Romania or Finland, but the regional powers of Turkey and Iran. Vigorous nation-building efforts in Kemalist Turkey through the 1920s and 1930s redefined the meaning of 'Turk' as the secular national identity of a new nation-state, Turkey. In Pahlavi Iran, nation-building over the same period centred on Persian history, culture and racial purity to portray the country's Turkic minority identity as an unfortunate accident of history. Both of these developments unfavourably reflected onto the AzSSR's Turkic identity. The Soviet lighthouse policy was exposed as being vulnerable to transformations in the external traditions of Turkishness it was meant to influence.[20] Ironically, the Soviet state confronted essentially the same problem that Mamed Emin Rasulzade had faced twenty years previously: to define a national identity in Azerbaijan that would contain unwanted synergies with Turkic spaces on its borders. A defensive reformulation of the ethnic character of Azerbaijan – as fortress, not lighthouse – was needed.

That reformulation was provided by a new tradition, which I term 'proto-Azerbaijanism'. Reflecting a wider Soviet shift towards more primordially conceived identities, the new doctrine stressed autochthonism and the quest for pre-Turkic ancestors in antiquity, with the emphasis on the homeland of the AzSSR rather than theories admitting migration. Proto-Azerbaijanism, developed among others by Soviet Azerbaijani academicians Igrar Aliyev (1924–2004) and Ziya Buniyatov (1923–97), embedded two highly significant divisions within subsequent imaginings of Azerbaijan. First, at the intra-ethnic level proto-Azerbaijanism resulted in a politically charged schism between the Turkic content of Azerbaijani identity and new theories of origin centred on the territory of Soviet Azerbaijan. The murder of thousands of citizens on charges of pan-Turkism further embedded this schism, and retrospectively lent a nationalist, anti-Stalinist legitimacy to turcophile ideas. This perception was enhanced by the fact that shortly after redesignation, the Azerbaijani language converted on 1 January 1940 to a cyrillicised script, after Latinisation had displaced Arabic in the 1920s.[21] In less than twenty years two generations of Azerbaijanis had been separated from their literary past; now they were renamed as a new nation and forced to use a Cyrillic script.

Second, proto-Azerbaijanism lent the division with Iranian Azerbaijan an air of historical authenticity. It asserted the existence of a contained geo-body north of the Aras, rather than a macro-Turkic geo-body traversing it. New theories minimised the role of medieval Turkic migrations in the origins of the Azerbaijanis, and emphasised autochthonous elements instead. The doctrine conjured pre-Turkic ancestors among the Iranian Medians and the Caucasian Albanians, a previously little-known Christian people inhabiting parts of the eastern Caucasus until the eighth century. Proto-Azerbaijanism thereby aligned symbiotically with the dominant, unitary concept of Pahlavi Iranian nationalism, *kasraviyya*, predicated on Persian high culture, ancient history and racial unity.[22] The two doctrines essentially concurred that Turkic ethno-linguistic continuity across the Aras – an imagined community of all Azerbaijanis – was the inauthentic residue of medieval migration that obscured a more fundamental historical divide.

The post-1937 Azerbaijanis were, as Charles King writes of the Moldovans – another Soviet nationality subject to the political winds of lighthouse and fortress policies – a 'stipulated nation': a bureaucratic requirement of super-ordinate Soviet political goals with an uncertain, contestable fit with local ethnographic realities.[23] Proto-Azerbaijanism would define orthodox nationalism in the AzSSR throughout the later Soviet decades. As in Moldova, it gave rise to a political and cultural elite habituated and committed to an identity separate from the cultural identities of external powers. This elite did not perceive a single geo-body partitioned into north and south Azerbaijans. But a minority position maintained a pan-Azerbaijani perspective, encouraged in part by the Soviet Union's own post-World War II foreign policy adventures in Iranian Azerbaijan.

Within just four years an unanticipated reprise of Azerbaijan's 'lighthouse' role challenged the new 'fortress' identity. As part of the Allied occupation of Iran in 1941–6, the Soviet Union occupied Iranian Azerbaijan and other northern regions of Iran. Pan-Azerbaijani sentiments were encouraged as a possible prelude to a longer-term Soviet presence. In 1945 a year-long regional rebellion ensued in Iranian Azerbaijan, establishing a Provincial Government of Azerbaijan (PGA), beyond Tehran's control and led by veteran communist Mir Jafar Pishevari (1893–1947).

Historians are divided on the relative roles of indigenous and external forces in the PGA episode, including Azerbaijani nationalism north and south of the Aras.[24] While ethnic mobilisation in Iranian Azerbaijan served to highlight regional neglect by Tehran, on key symbolic issues the PGA proved tractable with Tehran. This indicated the limited political horizons – regional autonomy at most – to a southern Azerbaijani geopolitical tradition. The speed with which the PGA collapsed in December 1946 after Soviet withdrawal further signalled its dependence on the opportunity offered by the occupation.

The 'Azerbaijan crisis' marked an early confrontation in the nascent Cold War. Soviet acquiescence with American–British demands for withdrawal from Iran invested the division of Azerbaijan with a consensus on spheres of influence in the Middle East, allowing the Cold War's frontline to relocate to Eastern Europe.[25] But locally the encounter had posited the possibility of unification of the two Azerbaijans. This idea was more popular in the north, notably with AzSSR First Secretary Mir Jafar Baghirov and the many emissaries and cultural workers dispatched during World War II to Iranian Azerbaijan.[26] Yet following the demise of the PGA, these sentiments became taboo. Expressions of pan-Azerbaijani sentiments were relegated to the cultural fringes such as the 'literature of longing', a subdued but consistent genre that lamented partition.[27]

A Failed Irredentism

Through the long years of Leonid Brezhnev's leadership orthodox nationalisms in the USSR increasingly cohabited with less orthodox and more competitive expressions of national identity. In the AzSSR these drew on the censored Turkic past, leading to a creeping turkification of national history.[28] A background trend encouraging this tendency was the demographic expansion of the Turkic peoples in the Soviet Union as a whole.[29] This shift subtly gave greater legitimacy to more turco-centric theories of origin for Soviet Turkic peoples, undermining official emphases on autochthonous non-Turkic components. Proto-Azerbaijanism was not immune in specialist publications to creative fusions with a more turco-centric tradition. These involved backdating a Turkic presence in Azerbaijan to allow, at last, the union of Turkic culture with the coveted status of indigenousness. But a historical deepening of Turkic theories of origin brought with it a spatial lengthening along the north–south axis of ethnographic continuity between the Turkic populations in the two Azerbaijans, and a concomitant interrogation of the AzSSR's borders.[30]

The imagined unity of a single Azerbaijani geo-body, a 'Greater Azerbaijan', burst out of the academic and cultural fringes with the rise of the Azerbaijani Popular Front in 1989. Although formally eschewing border change in its first programme, the trope of partition ran consistently through the Popular Front's discourse, imagery and symbolism. Popular Front feuilletons mapped an enlarged Turkic geo-body reaching from the Caucasus mountains to Hamadan in Iran (Figure 2.1). Its activists physically dismantled border installations with Iran in December 1989, resulting in a stream of euphoric border crossings and family reunions. The ethno-cultural premise of an Azerbaijani identity truncated of Turkic content was dismissed as colonial artifice. According to a former Popular Front official:

> The West doesn't understand us. In our genes we are Turks. Until 1937 the nationality of our passports was Turkish. In 1936 Moscow decided to rename our language Azerbaijani, and we all became Azerbaijanis: Turks, Jews, Armenians, Russians. They are all Azerbaijanis. This is not a nation, this is citizenship.[31]

Pan-Azerbaijanism found an ideologue in Abulfaz Aliyev (1938–2000), a graduate of oriental studies, one-time dissident and native of Nakhichevan, who had written his doctorate on the Tulunids, a ninth-century Turkic dynasty that briefly broke free of the Abbasid Caliphate. Aliyev chose to call himself Elchibey, meaning 'messenger' or 'prophet'. His rhetoric combined a post-colonial turcophilia with messianic overtones:

> The struggle for a united Azerbaijan is my life's mission. It is my sacred wish that Azerbaijan, which has been divided and separated for centuries, be physically reunited. Spiritually Azerbaijan has never

Figure 2.1 Visualising 'Greater Azerbaijan': President Elchibey stares out from an expansive Azerbaijani homeland on the cover of this 2003 book, whose title reads *The Path to Liberation and Unity*. Used with permission of Adalet Tahirzade.

lost its unity, as many simple examples show. In the north we have never lost our connection with the history and literature of the south. We have learned about Shah Ismayil as a great leader, a great military commander and great poet of our country. Tabriz has been the capital of several of our states, whose history we have learned. We consider the [medieval] Aq Qoyunlu, Qara Qoyunlu, Ilkhanid and Atabek states as our own. [Ninth-century insurgent] Babak Khurrami is from Bilalabad village of Ardabil and his Bazz Fort is in Savalan ... Azerbaijan is our united and common motherland. There are no moral or spiritual divisions between us ... Division and separation is a Russian policy, practised on Germany, Korea, then Vietnam ...[32]

Elchibey, who would wear a lapel pin depicting Ataturk at meetings with foreign dignitaries and insisted on speaking to Boris Yeltsin through an interpreter,[33] was elected president in 1992. Sharpening the Azerbaijani contours within Iranian space, his fundamental proposition was that the Republic of Azerbaijan was a homeland to irredenta within the Iranian geo-body. His rhetoric reverberated around the region, inciting Iranian fears of Azerbaijani irredentism.

Elchibey's precipitous exit from power in 1993 owed primarily, as we saw in Chapter 1, to disloyal lieutenants seeking to profit from war. Yet this should not distract from the ideological failure of Azerbaijani irredentism and Elchibey's project to unite the two Azerbaijans. This failure was the result of the disruption of multiple layers of consensus embedded within the AzSSR's borders over the latter half of the twentieth century among three key audiences. First, from 1946 stability in the Soviet–Iranian border that divided Azerbaijani ethno-space served as the index of a regionalised Cold War détente. An 'Azerbaijani question' never emerged – unlike Polish, Serbian and Armenian questions – because key external powers accepted the territorial delimitation as constitutive of their own borders or spheres of influence, and saw no vital interest in challenging it.

Second, a new Soviet Azerbaijani elite had been established from the 1940s that was violently severed from pan-Turkic ideals and intellectually committed to the autochthonous teachings of proto-Azerbaijanism. This elite formed a significant constituency invested in the separate and contained geo-body of the AzSSR. Even once in government the Popular Front found surprising resistance to signature policies symbolising Azerbaijan's Turkic turn. The law to change the name of the state language from 'Azerbaijani' to 'Turkic', for example, was accepted only by twenty-seven to fifteen votes, with nine abstentions, on 22 December 1992.[34]

Third, and most critically, Azerbaijani irredentism lacked willing irredenta. 'Greater Azerbaijan' was a *northern* Azerbaijani geopolitical tradition. It drew its constitutive building blocks – the Azerbaijani Turk tradition, the elaboration of theories of origin around Turkic elements, and a geopolitical vectoring towards Turkey – from the northern experience. Northern euphoria in the early 1990s resulted, as Brenda Shaffer observes, in 'a limited irredentist movement in the north, but no visible partner in the south'.[35] Unlike Soviet Azerbaijan, acculturated Iranian Azerbaijanis enjoyed largely uninhibited mobility through the wider state in which they lived. This coincided with rapid economic development in the late 1960s and 1970s, resulting in significant population movements, above all to Tehran, diminishing regional identities. To be sure, a strong tradition of dissent endures in Iranian Azerbaijan to the present day, protesting alleged discrimination, negative stereotyping of Azerbaijanis in central state media and the dialectalisation of the Azerbaijani language.[36] But by the late twentieth century, a southern Azerbaijani tradition faced the classic dilemma of groups enjoying high periphery-to-centre mobility: fissures between those who have reaped the benefits of mobility at the centre and adopted its norms and culture, and those in the periphery seeking to raise the status of the peripheral culture.[37] Shaffer's research in the 1990s identified several cultural obstacles to a single imagined community of Azerbaijanis. Post-Soviet Azerbaijanis found their southern brethren conservative and religious; Iranian Azerbaijanis found their northern brethren russified and inappropriately liberal. Each group subalternised the other as the natural periphery to its own centre.[38]

The return to power of former Azerbaijani Communist Party First Secretary Heydar Aliyev in 1993 brought with it – for the third time in the twentieth century – a repudiation of cross-border cultural continuity and renewed emphasis on borders in demarcating a sovereign Azerbaijani nation. Heydar Aliyev was a Soviet security official turned president of a fractured and demoralised country. He sought a new idea around which to stabilise and rebuild the fragmented Azerbaijani republic. We will meet the resulting doctrine, *Azerbaijanism*, in more detail in the next chapter. An updated but recognisable variant of proto-Azerbaijanism, its dominant ethos was the affirmation of international legal norms, above all territorial integrity and a civic national community. Affective ties with the Turkic world were not discarded, but became symbolic and strategic rather than foundational and existential. Aliyev selectively incorporated aspects of Elchibey's Turkic revival, such as re-latinisation – but significantly not the renaming – of the state language, but rejected all irredentist undertones to reinvest in a contained geo-body north of the Aras. He oversaw the transformation of Azerbaijan's unwilling 'irredenta' in Iran into one among many 'diasporic' communities with which the Azerbaijan Republic had no special relationship.[39] It was a state-building solution to the obvious discrepancy between advancing Azerbaijani irredentism abroad and fighting Armenian irredentism at home.

In sum, accepting a limited geo-body as the foundation of the Azerbaijani nation-state tradition won out as the dominant tradition in twentieth-century Azerbaijani geopolitical culture. As the continual intellectual ferment accompanying Azerbaijani theories of origin shows, bordered territoriality defines Azerbaijani nationhood with less ambiguity than any primordial community. It is the pivot from territory to ethnicity on which the winning definitions of community north of the Aras have turned. The fundamental frame that enables this construct, without which only the disruptive unities of culture remain, is territorial: the bordered geo-body of an Azerbaijani nation north of the Aras.

Borders and the Armenian Geo-body

Already in antiquity a succession of Armenian kingdoms had acquired a precarious buffer spatiality, appearing ephemerally at moments of political vacuum in the rivalries between Parthia and

Rome, and later Persia and Byzantium. A short-lived expansion in the second and first centuries BCE established a macro-template for Armenia, one that hangs on walls in Armenian classrooms today rendering all subsequent iterations of Armenian territory residual. Until the Middle Ages polities would intermittently emerge, albeit with markedly variable borders around a historical core, on the basis of recognisably Armenian kinship, spiritual and cultural genealogies: royal houses, the Apostolic faith, aesthetics in architecture and literature, and the Armenian language. When Armenians began to consider their place in a world of nations in the modern era, Razmik Panossian has argued that they did so 'multi-locally'. Geographically, three sets of parallel awakenings 'came from different directions, but were intertwined in their common goal of forming one nation'.[40] Panossian's perceptive argument highlights the plurality of territorial locales for the imagining of Armenian nationhood, and in turn the intractable question of territorialising a multi-local nation.

A Multi-local Awakening

Although one over-arching national identity was the eventual – and not inevitable – result, the dispersal of Armenians across numerous locales and two empires generated two cultural-linguistic patterns, two distinct geopolitical traditions and plural answers to different 'Armenian questions'.[41] A Western tradition drew on ideas of liberal reform, universalist values, literary realism and constitutionalism, and reflected the middle-class values of Ottoman Armenians integrated in the urban economies of Constantinople, Smyrna and further afield in Europe. An Eastern tradition characterised Armenians in Russian Transcaucasia, drawing on romanticism, social radicalism and populism and the experiences of Armenians in Moscow, St Petersburg and Tartu. Between Western and Eastern points lay a centre point composed of the six Ottoman *vilayets* (provinces), venerated by Armenians as the *Yerkir* ('the Country'). Although there was an urban Armenian elite in the towns of the *Yerkir*, its main Armenian demographic presence was a socio-economically marginal and politically vulnerable peasantry.[42]

Territory played an ambivalent role across this triadic structure. This was most evident in the Western tradition, in which physical and cultural distance characterised the relations between an urban elite far from the homeland and a rural peasantry, many among whom no longer spoke Armenian. In the Armenian language the distinct concepts of *azgaser* ('a lover of nation or community'), preoccupied with the *azg* ('nation', 'national community'), and *hayrenaser* ('a lover of the homeland', 'patriot'), more invested in the *hayrenik* ('homeland'), captured this distance.[43] Moreover, socio-economic and political concerns in the homeland threatened the (relatively) privileged standing of the urban Armenian elite in the Ottoman system. Yet neither did ethno-demography support an Armenian claim across the six eastern *vilayets* imagined as the *Yerkir*. The Ottoman demography of Armenians remains embroiled in political and methodological controversies, but it is clear that at *vilayet* level Armenians were at best a plurality and constituted majorities only in localised contexts, such as the city of Van.[44] Ottoman attitudes were no less complex, being shaped by an increasing sense of crisis at successive secessions from the empire.[45] The eastern *vilayets* were both a wild and vulnerable hinterland, beyond firm central control and neighbouring a rapacious imperial rival, Russia, which in 1878 had annexed Ottoman territories in Batumi, Kars and Ardahan. These territories' return was linked to reform commitments conceded by the Ottomans in the Treaty of San Stefano. An existential and contiguous threat of foreign annexation consequently underpinned Ottoman thinking about the Armenian *vilayets*.[46]

One solution was that put forward in the Armenian National Constitution of 1863. In a pattern analogous to the deterritorialised programme of cultural autonomy espoused by liberal Muslims in the Russian Empire, this proposed a reform of the Ottoman Empire's own system of communal (*millet*) institutions.[47] This would establish a network of community structures not tied to any specific territory, redefining Armenian nationhood '*within* the Ottoman domains, as a self-governing (and dispersed) nation within a reforming empire'.[48] The potential for reform of the deterritorialised *millet* system was superseded, however, by a deteriorating political situation, repeated massacres of Armenians in the 1890s and in 1909, and the challenge of the Eastern tradition emanating from Armenians in Russian Transcaucasia.

Territoriality was more central, yet still ambiguous, in the Eastern tradition. Ethno-demographically, despite sometimes being popularly referred to as 'Persian Armenia', the Armenian presence in the areas annexed by Russia in 1828 was tenuous. There were no Armenian majorities in any of the khanates under Persian rule prior to Russian annexation, although population exchanges between Muslims and Armenians following the treaties of Gulistan and Turkmanchay rapidly changed the demographic picture.[49] In 1828–40 the first territorial unit defined explicitly as Armenian since the collapse of the Bagratid Armenian kingdom in 1045, the Armenian oblast, appeared on the map as a constituent part of the Russian Empire. With minor changes, the oblast provided the basis for the Yerevan *guberniya* formed in 1849. Following further population movements in the 1870s, the Yerevan *guberniya* assumed a new significance as for the first time in the modern era Armenians became a majority population within a defined territorial unit. But this space still comprised only a fragment of the popular trope of 'historical Armenia'. Suffused with revolutionary, patriotic and populist ideals of romantic thinkers such as Johann Wolfgang von Goethe and Friedrich Schiller, the Eastern Armenian tradition embraced a wider concept of historical Armenia and linked it to ideals of radicalism, romanticism and national liberation.[50] The result was the imagining of an ethno-cultural Armenian community beyond temporal and spatial boundaries, not tied to any particular territorial unit or claim.

Between the distant imaginings of a reformed Ottoman citizenship or a transcendental Armenian ethno-space were the increasingly insecure conditions in the territories of the Ottoman Armenian *vilayets*. The need for self-defence and the emergence of local leaders such as Mkrtich Portukalian (1848–1921) and Mkrtich Khrimian (1820–1907) eventually bridged the urban–rural divide and introduced a new sense of territoriality into imaginings of the nation as an actor and agent, rather than passive abstraction. This led to a homeland-based nationalism that fused with the Eastern tradition in the programmes of several Armenian political parties, the Armenakans, Hnchaks and Dashnaktsutyun.[51] 'Revolutionary' Armenian political parties remained committed to a reformed autonomy within the framework of the Ottoman state for as long as this appeared feasible, including an ephemeral alignment with the Young Turks' reform agenda almost up to the onset of World War I. But by that time there was no unambiguous territorial referent or encompassing space that could territorialise 'Armenia'. In both Ottoman and Russian empires, Armenians remained divided between urbanised elites in Istanbul, Smyrna, Tiflis, Baku and other cities, and distant hinterland peasantries. They did not constitute ethno-demographic majorities in any of the territorial units in which they lived, with the single exception of a tenuous majority (53 per cent in 1897) in Yerevan *guberniya* interspersed with a substantial Muslim population, while there were substantial demographic enclaves of Armenians in Yelizavetpol' *guberniya* and the city of Baku.

The First Republic, Wilsonian and Soviet Armenias

The Armenians' uneven ethno-demography was considerably levelled by the 1915–16 genocide.[52] Genocide deterritorialised Ottoman Armenians in the most literal, physical sense. Yet it also territorialised Western Armenia, by sacralising it as the lost homeland of an 'orphaned nation'.[53] Genocide embedded the trope of 'lost lands' at the heart of Armenian geopolitical culture and, coinciding with a period of extraordinary territorial flux, rendered all real-world borders legitimately questionable. This was the context for the emergence of two vastly different geopolitical visions of Armenia. First was the unforeseen appearance in 1918 of the first Republic of Armenia (RA), led by the Dashnaktsutyun. Appearing by default, the RA left a deeply conflicted legacy to Armenian geopolitical culture. It was, on the one hand, the first sovereign polity bearing the name Armenia to appear on the map since the eleventh century, it featured an Armenian majority, and its armed forces won a clutch of symbolically transformative victories over Ottoman forces in spring 1918 permitting a short-lived survival. On the other hand, its territorial scope was so small that it was known pejoratively as the Yerevan or Ararat Republic. The Armenian National Council's declaration 'did not include the term "independence", for no one was sure if there was going to be an Armenia or, if there was, of its exact parameters'.[54] Nearly half of its population were refugees from Ottoman Armenia; disease and hardship took a devastating toll on the population.[55] It was in no position to pursue territorial claims, other than through purely symbolic moves such as the declaration of unification with Western Armenia of 28 May 1919, and it lost control over Kars and Ardahan to Turkey in October 1920. As a symbol of independence, the RA's legacy would be an enduring schism among Armenians: championed by the Dashnaktsutyun in diaspora, it was condemned in the Soviet Union.

Contrasting with the RA, the project for an Armenian state elaborated by President Woodrow Wilson for the Treaty of Sèvres immortalised an expansive and integral Armenian geo-body, comprising almost all of three of the eastern *vilayets* (Erzurum, Van and Bitlis), part of Trebizond *vilayet* to allow maritime access, and Eastern Armenia.[56] The scalar contrast between the 96,500 kilometres assigned to 'Wilsonian Armenia' and the rocky 7,200 kilometres declared as the RA could not have been starker. Although formally agreed to by the rump Ottoman government in August 1920, 'Wilsonian Armenia' remained a purely cartographic construct divorced from the realities of both military control on the ground and the viability of a state with only the most tenuous of hypothetical Armenian majorities.[57] Nevertheless, few images depict the deficit between aspirational and real-world Armenian homelands so starkly. 'Wilsonian Armenia' entered the visual iconography of the Armenian terrorist groups active in the 1970s, the Armenian Secret Army for the Liberation of Armenia (ASALA) and the Justice Commandos of the Armenian Genocide, as the symbol of a dissident geopolitical tradition.[58] Even then, it was divisive: diasporan militant (and ex-ASALA member) Monte Melkonian (1957–93) described 'Wilsonian Armenia' as 'grossly indefensible—morally *and* militarily'.[59] To this day the Wilsonian geo-body remains a visual staple of popular geopolitical culture in Armenia, appearing for example on calendars, memorabilia

Figure 2.2 A 2015 wall calendar commemorating 'Wilsonian Armenia'. Author photo.

and T-shirts on sale at the weekend at the Vernissage market in Yerevan (see Figure 2.2).

The cartographic efflorescence of 'Wilsonian Armenia' in the Treaty of Sèvres was quickly eclipsed by the Treaty of Lausanne, in which Armenia was not even mentioned. The fragment of this wider imagined space covered by the RA was sovietised as the Armenian Soviet Socialist Republic (ArmSSR). It was the USSR's smallest full union republic, covering 29,800 square kilometres or 0.13 per cent of Soviet territory, with a population of 880,000 in 1926. It was also the most ethnically homogenous republic, with Armenians accounting for more than 88 per cent of its population from the late 1950s. The disputed territories that the ArmSSR received as part of its Soviet delimitation, Lori in the north and Zangezur in the south, contrasted with multiple tiers of lost claims, from the regions of Nakhichevan, Javakheti and Nagorny Karabakh in Soviet Transcaucasia, to the briefly held provinces of Kars and Ardahan, and beyond them to the wider homeland, the *Yerkir*.

Two 'Repatriations'

Capitalising on the Soviet Union's post-war political standing within the Grand Alliance, in June 1945 Joseph Stalin resurrected the 'Armenian question' to lay claim to Kars and Ardahan, territories originally annexed by Russia from the Ottoman Empire in 1878 and then lost by the RA to Turkey in 1920.[60] Armenian diaspora organisations mobilised around the Soviet demands, and hundreds of thousands of diasporan Armenians were invited to repopulate a fragment of the homeland that would soon be restored. But Stalin rapidly backed down in the face of coordinated resistance from the United States, Britain and Turkey, and by October 1946 the territorial claims had been abandoned. Nevertheless, nearly 90,000 diasporan Armenians – about 10 per cent of all Armenians then living outside of the USSR – were 'repatriated' to the ArmSSR in 1946–8, a 'homeland' that as Western Armenians they had never been to.[61] Their experience was deeply ambivalent, as they were neither welcomed nor accepted by a homeland whose cultural codes, collective memories and political traditions were very different from their own. Repatriates and locals subalternised each other: repatriates were mocked locally as *aghpars* ('brothers'), 'a derogative term signifying both the claim and the negation of national unity'.[62] They in turn claimed more authentic national memories of the 'uncensored and often exaggerated history of the "*fedayee* past"'.[63] Although many repatriates eventually integrated, they became the largest category of those targeted by post-war Soviet deportations on grounds of political disloyalty in 1949; almost every second repatriate, or 40,000 people, were forcibly relocated as supposedly 'disloyal' citizens.[64]

In a lesser-known coda to the movement of diaspora Armenians to the ArmSSR in the late 1940s, a second 'repatriation' followed for part of that republic's Azerbaijani population. No longer classified as *tyurki* of indeterminate homeland but as *azerbaydzhantsy*, they were subject to a programme to resettle them from the ArmSSR to the cotton fields of the Kura-Aras basin in the AzSSR beginning in 1947. The campaign came at the request of the ArmSSR leadership, ostensibly to make room for Armenian repatriates. Post-Soviet Azerbaijani historiography frames the campaign, which lasted until Stalin's death in 1953, as 'an open policy of deportation'.[65] But while a degree of coercion was certainly present, the lack of preparation, resources and organisation appears to account better for its limited success. Azerbaijan – like Armenia – proved an unwilling homeland as resettled Azerbaijanis encountered a similar array of problems to those of the Armenian repatriates in the ArmSSR. Local authorities wilfully neglected them; insufficient accommodation was constructed and resources were misused.[66] On arrival some repatriates were left literally for days on the railroad with no accommodation to go to; since they lacked basic foodstuffs and commodities, conflicts emerged with locals. Of a planned 100,000 settlers, according to one contemporary report only 53,000 were ever actually settled in the Kura–Aras basin.[67] Others, including several thousand who voluntarily moved to the AzSSR outside of the resettlement programme, tried to settle in other less climatically forbidding parts of the republic.[68] But many also tried to return to their former homes in the ArmSSR: some 1,155 households (around 5,000 people) were reported to have returned to the ArmSSR by 1954, a community caught between two homelands and welcome in neither.[69]

An Ambiguous Homeland

In 1963 Vahakn Dadrian presciently observed that due to the ethnic homogeneity of the ArmSSR the confrontation between socialism and nationalism would be the most severe in this small Caucasian republic.[70] That homogeneity contrasted, moreover, with the heterogeneous memories of places beyond the ArmSSR to which a large part of its population traced its roots. This territorial memory, preserved in family histories, the names of several neighbourhoods in Yerevan and even the urban design of the Armenian capital, was tied to that of genocide.[71] Until the 1960s genocide formed the core of cultural, religious, psychological but as yet not the political meanings of being Armenian.[72] Politically taboo, genocide was a collectively owned but privately practised moral narrative and heuristic frame against which the current circumstances of Armenians could be evaluated. As genocide moved towards the centre of national identity from the 1960s, however, the questioning of borders was an inevitable undertow to political awakening. Memories of places beyond the ArmSSR nurtured a hidden transcript of territorial restoration that over time combined with sanctioned Soviet narratives and the experiences of Armenians beyond the ArmSSR to destabilise the Soviet Armenian geo-body.

In the post-Stalinist Soviet Union legitimate expressions of Armenian identity focused on rehabilitation of cultural figures purged in the 1930s, Armenian contributions to World War II, and the Armenian language. Yet already from the 1960s these expressions of orthodox Armenian nationalism cohabited with a subversive script of territorial restoration. Irredentist tropes, for example, were a consistent thread in late Soviet Armenian poetry.[73] Poet Hovhannes Shiraz's public recital 'upon repeated public demands' of poems reclaiming Ararat, Kars and Ardahan blemished the 1962 celebrations in Yerevan of the creation of the Armenian alphabet, generating – according to American Armenians invited to the event – 'an incredible atmosphere of national intoxication and massive obliviousness [to political consequences]'.[74]

The transgressive nature of territorial restoration was underscored by the fact that from the moment that dissidence was possible in Soviet Armenia, territorial claims were a primary idiom through which it was expressed. A dissident tradition focused initially on the three regions contested by Armenians in 1918–23 but given to their non-Armenian claimants: Nakhichevan and Nagorny Karabakh in the AzSSR, and Javakheti in Georgia.[75] Territorial claims to these areas were expressed in the 'affair of the seven' in 1962–3 and by the secret National Unity Party

(NUP) organisation in 1966.[76] Although NUP leaders were arrested, the organisation endured; a member openly burned a portrait of Lenin in central Yerevan in 1974.[77] These claims were reciprocated by letter-writing campaigns periodically emanating from the irredenta they sought to incorporate, notably in 1964 and 1967. Dissidence naturally focused on internal boundaries that the Soviet state could change. But the trope of 'lost lands' was as multi-local as Armenian geopolitical culture itself: beyond the claims to Armenian-populated territories in the Soviet Union lay the claims to Western Armenia. Territorial restoration was thus a bivalent idiom of dissidence that spoke to, and bridged, both Western and Eastern Armenian geopolitical traditions.

In addition to cultural elites and dissidents, Soviet Armenian scholarship of ethno-genesis – the primordial theories of origin coveted by Soviet cultural elites – became a third current destabilising the borders of the ArmSSR. Armenian ethno-geneticists shared a common preoccupation with their Azerbaijani counterparts to remove traces of migration. But while theories of Azerbaijani ethno-genesis focused on autochthonous ancestors to reify the AzSSR's borders, revitalised Armenian theories of origin led to the claiming – and eventual conflation – of the ancient polities of Urartu, Hayasa and Nairi as expansive ancestral precursors to modern Armenia.[78] Some of these genealogies, focused on the famous archaeological digs at Armavir, Artashat and Garni, claimed origins in the Ararat valley and hence *an* Armenian homeland within Soviet borders.[79] But claims of direct genealogical links between Urartu and Armenia also foregrounded the ArmSSR's residual character relative to ancestor-states reaching far beyond its borders. If some of the new theories of origin converged on the ArmSSR, they also dwarfed it. The ArmSSR became a mere microcosm of a macro-spatial 'artefactual Armenia': a popularly imagined, trans-historical ethno-space encompassing territories settled by Armenians past or present, and artefactually attested in ruins, inscriptions, churches, monasteries and *khachkars* ('stone-crosses'). Even if its scientific elaboration remained for most arcane, by the 1980s artefactual Armenia melded scientism, pop-ethnogenesis and popular literary tropes, such as the Armenian highland (*haykakan lernashkhar*), to tangibly expose the truncations of the Armenian homeland for wide audiences.

Poetics, dissidence and ethno-genesis, if independently of one another, expressed a multifaceted subversion of the Soviet Armenian geo-body. That this subversion was able to survive and thrive was in part owed to its successful hybridisation of Soviet and national frames.[80] Territorial restoration was never exclusively dissident but drew legitimacy from the identification of Armenian territorial claims with Soviet foreign policy concerns and indeed the official iconography of the ArmSSR, whose crest depicted Mount Ararat beneath a hammer and sickle. Elite stances on the borders of the ArmSSR were openly equivocal from 1945, when Catholicos Kevork VI (1868–1953) and Armenian Communist Party First Secretary Grigor Arutyunov (1900–57) addressed petitions regarding external and internal territorial claims directly to Stalin.[81] The half-centenary of the genocide on 24 April 1965 was the watershed moment when the Armenian communist elite lost control over the commemoration ritual. Mass demonstrations paralysed the whole of Yerevan, and protestors bearing placards calling for the return of 'lost lands' stormed a modest official ceremony in Yerevan's opera hall.[82] Although a purge of officials followed, this event augured two decades of Armenian nation-building that drew many of its affective symbols from beyond Soviet borders. The monumental and symbolic canon of the post-1965 ArmSSR consistently evoked places beyond its borders, such as the construction in 1967 of a genocide memorial (designed to face Ararat and in its structure to commemorate the lost *vilayets* of Ottoman Armenia) on a hilltop overlooking Yerevan, Tsitsernakaberd, and the 1968 commemoration of 2,750 years since Yerevan's founding as an 'Urartian' city. The borders of the ArmSSR increasingly constituted a publicly questionable injustice, the articulation of which flowed seamlessly into the legitimacy of the republic's elite.

Outside of the Soviet Union, the ArmSSR was alien to the post-1915 diaspora in multiple ways. Spatially, the geo-body of the ArmSSR was entirely different from the much larger Western Armenia. It was 'a mangled bit of land, that for lack of a better term, [was] called a republic', a vestigial space depicting truncation even within its own, Eastern Armenian, tradition.[83] Ideologically, the sovietisation of Armenia posited a profound fracture within the post-1915 diaspora between the Dashnaktsutyun, excoriating the ArmSSR and celebrating the first republic as the true symbol of Armenian independence, and the Apostolic Church and Ramkavar and Hnchak parties, more sympathetic to the ArmSSR.[84] This division split the diaspora for generations. Culturally, the formation of the ArmSSR embedded a divide between the Eastern Armenian dialect, institutionalised as a state language, and the Western Armenian dialect, stateless and subjected to new socio-linguistic pressures as a diasporan language. As Gerard Libaridian observes: 'Few [in the diaspora] had much to do with the First Republic or imagined present-day Armenia—whose people spoke a different dialect and used a different orthography, not to speak of the mores—as their homeland.'[85] Over time, the real-world territoriality of the ArmSSR was invested with a contingent expedience, a making-do, pending the restoration of the 'real' Armenia, itself increasingly abstracted as 'an idea and a museum'.[86] If the intensity of the nation-building process in Soviet Armenia would eventually be recognised in the diaspora, this did not translate into practical attraction or real substitution. Writing about diaspora migration to the ArmSSR in 1986, militant Melkonian – who as a Marxist revolutionary was sympathetic to the Soviet Union – concluded: 'Soviet Armenia should not be expected to be what its geographic boundaries preclude it from being'.[87]

To sum up, the interrogation of borders and the symbolism of larger homelands lost to truncation dominate twentieth-century Armenian geopolitical culture. While expansive geo-bodies also cue nationalist conceptions of wider Armenian state traditions in antiquity and the medieval era, they are inseparable from the master-narrative of genocide. The territorially revisionist Armenian gaze traces more than an ethno-nationalist dissatisfaction – hardly unique – with incongruent political and cultural borders, but also draws on the legitimacy of a collective unity of feeling on the historical cataclysm of genocide. Ambivalence towards Armenia's borders reflects what might be called the *metonymic illegitimacy* of the Armenian geo-body inherited from history, meaning that it is unable to symbolise on its own the plurality of Armenian traditions, places and indeed human bodies destroyed by genocide. By implication the attainment of a 'moral' Armenian geography assumes spatial flux in the 'immoral' territorialisations in which the demand for such a geography originates. In Armenian geopolitical culture, then, malleability of the geo-body is a route to more satisfying identities embodying resistance, recovery and release from victimhood.

By the 1980s metonymic illegitimacy had coalesced into a multifaceted questioning of the ArmSSR's borders as an inadequate reconciliation of fact, artefact and resistance. In the cultural sphere, Soviet Armenia increasingly 'filled in' as an Armenian homeland, bolstered by the congealing of ethno-genesis to the territory it covered. But its borders were increasingly overshadowed by an artefactual Armenia territorialising wide areas far beyond its borders as Armenian. By the onset of Gorbachev's campaign to reform the USSR, the contestation of Soviet Armenian territoriality was normalised and variously legitimated as the expression of post-genocide consciousness, anti-Soviet dissidence and legitimate orthodox nationalism. Yet the claims attaching to different territories – and the circumstances within them – were extremely diverse. Some claims implicated Armenians in an unlikely politics of international revisionism, without Armenian communities on the ground. Others involved contiguous Armenian minorities in neighbouring federal units of the same state; among these one, in Nagorny Karabakh, had autonomous institutions, others did not. Politicised, self-aware but fragmented, Armenian geopolitical culture lacked a single moment of unity. The resolution requesting unification with the ArmSSR, passed by the Armenian members of the NKAO's regional assembly on 20 February 1988, provided that moment.

'Seeing' Each Other

Over a tumultuous twentieth century territorialisations of Armenia and Azerbaijan have been plural, mobile and contingent (see Tables 2.1 and 2.2). Only the concerted efforts of

Table 2.1 Traditions and territorialisations in Azerbaijani geopolitical culture

Tradition	Associated with	Territorial referent/spatial extent
Northern Azerbaijan	Russian Empire, treaties of Gulistan (1813) and Turkmanchay (1828)	Khanates of Baku, Quba, Shirvan, Talysh, Sheki, Karabakh, Ganja, Erivan, Nakhichevan, Javad and Derbent; plus smaller sultanates and communities
Azerbaijani Turk	M. E. Rasulzade, Musavat, and the Azerbaijan Democratic Republic (ADR)	1911–18: federalised autonomy, based on Baku, Yelizavetpol and part of Yerevan *guberniyas* 1918–20: integral nation-state; western areas disputed with Armenia
	Soviet Union, 1920–37	Federated mainland-exclave republic, based on ADR minus Zangezur
Proto-Azerbaijanism	Soviet Union, 1937–91; ethno-genesis school	Soviet Azerbaijan; historical antecedents in Media, Atropatene, Caucasian Albania
Azerbaijanism	Heydar Aliyev, 1993–present	Internationally recognised Azerbaijani Republic, co-extensive with Soviet Azerbaijan
Southern Azerbaijan	Iran, 1813 and 1828	Khanates of Maku, Khoi, Urmiya, Tabriz, Qaradagh, Serab, Ardebil, Maragha, Gilan, Zanjan
Autonomist	1906–8: Tabriz Democrats 1920: M. Khiyabani and 'Azadistan' regional autonomy 1945–46: Mir Jafar Pishevari, Provincial Government of Azerbaijan	Autonomous local government based on *iyalat* of Azerbaijan (1920), later the *ostans* of Western and Eastern Azerbaijan (1930)
Greater Azerbaijan	Abulfaz Elchibey, Azerbaijani Popular Front 1989–93	Unclear: Turkic-speaking areas north and south of Aras River

Table 2.2 Traditions and territorialisations in Armenian geopolitical culture

Tradition	Associated with	Territorial referent/spatial extent
Western Armenia	Ottoman Empire; Armenian revolutionary parties: Armenakans, Dashnaktsutyun, Hnchaks	Ottoman *vilayets* of Erzurum, Van, Bitlis, Diyarbakir, Harput, Sivas
	'Wilsonian Armenia' and the Western Allied Powers, Treaty of Sèvres, 1920	Eastern *vilayets* of Erzurum, Van, Bitlis; part of Trebizond (Trabzon) *vilayet*
Eastern Armenia	Persian Empire 1639–1828	Erivan and Nakhichevan khanates
	Russian Empire 1828–1918	Armenian oblast' 1828–40; Yerevan *guberniya* 1849–1918
	First Republic of Armenia (RA); 1918–20, Dashnaktsutyun	Most of Yerevan *guberniya* plus Ardahan and Kars to October 1920
	Soviet Armenia, 1920–91	RA minus Kars and Ardahan, plus Zangezur
	Republic of Armenia, 1991–present, Pan-Armenian National Movement	Internationally recognised state of Armenia (co-extensive with Soviet Armenia)
De-territorialised Armenia		
National Constitution	Armenian liberals in the Ottoman Empire, 1863	
Diaspora	Communities in Middle East, South Asia, Europe, Russia, North and South Americas	
Imagined Armenia The Armenian plateau		Mountainous plateau bounded by Rivers Kura and Aras (east), Pontus range (north), Taurus range (south), River Euphrates (west)
Artefactual, historical, Greater Armenia	*Zartonk* 1650s–1800s; revolutionary nationalist parties, Dashnaktsutyun, Hnchaks	Unclear: wherever Armenian communities or artefacts exist on the Armenian plateau, that is Armenia: from Sivas in the west to Karabakh in the east

ethno-geneticists and patriotic historians – armed with the alluring trope of 'Armenian/Azerbaijani lands' – have rendered the cross-hatched pluralities of the historical evidence into unitary traditions and exclusive national claims. Yet if there is an overall pattern to be discerned, it is the persistent destabilising effects of trans-border ethno-spaces on the emergence of singular or hegemonic Armenian and Azerbaijani nation-state traditions. The Soviet territorialisations of both Armenian and Azerbaijani homelands were dramatic truncations of larger geo-bodies celebrated in dissident geopolitical traditions. National homelands constructed on only parts of these wider spaces incited what might be understood as a persisting hinterland consciousness: an affective awareness of perceived heartlands 'lost' elsewhere, captured in the poetic landscapes of poets and writers and perennially available for activation by political elites. This duality of homeland and hinterland identities, and the tensions between them, characterises both republics and implicates their borders in the perpetual politics of residuality. Azerbaijani geopolitical culture makes sense of truncated borders by reifying them, and its Armenian counterpart by challenging them.

There is, consequently, much more than legal principle at stake in contemporary invocations of territorial integrity or self-determination. Behind Azerbaijani appeals to the former lies an existential uncertainty as to the scope of the homeland and indeed the nature of the nation itself. Armenian evocations of self-determination see it as the only perceived alternative to the risk of repeated genocide. It is tempting to see the classic juxtaposition of two visions of nationhood – the civic *demos* versus communal *ethnos* – in this standoff. This reading has persuasive advocates, especially among liberal Azerbaijani intellectuals. But it is too simple and too absolute. As this chapter has argued, ethno-nationalist and civic conceptions coexist in Azerbaijani geopolitical culture. In the next chapter we will see that a similarly fraught cohabitation was a defining feature of post-independence Armenia.

Implicit throughout the foregoing analysis is the question of how the two geo-bodies of the ArmSSR and AzSSR came to 'see' each other. Two spatial scripts capture their relationship. A script of *assimilation* structured Armenian perceptions of the

Azerbaijani geo-body. This drew on a pre-existing storyline of Armenia's absorption into larger, alien-ruled states, driving historical fears of assimilation into incoming cultures perceived as politically dominant but culturally inferior. Since nationality was ascribed to all Soviet citizens at the age of 18, and could not be changed, Armenians could not be formally assimilated into other nationalities. However, they could be acculturated into an indeterminate Soviet identity, bureaucratically Armenian but primarily Russian-speaking and inflected with the cultural mores of the republic in which they lived. This was a concern for a dispersed nationality whose numerous communities outside of the ArmSSR always constituted minorities in politically significant ways. Popular terms in the Armenian language reveal a preoccupation with the policing of cultural boundaries. The Armenian term *otar* can be glossed as 'foreign', 'exotic', 'eccentric' or 'unfamiliar',[88] but can also assume a derogatory meaning implying not only non-Armenian, but *un*-Armenian. Another more colloquial expression, *shurtvats hayer* (literally, 'overturned Armenians'), connotes Armenians who are, in various senses, insufficiently 'Armenian'. This part-ironic, part-pejorative term applied, for example, to Armenians in other Soviet republics not conversant with a full Armenian cultural repertoire, such as russified Armenians from Baku or Tbilisi, no longer fluent in Armenian or over-reliant on Russian loanwords, and insufficiently invested in the Armenian national cause.[89]

Beyond the individual, the mass of the geo-body itself could also be assimilated into alien ethnic space. If in the Armenian–Turkish relationship a script of genocide applied to this process, in the Armenian–Azerbaijani relationship this was narrated as encirclement and depopulation. The perceived threat of encirclement was symbolised, for example, by Azerbaijani claims presented to the Paris Peace Conference in 1919, which at their widest extent would have left Armenia as a small island encircled by Azerbaijani territory: an Armenian Lesotho to an Azerbaijani South Africa. After Soviet incorporation, the absorption of Armenian space was narrated, at least until the late 1980s, as depopulation as a result of migration. The tropes of assimilation and genocide mingled easily, however, as in the expression 'white genocide' or 'Nakhichevanisation'. This dramatised Nakhichevan as the archetypal precedent of assimilated Armenian ethno-space and a prior script for the interpretation of developments in Nagorny Karabakh. Although Nakhichevan lost more of its Armenian population during the hostilities of the post-World War I independence era, popular narratives situate Armenian demographic decline as a Soviet-era phenomenon associated with Nakhichevan's incorporation into the AzSSR.[90] Underlying these perceptions is a commonly encountered assertion in Armenian geopolitical culture that an Azerbaijani nation-state north of the Aras is an artificial construct, and that Azerbaijanis are by implication 'really' Turks or Persians.

A script of *encroachment* captures Azerbaijani perceptions of the Armenian geo-body. Of course, encroachment and assimilation are two sides of the same coin, but the difference is one of minority or majority perspective. Azerbaijanis have always been the most numerous nationality in the South Caucasus – as well as being culturally affiliated with larger surrounding Turkic groups – and interacted overall with Armenians from a position of numerical preponderance. The script connects separate threads into a single narrative of encroachment by Armenian elements on the Azerbaijani geo-body: the 1828 transformation of the Muslim-majority Erivan and Nakhichevan khanates into the Armenian oblast, nineteenth-century Russian-sponsored Armenian resettlement in Transcaucasia, the 1920 allocation of Zangezur to the ArmSSR, and the penetration of an already residual Azerbaijani geo-body by the formation of the NKAO in 1923. The encroachment script parses the presence of Armenians in the South Caucasus as recent, externally mediated and illegitimate. Azerbaijani geopolitical culture locates the 'real' Armenian homeland in Anatolia, while also maintaining an even stronger denialist stance on the Armenian genocide than in Turkey itself. Moreover, encroachment is visually embedded by the fact that as a result of the Soviet delimitation of the AzSSR into a mainland and exclave, any map of Azerbaijan simultaneously portrays the borders of most of Armenia (its roughly 220-kilometre border with Nakhichevan and its more than 700-kilometre border with mainland Azerbaijan). Maps of Azerbaijan are hence simultaneously maps of Armenia, imposing a set of choices around representation and the design elements to be deployed in portraying Armenian, as well as Azerbaijani, space. The duality of simultaneous depictions of one's own and an adversarial geo-body is a specific feature of Azerbaijani cartography, often resulting in a 'second text' to post-Soviet maps of Azerbaijan.[91] A second relational dilemma lay in the representation of the NKAO within the Azerbaijani geo-body. The Soviet intertwining of Armenian and Azerbaijani geo-bodies thereby imposed two registers of an Armenian presence on the cartographic depiction of the Azerbaijani geo-body.

The bordered Azerbaijani geo-body and the metonymic illegitimacy of its Armenian counterpart meet on the ground in Nagorny Karabakh. Since the late 1980s these conflicted geopolitical visions have driven the transformation of this borderland, where Armenian and Azerbaijani geo-bodies overlap, into the cornerstone of their nationhood.

3 Borderland into Cornerstone

On a late summer's evening in 2014, Armen, an Armenian settler in the occupied town of Lachin (a place that he knew as Berdzor), told me a story. In the early 1980s a relative had married into a Karabakh Armenian family. The families decided to hold two parties, first in Yerevan and then in Karabakh. The Yerevan wedding band was so popular that Armen's relatives decided to hire them for the party in Karabakh too. The party in Stepanakert was in full swing when the band struck up songs celebrating Armenian *fedayi* of the World War I era. Armen recalled how a ripple of consternation passed through the hall. Although formally forbidden, *fedayin* songs were widely performed in Armenia. But performing them in Karabakh was another matter. Even though there were no Azerbaijanis at the party, the embarrassed hosts had a quiet word with the bandleader. Moderating their repertoire, the band played on and all was well. This anecdote is indicative of the fraught layering of twentieth-century Armenian–Azerbaijani experiences. The wedding band's playlist cued memories of historical violence overlaid by the Soviet internationalist order and its dictates of interethnic friendship. After the elapse of sixty years, however, Armen's story shows how variable – and spatially contingent – the policing of collective memory was. Informally tolerated in Armenia, *fedayin* songs disrupted a fragile modus vivendi in Nagorny Karabakh. They were the height of political incorrectness, and a reminder that even if the region had an Armenian majority, it was less than fully Armenian.

A Quintessential Borderland

Nagorny Karabakh, the territory at the heart of the Armenian–Azerbaijani rivalry, is a quintessential borderland. It is, first, a physical borderland where two geographies meet. The Karabakh mountains, the easternmost promontory of what Armenians call the 'Armenian plateau', descend rapidly to the plains. If you stand on the foothills above the River Khachen, a short distance from the capital Stepanakert, the steppe of central Azerbaijan stretches out below you to the east, close and immediate. Behind you to the north-west, invisible behind the formidable Karabakh mountain range, lies Armenia. This geography elicits two competing logics of belonging, access and identity, central to the region's modern history. The term Karabakh itself has attached inconsistently to highland and lowland spaces. Whereas Azerbaijani geographies see both as indivisible components of a single, wider space encompassing the territory between the Aras and Kura rivers, Armenian geographies more often differentiate an Armenian-majority highland as a separate space.

Like the Great Caucasus to the north, Karabakh has been both barrier and bridge. Between the thirteenth and eighteenth centuries terrain demarcated Christian and Muslim populations, the former dominant in the highlands and the latter increasingly so on the plains. Religious distinction was reinforced by different ways of life among nomadic lowlanders and sedentary mountaineers. Community structures were nonetheless linked by seasonal transhumance among Turkic groups along established routes to highland pastures.[1] Populations varied significantly according to the time of year, complicating the demographic snapshots captured by early censuses. Communities interacted symbiotically for much of history but also competed for resources and space; conceptions of place and identities overlapped rather than merged. In the early fifteenth century German traveller Johann Schiltberger, an Ottoman then Mongol prisoner and a regular visitor to the lowland plain he knew as *Karawag*, observed: 'The Infidels possess it all, and yet it stands in Ermenia.'[2] Schiltberger's observation appears to capture the liminality of a borderland between Muslim political mastery and a cultural narrative about Armenia that he may have heard from his Armenian hosts (and whose language he learnt). Although traditions of cultural borrowing and tolerance existed, especially from the eighteenth century when Christians and Muslims began to share highland space, overlap did not result in synthesis. Distinct local identities developed in Karabakh as variations on matrix Armenian and Turkic identities. A uniquely Karabakhi identity beyond the geographic did not emerge. This is evident in the border retained to this day in customary reference to 'Karabakh Armenians' and 'Karabakh Azerbaijanis'.

A borderland space is also manifest in the profusion of names, spellings and transliterations used of the territory, each a cue for different geo-cultural traditions. The term Karabakh, rendered *Qarabağ* in Azerbaijani and *Gharabagh* (Ղարաբաղ) in Armenian, is the Russian form of a Turco-Persian compound dating from the thirteenth century, meaning 'black garden' – popularly parsed as reference to the area's rich, dark soil. Artsakh is an older name preferred by many Armenians, evoking one of the peripheral provinces of ancient Armenia. With different meaning, as we will see, the term Artsakh also appears in Azerbaijani historiography.[3] Within each tradition territorial referents have been far from consistent. Whether your preferred term is Karabakh or Artsakh, it has come and gone and it has moved around. Neither term provides an all-encompassing frame for the region's tumultuous history.

Karabakh consequently offers fertile but unstable ground for nationalist imaginings. Over centuries when there was no geopolitical unit called Armenia, and before a geopolitical understanding of Azerbaijan had been imagined, local rulers exercised varying degrees of self-rule in a history that resists seamless integration into a national thread. Contemporary conceits asserting nationalist singularity deny this history, which defies reduction and is best understood in all its pluralities. An alternative framework is to see the region's history as a cyclical interaction between two other traditions of political authority, those of the distant suzerain and the local potentate. The list of suzerains who have ruled today's Karabakh from afar is long, encompassing Sasanid Iran, Arab Umayyad and Abbasid Caliphates, Bagratid Georgia, Ilkhanid and

Timurid Mongols, the Qara-Qoyunlu and Aq-Qoyunlu Turkmen tribal confederations, Safavid Iran, Nadir Shah, and finally the Russian Empire. With the single exception of the latter, suzerains were unable or unwilling to incorporate this distant periphery at the far range of their power in a sustained way, instead crafting expedient, transactional relations with local potentates.

During relatively brief periods when suzerains were at war or otherwise distracted, local potentates intermittently consolidated power into more independent traditions. Three such periods stand out. From the ninth century the princely house of Khachen, based around the eponymous river in today's eastern Karabakh, emerged as one of several houses claiming descent from the dynasties of early Christian eastern Caucasia.[4] In around the year 1000, converging lineages endowed the princes of Khachen with royal title. Plural lineages permitted a range of kingly titles. The princes of Khachen variably referred to themselves as kings of Artsakh and Syunik, titles situating them within the Armenian dynastic world whose culture and language they upheld, but also Albania, signifying a royal claim to the Christian domains of the defunct Caucasian Albanian kingdom in the eastern Caucasus. Dignitary title, like any other identity, was presumably contextual. More principality than kingdom, Artsakh-Khachen lasted fitfully for some 250 years with no permanent capital, no cities and no army; it nevertheless left a significant cultural legacy, for example, in the monasteries of Gandzasar and Dadivank. Between the seventeenth and nineteenth centuries vestiges of medieval Armenian kingdoms survived as small dynastic houses known as melikdoms after the Arabic term *melik* (meaning 'ruler'). The meliks retained autonomy as frontier garrisons for Turkmen then Iranian overlords.[5] And for sixty years in the turmoil following Nadir Shah's assassination in 1747 the Javanshir khans ruled the Karabakh khanate, a multi-facing frontier over which the stars of Muslim khans, Georgian kings and Armenian meliks would rise and fall with the ebbs and flows of both imperial and natural forces.[6] Local potentates were neither able to sustain their rule, nor did they have the ambition to expand and create states of their own. Statehood was a memory only for some, and a programme for none. Relative to the traditions of suzerain and potentate, that of the sovereign – and the associated concepts of territorialised sovereignty and nationalism – is the newcomer, indeed intruder. Karabakh became an object of competition because of the rise of two potential sovereigns disrupting a prior dynamic of great historical longevity.

By the 1980s Karabakh was caught between the boisterous national revival in neighbouring Armenia, and an uncertain status in Azerbaijan as new varieties of nativism also increasingly displaced Soviet internationalism in that republic. Two national projects met on the ground in the Nagorno-Karabakh Autonomous Oblast (NKAO), a formally shared space where each was at its most vulnerable. This chapter examines the geopolitical visions accumulating around Karabakh since the late 1980s. Their evolutions are deeply paradoxical. The claim to Karabakh settled the internal contestations of Armenian and Azerbaijani geopolitical cultures examined in the previous chapter. But their regrouping around a fractious borderland diffused its ambiguity across both. Spatial conceptions of Karabakh, always an elusive geographic concept, have not been stable but have metastasised to encompass wider spaces over time, and the overlap between spaces imagined as Armenian or Azerbaijani has grown. For the Armenian side this has meant the merging of territorial regimes of self-determination and occupation, with concomitant costs to legitimacy. On the Azerbaijani side the claim to Karabakh has driven the conjuring of new homeland spaces projected not only across contested space in Karabakh but also Armenia itself. As lands imagined as Azerbaijani or Armenian have increasingly overlapped and flowed into one another, the boundaries between them have begun to fray. Karabakh consequently emerges as both crucible and solvent, continually making and unmaking the matrix territorialities in whose name the claim to the territory is made.

Karabakh in Armenian Geopolitical Culture

In the Artsakh National Historical Museum in Stepanakert there is a large map depicting *Meds Hayk*, the 'Great Armenia' of antiquity, an expansive space reaching from the Caspian to within a few kilometres of the Black Sea. Against this backdrop, a small red outline traces the borders of the modern Republic of Armenia. It is a striking visualisation of the metonymic illegitimacy of the modern Armenian geo-body, and an image replicated in many atlases and history books about Armenia. But there is a particular resonance to the exhibition of this map in Karabakh. As anyone gazing at this map will be aware, the point where they are now standing does not fall within the narrow shard outlined in red. They are standing in that one small part of the artefactual Armenia dwarfing it where Armenians still live. The act of gazing upon this map, truly a map of pride and pain,[7] establishes Karabakh as a metonym for Armenias won and lost. Since 1988, Karabakh has demonstrated a seemingly boundless metonymic rapaciousness in symbolising disparate Armenian goals and values extending far beyond the territorial.

For a geopolitical culture overwhelmingly preoccupied with loss, Karabakh exerts a special fascination as the exception that proves the rule of genocide, truncation and artefactual decay. It first appeared as a significant site in Armenian spatial imaginations in the late nineteenth century, when its exceptionality to the dominant narrative of Armenian subordination attracted patriotic authors active in the national revival. In an epic history of the five melikdoms novelist and publicist Raffi (1835–88) wrote a counter-narrative, that of the last bastion of the fallen Armenian throne, a missing link to a glorious past and inspiration for the Armenian cause in the present.[8] The bastion trope assumed new meaning after genocide eliminated the Armenian population in Ottoman Turkey, violence in Karabakh itself in April 1920 and its incorporation as the NKAO into Azerbaijan in 1923. The Armenian population of the NKAO now constituted the largest territorialised Armenian community outside of a dramatically reduced Armenian geo-body. Reiterating the claim to Karabakh whenever political conditions permitted, the Armenian communist elite kept alive the notion that the Soviet delimitation was provisional, but Moscow held fast in refusal.

From the 1960s a different kind of exceptionality, as warning not example, began to attach to Karabakh. Political isolation from the cultural national revival taking hold in Armenia jarred with Karabakh's powerful demographic, historical and cultural resonance with that same nationalism. It was the only area of historical Armenia outside of Soviet Armenia that had retained a consistent Armenian majority, and held a distinguished place in popular narratives of historical resistance against political overlords. Karabakh's aesthetics – spectacular mountains and a profusion of precarious and overgrown monasteries – cued the archetypal poetic spaces of the 'Armenian plateau' and membership of an essentialised spiritual-geological unity. But by the 1980s this imagined unity confronted an enclave geography, a diminishing demographic majority and an internationalist ideology that, although withered, still censored nationalist expression considered unorthodox. The onset of perestroika gave an opportunity for Karabakh's allocation, an issue that had lingered since the beginning of the USSR, to be framed as a test case of Gorbachev's new policy. In pitching their claim, the Armenians again stressed Karabakh's exceptionality, this time as an error in applying the founding principles of the Soviet Union. (The profuse pamphlets and brochures advocating revision of the NKAO's status never made parallel or comparable claims for other territorial units in the USSR.) This allowed them, at a time of promised policy change, to frame the NKAO's enclave geography as a *policy* – as well as demographic, historical and cultural – aberration.

Since 1988 there have been essentially three distinct geopolitical visions of Armenia, each defined by its relationship to a corresponding vision of Karabakh (see Table 3.1). A post-Soviet flowering of the artefactual Armenia discussed in the previous chapter provided a backdrop to them all.

'Integral-Reformist Armenia'

The first vision, emerging in 1988, I term 'integral-reformist Armenia'. This awkward compound is deliberate, to emphasise that this geopolitical vision of Armenia was always a compound of a new, geopolitically imagined ethno-territorial order, and a reformist agenda seeking to test-run perestroika on the Karabakh issue. The link between the human rights of Armenians in Karabakh and an expanded Armenian geo-body effectively territorialised a

Table 3.1 Territorial visions and conceptions of Nagorny Karabakh in post-Soviet Armenian geopolitical culture

	Dominant expression	Primary divide	Political imperative	Leading proponents	Conception of Karabakh
Integral-reformist Armenia	Achieve contiguity/ rectify Stalinist injustice	Perestroika reformism versus Stalinist past	Reverse perceived cultural and demographic decline in NKAO; promote union-wide reform	Karabakh Committee, perestroika liberals	Armenian enclave unjustly separated from Armenia; ancient Armenian province of Artsakh
Compliant Armenia	Independent Armenian statehood	Sovereign Armenia versus Soviet Union; pragmatism versus external dependency	Secure viable Armenian state, including as a means to secure Karabakh	Levon Ter-Petrossian, Armenian National Congress	Self-determining republic consisting of NKAO plus Shahumyan; sovereign but with uncertain relationship to Armenia
Augmented Armenia	Viability of a single but bifurcated Armenian state; defensible borders	Nagorno-Karabakh Republic (NKR) versus Azerbaijan	Preserve post-1994 status quo	Nationalist consensus	NKR (2006 borders) as a mono-ethnic de facto state attached to Armenia; 'liberated territories'
Greater Armenian homeland	Wherever there is Armenian heritage, that is Armenia	Armenians versus 'Turks'; Armenian Christianity versus Oriental Islam	Preserve Armenian identity	Nationalist consensus; Samvel Karapetyan	Recovered fragment of historical homeland

communal morality responding to both Stalinism and genocide. This was the foundational moment of the Armenian national movement, establishing a moral deficit for any subsequent vision of Armenia that did not include Karabakh.

Geography mediated the emphasis in this compound.[9] In Armenia it was the reformist element that predominated: a revised ethno-territorial order was the means to substantiate and pave the way for wider political reform. Through this prism Karabakh became a cause célèbre among many reform-oriented Russian intellectuals, lending the Armenian agenda a formidable congruence with Gorbachev's stated goals for perestroika.[10] Karabakh thereby became a bridging metonym for 'de-Stalinisation' at local and all-union levels. In the NKAO the geopolitical vision was more paramount. The reform agenda was the means to realise the union of the oblast with Armenia, creating an integral Armenian geo-body – summed up in the rallying cry *miatsum* ('unification'). In the words of Igor Muradyan, a founder figure in the Karabakh movement and early member of the Karabakh Committee:

> The NKAO was a ghetto for Armenians, surrounded and unsustainable. We needed a different configuration. We needed contiguity as a strategic imperative. If there is a solution we can adjust the borders, but not to that former isolation; it has to be defensible and contiguous.[11]

The procurement of light weapons even at the earliest stages of the movement indicates that those pursuing this vision were fully aware of its conflict potential.[12] This was the darker alter ego to the reformist wing that presented itself as reasonable and law-abiding and which captured liberal imaginations in Moscow. The Karabakh Committee tried to contain it by ousting Muradyan and stressing the movement's peaceful and democratic character.[13]

For two years the ratio between the geopolitical and reformist components in the 'integral-reformist' vision of Armenia would fluctuate against the rapid and chaotic unfolding of events in Gorbachev's Soviet Union. The reformist component presumed a system-wide transformation of the Soviet Union that looked increasingly unlikely, leaving only the securitised geopolitics of territorial control. Moscow's imposition of direct rule in 1988–9 – a de facto secessionist policy removing the NKAO from Azerbaijani jurisdiction – appeared to admit the possibility of border change. Moscow's abandonment of this policy at the end of 1989 and the NKAO's return to Azerbaijani jurisdiction prompted more openly irredentist responses in Armenia. Armenia's increasingly sovereign governing institutions ruled formally on accepting unification and incorporated the NKAO into Soviet Armenia's budget in December 1989 and January 1990 respectively.[14] By this time national awakenings across the USSR had foregrounded myriad territorial claims and possible revisions of internal and even external borders. The March 1991 referendum on the preservation of the Soviet Union attempted to fold these myriad claims into a single commitment to the preservation of the Soviet state. Instead, it revealed the chasm between those republics pursuing alternative geopolitical visions as independent states and those still committed to their Soviet borders. Armenia was among the former, boycotting the referendum.

As the Soviet reform horizon faded away, so too did Soviet territorial categories keeping the NKAO within that horizon. The possibility of upgrading the NKAO to the next level up on the ethno-federal hierarchy, an autonomous republic, was half-heartedly discussed in 1988–9.[15] But Soviet geographies increasingly yielded to an insurgent reterritorialisation of Karabakh as 'Artsakh', a name associated in Armenian geopolitical culture with one of the fifteen provinces of *Meds Hayk*, the expansive Armenian kingdom of antiquity. Reconceiving Karabakh as Artsakh expressed an Armenian *prior tempore, prior jure* (first in time, first by right) claim to the territory. Chiming with the millenary timeframes favoured in Soviet theories of origin, the term exposed the name 'Karabakh' as an inauthentic Turco-Persian overlay. It also came with strong support from classical sources. As a widely disseminated information brochure produced by the Armenian Academy of Sciences pointed out, references to Artsakh as *Orchistene/Orchistena* abound in classical authors such as Strabo, Pliny the Elder and Ptolemy.[16] Artsakh thus imagined traced a bi-millenary

– if in fact intermittent – lineage to the very origins of Armenian culture. Of course, conceiving of the boundaries of Artsakh involves the imposition of a modern, homogenous and bordered territoriality on pre-modern, dynastic conceptions of territorial claims admitting considerable diversity, overlap and fluctuation. Different iterations of Artsakh across antiquity and medieval periods were consistently incongruent, and appear to have been larger than the modern NKAO.[17]

'Compliant Armenia'

In 1991 the imminence then fact of Soviet collapse transformed the context and parameters of the Karabakh issue in Armenian geopolitical culture. A new moral equation came into play: revising the ethno-territorial order in Karabakh now needed to be weighed up against the priorities and interests of a sovereign and internationally recognised Armenian state. In particular, the advent of sovereignty, and the transition from internal boundary dispute to interstate conflict, transformed two important parameters in the conflict to date.

First, the content of self-determination changed. In its evocation of the Soviet Union's founding principles, the early Karabakh movement appealed to a specifically Leninist conception of self-determination. Lenin's vision on the issue was contrasted with that of Stalin as more democratic and sensitive to local nationalism, including through the holding of localised plebiscites in the early 1920s.[18] This ignored Lenin's underlying dismissal of nationalism as anything other than an epiphenomenon of class struggle. But it made for a cogent argument in support of 'right-sizing' internal Soviet boundaries, something that if not common had happened several times in the USSR. With the Soviet collapse international law replaced the Leninist frame of reference for self-determination. Even if international law formally recognised the self-determination of peoples as a human right, it was considerably more ambivalent on border change. Outside of the context of decolonisation, international recognition of secession without the consent of the parent state was so exceptional as to have only one precedent since World War II: Bangladesh in 1971. A more likely prospect – especially in the light of the multiplicity of territorial conflicts accompanying Soviet and Yugoslav dissolutions – was international adherence to the *uti possidetis juris* ('as you possess') norm prescribing the recognition of new states within prior internal administrative boundaries.[19] An integral vision of Armenia and Karabakh confronted the fact that the territorial integrity of states was much better protected under international law than the territory integrity of union republics in the Soviet Union. Second, sovereignty accentuated the irredentist aspect to the Armenian campaign over its secessionist aspect. 'Integral-*reformist*' Armenia became 'integral-*revisionist*' Armenia in a conflict that now clearly had an interstate dimension easily read as irredentist, even if this reading often understated the agency of Karabakh Armenians.

A second vision of Armenia took note, and formally complied with, international sovereignty norms. This 'compliant Armenia' was the Armenia recognised and accepted by most of the international community and represented in formal cartography, that is, within its Soviet boundaries without Karabakh. The problem within Armenian geopolitical culture was that this vision of Armenia was also 'compliant' with its Soviet territorialisation, the revolt against which had been core to the national revival movement. Against an integral Armenian geo-body, a 'compliant Armenia' shorn of Karabakh regressively embodied the metonymic illegitimacy dogging Armenia's Soviet borders for decades, and consequently, an incomplete national self-determination. Karabakh had become a metonym of Armenian self-determination *tout court*.

Yet 'compliant Armenia' was far from being just window-dressing for international audiences. It embodied an extremely ambitious geopolitical project of its own. The Karabakh Committee and then the Pan-Armenian National Movement (PANM) attempted to link the successful building of an independent Armenian state to a fundamental paradigm shift away from the traditional Armenian preoccupations with Turkey, victimhood and reliance on an external patron.[20] Given the prominence of these concerns and fears of further violence in Karabakh, the PANM project was a far-reaching revision of the founding postulates of

Armenian geopolitical culture, one that might be called *étatiste* not so much in relation to the individual citizen but to the ethnic nation and, in particular, the Armenian diaspora.[21] Compliance in this vision was not restricted to international concerns over territorial integrity. It went much further to emphasise the imperative of realignment with what its advocates deemed the normal path of development of a sovereign nation-state, from which the twin spectres of pan-Turkism and Russian rescue had long distracted Armenians. Compliance meant normalcy, and the quest for answers to the salient problems of Armenians' place in the world in statehood, rather than the affective geopolitics of eternal enemies and friends. In the context of the dominant narratives of Armenian history and ongoing war in and around Nagorny Karabakh, this was an extremely radical proposition.

In the vision of an Armenia compliant with normal international relations, Karabakh's position was ambivalent. How would a 'normal' Armenian state deal with a situation that most international actors saw as abnormal and indeed transgressive of fundamental norms? Prominent PANM figures expounded an 'Armenia first' strategy, arguing that a secure and strong Armenian state would ultimately be the *sine qua non* of any favourable outcome in Karabakh. The Karabakh Armenians' own self-reliance was evoked as the archetype of the kind of sovereign action that PANM was advocating over the 'politics of demand' for which it roundly criticised the diaspora. In practice, the PANM attempted to preserve as much room for future manoeuvre as possible. The Republic of Armenia's Declaration of Independence, adopted 23 August 1990, evoked the 1 December 1989 joint decision of the Armenian Supreme Soviet and the Artsakh National Council on 'reunification', but did not define the republic's borders.[22]

The failed August 1991 putsch by Soviet hardliners, Azerbaijan's declaration of independence on 30 August and its abolition of the NKAO on 26 November accelerated the need to form a distinct state-political identity in Karabakh. In the final weeks of the Soviet Union's existence, ballots were held founding a successor entity in the territory, the Nagorno-Karabakh Republic (NKR). Although demographic unravelling within the territory was far advanced (see Chapter 4), the NKR's founding ballots consciously framed the polity as multi-ethnic. Voting forms for the 10 December 1991 referendum were printed in Azerbaijani and Russian, as well as Armenian, but Azerbaijanis did not participate. The result was a foregone conclusion in favour of independence at 99.9 per cent. A declaration of independence followed on 6 January 1992.[23] In parliamentary elections on 28 December 1991 and 11 January 1992 six (out of eighty-one) mandates were reserved for Azerbaijani-populated districts, although Azerbaijanis did not participate and no deputies were elected for these districts.[24] The parliament reserved a seat for an Azerbaijani deputy speaker – also left vacant.

If the founding of the NKR provided an expedient foil to accusations of irredentism, it invited others. Karabakh Armenian and PANM leaders framed the NKR as a self-determining unit, one of many such claims responding to the disintegration of socialist federations in the USSR and Yugoslavia. But how did the Karabakh Armenians qualify as a people separate from Armenians who could claim the self-determination right? What did the formation of a second Armenian state-political entity mean for the prior emphasis on unification? If the NKR had, as its representatives argued, observed Soviet legal requirements in seceding from Azerbaijan, how relevant were these arguments now that the Soviet Union was gone? Whose territorial regime counted? This last question was further complicated by the fact that the area claimed by the NKR expanded on that of the NKAO. In the first of a series of territorial accretions, it incorporated the Armenian-majority Shahumyan district that had shared a 40-kilometre border with the north of the NKAO. The claim was based on this district's unique status as the sole Armenian-majority district in the AzSSR outside of the NKAO.[25] In effect, the Armenia-Karabakh script of repressed unification was played out in microcosm in the dynamic between the NKAO and the Armenians of Shahumyan, again on the 'wrong side' of an 'artificial border'. But if an ethno-demographic Armenian claim could be asserted in Shahumyan, no such claim could be made in those regions interposing between Armenia and the self-proclaimed NKR – all of which were populated by overwhelming ethnic Azerbaijani majorities. The ethno-demography of the former oblast might have provided arguments for a contested self-determination but, emphatically, it did not solve the fundamental issue of enclave geography.

These issues were rapidly overtaken by the course of events on the battlefield. Karabakh's enclave geography was transformed by the military conquests of May 1992–October 1993 occupying a wide belt of territory, encompassing (in whole or in part) the seven Azerbaijani districts of Lachin, Kelbajar, Agdam, Jebrayil, Fizuli, Qubatly and Zangelan surrounding the former NKAO. Together they comprised more than the original surface area of the NKAO's 4,400 square kilometres. Their capture and occupation reached beyond the imperative of security to introduce conditionality as a possible future negotiating strategy: the territories – or some of them – would be returned on securing Armenian demands. Ostensibly they established a negotiating position of strength wielding bargaining collateral. But territorial overspill created critical new impediments to the realisation of a compliant Armenia in juridical, geopolitical or wider philosophical terms. It was a wartime geography that absorbed 'compliant Armenia' and never went away.

'Augmented Armenia'

By the mid-2000s there was increasing evidence that the expanded wartime geography of the NKR, and the occupation of territories it subsumed, had become an accepted reality in Armenian geopolitical culture. While the rhetoric of security continued to formally justify the NKR's expansive geography, symbolic attachments to all of the territories under Armenian control grew. An evolving scale of spatial metaphors naturalised possession of these territories, transforming the expedient into the existential. These dynamics, a kind of inexorable geopolitical mission creep, gave rise to a third geopolitical vision of an 'augmented Armenia'.

Mission creep manifested in the metaphors and visuals used of the territories surrounding the NKR. These shifted from functionalist-strategic euphemisms such as 'buffer zone' or 'security belt' (*anvtangutyan goti* in Armenian) to the affective claim of 'liberated territories' (*azatagrvatz taratskner*). In the late 1990s this term was radically nationalist; by the early 2010s it was normal in the Armenian media.[26] The slogan of '42,000 kilometres', the combined surface area of Armenia and Armenian-held territories in and around Karabakh, became popular.[27] Lexical and cartographic shifts ran in tandem. From the mid-2000s a new genre of 'cartographic exhibitionism' challenged compliant cartography depicting Armenia without Karabakh.[28] Exhibitionist mapping became the dominant practice outside of official government maps, deploying a wide range of iconographic and visual devices to smooth over distinctions between the NKR and the surrounding occupied districts. A new composite space and unified visual image became dominant. Through chloropleth technique, this image homogenised the complex and politically highly consequential interactions between three distinct geopolitical referents: a sovereign and internationally recognised state, Armenia; an unrecognised, de facto jurisdiction ostensibly aspiring to a separate sovereign identity but informally integrated with that state; and the wartime regime of occupied territories. Formerly Azerbaijani settlements were renamed with Armenian names often evoking local medieval geographies, settlements in the former AzSSR or even settlements in Eastern Anatolia. Revived medieval toponyms include the resuscitation of Varanda (one of the melikdoms described by Armenian novelist Raffi) and the renaming of the republic itself as Artsakh. Numerous place-names in the occupied territories evoke the names of sites left under Azerbaijani control in 1994, such as the villages of Nor ('new') Getashen, Nor Maragha and Nor Verinshen and Shahumyan district. In the former Azerbaijani district of Zangelan, renamed Kovsakan, several villages evoke sites formerly inhabited by Armenians in Anatolia, such Mush, Van and Alashkert (Eleşkirt). Multiple conceits of territorial revival coalesced on the occupied territories, evoking disparate times and spaces in Armenian geopolitical culture.

These strategies solidified into a formal transformation of de facto space in the NKR. The NKR's first constitution, adopted in 2006, affirmed the reconfiguration of the entity's internal administrative boundaries submerging the former NKAO within the wartime spatiality of conquered territories.[29] To the east and south, expanded Mardakert, Askeran, Martuni and Hadrut regions (*shrjan*) flowed outwards to the Line of Contact. In the more sensitive area interposing between the former NKAO and the border with Armenia two large new regions were created, Kashatagh and Shahumyan. Shahumyan encompassed both territory under Armenian occupation (the Azerbaijani district of Kelbajar) and areas that remained under Azerbaijani control at the end of the war in 1994 (former Shahumyan district). The easternmost 'fingers' of the former NKAO are also still controlled by Azerbaijan. These pockets of territory beyond Karabakh Armenian control cue Armenian references to Azerbaijani 'occupation' of parts of the NKR and the entity's own putatively incomplete territorial integrity as a mirroring riposte to the Azerbaijani discourse of Armenian occupation.

Justifying territorial augmentation came in different forms. Defensible borders and the strategic viability of the NKR is a common argument in the territory itself.[30] By this argument the current frontline establishes the optimum – shortest – interface with more numerous Azerbaijani forces. But it also supplies Armenia with security by adding 'strategic depth' to the latter's southernmost Syunik region, a mere 20 kilometres across at its narrowest point.[31] The expanded NKR thereby becomes a metonym for Armenian security, in Karabakh *and* Armenia. Returning regions to Azerbaijani jurisdiction would only lengthen the Line of Contact, so this thinking goes, and deepen insecurity. These arguments mediate a hierarchical coding of the various regions under occupation that slogans of 'not one centimetre' obscure. Lachin and Kelbajar, as districts interposing between the former NKAO and Armenia, have special significance. This is recognised in the framing of the 'Lachin corridor' as a core Armenian demand and is more subtly reflected in the submerging of both districts within larger macro-regions of the revised NKR in its 2006 borders. These two districts have been the focus of renaming efforts, their formerly eponymous administrative centres being renamed Berdzor and Karvajar respectively, and of material entrenchments. The road connecting the town of Goris in Armenia with Stepanakert was for many years the best in the South Caucasus. Construction of a second road, running between Mardakert and Vardenis in Armenia, was completed in 2015.

Resettlement efforts have also focused on these two regions, if with limited impact (see Chapter 8).

Populating a 'security zone' was always an inherently contradictory project. *Pace* claims of demographic engineering, exaggerated on both sides of the conflict, the reality of the expanded NKR was vast swathes of territory liberated of any human geography, Azerbaijani or Armenian. But where human bodies have feared to tread, the sticky attachments of sacralised territory have little hesitation. Reputable scholarship has long discerned the significant place of heritage in the former NKAO for the study of Armenian religious architecture and art.[32] But alongside such scholarship a more nationalistically inflected activism, driven by what Gerard Toal and John O'Loughlin call an *ecclesio-topographical gaze*, has played a significant role in imagining the ancient and expansive Christian palimpsest of artefactual Armenia as the sacred patrimony of the modern Armenian nation.[33] Exemplified by the work of Samvel Karapetyan, director of the Research on Armenian Architecture (RAA) NGO, this endeavour has traditionally enjoyed legitimacy within Armenian geopolitical culture as a response to genocide. Founded in 1982 in Germany and registered in Armenia in 1998, RAA frames its activities as a response to 'the premeditated destruction [of heritage] particularly in the lands annexed to Turkey, Azerbaijan and Georgia', and it has published an extensive library documenting Armenian heritage from hundreds of research expeditions.[34] Transposed to a context of Armenian military conquest, however, cultural restoration melds easily with territorial revisionism, legitimating de facto possession of territory as *repossession*.[35]

Yet the act of sacralisation remains partial. Satiating desires to recoup fragments of a lost homeland, the sacralisation of Karabakh simultaneously triggers the ecclesio-topographical gaze to look beyond its borders. Reprising Raffi's work of more than a century before, Karapetyan's ecclesio-nationalist literature also documents the lost territories of 'Northern Artsakh', the area to the north of the NKR, and to the west, Gandzak, the Armenian name for Azerbaijan's second city Ganja.[36] Beneath the western half of the modern Azerbaijan Republic an expansive Armenian palimpsest is revealed. In a recurring loop of territorial truncation, today's Artsakh is consequently revealed as incomplete and residual relative to a historically more expansive 'Northern Artsakh'. This is the circular lure of artefactual Armenia and its geopolitics: perhaps the core visual register of Armenian territoriality, in its expansiveness it destabilises any real-world Armenian polity built upon it.

Popular consensus on the expanded boundaries of 'augmented Armenia' has penetrated wider Armenian geopolitical culture to become widely consumed as a cartographic product, reproduced in innumerable maps, T-shirts, children's puzzles, key rings and organisational logos, such as that of Birthright Armenia, an organisation that introduces young Armenians from the diaspora to the homeland.[37] 'Augmented Armenia' reaches out to the diaspora through annual fundraising events for the construction of infrastructure in the occupied territories.[38] Citizen activists police its boundaries by lobbying Armenian politicians and media to reproduce them.[39] Depictions of Armenia without the occupied territories in public spaces are defaced and 'corrected' (see Figure 3.1). In a public opinion survey carried out in Karabakh in 2011, 60 per cent of respondents supported a maximalist definition of the NKR: all areas under Armenian control, plus the Shahumyan district and eastern fingers of the NKAO currently under Azerbaijani control.[40]

'Augmented Armenia' is problematic because it combines the legitimacy of self-determination with the illegitimacy of occupation and ethnic cleansing. Karabakh, a former rallying cry for liberals and human rights activists, morphed into a theatre for the very kinds of practice – exclusive nationalism, cultural suppression – denounced by the Karabakh movement and winning it popularity. That there is no resolution of this ambivalence is quietly recognised by elites in both Armenia and Karabakh. One senior Armenian official identified a zero sum schism within differing territorial conceptions of the NKR: 'the more the claim to these [occupied] territories is asserted, the more the claim to self-determination in Karabakh is invalidated'.[41] Another admitted: 'yes, of course it will be difficult to give the territories back, it's a problem waiting for us in the future'.[42] Senior de facto officials in Karabakh still privately recognise – at least in off-the-record

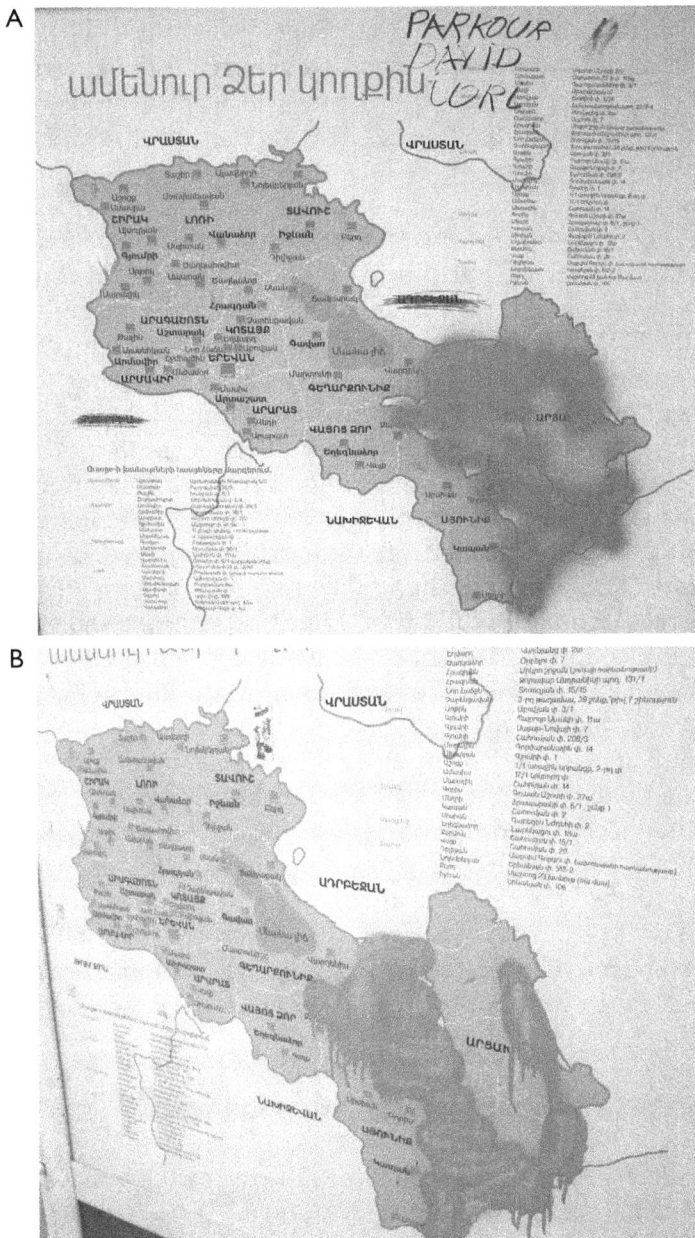

Figure 3.1A and B Policing 'augmented Armenia': graffiti at bus stops in Yerevan, 2015. Author photos.

conversations with Western researchers – a transactional basis for holding the territories.[43] But affective ties to these territories have far outstripped such calculations. In neither Armenia, nor especially in Karabakh, are elites able to take a firm public stance in defence of this position.

In sum, the three dominant visions of post-Soviet Armenia have all been defined by their relationship to Karabakh. 'Compliant Armenia' survives as a geo-juridical construct: it is the Armenia of formal statehood, legitimate interaction and foreign policy. But the PANM's political project to normalise Armenian geopolitics did not survive, and 'compliant Armenia' is not the territorial image that prevails in Armenian geopolitical culture today. Suffering from the same metonymic illegitimacy as its Soviet predecessor, it is eclipsed by the 'augmented Armenia' of nationalist consensus, popular geopolitics and diasporic mobilisation, centred on the cornerstone of Karabakh. Moreover, defending augmented Armenia necessitates the same geopolitics from which the first generation of post-Soviet Armenian leaders sought to liberate their country. Militarily, maintaining augmented Armenia over the long term was a prospect auguring the kinds of external reliance decried by the Karabakh Committee. Philosophically, defending the ethnic cleansing and seamless incorporation of Azerbaijani territories necessitated the kind of stable, historicised and essentialised narratives that Levon Ter-Petrossian and the PANM had rejected. Legitimating the casting out of ethnic others and the effacement of their culture – prevailing tragedies in Armenians' narrative of their own history – required those others to be represented as transient trespassers, 'nomads without culture', 'Turks' without an identity or heritage of their own.

Karabakh in Azerbaijani Geopolitical Culture

'Facts are facts: in Azerbaijan, the history of Armenia and of Karabakh had never been seriously studied.' Thus laments Rasim Agaev, former press secretary to Azerbaijani Communist Party First Secretary Abdurahman Vezirov, in his memoir.[44] It was undeniably true: until the 1980s Karabakh was marginal in Azerbaijani

Table 3.2 Territorial visions and conceptions of Nagorny Karabakh in post-Soviet Azerbaijani geopolitical culture

	Dominant expression	Primary divide	Political imperative	Leading proponents	Conception of Karabakh
Caucasian Albanian school	Albania is an ancestor community and state tradition of modern Azerbaijanis	Albanian versus Armenian	Indigenise Azerbaijanis and counter Armenian *prior tempore, prior jure* claim to Karabakh	Ziya Buniyatov, Farida Mamedova	Ancient Albanian provinces of Artsakh/Uti
Integral Azerbaijan	Self-determination of Azerbaijanis	Sovereign Azerbaijan versus Soviet Union	Regain Azerbaijani independence	Ayaz Mutalibov post-August 1991	NKAO is a Soviet imposition to be abolished
Greater Azerbaijan	Unification of north and south Azerbaijan	Turks versus imperialist Great Powers	Rectify partition and fulfil 'Turkic destiny'	Abulfaz Elchibey, Azerbaijani Popular Front	Karabakh is primordial Turkic land
Azerbaijanism	Azerbaijan is a multi-ethnic homeland within recognised borders	Pragmatic state-building versus romantic ethno-nationalism	Preserve Azerbaijani state; integrate minority groups	Heydar Aliyev	Negotiable space; Armenians are a national minority
Wide Azerbaijanism	Armenia is an imperial project located on historical Azerbaijani lands	Azerbaijani versus Armenian	Challenge Armenian statehood	Policy elites under Ilham Aliyev	Primordial Azerbaijani land; Armenians are a later addition

geopolitical culture, whose more dissident strands remained preoccupied with the wound of partition and Iranian Azerbaijan. The invisibility of Karabakh – and of Armenians within it – was also owed to ideological factors. Marxism and Soviet preferences for the ancient past skewed Azerbaijani scholarship away from more historically proximate Azerbaijani geographies of the territory: the khanate that had appeared in Karabakh in the latter half of the eighteenth century, or the region's incorporation, even if locally contested, into the Azerbaijan Democratic Republic (ADR) of 1918–20. Instead, Karabakh's place in Azerbaijan was interpreted through the prism of proto-Azerbaijanism, the doctrine that from the late 1930s gave the Azerbaijanis a narrative of autochthony.

The Caucasian Albanian School

In 1937, as we saw in Chapter 2, national ideology in the AzSSR turned inwards in a quest for autochthonous ancestors dispelling unwanted connectivity with Turkic spaces beyond Soviet borders. In doing so, Azerbaijanis encountered a problem confronting most of the Turkic peoples of the Soviet Union. The 'objective' conjuncture of territory and language as the preferred Soviet basis for claiming autochthony met with the unfortunate and widely known fact that Turkic languages were not of local origin for most Turkic nationalities. A dilemma appeared between claiming autochthony but 'admitting' the well-established fact of medieval language shift, or claiming Turkic identity and thereby 'confessing' to non-autochthony.[45] For both broader ideological and narrower foreign policy reasons, the latter was not an option in Azerbaijan and the role of migration in Azerbaijani origins became taboo.

Finding autochthonous ancestors for modern Azerbaijanis necessitated an inclusive approach towards prior groups and polities on the territory of the AzSSR. Proto-Azerbaijanism was a doctrine that consequently admitted considerable diversity into the Azerbaijani national narrative, recasting the Azerbaijani nation as primordially multicultural, inclusive of diverse pre-Turkic Iranian and Christian elements. Imagining these elements as flowing into a single, modern Azerbaijani identity in turn implied a certain plasticity to identities. The theory effectively required that disparate elements within the territorial frame of Azerbaijan be assimilated into a singular Azerbaijani identity. The resulting theory of primordial amalgam provided the requisite autochthonous ancestors, but it also simultaneously recast the meaning of the republic's diversity in the present. The autochthonous boot was now on the other foot: Azerbaijanis were no longer descended from invading Turkic tribes disrupting 'earlier indigenes' but had diverse autochthonous ancestral lineages of their own mirroring the contemporary diversity of the republic. Disparate cultures in the AzSSR could now be emplotted as 'genetic' sub-elements within an elastic Azerbaijani theory of origin. The implications for minority groups in the AzSSR were subtle and perhaps not immediately obvious. They were nevertheless far-reaching, as inclusivity in antiquity could easily be read as exclusivity in the present.

This was the context for the emergence of the Caucasian Albanian school as the primary focus of Azerbaijani interest in Karabakh prior to the conflict. Unrelated to Balkan Albania, Caucasian Albania was a state existing in the eastern Caucasus from antiquity to the eighth century. It converted to Christianity in the fourth century, forming its own doctrinally Monophysite church that remained closely related to the Armenian Apostolic Church. The kingdom began to disintegrate after Khazar, then Arab, invasions of the mid-seventh century; by 705 it no longer existed as a coherent polity. But its name lived on as a loose geographical denomination; as a separate branch (Catholicosate) of the Armenian Church, with which the Albanian Church merged in the eighth century; and as a royal title to an ancient throne and its associated titular claim to the Christian population of eastern Caucasia.[46]

Initially the recruitment of the Albanians as an ancestral community for the Azerbaijanis served Soviet goals well, indigenising the new Azerbaijani identity and differentiating it from neighbouring Turkic populations. But from the 1960s two more subversive implications began to become obvious in the works of Azerbaijani historians. The first was that Azerbaijan had its own, indigenous Christian tradition separate from an Armenian one. Second, it was only a short intellectual step to then suggest that there were no indigenous Armenians in Azerbaijan. These ideas were developed in the Caucasian Albanian school, a tradition of polemic as history, premised on a foundational conceit that Armenians are foreign to Azerbaijan.

Pioneered by Ziya Buniyatov and continued by his doctoral student Farida Mamedova, the Caucasian Albanian school crafted a national narrative for the Albanians that was strikingly similar to the Armenians' own: a once great state that introduced Christianity to the Caucasus, Albania disintegrated owing to foreign invasions but its culture lived on as a separate Albanian Catholicosate in the bastion of Karabakh.[47] The ethnic archaeologists of the Caucasian Albanian school indiscriminately read any historical reference to Albania or Albanians as evidence of hard ethnic identity. That the princes of Khachen sometimes referred to themselves as the 'kings of Albania' made them 'ethnic Albanians', rather than shrewd manipulators of dignitary title in a feudal era. Albanologists recast the principality of Artsakh-Khachen as a medieval revival of the fallen Albanian state. The survival of an Albanian Catholicosate at Gandzasar in Nagorny Karabakh until 1836 conjured an ethnic Albanian minority in the territory right up to the nineteenth century, repressed not by Turks or Muslims but by Armenians. The Caucasian Albanian school was, with Soviet inflections, a discursive pastiche of the 'Greater Armenia' tradition it set out to repudiate, and it raised more questions than it answered. An obvious problem was how to explain the near-total disappearance from the Caucasus of an Albanian identity supposedly buttressed by millennial traditions of statehood and a separate church, yet the survival of an Armenian one, supposedly recent, 'foreign' and stateless. Answers were found in the wilful neglect of countervailing evidence, the toleration of omissions and non sequiturs, the massaging – in Buniyatov's case – of source materials, and after perestroika's relaxation of censorship, Russian malfeasance and 'divide and rule' policies.

These ideas, and the feud among Azerbaijani and Armenian intellectuals they generated, remained restricted to specialist publications through the latter Soviet decades.[48] Yet they impacted on popular culture indirectly. At around the same time as Armen's family wedding, in 1980 an Azerbaijani Voluntary Association for the Preservation of Historical and Cultural Monuments published a pictorial map depicting ancient and medieval monuments of Azerbaijan.[49] The accompanying text lauds the republic's historical diversity, including architectural marvels of the early Christian state of Caucasian Albania surviving to the seventh century of the Common Era.[50] The map depicts seven cultural heritage sites for the NKAO. One, the monasterial complex at Gandzasar, is Christian. Despite this being dated to 1238, and hence by the text's own definition, a post-Caucasian Albanian monument, the map is silent on its cultural provenance. In this way Armenian heritage – and a visibly shared space – disappeared. But it took the removal of Soviet constraints of political correctness for the same device to be used on people.

1988–93: Extreme Fracture

In contrast to Armenia, where a national consensus on the Armenian cause in Karabakh rapidly emerged, from 1988 there was a profusion of reactions to the Karabakh movement in Azerbaijan. Armenian secessionism and the unravelling of Soviet power both exposed and created multiple fractures in Azerbaijani society – between Azerbaijanis and minorities, Russian-speaking and Azerbaijani-speaking Azerbaijanis, cosmopolitan cities and ethnic peripheries, urban communities and rural migrants, street and elite, regional clans and elite factions, locals and refugees from Armenia, nationalists and democrats, and northern and southern Azerbaijans. The precedent and persistence of the Armenian self-determination claim exacerbated these fractures, preventing the formation of political coalitions around broad-based values or consensual positions.[51]

Between 1988 and the exit of the Azerbaijani Popular Front government in 1993 there was consequently little consistency in Azerbaijani positions on Karabakh. Until the end of 1991, the Azerbaijani elite was caught in the unfortunate position of upholding Soviet territorial arrangements even as the legitimacy of the political order that had created them drained away. In complete conflict with this position, the Popular Front evoked historical truncations of Azerbaijan to mobilise a popular sense of injustice at its Soviet contours. Distinct geopolitical traditions evoked multi-scalar templates of Azerbaijani territoriality that were at odds with each other – at times suggesting border revision, at others demanding that borders be left as they were. Against a backdrop of continuous political tumult, numerous positions competed to define the nature of the Karabakh problem from an Azerbaijani perspective and how to solve it. Hardly coherent or consistent among themselves, the following distinctions simplify a chaotic and still poorly understood period in Azerbaijani history.

The Azerbaijani party elite adopted a status quo stance that still looked for solutions within a Soviet framework. Ossified, conformist and utterly unprepared for the Karabakh crisis, the Azerbaijani party elite had no idea of how to parse the crisis in a reforming climate.[52] For several months party bodies and the press continued to intone stock internationalist slogans on the preservation of Soviet brotherhood.[53] Without an effective narrative marrying Azerbaijani possession of Nagorny Karabakh to perestroika, the party elite sided with Moscow in framing the problem as a socio-economic one. As rising violence in 1990 obviated economic solutions, the Azerbaijani party elite under Ayaz Mutalibov approached the situation as a bargain between territorial control and loyalty to Moscow. Frequently exclaiming that Karabakh was a Soviet, not Azerbaijani, problem, Mutalibov traded Azerbaijan's support in the March 1991 referendum on the preservation of the Union for Moscow's collaboration in pursuing a military solution.[54] The August putsch revealed the shortsightedness of this approach as within six months Azerbaijan confronted a prepared Armenian army without having created one of its own.[55]

Slow to catch up with the well-organised information campaign of their Armenian counterparts, the response of the AzSSR's intellectual elite was to reify the Caucasian Albanian school.[56] Increasingly free of censorship and Soviet political correctness, perestroika-era expressions of the Caucasian Albanian school extended its Albanianising gaze over the Armenian population, as well as monuments, of the NKAO. According to a brochure issued by the Azerbaijani Academy of Sciences in 1989:

> The so-called Armenians of Karabakh, and the actual Azerbaijanis (being descendants of the Albanian population) of northern Azerbaijan are ancestral brothers. Both groups are without a doubt former Albanians. The so-called Armenians of Karabakh became adherents of the Armenian Gregorian Church [*grigorianizirovalis*] and armenianised, while today's Azerbaijanis adopted Islam in the past and turkified.[57]

Arguments turning on readings of medieval – and earlier – geographies were used to depict contemporary ethnic difference as false consciousness. 'Albanianised' Armenians found themselves in the same position as Muslim Bosniaks, depicted by Serbian and Croatian nationalists as 'really' being Serbs or Croats respectively, or Abkhaz depicted by Georgian nationalists as 'really' being Georgians.[58] This sleight of intellect turned the tables on the Armenian *prior tempore, prior jure* claim to Karabakh, affirmed the territory's Christian – but *not* Armenian – character, and allowed the historical eviction of any Armenians prior to the nineteenth century. These arguments hardly sat well with affirmations of the NKAO within the same publication as the 'painstaking work of the party' and a 'triumph of Soviet power', or indeed with discussion of an upgraded autonomy for the NKAO.[59] Territorial autonomy was being defended even as the minority group for which it had been created was written out of history.

In the oppositional Popular Front, early commitments to liberal-democratic values and efforts to elaborate an Azerbaijani position on Karabakh suitable for the reforming times were rapidly eclipsed by more nationalistic views. In July 1989 the Popular Front's original founders saw the organisation they had founded hijacked at its first congress, as Abulfaz Elchibey was elected chairman.[60] A heady mix of pan-Turkism, pan-Azerbaijani nationalism, recriminations against Russian-speaking Azerbaijanis, populist messianism and anti-Armenian rhetoric displaced appeals to legal principle and democratic reform. 'Exhibitionist' cartographies of Turkic unity across the Aras unnerved non-Turkic minorities and aggravated feuds with establishment intellectuals who had built their careers on theories of autochthony eschewing Turkic influences. Policy-wise, Elchibey offered few options for resolving the Armenian–Azerbaijani conflict other than rhetorical flourishes that the route to Stepanakert lay through Tabriz.[61] Once in power, such heroic aesthetics were quickly eclipsed by war and internal insurrection.

A final position emerged largely by default. This was Azerbaijan as an integral republic within its Soviet borders, but shorn of ethno-federalism; in other words, Azerbaijan without the NKAO. This concept had a historical precedent in the independent Azerbaijani republic of 1918–20. An integral Azerbaijan was also the formal legal situation at the time of Azerbaijan's entry into the United Nations in March 1992 after the Azerbaijani Supreme Soviet had formally abolished the NKAO on 26 November 1991. The NKAO was formally dissolved, its capital renamed Khankendi and a new cartography of *Yuxari Qarabağ* (Upper Karabakh) created. Five new undifferentiated Azerbaijani districts (*rayonu*) – Terter, Kelbajar, Khojaly, Shusha and Khojavend – were created, comprising an inexact over-layering of the NKAO. The latter's familiar outline disappeared from Azerbaijani maps, and several district capitals were moved from Armenian- to Azerbaijani-majority settlements. These changes remained cartographic rather than practical. Having taken control of most of the northern part of Karabakh by autumn 1992, in the following year Azerbaijani forces lost control over almost all of the former NKAO, in addition to the seven neighbouring regions. Azerbaijan ended the war a fractured country, with 13.6 per cent of its territory beyond its jurisdiction.[62]

Azerbaijanism

The disintegration of the Soviet Union, independence and the battlefield outcomes of the Karabakh war transformed political geographies in ways that strengthened Azerbaijan's legal-political claim to the territory even as it endured military defeat. Both the weight of the international *uti possidetis juris* and territorial integrity norms, as well as Western investment in Caspian oil production, now backed Azerbaijan's position as former Communist

Party First Secretary Heydar Aliyev returned to power in the Azerbaijan Republic. Aliyev's rejection of irredentism resumed a prior emphasis on indigenous factors in defining an Azerbaijani nation. The resulting doctrine, Azerbaijanism (*Azərbaycançılıq*), was a post-Soviet rebrand of proto-Azerbaijanism that absorbed the Soviet emphasis on autochthony, and paired it with a rigid deference to internationally recognised borders (see Figure 3.2). It courted the legitimacy of consensus as a dialogically conceived discourse of nation-building assuaging both domestic secessionism and fears of Azerbaijani irredentism abroad. Remaining the official ideology of the republic to this day, its success lies precisely in its ambiguity. Azerbaijanism pivots around the ambivalence between territorial and ethnic understandings of Azerbaijan dating from the late 1930s. As a territorial concept, it is inclusive of all minorities and mitigates minority anxieties about Turkic cultural hegemony. As an ethnic concept, it expresses the nationalism of a Turkic majority significantly consolidated since independence (Azerbaijanis accounted for 91.6 per cent of the population in 2009), and can be seen as a continuation of the Turkic revival.[63]

Figure 3.2 Visualising Azerbaijanism: poster board of Heydar Aliyev, Sheki, 2011. Author photo.

Azerbaijanism tacitly recognised that in ideological terms it was Soviet theories of autochthony – not Turkic solidarity – which provided more usable tools to counter Armenian secessionism. Azerbaijanism brought with it a popularisation of the Caucasian Albanian school. In 2002 an Institute for Research on Caucasian Albania was established, with Farida Mamedova as its academic director, and the first international conference on Albanology was convened.[64] The utility of a Christian heritage community for a Muslim-majority state espousing a civic-secular nationalism and facing a secessionist Christian minority was not lost on either the state or Albanologists. According to Mamedova, 'this is where our tolerance comes from'.[65]

As a result two contradictory trends marked the latter years of Heydar Aliyev's presidency. On the one hand, Armenian–Azerbaijani negotiations experienced their most intense period in which a wide range of different territorial-federal solutions was considered (see Chapter 9). These suggested that Karabakh was negotiable space. On the other, an ideological structure based on Soviet titular nationalism that wrote the Armenians out of the history of Karabakh was institutionalised. After Heydar Aliyev's son Ilham became president in 2003, these trends diverged. The former atrophied, while the latter hypertrophied.

'Wide Azerbaijanism'

In June 2014 I met Akif Nagi, president of the Karabakh Liberation Organisation (KLO).[66] The walls of Nagi's office were covered with maps and in what seemed like a well-rehearsed routine, our meeting began with them. First, Nagi showed me a small standard map of Azerbaijan next to his desk, on which the Line of Contact with Armenian forces around Nagorny Karabakh had been drawn by hand. He then walked over to a large map of the first Azerbaijani republic of 1918–20, and traced its western border with Armenia, bifurcating Lake Sevan and running through what is today southern Armenia. Demonstratively moving his finger across the map to where the Line of Contact now lies, Nagi said, 'and now the Armenians want to put that border here'. Sitting at his desk, he then pointed to a third map covering the wall behind him, of Russian Transcaucasia in 1903, and said, 'See how none of the places in what is now Armenia had Armenian names then?'

Nagi's cartographic tour was striking for two reasons. First, his perspective was remarkably congruent with that of Azerbaijan's political leadership. As he pointed out, President Ilham Aliyev's speeches had begun to refer to Armenia as an artificial construct on Azerbaijani lands. A few months after my meeting with Nagi, staff in the presidential apparatus shared with me proofs of a new book about Azerbaijani heritage destroyed during the Soviet construction of Yerevan in the 1930s.[67] The existence of an Azerbaijani palimpsest under the modern state of Armenia had become a ubiquitous narrative, articulated in unison by government and what was supposedly one of the most radical organisations in the country. Nagi's sole disagreement with the government was on method. He showed me the KLO's logo: a map of Azerbaijan with a scimitar curving from Baku to Karabakh, symbolising the need for military action. A second striking feature of Nagi's maps was the torsion of the Azerbaijani atlas of affect over time. President Abulfaz Elchibey's insurgent tradition of 'Greater Azerbaijan' had felt its phantom pains in southern Azerbaijan: in the city of Tabriz, on Mount Savalan in Ardabil and in the *Qalleh Bazz* (Fort of Bazz) of ninth-century rebel Babak Khorramdin (798–838).[68] Nagi's geopolitical coordinates were entirely different. They exemplified a revectoring of Azerbaijani geopolitical culture from a north–south axis preoccupied with partition to an east–west axis preoccupied with Armenia.

Heydar Aliyev's vision of Azerbaijanism recentred geopolitical culture on Azerbaijan's recognised borders and effaced earlier irredentist concerns. But this proved only a provisional stability. From the mid-2000s a new geopolitical imagination took hold, formally observant of Azerbaijanism, but expanding with new geographies selectively recruited from Turkic historical, ethnocultural and political templates. I call this 'wide Azerbaijanism'. This is, of course, a contradiction in terms: an ostensibly civic nationalism defined by a fixed territorial referent can *a priori* be neither wide nor narrow. Yet the term captures the discursive and cartographic widening of Azerbaijani territoriality to laterally project a historical Azerbaijani palimpsest westwards beneath the modern Republic of Armenia. 'Wide Azerbaijanism' remains true to the doctrine's foundational concerns to delink northern and southern Azerbaijan and assuage fears of Azerbaijani irredentism in neighbouring states. But it appropriates the latter's insurgent spatial imaginary and redirects it towards a new space, 'western Azerbaijan', a space beyond Azerbaijan's borders and largely coextensive with modern Armenia. It is an eclectic school of nation-building that allows civic and ethnic codes of nationhood to cohabit, even on the same map. Civic codes cue the territorial integrity norm for international audiences; ethnic codes mobilise nationalist grievance.

'Wide Azerbaijanism' is a geopolitical confection emerging at the meeting point of two previously subdued geographies made relevant by both sovereignty and the Armenian–Azerbaijani conflict. The first is that of the more than two dozen khanates appearing north and south of the Aras after 1747. Marginalised in Soviet historiography as relics of a backward feudal order, the khanates have been rehabilitated in post-Soviet Azerbaijani historiography. In their transience, plurality and incessant in-fighting they are awkward building blocks for a national narrative; in their structure they were 'miniature replicas of the Iranian monarchy'.[69] But as Turkic-ruled and Muslim-majority entities both coinciding with the first modern population surveys and forming the last local political tradition before Russian incorporation, they are invaluable for contemporary territorial claims. Disparaged in the Soviet Azerbaijani narrative, all of the khanates north and south of the Aras are depicted by contemporary Azerbaijani scholarship and history textbooks as 'Azerbaijani khanates', reframing them as precursors of modern Azerbaijani statehood.[70] Among them the Karabakh khanate was both one of the largest, encompassing the area between the Kura and Aras rivers and bordered by Ganja to the north and Nakhichevan in the west, and more powerful.[71] As a political geography of Karabakh the khanate offers an integral highland and lowland space, an overall Turkic majority, and a political narrative of the Javanshir khans as founding fathers. This tradition stresses, for example, that it was Javanshir khan Panah Ali – and not Armenians – who founded the fortress in

Shusha (known briefly as Panahabad). The second building block of 'wide Azerbaijanism' is 'western Azerbaijan'. A colloquialism among some Azerbaijani refugees referring to Soviet Armenia, the term began to assume a more geopolitical meaning in the late 1990s as a revivalist project recovering the history of this population after displacement.[72] With return to Armenia never seriously considered politically feasible (see Chapter 4), refugees integrated into Azerbaijani society. The community melted away but the historical geography of an Azerbaijani palimpsest under modern Armenia remained.

From the mid-2000s the notion of western Azerbaijan converged with revived interest in the khanates in a wide-ranging fetishisation of the Erivan (Irevan) khanate as a historically Azerbaijani entity. Covering some 7,500 square kilometres and most of present-day Armenia (if not exactly coextensive with it), the Erivan khanate has undergone the same kind of transformations as Caucasian Albania before it. Contemporary Azerbaijani historiography depicts the Erivan khanate as an 'Azerbaijani state', populated by autochthonous Azerbaijani Turks and sacralised as the burial ground of semi-mythological figures from the Turkic pantheon.[73] 'Azerbaijani Turk' and 'Muslim' are used interchangeably in this literature, although contemporary demographic surveys differentiate the latter into Persians, Shia and Sunni Kurds and Turkic tribes.[74] Emulating the nationalist scientism of Samvel Karapetyan, catalogues of lost Azerbaijani heritage depict a Turkic palimpsest beneath almost every monument and religious site in Armenia – whether Christian or Muslim.[75] Cartographically, from around 2007 the standard map of Azerbaijan began to feature Turkic toponyms printed in red beneath Armenian ones on the large part of Armenia that it shows. Familiar Armenian toponyms appear on the regular reissues of this map to this day with a Turkic double: Jermuk/Quşçu, Spitak/Hamamlı, Vanadzor/Böy Kilsə, and so on. Rhetorically, an Azerbaijani palimpsest beneath Armenia reaches into the future as a prospective territorial claim: from around 2010 President Ilham Aliyev began to make regular reference to Irevan, Göyçə and Zangezur as once and future 'Azerbaijani lands'.[76] His address after being nominated as presidential candidate by the New Azerbaijan Party in 2018 called for the return of Azerbaijanis to these lands.[77] Yerevan is a particular focus: its eighteenth-century fortress and Sardar Palace, demolished in the Soviet building of the Armenian capital, have become widely disseminated symbols of lost Azerbaijani heritage recalling the fetishised contours of a severed body part.[78] Another is Lake Sevan, reclaimed by its Azerbaijani name, Göyçə.

'Wide Azerbaijanism' is not only a discursive tit-for-tat responding to 'augmented Armenia'. It is a geopolitical vision that absorbs a modern Armenian territoriality in its entirety. Its implications are obvious: a historically deepened and horizontally elongated Azerbaijan edges Armenia out of the Caucasus. The theatre of contested space is shifted from Nagorny Karabakh to Armenia itself, revealed as a lesion on a wide Azerbaijani geo-body. But selectivity is key: no Turkic palimpsest is marked on Azerbaijani maps beneath Georgia, Russian or Iranian space. 'Wide Azerbaijanism' is consequently a measured flexing of nationalised space to depict not only the current situation in the Karabakh, but modern Armenia in its totality through the lens of occupation. There are numerous borrowings and similarities with Armenian geopolitical culture here. The fetishisation of Yerevan recalls the latter's own fetishisation of Mount Ararat as the ultimate contour of a lost geo-body. There is also convergence on essentialised narratives and the factuality of maps as vehicles to express territorial claims. Mirroring Armenian geopolitical culture's own depictions of 'Turks', Armenians are portrayed as usurping interlopers with neither an indigenous state nor a culture of their own. There are differences in scale and implication, however. First, whereas Armenian practices trace their palimpsest across large swathes of western Azerbaijan, Azerbaijan's is more total in extending over all of Armenia. Contemporary Azerbaijani textbooks depict early nineteenth-century Azerbaijan as a wide, homogenous geo-body stretching from the Caspian to Igdir in the west.[79] Second, while Armenian scenarios of secession and ultimately recognition of the NKR are at best indifferent to permanent demographic segregation, Azerbaijani scenarios are predicated on future coexistence. The retroactive ethnic homogenisation of 'wide Azerbaijanism' hardly supports such scenarios, dating Armenian arrival to the nineteenth century – an unforgivably recent date for legitimate national claims in the Caucasus.

In sum, Azerbaijani geopolitical culture converged on the same dualistic instability as its adversary. There is the Azerbaijan of formal statehood, fixed boundaries and inclusive civic nationalism, and the Azerbaijan of an amorphous, expansive and exclusive Turkic palimpsest and its associated ethno-cultural narrative. No contemporary political geography admits an Armenian presence, yet the Azerbaijani geopolitical gaze is continually drawn to signs, spaces and markers of this presence. The antagonism with Armenia has become the cornerstone of post-war Azerbaijani geopolitical culture, bringing with it a disconcerting duality as Azerbaijani and Armenian geo-bodies are increasingly found to occupy the same space. Urges to 'inhabit' all spaces and communities historically associated with Armenians in the Caucasus also contradict the normative prizing of territorial integrity as the marker of Azerbaijani nationhood. As qualifying adjectives multiply – northern, southern, western – the boundaries of the noun Azerbaijan, and its associated identity, become ever more blurred.

Far from frozen, since the late 1980s Nagorny Karabakh has moved from the margins to the core of Armenian and Azerbaijani geopolitical cultures. New understandings of history, identity and space, much of it far from the territory itself, have accreted around this movement. Memories of lived coexistence have given way to the rhetoric of maps, the homogeneity of fixed territorial units and the denial of real-world human geographies. There is deep irony in the fact that it is the very extent of historical mingling among the ancestral communities of modern Armenian and Azerbaijani nations that enables, and indeed requires, reciprocal purges of cultural memory extirpating the omnipresence of the other. As 'augmented Armenia' became entrenched, and as Azerbaijan developed its own historicised geopolitical narratives, exclusive Armenian and Azerbaijani geo-bodies have come to inhabit more of the same territory over time. Popular perceptions on either side have come to think of increasingly more of the same space as 'theirs', while granting ever less space to the other. It is a path to mutual existential denial, entrapping Armenians and Azerbaijanis in mirror images of each other.[80]

Yet when no border is sacrosanct, the 'contingency' of an adversarial territorial body becomes the destabilisation of one's own. Karabakh's capture of both countries' geopolitical imaginations has shifted the geographic periphery to the conceptual centre, imposed the liminal as canonical and redefined the residual as essential. The founding of national projects on this fractious borderland and the quest for singular histories has resulted instead in the congealing of new ambiguities around the borders of both nations. As territorial regimes and palimpsests have proliferated, territorial referents have multiplied: 'Artsakh' is repositioned relative to 'Northern Artsakh', 'Azerbaijan' relative to 'western Azerbaijan'. Discourses of individuation and segregation furnish unwitting evidence of the impossibility of either project, locking Armenia and Azerbaijan into a continuous dynamic of simultaneous definition and dissolution. Silenced by the rhetoric of maps, the heterogeneous human geographies in which Armenians and Azerbaijanis historically lived have receded into obscurity. It is to the mass forced displacements of people that were required to destroy these geographies that the next chapter turns.

4 Displacements

In 2007 Elmira, an Azerbaijani woman living in Nagorny Karabakh, told her tragic story to a team of Armenian filmmakers. Elmira met Slavik, her future husband, when he was on his military service in Baku in the 1960s. Despite the disapproval of their parents – because he was Armenian – they married. They settled in Karabakh, where Elmira quickly learned fluent Armenian, and had five children together. Two met untimely deaths. Their eldest daughter Irina was murdered in 1980 in their home village of Berdashen. A son, Yernik, was later killed fighting Azerbaijani forces in 1994. Apart from a letter delivered by the International Red Cross after the war, Elmira knew nothing of what had become of her two sisters in Baku.[1]

Elmira's story is truly exceptional. A 2005 census showed that she was one of only six Azerbaijanis still living in Nagorny Karabakh, out of a pre-war population of more than 40,000. The rest had been forcibly displaced from the territory in 1992. Attrition rates among Azerbaijanis in post-war Armenia, and Armenians living in post-war Azerbaijan outside of the former oblast, were nearly as dramatic. Almost all of those who remained were, like Elmira, spouses in mixed marriages and often of mixed parentage.[2] By the turn of the millennium there were not more than a few hundred Azerbaijanis remaining in Armenia, and between 3,000 and 5,000 Armenians in Azerbaijan. The demographic purge of each nationality in the other's republic was all but total.

Forced displacement is the most easily grasped and leveraged human story of the Armenian–Azerbaijani conflict. For this reason, it is an issue that policy-makers rarely lose sight of, while nationalist narratives compete for the refugee as an icon of pathos and for human bodies in a competitive game of numbers. Quantifying displacement in the Armenian–Azerbaijani conflict is correspondingly contentious, and methodologically fraught. Arriving at precise numbers for those displaced in 1988–94 is complicated by the chaos prevailing through this period; many people were displaced several times, some permanently and others temporarily. Forced movements began before the last Soviet census was conducted in January 1989, making it a snapshot of demographic unravelling in motion rather than a reliable picture of the status quo ante. Movements of those displaced by the conflict also coincided with other mass movements, including those displaced by the December 1988 earthquake in Armenia and the arrivals of both Armenians and Meskhetian Turks fleeing persecution in Central Asia. Many refugees, especially Russian-speaking Armenians, disappeared from national statistics by moving on almost immediately to Russia. Conversely, popularly cited numbers of internally displaced often date from movements at the height of hostilities; some communities were able to return to their homes after the recapture of territory. The contested borders of the de facto Nagorno-Karabakh Republic (NKR) also mean that sources on each side disagree over definitions of refugee and internally displaced person (IDP), sowing further confusion.[3]

There were two phases of displacement in the Armenian–Azerbaijani conflict. In a first phase, lasting from the winter of 1987–8 to 1990, mass movements of externally displaced Armenians and Azerbaijanis (and some smaller groups) unravelled the mingled demography of the Soviet Armenian and Azerbaijani republics (ArmSSR and AzSSR respectively).[4] Azerbaijani scholar Arif Yunusov estimates that some 360,000 Armenians were forcibly displaced from the AzSSR outside of the former oblast in Nagorny Karabakh.[5] Yunusov's calculations accord with data later published by Armenia's State Migration Service, which put the total number of Armenians displaced from the AzSSR outside of the Nagorno-Karabakh Autonomous Oblast (NKAO) at 361,453.[6] With regard to refugees from Armenia, Yunusov cites official Azerbaijani statistics indicating some 205,000 people by September 1990, composed overwhelmingly of ethnic Azerbaijanis with small numbers of Muslim Kurds and Russians. This data broadly corresponds with that of the United Nations High Commissioner for Refugees (UNHCR) for 1996.[7] The total number of refugees consequently comes to roughly 570,000.

In a second phase, coinciding with large-scale hostilities in 1991–4, a rather larger number of people became IDPs. On the Armenian side, up to 80,000 were internally displaced from border areas at the peak of hostilities.[8] In addition, the de facto authorities in the NKR claimed an internally displaced population of 30,000 in the mid-2000s.[9] The vast majority of IDPs, however, are Azerbaijanis from the former oblast and the surrounding regions occupied in 1992–3. At its peak, internal displacement in Azerbaijan reached figures of around 780,000, but part of this population was able to return in the aftermath of war. Official Azerbaijani statistics in the late 1990s put the number of those still internally displaced at around 600,000; Yunusov's estimates and UNHCR statistics come in a little lower at 520,000 and 550,000 respectively.[10] Overall, the total number of internally displaced across the conflict exceeds 600,000. In sum, then, it is reasonable to assume that somewhere in the region of 1.2 million people lost their homes because of the Armenian–Azerbaijani conflict in 1988–94. For two republics with a combined population of some ten million in 1989, this was a demographic cataclysm.

In this chapter, however, I am more concerned with the qualification than quantification of forced displacement, and its significance as a geopolitical practice remaking space and ethno-territorial orders. It is now time to return to questions that Chapter 1's discussion of causal factors driving violence in the late 1980s left open. These concern a crucial aspect to the Armenian–Azerbaijani case typically overlooked in the wider literature on post-Soviet conflicts: communal violence. Although numbers are difficult to verify, several hundred people died as a result of communal violence in 1988–90 in Azerbaijani cities, across Armenia and in Nagorny Karabakh. In each instance the violence targeted Armenian and Azerbaijani minorities, with the explicit goal of inducing them to flee, and came early in the mobilisation cycle. Moreover, most of this violence was enacted not by soldiers, paramilitaries or other entrepreneurs of organised violence, but by ordinary citizens. Ritualised violence imbued with symbolic meaning was present in many cases. Preceding the onset of large-scale, organised violence in 1991, this is a troubling story of a collective eviction that cannot be wholly explained by security concerns. This story raises the question of why communities were attacked and displaced from areas where they formed small and non-dominant minorities. Put differently, why were people attacked and evicted in the absence of threat?

Another feature of forced displacements in 1988–90 that demands attention is its totality. People were not only, and not *initially*, displaced from areas within or near the disputed oblast. Chronologies are contested, but displacement appears to have begun with movements of Azerbaijanis from southern Armenia in the winter of 1987–8 and of Armenians from Sumgait, an industrial suburb of Azerbaijan's Absheron peninsula, a few weeks later in February.[11] Although people were also displaced within and around the borders of the oblast in the earlier stages of the conflict in 1988–90, the vast majority were displaced from locations nowhere near it. Forced displacement therefore indelibly transformed not only the ground zero of conflict in Nagorny Karabakh, but also the entirety of spaces identified as Armenian or Azerbaijani. Given the extent of mixed settlement prior to 1988, why was displacement so complete? Outside of a dwindling number of mixed marriages, why did no microclimates of cohabitation survive the conflict, as they did – however problematically – in other theatres of conflict in the South Caucasus, such as Georgian-populated Gali district in Abkhazia and Georgian villages in South Ossetia until 2008? There is clearly a need to explain this outcome through factors other than contested territorial autonomy in Nagorny Karabakh itself.

Ethnic cleansing – the murder and expulsion of ethnic others – is never straightforwardly 'ethnic', but subsumes a range of motives, including military-strategic goals, criminal opportunism, local grievance, revenge and thrill-seeking nihilism.[12] To apply this insight to the above questions, I distinguish between 'communal ethnic cleansing', enacted by civilians and dominant in the first phase of displacement in 1988–90, and 'strategic ethnic cleansing', enacted by armed forces and dominant in the second phase of 1991–4. There is, to be sure, a certain arbitrariness to this distinction, as ethnic cleansing may always be said to be strategic in its targeting of a specific community. The key distinction lies in the agency and motives driving the expulsion of others. Communal ethnic cleansing is a collective act drawing on deeply rooted perceptions of group relations, and may be enacted to 'cleanse' territory that is not necessarily contested by those being expelled. Strategic ethnic cleansing entails the expulsion of others as a necessary condition for claims to contested territory to be pursued, and fulfils military-strategic goals. The chapter proceeds by considering each in turn, before examining post-displacement trajectories and the politics and prospects of return.

Communal Ethnic Cleansing

In Armenia and Azerbaijan today a narrative of the peaceful and compensated departure of refugees belonging to the other nationality prevails. The communal violence that in reality drove their departure is a prominent omission or focal point of conspiracy theories. Where local agency is admitted, it is attributed to the vengeful feelings of people who were themselves victims of displacement. This forms the basis for the 'revenge thesis', the idea that refugees from earlier waves of displacement perpetrated communal violence in revenge. It is an explanation closely intertwined with justification: refugees were only doing to others what had been done to them. There is no doubt that some refugees did participate in communal violence. But there is no evidence to suggest that their role was primary. Locals dominated in the small number of convictions arising from the trials relating to the February 1988 pogrom in Sumgait, the only legal proceedings ever held in connection with communal violence in the AzSSR. This is confirmed by eyewitness accounts, which indicate a variety of perpetrators. Some eyewitnesses at Sumgait in 1988 recalled rural youths, while others spoke good Russian and others still spoke flawless Armenian and were clearly from Armenia. But some eyewitnesses recognised their attackers from the neighbourhood, a place of work, or their own building. Eyewitness and victim Lyudmila Grigorevna M. observed: 'the group [of refugees] that went seeking "revenge" ... was joined by people seeking easy gain and thrill-seekers'.[13] Actual violence was in any case only one strand in the political ecology of collective eviction. In Baku acquisitive neighbours directed crowds towards desirable apartments inhabited by Armenians; local housing officials acquiesced in these designs, while doctors signed death certificates indicating more innocent causes.[14] In Armenia, eyewitness accounts point to the role of local party bosses in leading the violence.[15] In Karabakh, 'it was former neighbours who were in deadly combat'.[16] There is, in short, little reason to believe that refugees dominated, still less led, the forced evictions of others. On the contrary, the trope of the 'refugee as perpetrator' risks a second, moral displacement obfuscating the multiple roles and motives of local actors.

To explore these motives, I turn to theories of collective violence that emphasise the roles of emotion. Emotion-centred theories have traditionally been marginal in the scholarship on ethnic mobilisation and violence on account of the difficulties of empirical measurement or prediction. Yet there is an emotional narrative at the heart of almost any theory of nationalism or collective violence. This is increasingly recognised in a scholarly literature acknowledging the importance of *affective dispositions* as culturally embedded tendencies to appraise ethnic others in moral terms, and emotions as micro-mechanisms triggering action tendencies towards satisfying particular, situationally salient concerns.[17] Which emotions predominate in any given context requires an understanding about the salient beliefs that different groups have about one another. In his study of ethnic violence in Eastern Europe Roger Petersen observes: 'Beliefs about threat lead to fears; beliefs about status inconsistency lead to resentments; beliefs about history and vengeance lead to hatreds.'[18] I use Petersen's insight here to argue that Armenian–Azerbaijani communal violence in 1988–90 was driven not by the mechanical revenge of refugees, but by popular beliefs about threat, status and history.

To understand the origins of these beliefs and the affective dispositions they generated it is necessary briefly to step back into history in order to examine the trajectories of Armenians and Azerbaijanis as constituent peoples in wider imperial projects of modernisation. Over nearly two centuries of alien rule, Russian and Soviet, it was the Armenians who achieved a greater congruence with metropolitan ideals of progress and group worth. Co-religionist identity fuelled a tactical détente between the Russian imperial state and the Armenians of Transcaucasia for much (although not all) of the nineteenth century.[19] Armenians were demographic beneficiaries of Russian rule, and by the end of the nineteenth century formed influential bourgeoisies in the Transcaucasian urban economy and notably in Baku's oil industry. Forming rural majorities in most of the districts of Baku and Yelizavetpol' provinces and several in Yerevan province, Azerbaijanis were typically under-represented in civil administration, especially in large towns, and in capitalised industries. Azerbaijanis, in other words, were in a typical position of many Eastern European groups confronting urban environments dominated by ethnic others, of which Armenians were one. This situation reversed the centuries-old dominance of Muslim beys and khans, and the subservient position of Christians, that went back to the advent of Safavid Iranian suzerainty in 1501 and to Turkmen and Seljuk rule before it.[20]

Ironically, given its socialist creed, this situation was further embedded by the Soviet Union. From the beginning of Soviet rule a broad developmental division separating 'advanced' Western nationalities and 'backward' Eastern ones shaped the respective emphasis in its policies of indigenisation.[21] The 'cultural backwardness' (*kul'turno-otstalost'*) of Eastern nationalities mandated a policy emphasis on the creation of literate, indigenous elites, while Western nationalities proceeded directly to the deepening of local language use across new bureaucracies. The Soviet discourse of backwardness was, so to speak, a corrective orientalism intent on dissolving developmental disparities. Yet it maintained an implicit hierarchy. While comparing poorly with those nationalities that the Soviet Union considered its most advanced (Baltic, Jewish and German nationalities), Armenians were closer to the ideal of urbanised, literate nations and were classified as a 'Western nationality' (see Table 4.1). Azerbaijanis were classified

Armenia and Azerbaijan

Table 4.1 General development indicators in early Soviet Armenia and Azerbaijan (%)

Variable	1926	1939
Urbanisation by republic		
ArmSSR	19	29
AzSSR	28	36
Urbanisation by nationality		
Armenians – all-Soviet	36	41
Armenians in the ArmSSR	20.1	30.4
Azerbaijanis – all-Soviet	16	21
Azerbaijanis in the AzSSR	17	22.7
Literacy by republic[a]		
ArmSSR	38.7	83.9
AzSSR	28.2	82.8
Literacy by nationality[a]		
Armenians	47.5	88
Azerbaijanis	12.7	75.4
Titular nationality shares, 1939		
ArmSSR, total population		82.8
ArmSSR, leadership posts (average)		86.8
ArmSSR, leadership posts (highest, republican level)		95.2
AzSSR, total population		58.4
AzSSR, leadership posts (average)		50.3
AzSSR, leadership posts (highest, republican-level)		33.1

Source: Compiled from Robert Kaiser, *The Geography of Nationalism in Russia and the USSR* (Princeton, NJ: Princeton University Press, 1994), Tables 3.3 and 3.6; Yu. A. Polyakov, *Vsesoyuznaya perepis' naseleniya 1939 goda: Osnovnye Itogi* (Moscow: Nauka, 1992), Tables 16, 19 and 55.
[a] Percentage of population aged 9–49 years.

as an 'Eastern nationality' and especially in their role as lighthouse to the Middle East, were thought of as part of the 'Orient' (*Vostok*).

These broad structural conditions interacted with the expectations of entitlement proceeding from Soviet indigenisation policies, external events such as the Armenian genocide, and local demographic balances to generate disparate affective dispositions among Armenians and Azerbaijanis in different contexts. I argue that the dominant affective dispositions mediating the mass expulsions of the late 1980s–90s were resentment in Azerbaijan, hatred in Armenia, and fear in Nagorny Karabakh. These supply the causal elements to different scripts, or what Lee Ann Fujii calls 'dramaturgical blueprints' for imagined worlds – in this case worlds defined by more legitimate, just or secure group relations – that drove violence and expulsion.[22] Affective dispositions structured around scripts of resentment, hatred and fear defined tacit understandings of the appropriate targets, objectified and deindividuated them, and substituted for leadership among those directly perpetrating, facilitating, or otherwise condoning communal violence.[23]

Several important caveats apply to this argument. It does not, emphatically, evoke the romantic passions of exotic peoples. The same emotional mechanisms are visible across the world, and have their roots in the interactions of human biology and political modernity.[24] Second, I do not propose that because a particular affective disposition predominated in a given context, all members of a given category of people were gripped by it. This would be an irresponsible extrapolation. It is only the motivations of those actually perpetrating violence, facilitating it or simply seeking to exonerate or explain it in favourable terms, which concern me. There are many examples of individuals who did not act according to scripts of resentment, hatred or fear, but according to other emotions such as empathy, compassion or shame. Affective dispositions cohered around scripts of ethnically coded storylines – not ethnicity as such – inciting corresponding action tendencies. I therefore do not argue that people acted as ethnic blocs – my point, rather, is that relational meanings associated with being identified as Armenian or Azerbaijani varied according to place and circumstance. There is indeed much that future research might reveal about how local circumstances mediated prevailing scripts of group relations to shape the occurrence, non-occurrence and patterns of violence. This leads to a third caveat, which is that affective dispositions must be seen as only one element of a complex, causal conjuncture in the late 1980s interacting with institutionalised cultures reifying 'indigene' and 'non-indigene' identities, symbolic funds of traumatic collective memories, uncertainty generated by an unprecedented attempt at reforming the USSR, and a series of precipitating events. What the role of emotions can illuminate is why ordinary people participated in or condoned the mass expulsion of ethnic others, and accepted the remaking of ethnic space that resulted as legitimate and irreversible.

Azerbaijan: Resenting Delayed Indigenisation

Since the late nineteenth century non-natives had played a dominant role in the industrialised metropolitan area on Azerbaijan's Absheron peninsula. As Arif Yunusov observes of the Azerbaijani capital, Baku:

> Locals had become 'strangers' in their own home town ... they were moved to the periphery of the city, not only in the geographical but also in the cultural sense as well. Local people lived among people who spoke Russian, called the streets by Russian names and considered [Baku] to be a Russian city.[25]

Early Soviet rule also showed 'colonial' characteristics. A substantial influx of Russian settlers and skills took place in the 1920s, and an intrusive language policy estranged many native speakers through script reforms of the Azerbaijani language in 1926 and 1940. In terms of the AzSSR's leadership, indigenisation remained more programme than reality. After two decades of Soviet rule ethnic Azerbaijanis accounted for only half of the republic's leadership posts in 1939 (see Table 4.1), concentrated at municipal and regional levels. At the higher, republican-level structures Azerbaijani representation dropped to just a third.[26] As under tsarist rule, Russian stewardship of the AzSSR's modernisation was shared with Armenians. Armenians were fewer in overall numbers than Russians until the 1970s, but played visible roles in the technical elite, showed robust demographic growth through to the 1960s, and most tellingly, remained significantly over-represented in Azerbaijani Communist Party membership throughout Soviet rule (see Table 4.2).

After World War II, Azerbaijanis closed the gap in a pattern I term 'delayed indigenisation'. A key development was the renaming of the republic's Turkic population: *tyurki* became *azerbaydzhantsy* in 1937 (see Chapter 2). This defined an eponymous

Table 4.2 Armenian (ArmCP) and Azerbaijani (AzCP) Communist Party membership by nationality (%) in major census years (with minority nationality shares of overall republican population in parentheses)

	ArmCP		AzCP	
	Titular	Azerbaijani	Titular	Armenian
1922	93.4	1.6 (no data)	39.4	9.4 (no data)
1926	91	4.3 (8.7)	39.7	17.5 (12.4)
1939	89.7	7.4 (10.2)	44.9	24 (12.1)
1959	92.2	4.2 (6.1)	54.1	19.4 (12)
1970	92.6	4.2 (5.9)	66.4	13.7 (9.5)
1979	93.2	3.6 (5.3)	72.9	10.8 (7.9)

Source: Compiled from Institute for the History of the Party under the Central Committee of the Armenian Communist Party, *Kommunisticheskaya Partiya Armenii v tsifrakh i dokumentakh* (Yerevan: Ayastan, 1980); Institute for the History of the Azerbaijani Communist Party, *Kommunisticheskaya Partiya Azerbaydzhana v tsifrakh. Statisticheskiy Sbornik* (Baku: Azerbaijan State Publishing House, 1970), *Kommunisticheskaya partiya Azerbaydzhana – boevoy otryad KPSS* (Baku: Azerbaijan State Publishing House, 1979).

titular nationality, and consequently an explicit ethnic hierarchy, for the first time. Social mobility came to reflect this hierarchy through recruitment policies that no longer admitted senior roles to Armenians or Russians. If in 1939 Azerbaijanis had accounted for only half of leadership posts in the republic, indigenisation proceeded rapidly in the post-war era with Azerbaijanis accounting for 91 per cent of leading positions between 1955 and 1972.[27] But exceptions to increasing indigenisation remained in the AzSSR's urban spaces, especially its metropolitan area on the Absheron peninsula. Nationalising this space confronted embedded Russian and Armenian communities, constituent elements of a supra-national identity summed up in the word *bakinets* ('Bakuvian'), a distinct, ethnically unmarked but Russian-speaking identity defined by cosmopolitan ideals.[28]

By the 1970s, delayed indigenisation had reconfigured the implicit hierarchies shaping interethnic relations in the AzSSR. These structural changes gave rise to one of the commonest anecdotal narratives among Armenian refugees displaced from the AzSSR: the Armenian 'second-in-command'. The stereotypical arrangement in such anecdotes is of the Azerbaijani director of a Soviet factory or institute, both entitled and work-shy by right of their titular claim, undermined by an Armenian deputy who has to work twice as hard, yet is forever frustrated by an invisible ethnic ceiling. The two might even be close friends, attending each other's family celebrations and sharing fond memories, yet their structural disparities remained a silent barrier. Armenians saw previous horizons of opportunity disappear: 'I had a good job in a factory in the food industry in Baku, when a new post became available. The director said to me: "You've reached your limit here, I have to appoint an Azerbaijani."'[29] It was not only mobility at stake, but also the symbolic rewards affirming the existence of a new hierarchy and the overturning of the previous order:

> When there was talk of who was to receive awards at work, then of course it would have to be Mamedov or some Alekperov [two common Azerbaijani surnames]. When a delegate was to be sent to a meeting, conference, or congress etc., then, of course, again it would be some Mamedov or Alekperov.[30]

Resentments accumulated on both sides, Armenians at domination by a group that the state had within living memory classified as 'backward', Azerbaijanis at the lingering presence of an urban minority always perceived as profiting from metropolitan favouritism.

It is against this backdrop that several precipitating events in late 1987–8 should be considered. Heydar Aliyev, the most powerful Azerbaijani in the Soviet Union and the anchor, even from afar, of the AzSSR's patronage structure, was dismissed from the Politburo in October 1987. His dismissal could only bode a decline in Azerbaijani influence at a time of growing uncertainty. The more direct challenge was the 20 February 1988 resolution by the local assembly in the NKAO calling for unification with the ArmSSR. This unprecedented act by a lower-level Soviet autonomy challenged Azerbaijan's still fragile ethnic hierarchy, and effectively proposed its reversal in the NKAO. An emotional narrative focused on resentment of Armenians was formed, running approximately along the following lines. Against a backdrop of uncertain structural change, Azerbaijani leadership had been weakened. Armenians had taken advantage of the situation to make a bid for secession, which if successful would be a humiliating loss for the AzSSR. Who, in this context, were the Armenians? They were a long-privileged minority that had finally been brought to heel in the AzSSR. Now they were seeking to reverse the hierarchy and senior policy-makers in Moscow had come out in support of their plan. There were rumours that Armenians were terrorising Azerbaijanis in the ArmSSR and they needed to be 'put in their place'.

A preoccupation with status and symbolic reversals is evident in eyewitness accounts of the communal violence in the AzSSR that followed. Sumgait resident Tatyana Arutyunian, returning under military escort to her apartment in the aftermath to collect possessions, observed: 'especially with the young people, you could sense the delight at our misfortune, the grins, and they were making comments, too'.[31] Vladimir Marutyan, attacked by his neighbour Adil Shafiyev, recalled: 'Normally he was scared to death of me, but now . . .'.[32] In Baku in November 1988 Russian army general Aleksandr Lebed' witnessed Azerbaijani demonstrators with placards, allegedly quoting Russian poet Aleksandr Pushkin, offering a reminder of historical Armenian subservience: 'You're a slave, you're a thief, you're an Armenian' (*ty–rab, ty–vor, ty–armyanin*).[33] In December at Baku's railway station Lebed' observed how 'Azerbaijani porters demonstratively ignored Armenian families with all their suitcases and bundles.'[34] Just over a year later in January 1990 Armenian refugees remember petty humiliations accompanying their departure: mockingly painstaking inspections of the few belongings they had managed to grab as they queued for hours to board at the port, and demands for payment to be allowed to sit indoors out of the January cold once aboard.[35] Symbolic redress, enacted through public humiliation, was an intrinsic aspect to the communal violence in Azerbaijan.[36]

The most severe communal violence, in Baku in January 1990, was enacted against a residual population. According to Armenian human rights activist and former ombudsman Larisa Alaverdyan, not more than 25,000 Armenians remained in Baku by then, out of an already depleted population of 180,000 recorded in the 1989 census.[37] They had been subjected to persistent demands by local housing officials to leave, to periodic electricity and gas supply cuts, and even to bread blockades. Most were in the process of leaving; others were hanging on in order to sell or exchange their apartments. Violence was already a fact of everyday life: 'all of our window sills were stocked with knives and axes'.[38] Many Armenians were literally sitting on their suitcases when the pogrom broke – attackers just carried out already packed up goods and possessions; they were also able to identify some Armenian flats because possessions were boxed up. Why was a residual population targeted in this way? One explanation is that Armenians were sacrificed in the struggle for power between the Azerbaijani Communist Party and the Azerbaijani Popular Front, who both believed that violence would benefit them.[39] Yet the violence also served as a crucible forging a national identity in the capital where an alternative cosmopolitan identity was strongest. Violence nationalised previously ethnically indeterminate, Russian-speaking urban space, and removed its most numerous, most successful, and most resented non-indigenous exemplars – Armenians. Mixed marriages involving Armenians, an icon of Bakuvian cosmopolitanism, were not spared in many cases. Irina Mosesova recorded the presence of families bearing the Azerbaijani surnames Mamedov and Askerov among the lists of refugees from Baku: evidence of an Armenian grandparent or spouse that only locals could have known about.[40]

Communal violence in the AzSSR in 1988–90 was indeed, then, a 'revenge attack', but far wider in scope and meaning than the extraction of 'an eye for an eye' by refugees. This was a collective enactment of vengeance against a minority that had forgotten its 'rightful place' in Azerbaijan's fragile ethnic hierarchy, and which also served as a surrogate target for two centuries of accumulated resentment at metropolitan labelling of Azerbaijanis as 'backward' – and Armenians as 'advanced'.

Armenia: Enacting Historical Justice

A different set of circumstances shaped affective dispositions towards Azerbaijanis in the ArmSSR. Unlike the AzSSR, the ArmSSR was thoroughly indigenised from the beginning of Soviet rule. Russian skills, culture and settlers played no equivalent role in its modernisation. In the first two decades of Soviet rule Armenian demographic dominance was overlaid with a near-total political dominance: in 1939 Armenians accounted for 95.2 per cent of leadership roles at republican level (see Table 4.1); at the regional level they were also over-represented at 88.5 per cent. In the latter Soviet decades Armenians enjoyed mobility across the Soviet Union to the extent that they were the nationality least likely to live in their own republic (only 65.5 per cent did so in 1979), and frequently came close to the top of all-union indices in areas such as education.

Despite depletions through the forced resettlements of 1947–53, Azerbaijanis were the ArmSSR's largest minority throughout the Soviet period. But in almost every other sense, their position was structurally the opposite to that of the Armenian minority in the AzSSR. Ninety per cent of the community was rural in 1979, and Azerbaijanis accounted for less than 1 per cent of the ArmSSR's overall urban population. They were consistently under-represented in the Armenian Communist Party (see Table 4.2), and in urban settings popular stereotypes associated Azerbaijanis with market trade and the vegetable bazaar. There were few grounds for this minority to arouse resentment among the Armenian majority. Azerbaijani demographic resilience, however, was a publicly expressed concern in the 1980s.[41] This was the flipside of high Armenian mobility and migration, as well as higher Azerbaijani birth rates and some rural-to-rural migration into the ArmSSR from the AzSSR.[42]

This was leading, in some areas, to a 'rural thinning' among Armenians. In 1979 three of the ArmSSR's thirty-six regions featured Azerbaijani majorities; in another seven, Azerbaijanis accounted for 20–40 per cent of the population (see Table 4.3). All of the Azerbaijani-majority regions were in the periphery, in the north-west region of Amasiya, and its outer rim to the east of Lake Sevan (Krasnosel'sk and Vardenis). The latter became Azerbaijani-majority regions during the 1960s, evidence of robust Azerbaijani growth. In the late 1980s social anthropologist Nora Dudwick documented an Armenian mindset giving credence to a 'social Darwinist model of expanding and predatory populations'

Table 4.3 Azerbaijani population growth in regions of the ArmSSR, 1959-79

Region	1959	%	1970	%	1979	%
Amasiya	9,431	71.9	15,002	80.9	17,109	81.5
Vardenis	17,632	49.5	25,781	52.7	31,226	54.9
Krasnosel'sk	9,283	38.7	13,352	50.8	13,827	52.3
Kapan	7,345	27.7	9,926	37.3	9,307	41.4
Gugark	3,910	16.8	7,250	27.3	8,128	29.2
Meghri	3,351	28.5	3,852	27.0	3,948	29.1
Azizbekov	2,306	20.3	3,455	24.0	4,117	26.9
Kalinino	4,985	19.7	7,786	24.5	9,047	26.0
Masis	9,850	34.0	13,576	29.8	14,169	24.8
Sisian	6,212	21.6	7,526	23.9	7,061	21.9

Source: Adapted from Central Statistical Committee of the ArmSSR, *Itogi Vsesoyuznoy Perepisi Naseleniya 1979 goda po Armyanskoy SSR* (Yerevan: Central Statistical Committee, 1980), Table 6, pp. 232-44.

at 'demographic war' - which only one group could win.[43] These developments suggest that fear, arising from localised demographic contractions, could explain the mass eviction of Armenia's Azerbaijanis. This is indeed how their exodus has been explained, often cynically, to outsiders in the post-war era: a regrettable but inevitable step, as a result of which Armenia's demography - at least in its ethnic character - is secure.[44]

A collective act of self-preservation perhaps offers a more justifiable rationale for the mass eviction of Azerbaijanis from the ArmSSR in 1987-90, but it is unconvincing. By 1979 Armenians accounted for 90 per cent of the ArmSSR's population, making it the most homogenous in the USSR. Armenians were hardly in the same situation as Estonians or Kazakhs, struggling to preserve or attain a majority in the face of substantial Soviet-era in-migration. Pockets of local resilience aside, proportional overall decline in the ArmSSR's Azerbaijani population had been consistent since the 1930s. Moreover, if fear of Azerbaijani demographic growth were the driver of anti-Azerbaijani violence in Armenia, one would also expect violence to have been worse in those areas where Azerbaijanis were most populous. It is true that the highest number of violent deaths, around forty, recorded by Azerbaijani researchers at the time occurred in the region of Vardenis, home to the second-largest Azerbaijani population in the AzSSR. But the demographic factor proves a poor guide to the distribution of Azerbaijani fatalities. In some regions with large Azerbaijani populations, such as Amasiya and Kapan, violence in 1988–9 was considerably lower than in others that had significantly smaller Azerbaijani populations. The most brutal violence, involving thirteen cases where victims were allegedly set alight, took place in Gugark, far from the border with the AzSSR and with no rural Azerbaijani majority.[45]

The structural context of Soviet Armenia's Azerbaijani minority and the patterns of violence against it suggest that rather than resentment or fear, it is hatred that was the predominant emotion towards this community in the ArmSSR. Hatred is a loaded term, and I use it in a specific sense. I do not imply the 'ancient hatreds' that achieved notoriety as a misleading explanation of Balkan violence in the 1990s. Rather, I use the term to denote an established schema of historically recursive violence between two groups understood in terms of 'innate', unchanging characteristics. Hatred is not ancient, but it requires sufficient duration to become fixed as a cultural schema with ritualised roles for in- and out-groups. It is, as Roger Petersen observes, often a latent dimension within broader historical schemas. In the face of dramatic structural change, hatred can be activated as a 'desire for historically framed violence', to 'settle scores' and 'take back what is ours'.[46]

By the 1980s the figure of the warrior-martyr, defeat by more powerful foes, and redemption through collective suffering were recurring tropes in a historical schema of Armenian identity reaching back to the fifth century.[47] Already since 1965, genocide commemoration had bridged the divide between official and unofficial transcripts of Armenian identity, and by the late 1980s genocide was a ubiquitous interpretive routine for understanding the Armenian experience across multiple domains.[48] This historical schema clearly identified 'innate' roles for in-group martyrs and heroes, and out-group villains. As cultural anthropologist Harutyun Marutyan's study of posters during the Karabakh movement in Yerevan shows, the massacre of Armenians in Sumgait cued this schema instantly, foretelling a resurgence in

'Turkish barbarity'.[49] Sumgait, and all subsequent outbreaks of anti-Armenian violence in the AzSSR (and even local incidents in the ArmSSR, such as outbreaks of disease), were merged into a unified narrative of 'serial genocide'. The schema of hatred scaled local Azerbaijani communities up to the level of the Armenian–Turkish antagonism, essentialising them as 'Turks' playing the 'traditional' Turkish role. Rather than demographic fear, a historical schema of hatred not only reduced a vulnerable and defenceless minority to a single categorical identity as 'Turks', but also prescribed violent role-play against them as a historically legitimate 'response'.

Nagorny Karabakh: A Fearful Security Dilemma

Until 1991 the former oblast in Nagorny Karabakh was the ground zero of conflicting territorial claims, but not of forced population movements. The territory actually provided refuge for some of the Armenians fleeing metropolitan areas of Azerbaijan and – temporarily – for some Azerbaijanis fleeing Armenia. These incoming movements further embedded an already complex strategic context of double encirclement, driven by each group's blockading of the other's access to friendly territory. Karabakh Armenians could commute safely only by helicopter with Armenia, while Karabakh Azerbaijanis could not travel securely between Shusha and the rest of Azerbaijan. While other emotions were also present, fear emerges as the pre-eminent affective disposition among both communities in the oblast.

Among the province's Armenians, anxieties stemmed from the ambiguity of autonomy, which did not formally define a titular nationality (see Chapter 1). This reduced 'ownership' to a question of demography: without an Armenian ethnic majority, the NKAO could become, like Nakhichevan, a purely formal autonomy that was to all intents and purposes an undifferentiated Azerbaijani province. This lent the disproportionate growth rates of the two populations in the NKAO in the post-World War II era a particular political charge. Between 1959 and 1979 the Azerbaijani population increase exceeded Armenian growth by a factor of nearly ten. In an oft-cited speech dating from July 2002 Heydar Aliyev took credit for policies encouraging the movement of Azerbaijanis into the oblast in the 1970s.[50] Politicians, of course, calibrate their message to their audience, in this case a post-war Azerbaijan hungry for culprits. Anecdotally, securing residency permits for Azerbaijanis to resettle in the NKAO was in practice more difficult than Aliyev's *ex post* comments implied.[51] Yet Aliyev's claim seems credible to many Armenians today because the empirical reality appeared to reflect it. Disproportionate growth rates were nevertheless evident before Aliyev became Azerbaijani first secretary and resulted from a complex combination of factors, including different birth rates, stagnant Armenian rural population growth and Armenian mobility out of the province to the ArmSSR.

Demographic fear is a prominent thread in post-war characterisations of the context facing Karabakh Armenians in the late 1980s:

> To this day we cannot explain why the people followed us, why we were able to get people behind us . . . There were language concerns, about TV and radio; we had empty kiosks standing in the street in Hadrut, and shops stocked to the ceiling with goods down the road in Fizuli. There was assimilation: Armenians in mixed villages were losing their traditions, they were starting to speak Azerbaijani, losing their Christianity, not naming their children with traditional Armenian names . . . Shahumyan, for instance, was a marchland. We didn't even consider it part of lowland Karabakh. They were not the same Armenians as us. They spoke Azerbaijani amongst themselves, they did things 'their' way. Yes, there was concern about assimilation, but you could never say that out loud . . . There was an encirclement strategy – they would put Azerbaijani villages between two Armenian villages, and their settlers would be a specific kind of person, they were people with a mission. Transport routes took us via Azerbaijani population centres, while our own internal communications and roads were left to disrepair. There was a process of internal fragmentation. If we had left it another five years we would have lost Nagorny Karabakh.[52]

Perception is everything. Incited by nationalist intellectuals and perestroika-era media reporting, demographic fear became the prism through which Armenians perceived the policy initiatives emanating from the centre in 1988–9, even though they still accounted for nearly 80 per cent of the oblast's population. Moscow's programme for economic aid was depicted as being redirected into construction of new settlements for Azerbaijanis, with particular anxieties focusing on the town of Khojaly. The construction there of new housing for a few hundred Azerbaijani refugees from the ArmSSR was reported to be proceeding rapidly in late 1988, allegedly without *raispolkom* permission and with the assistance of AzSSR Interior Ministry units. This was framed as an attempt to create a 'second Shusha', that is, another purely Azerbaijani-settled population centre in the NKAO.[53] The perceived threat of Khojaly as a demographic bridgehead into Armenian ethno-space made it a focal point of local disputes. On 18 September 1988, a convoy organised by Armenian students headed for Stepanakert sustained injuries when it was shot at from Khojaly.[54] This precipitated the expulsion of Armenians from Shusha and of Azerbaijanis from Stepanakert.

The NKAO's Azerbaijani population was also fearful. Karabakh Azerbaijanis may have shown robust demographic growth, but this was not patterned to form a unifying ethno-space linking Azerbaijani settlement points within the oblast with Azerbaijani-settled areas outside of it. Azerbaijanis were an overwhelming majority only in Shusha, enjoying a strategic position on commanding heights over the capital, Stepanakert, yet isolated deep within the oblast. Moreover, the last Soviet census, conducted in January 1989 after the conflict had begun, was indicative of a wider demographic dilemma from an Azerbaijani perspective. The census revealed a sharp spike (43.5 per cent) in the Armenian urban population since 1979, driven by migration by Armenians from other urban settings in the AzSSR.[55] In other words, the more Azerbaijani the AzSSR's urban spaces became, the more Armenian the NKAO would become. The reluctance of Armenians from the AzSSR to resettle in the ArmSSR, a 'homeland' many had never been to and whose language many did not command, is well documented.[56] If Russia was the destination of choice for a majority, some elected to resettle in the NKAO, where they may have had relatives, ancestral roots or simply no other choice.

Refugees and migrants brought with them narratives of trauma (if not exclusively so: some memories of friendship and peaceful co-existence survived). In the still strategically intermingled context of the NKAO and the receding security guarantees of the Soviet state, neighbours were reidentified as enemies and their defensive actions perceived as threatening. The mechanism of the security dilemma was sprung. Communal violence in Nagorny Karabakh took the form of individual attacks 'mainly at night, aimed at destroying livestock and harassing people. There was also hostage-taking, which frightened people in neighbouring villages.'[57] Stoning passing vehicles was common; Khojaly and Askeran were known as rock-throwing trouble-spots. As a result, between 1988 and 1991 large swathes of the NKAO, in addition to the districts of Khanlar and Shahumyan to the north, were transformed into a series of interlocking micro-security dilemmas between neighbouring villages, demarcated by ethnicity and strategic advantage or vulnerability.

Strategic Ethnic Cleansing and 'Refuchess'

By early 1990 the demographic unravelling of Armenian and Azerbaijani populations was all but complete. It was only in the NKAO that they continued to share the same geopolitical space, albeit now segregated by internal displacement into single-community settlements, many subjected to strafing, arson and hostage-taking raids. From 1991 forced population movements resulted from military operations and served strategic goals of limiting sources of support to enemy combatants or consolidating territorial gains. Strategic ethnic cleansing created new 'empty spaces', bereft of inhabitants, which became blank canvases for the creation of new human geographies in which previously displaced persons themselves became an important instrument. Anthropologist Stef Jansen has defined the ensuing process as 'refuchess': 'the strategic deployment and movement of nationalised persons across nationalised places'.[58] In the game of refuchess displaced persons are made symbolically central to the story of national suffering, but at the same time are moved to the geographic and political margins of society, or inserted as demographic ramparts fortifying recently abandoned spaces against the return of their former inhabitants.

There were three core contexts for the strategic ethnic cleansing of Armenians and Azerbaijanis in 1991–4. The first was 'Operation Ring' in April–June 1991 (see Chapter 1). Publicly justified as an internal passport-checking operation, the aim of Operation Ring was to flush out Armenian fighters taking cover in Armenian-populated villages, mainly on the borders of the NKAO.[59] Villages were surrounded and cut off from the outside world, hence the operation's codename, before Azerbaijani forces combed through the settlements, looting, taking hostages and deporting their inhabitants. More than twenty Armenian villages were cleared of their populations over the spring and summer of 1991, 'with an unprecedented degree of violence and a systematic violation of human rights'.[60] Although not limited to them, the Armenian-populated areas of Shahumyan and Khanlar to the north of the NKAO emerged as the operation's epicentre. Armenians displaced from several villages in Shahumyan during Operation Ring later returned when Armenian forces recaptured them during the summer. In September 1991 Shahumyan's Armenians declared themselves part of the NKR, but were displaced for a second and final time when Azerbaijani forces retook control of the area in 1992. In all, some 40,000 people lost their homes in the Shahumyan and neighbouring districts of Khanlar, Kasum-Ismayilli and Dashkesan.

The second context was the struggle for territorial control of the former oblast itself in 1992, with forced movements accompanying all major military offensives and retreats, motivated, inter alia, by the perpetration of atrocities against civilian populations on both sides. The former oblast's mixed demography finally unravelled with the expulsion of Karabakh Azerbaijanis after the massacre at Khojaly on the night of 25–6 February 1992. Azerbaijani forces attacking from the north also committed atrocities, if on a smaller scale, notably in the village of Maragha on 10 April. The last Azerbaijani presence in the former oblast was expunged with the fall of Shusha on 8–9 May. One month later in June, an Azerbaijani counter-attack overran Karabakh's

Mardakert region, resulting in a flow of some 40,000 displaced Armenians to other locations in Nagorny Karabakh.

The third context was the conquest of Azerbaijani regions around the former oblast by Armenian forces in 1992–4. In May 1992 Armenian forces broke out of their encirclement by taking the Azerbaijani region of Lachin, populated before the war by nearly 50,000 people. Its Azerbaijani and Muslim Kurd population fled. After repelling the Azerbaijani counter-offensive over the latter half of 1992, Armenian forces reprised the method of Operation Ring on a larger scale as they carved out their own 'security belt' of occupied territories around the former NKAO in 1993.[61] Azerbaijanis internally displaced as a result of the conquest of the seven regions account for the single largest category of people displaced by the Armenian–Azerbaijani conflict, at around half a million. They were displaced from largely mono-ethnic territories that had never formed part of the dispute, and there was no communal aspect to their displacement. Rather, the conquests were understood in terms of territorial control providing for security for the NKR within 'defensible borders', and as collateral against its eventual recognition.

Following the logic of refuchess, after displacement refugees have been relocated in order to validate territorial claims. In the aftermath of Operation Ring, Azerbaijani refugees from Armenia were brought in to settle recently abandoned Armenian settlements.[62] Post-war, many new settlements constructed for Azerbaijan's internally displaced population were located near the Line of Contact. The logic was to uphold a returnee identity through spatial proximity to former homes a short distance away on the other side of the frontline.[63] Yet in a context of escalating violence, communities located along the frontline are increasingly in harm's way, even if state officials claimed that none were built closer to the Line of Contact than pre-existing villages.[64] Over the long term, location near a live conflict zone precludes stable or secure livelihoods, but to relocate displaced Azerbaijanis confronted a confining regime of residency registration. In the 2000s residence permits for large cities, especially Baku, were notoriously difficult to obtain. As a state official put it to Amnesty International in 2006, displaced persons are easier to count and provide for in compact settlements, whereas in Baku or Sumgait they 'disappear and run their own businesses and livelihoods'.[65]

In Armenian-occupied territories, the logic of refuchess is clear in the view that 'if we had 500,000 people in Karabakh, the issue would be settled'.[66] The demographic realities in Nagorny Karabakh, however, fall short of this ambition (see Chapter 8). De facto officials concede that efforts to encourage settlement have yielded disappointing results: 'we have offered incentives but we have not been able to really change the demographic reality'.[67] But displaced Armenians have provided one source of new demographic mass for the consolidation of territorial gains. In the mid-2000s de facto authorities estimated that around a third of the territory's population was composed of displaced persons.[68] In some sites this proportion rises. In 2005 local residents of the town of Shusha estimated that two-thirds of its population of 3,000 were displaced.[69] Many of those displaced from metropolitan Azerbaijan have traumatic memories of the communal violence there in 1988–90. Essentialised views that Armenians must not live among Azerbaijanis, Turks or even Muslims at large are easily heard here, sometimes from older generations raised as convinced advocates of Soviet internationalism.[70] These collective fears form a communal firewall against the possibility of return for Azerbaijanis displaced from these territories in 1992–3.

Return and Its Alternatives

The right of displaced persons to return will be a central issue of contestation and litmus test by which any eventual Armenian–Azerbaijani peace agreement is seen as just. Reversing ethnic cleansing – at least in part – is likely to assume a far greater symbolic significance than the practicalities, advisability and sustainability of returns in reality.[71] While displacement was a fate that befell both nationalities with terrible thoroughness, the agenda for return revolves overwhelmingly around Azerbaijan's internally displaced population. This is because the return of refugees evicted through communal ethnic cleansing has never been seen as practical or desirable, on either side of the conflict. In Azerbaijan refugees from Armenia were naturalised as citizens with full political and property rights. Already in November 1991 the former Supreme Soviet recognised a refugee right to private ownership of properties exchanged with Armenians or new housing constructed since 1988.[72] Known, somewhat pejoratively, as *Yerazi* ('Yerevan Azerbaijanis'), Azerbaijanis from Armenia developed into one of the most successful informal networks in post-war Azerbaijan and a support base for Heydar Aliyev, himself long rumoured to have been born in Armenia. In Armenia the fate of refugees from Azerbaijan is a largely forgotten story. Some 97 per cent came from urban locations in Azerbaijan and faced considerable hardship adapting to the rural accommodation in which many found themselves in Armenia.[73] Poor knowledge of Armenian, and an identity gap between older refugees habituated to Soviet internationalism and local stereotypes depicting refugees as 'Turkified Armenians', compounded socio-economic difficulties. Many feel abandoned by the state: 'There is no prospect for our return, so the government says that integration is our only option. So donors don't give money and the issue is forgotten. We are slowly dying out and that suits everyone.'[74]

Conversely, Azerbaijan sees the return of internally displaced Azerbaijanis as an essential aspect to the restoration of territorial integrity and the resolution of the conflict. Policies towards its internally displaced population have been designed to maintain this population's social coherence and prospective returnee identity. Referring to new, state-constructed housing for IDPs, the Head of the State Committee for Refugees and Internally Displaced Persons explained in 2007: 'we haven't given internally displaced persons property rights because they must return'.[75] These policies are not without support among internally displaced, especially in older generations. Yet the reluctance to integrate IDPs has resulted in long-term dependency on state assistance, and consigned many to the literal and political margins of Azerbaijan. Throughout the 1990s and early 2000s improvised tent camps and provisional shelter of great hardship dominated imagery of displacement in Azerbaijan. Beginning in 2001 the state began to move those in makeshift accommodation into newly constructed settlements. By 2007 the last of the country's tent camps was closed and up to

100,000 displaced persons had been relocated to new settlements. This was not necessarily a consultative process, as many were relocated to homes they could not own, or sublet, in isolated locations across the country.[76] In 2011 73 per cent of IDPs still reported government assistance to be their primary source of income.[77] By then 35 per cent of the internally displaced population was living in newly built settlements. The majority continued to live in non-residential accommodation, such as public buildings, former dormitories and improvised shelter, or with relatives.

The prospects for return in the foreseeable future, however, are dim. For many years the return of internally displaced Azerbaijanis to the provinces of Agdam, Fizuli, Jebrayil, Zangelan, Qubatly and Kelbajar could be considered relatively straightforward if security and status issues were resolved. These areas had never formed part of the original dispute, and offered clear scope for returns to areas where Azerbaijanis had formed overwhelming pre-war demographic majorities. Yet the growing hegemony of 'augmented Armenia' in Armenia's geopolitical culture challenges readings of these spaces as uncontested. While demographic crisis in Armenia (see Chapter 6) has limited the capacity of settlement to keep up with such claims, small but established settler communities and multiplying infrastructure in areas to the west and south of the former oblast makes this a possibility in the future.

Return to areas inhabited by members of the adversarial group is inherently more complex, requiring not only rehabilitation and physical reconstruction but also reconciliation. For Azerbaijanis, the litmus test for a future peace agreement will be the degree of return possible to Shusha.[78] As the former historical and cultural capital of Nagorny Karabakh, Shusha retains enormous symbolic importance for both Armenians and Azerbaijanis. Its geopolitical significance lies in its status as the only major town in the former oblast with an Azerbaijani majority (comprising 98 per cent of its population in 1989) and its location commanding strategic heights above Stepanakert, upon which rockets indiscriminately hailed down from Shusha in early 1992. Gradually restored from the late 2000s, the town had a population of some 4,200 (as noted, mostly displaced) in 2016, and several de facto ministries and state institutions had relocated to it.

Displacements

Lachin and the former Shahumyan region form two other critical contested spaces. Lachin has long held a central place in Armenian reasoning as the shortest corridor between the former oblast and Armenia. Local statistics indicated that, submerged within reconfigured internal borders, in its new identity as Berdzor, Lachin town held a population of nearly 2,000 in 2016. The former district of Shahumyan, as noted, was the sole area in Soviet Azerbaijan outside of the former NKAO with a pre-war Armenian majority. Incorporated in 1991 into a reconfigured Azerbaijani region of Goranboy, former Shahumyan is today populated by Azerbaijani refugees from Armenia, and internally displaced communities from Khojaly and Kelbajar.[79] Across the de facto border from former Shahumyan, displaced Armenians live in occupied Kelbajar, renamed and rebordered as part of the 'new' Shahumyan region of the NKR. These mirroring geopolitical conceits generate bewilderingly complex dialectics of place-making and unmaking, sowing seeds of confusion for any future process of return.

Secessionists seeking international legitimacy for ethnically cleansed territories can become disingenuous 'advocates' of the return of displaced communities to them. There is evidence of such posturing in the NKR's de facto President Bako Sahakyan's comments to the effect that 'Azerbaijani refugees naturally can return to Artsakh, to the Artsakh Republic, if they recognize its jurisdiction'.[80] Azerbaijani return to Nagorny Karabakh could, in theory, mitigate wartime legacies of ethnic cleansing and move the de facto republic in the direction, if not of multi-ethnic democracy, then at least liberal ethnocracy. Karabakh Azerbaijanis have also advocated for their return to the territory as the single most effective security guarantee for Karabakh Armenians.[81] However, there are few indications that outside of statements for international audiences there is readiness in Nagorny Karabakh to begin dialogue on more inclusive cultural conceptions of identity. In 2014 Sergey Shahverdyan, director of the NKR's Department of Tourism, sarcastically dismissed my questions about cultural heritage as a means to build bridges, arguing that the territory's Muslim monuments represented a symbiosis of Iranian and Armenian styles.[82] In the wider population, reconciliatory attitudes towards Azerbaijanis are the lowest in any post-Soviet secessionist space vis-à-vis representatives of the parent state nationality. More than 80 per cent of those interviewed in a 2011 survey held negative or very negative attitudes towards Azerbaijanis.[83]

The fact that displaced Azerbaijanis are often evoked as voices of impatience, or voices calling for war, compounds these divisions. Yet any face-to-face discussion with groups of internally displaced Azerbaijanis reveals that no single narrative encompasses their experiences. Individual life cycles, and where displacement falls within them, shape differing outlooks. Genuine nostalgia and loss among older generations gives way to affective compliance with an idealised narrative of return among younger generations, who only know of ancestral homes from the memories of parents and grandparents. For some in future generations well established in mainstream life, an identity associated with a historical displacement may be attractive as a symbolic choice. But for many younger people within displaced community settings today, especially those in the geographic and political margins of the country, a displaced identity is one precarious identity among many. Reifying this identity – and return as an exit from it – can embed already multiple disadvantages on the path to social mobility, professional fulfilment and economic security.

Restitution as a Return to Agency

Powerlessness and dependency on a neglectful state, or one driven by geopolitical agendas, is a common thread among displaced communities across the Armenian–Azerbaijani conflict. *Return* in these contexts takes on a different meaning, as the return of agency and decision-making powers to the displaced individual and their descendants to make choices about where to live. This raises the difficult and often unwelcome theme of restitution: the conversion of a lost title to property into resources that can be used to rebuild a home elsewhere. Property restitution endows displaced persons not only with resources, but also with choice and agency to finally sever ties to a former home. By the same token, restitution disrupts both geopolitical narratives and strategies of staking out claims to territories by embedding displaced persons within them. This is one reason why popular narratives of the compensated departure of refugees still hold. In reality, it appears that most of the restitution that took place in the late 1980s was informal and derived from exceptional circumstances where village communities agreed to swap their homes.[84]

On the same day in June 2015 the European Court of Human Rights (ECtHR) handed down two judgments upholding the rights of people displaced on both sides of the Armenian–Azerbaijani conflict. In both cases, the court upheld the claimants' complaints that their rights under the European Convention to the peaceful enjoyment of property, the right to private and family life and home, and to the right to effective remedy, had been violated. The juxtaposition of the two judgments, delivery on the same day and by the exact same composition of judges, gave the impression of symmetry. The two cases did indeed assert a presumption of jurisdiction with regard to the governments of both Armenia and Azerbaijan.

In *Chiragov and Others v. Armenia*, six Azerbaijani Kurds displaced from Lachin brought a complaint against Armenia. Much to Azerbaijani satisfaction, the ECtHR overturned Armenia's objections that it had no jurisdiction in Lachin. The court argued that by weight of its military, political and economic support to the NKR Armenia exercised 'effective control' over it and thereby exercised extra-territorial jurisdiction.[85] This was a significant win for Azerbaijan's wider legal position as it can easily be interpreted as confirmation that Armenia is an occupying power in Nagorny Karabakh. In *Sargsyan v. Azerbaijan*, Armenians displaced from the village of Gulistan in the former district of Shahumyan brought a complaint against Azerbaijan. In this case, the ECtHR again asserted a presumption of jurisdiction, this time Azerbaijan's, over a deserted settlement lying between Azerbaijani and Armenian forces on the Line of Contact itself. Despite losing de facto control over Gulistan, the court held that Azerbaijan was accountable to its former inhabitants. This judgment was not without controversy. As one of the judges argued, the context in

Gulistan could only be properly understood in terms of responsibility shared between Armenia and Azerbaijan.[86]

Although the two cases raised different sets of issues, concurrent responsibility of the two states for the (non-)fulfilment of displaced persons' rights was undoubtedly the political message behind their choreographed delivery. In both judgments, the ECtHR used the same wording to advise the establishment of 'a property claims mechanism ... allowing the applicant[s] and others in [their] situation to have their property rights restored and to obtain compensation for the loss of their enjoyment'.[87] The judgments framed the indefinite postponement of conflict resolution as continuous violations of individual citizens' rights, for which states were liable. Yet what the two cases also revealed were the likely future contours of obstructionist tactics seeking to stall and prevent return. Here the judgments showed a different kind of symmetry, in mirroring claims by each state that documentation of property ownership was inadequate, missing or fake, or that claimants had not even proven that they were who they said they were. At times these bordered on the absurd, such as claims that titles to properties in areas subjected to sustained blockade and bombardment in 1991–2 bore the 'wrong stamp', after these areas had been gerrymandered into new regional configurations without even the knowledge – let alone consent – of their inhabitants.[88] Both Armenian and Azerbaijani governments sought to avoid responsibility by arguing that events had occurred before they acceded to the relevant legal instruments. Contradictory claims were in turn wrapped within interpretations of pre-privatisation Soviet legal codes that do not map across into unambiguous claims of private ownership.

In conclusion, the incomplete yet still considerable reversal of ethnic cleansing that to a degree reconstituted multi-ethnic societies in post-war Bosnia in the 1990s is unlikely in the Armenian–Azerbaijani case. Displacement has gone on for a much longer period of time, embedding new, post-war conceptions of space and ethno-territorial order. Victor and victim identities are more entrenched, by both the outcomes of war and the passage of time. With the heyday of liberal interventionism long gone, the extent of international presence on the ground in the event of an

Armenian–Azerbaijani peace is also likely to be much smaller. In the years to come we will likely see increasing activism and grassroots memorialisation around the theme of displacement, particularly in Azerbaijan. Yet it is at best uncertain whether displaced individuals will be able to effectively assert their rights. Even less certain is whether sufficient reconciliation can be achieved to make even symbolic levels of return to contested spaces possible. Ultimately, the prospects for either outcome depend on the nature of the regimes that have developed in the context of enduring rivalry.

5 Regime Politics and Rivalry

'We need to democratise first, then solve the Karabakh problem!' It was February 2005, and my interlocutor was a civil society activist in Baku. His view was one I would repeatedly encounter across the conflict in the years that followed. But more than a decade later in 2016, and a quarter-century after independence, Armenia and Azerbaijan counted among the longest-lived regimes in the former Soviet Union. Electoral fraud was routine, 'colour revolutions' had passed the two states by and through repeated referendums their regimes had mapped onto constitutions, rather than the other way around. In longevity only Belarus and regimes in Central Asia rivalled them. Yet nowhere else was the contrast between mass mobilisation on the path to independence and regime endurance since then so stark. What had happened to the public demand for political participation articulated in the mass demonstrations of 1988–9? And what was the role of the rivalry between the two states in muting this demand? These questions raise the issue of regimes, democratisation and the institutional sources of the Armenian–Azerbaijani rivalry today.

One of the most empirically grounded findings in political science is that mature democracies have rarely – if ever – gone to war with one another.[1] Scholars refer to this as the 'democratic peace'. As this finding would lead us to expect, very few democratic states have entered into enduring rivalries either, and there has only been one case (Britain's nineteenth-century rivalry with the United States) of an enduring rivalry waged for its duration between two democratic regimes.[2] Enduring rivalry is therefore overwhelmingly associated with non-democratic regime types. Once a rivalry has locked in, however, a joint transition to democracy can attenuate it. In such 'regime-change rivalries', featuring both democratic and non-democratic periods, the evidence suggests that militarised conflict declines (though does not disappear) when both rivals experience periods of democracy.[3] If democratic norms and institutions go on to become embedded, however, rivalry becomes difficult to sustain over the long term. There is consequently an empirical basis for my Azerbaijani colleague's popular intuition that democracy offers the best hope for an eventual resolution of the enduring rivalry between Armenia and Azerbaijan.

These findings come with several significant caveats, however. First, both rivals must transition for the democratic peace to take effect. Mixed-regime rivalries, when only one rival is democratic, can thrive, as the Cold War, North and South Korean and, with significant reservations, the Arab–Israeli rivalries show.[4] Second, if consensus exists on the long-term pacifying effect of democracy among mature democratic regimes, scholars have significantly qualified it by highlighting transitions *to* democracy as an especially dangerous time.[5] Armenia and Azerbaijan in 1988–91 are indeed brought as examples of this dynamic, where democratisation in the context of weak institutions and the escalation of conflict were closely linked.[6] Even where two rivals experience democratic – or democratising – periods, rivalries can be maintained. The India–Pakistan rivalry has passed through periods of joint democracy, yet these have never been of sufficient length and stability in Pakistan's case to generate the democratic peace effect.[7] At least in the short to medium term, then, rivalries can persist independently of regime effects. Armenia's 'Velvet Revolution' in April 2018, which saw a civil uprising overthrow a long-established authoritarian regime, is a test of these dynamics. Patterns in other enduring rivalries suggest, however, that over the short to medium term unilateral democratisation in one rival, even if sustained, may not have any significant attenuating effect.

These ambiguous causalities suggest that while democratisation does offer a long-term perspective for rivalry termination, in the short term it is not a panacea and democratic openings are fraught with the risk of renewed violence. Armenia and Azerbaijan begin their rivalry without the requisite democratic dyad, and since the ceasefire of 1994 have experienced neither periods of joint democracy nor simultaneous shifts towards democratisation. Looking back at the Armenian–Azerbaijani rivalry over its first quarter-century, then, what needs to be explained are the institutional constraints to de-escalation in a stably non-democratic dyad. How has the factor of pre-existing conflict shaped the development of regimes, and how have the resulting regime types fed back into the rivalry dynamic? The strong gravitational pull of democratisation narratives means that this question is primarily understood in terms of an absence of democracy. In this chapter I flesh out this understanding by arguing that the institutional sources of the Armenian–Azerbaijani rivalry can be understood in terms of three dynamics. The first is the mutual interaction of two hybrid regimes. Neither democratic nor wholly autocratic, regimes have been neither open enough to allow for new policy entrepreneurs to enter the political arena, nor closed enough for incumbents to risk controversial policy shifts towards de-escalation. The second dynamic is the resilience of what I will call networked power in each state, constituted by informal networks and guided by unwritten, extra-legal rules and norms of interaction. There is now a broad consensus that phenomena once bracketed under rubrics of dysfunction such as 'corruption', 'clans' or 'state capture' are more properly understood as the primary agents of post-Soviet politics. Networked power, wielded by unaccountable elites, stunts the development of the necessary institutional capacities, as set down in formal constitutions, to negotiate and implement a politically challenging peace agreement. The origins of networked power are wider than the conflict itself, but in a third dynamic unresolved conflict affords significant resources contributing to its resilience. The generalised insecurity associated with the prolonged militarised competition inherent to enduring rivalry enables elites to use discourses of threat and security to marginalise and silence domestic challenges to their power.

Not Enough (or Too Much) Democracy?

There is little consensus on the terminology to describe post-Soviet regimes in Armenia and Azerbaijan. They have been analysed with other post-Soviet states as 'semi-authoritarian' or 'hybrid' regimes.[8] These perspectives emphasise two fundamental characteristics. The first is the inadequacy of linear transitions to democracy as a lens through which to understand hybrid regime dynamics. The second is that while not democratic, neither regime is devoid of political competition. This leads, as Nina Caspersen argues, to an important explanation of how regime types have locked in rivalry. This is the *mutual hybridity* argument, meaning that in this dyad of hybrid regimes there is both not enough and too much democracy for compromises to be made.[9] By this argument, it is the extremely partial nature of the democratisation that has taken place that is the greatest obstacle to resolving the rivalry. Simply put, Armenian and Azerbaijani leaders have been authoritarian enough to block challengers from entering the political arena, and to dominate the policy-making process, but when they have proposed compromise solutions themselves they are not authoritarian enough to enforce them (or even to survive politically). Unable to count on either popular legitimacy or intra-elite loyalty, elites have had few incentives to pursue 'soft' alternatives to hyper-realpolitik strategies embedding rivalry.

Failed Democratic Transitions

While scholars struggle to define the kinds of regime present in Armenia and Azerbaijan today, what is certain is that after twenty-five years of independence they had become less democratic than when the war between them ended in 1994. Freedom House's Freedom in the World Index scores countries along a seven-point scale; states at 5.5 or above on this scale are deemed 'not free'. States between 5.0 and 3.5 are 'partly free'; states below 3.0 are 'free'.[10] Figure 5.1 illustrates Armenian and Azerbaijani trajectories since independence. Since the ceasefire the two states have never been in a democratic, or even jointly democratising, dyad. They have only shared a 'partly free' status for three years in 1997–9 – years indeed coinciding with one of the more productive periods of negotiations (see Chapter 9). Since then Azerbaijan has been consistent in flatlining near the upper, more repressive end of the Freedom House scale and in 2015–16 broke new

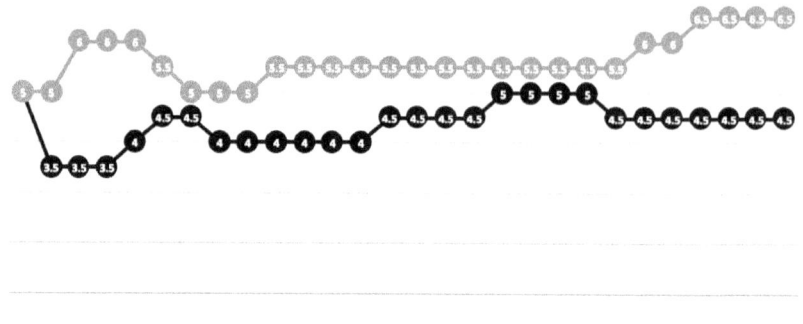

Figure 5.1 Armenia and Azerbaijan Freedom House Ratings, 1991–2018.
Source: Compiled from <https://freedomhouse.org>.

ground, becoming in Freedom House's parlance a 'consolidated authoritarian regime'. From the late 1990s Armenia consistently rated as a 'partly free' regime, albeit increasingly at the higher, more oppressive end of this category. Its trajectory wavered within a narrow margin, indicating that democratising shifts were slight and not sustained. Freedom House reflected this in parsing Armenia as a 'semi-consolidated authoritarian regime'.

A second gauge of the vector of democratisation is the quality of elections. The meticulously researched reports of the election monitoring missions fielded in Armenia and Azerbaijan by the Office for Democratic Institutions and Human Rights (ODIHR) of the Organization for Security and Co-operation in Europe (OSCE) make for repetitive reading. None of Azerbaijan's elections have been deemed free and fair, as incumbent presidents have cruised to victory and no major opposition party has been represented in the Azerbaijani parliament since 2010.[11] ODIHR monitoring mission reports on Armenian elections have been less categorical in comparison. They have noted competitive and vibrant campaigns, and parliamentary elections in 1999 and 2007 that respectively 'represented a step towards' and 'were conducted largely in accordance with' OSCE commitments and other international standards.[12] In 2012–17 ODIHR reports on Armenian elections shifted their critical emphasis to a pervasive lack of trust in the integrity of the electoral process, as vote buying in an atmosphere of general apathy obviated cruder forms of electoral fraud. These trends are consistent with Armenia's characterisation as a competitive authoritarian regime, in which competition is 'real but unfair'.[13]

The World Bank's World Governance Indicators (WGI) provide a third gauge of failed transitions in Armenia and Azerbaijan. The WGI's Voice and Accountability rating is one of six governance indicators produced since 1996. It draws on qualitative surveys to capture perceptions of 'the extent to which a country's citizens can participate in selecting their government', and the state of freedoms of association, expression and the media.[14] Countries are scored from 2.5 (high) to -2.5 (low). As Table 5.2 shows, stagnation and decline mark the two states' trajectories. In 2016 citizens of Armenia felt that they had no more influence over the selection of their government than twenty years earlier; in Azerbaijan, citizens felt they had even less of a voice than their parents' generation. In the light of these findings, we must concede that the lens of transition is largely irrelevant to understanding Armenian and Azerbaijani regime dynamics over their first twenty-five years as independent states. The implications for peacebuilding programmes are hardly comforting. If, as Western policy perspectives suggest, 'all good

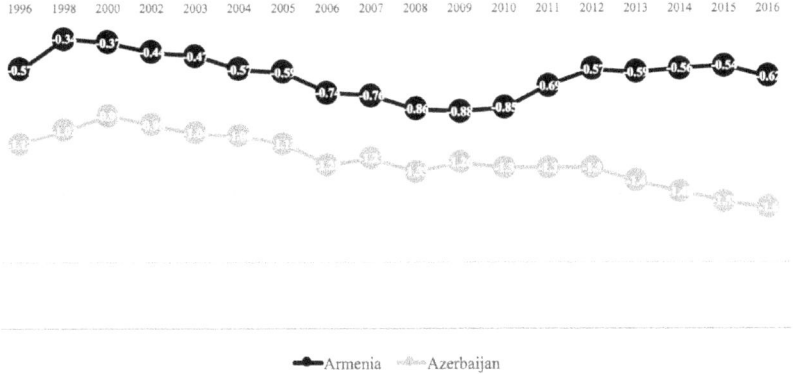

Figure 5.2 World Bank Governance Indicators: Voice and Accountability in Armenia and Azerbaijan, 1996–2016. *Source:* Compiled from <http://info.worldbank.org/governance/wgi/index.aspx#home>.

things go together' – democracy, civil society, human rights and peace – Armenians and Azerbaijanis must wait a long time for peace.[15] But if leaders were effectively insulated from electoral challenge for more than two decades, why were they unable to secure an elite deal?

Elite Loyalty

A commonplace answer to this question invokes 'political will' and its absence. But this diplomatic euphemism gives us little traction on the interests and constraints limiting leadership. Another explanation more congenial to leaders is that they are in fact representative of popular opinion on the Karabakh issue. This glosses over more complex realities. While elite and popular visions may be more congruent today, in the intervening quarter-century since the ceasefire Armenian and Azerbaijani leaders have often portrayed themselves as being less hardline than their populations. The idea that the 'presidents are ahead of their peoples' enjoyed wide currency among mediators in the early 2000s. Insulated from electoral punishment, it was not public backlash that leaders feared most (although neither could they ignore it), but elite revolt. This leads us to a third explanation, which is that while neither state is democratic, neither are they sufficiently closed for leaders to act with complete autonomy, at least on an issue with such high public resonance.

Armenian and Azerbaijani elites have twice rebelled against proposed compromises in the negotiations. In February 1998 Armenia's first president, Levon Ter-Petrossian, resigned under pressure, not from his antagonists in opposition parties but from his closest associates.[16] The primary reason was differences over approaches to the negotiations with Azerbaijan. His prime minister, Robert Kocharian, and the latter's associates rejected Ter-Petrossian's advocacy of a phased approach that did not tie in at the first stage the determination of Nagorny Karabakh's political status (see Chapter 9). Although other factors, such as Ter-Petrossian's flagging popularity, economic hardship and a contested election re-electing him in 1996, were certainly present, it was elite defection in favour of a harder negotiating line that sealed his fate. Kocharian, former de facto president of the Nagorno-Karabakh Republic (NKR), replaced him as president, establishing a twenty-year tradition whereby natives of Karabakh served as presidents of Armenia.

In October 1999 Azerbaijani President Heydar Aliyev encountered similar resistance. Following discussions of proposals entailing territorial exchange, three of Aliyev's closest advisors resigned. Subsequently in 2001 four prominent politicians, including two of those that had resigned, published a Karabakh Charter (also referred to as the Charter of Four). According to one of its authors:

> we needed a consensus document: it was less than one page long, and it aimed to be an expression of public opinion rather than our work as authors ... It is a set of principles – territorial integrity, the return of displaced people, autonomy – and we got more than 600 organisations to sign up to it.[17]

The Charter established a 'maximum tolerance level' of compromise for Azerbaijan, setting down society's red lines as its authors interpreted them.[18] Significantly, Azerbaijan's publicly stated negotiating position has remained largely consistent with the Charter ever since.

Periods of unsettled domestic politics followed these precedents of elite defection or disloyalty: the assassinations of Prime Minister Vazgen Sargsyan, Parliamentary Speaker Karen Demirchian and six other senior officials in the Armenian parliament in October 1999 and Azerbaijan's succession election in October 2003, when Ilham Aliyev was elected to replace his father as president. Over the next few years the successive toppling of post-Soviet leaders in the 'colour revolutions' demonstrated that unpopular leaders of hybrid regimes were vulnerable. In 2004 and 2005 Armenian and Azerbaijani regimes both fended off mobilisations by oppositional forces seeking to emulate the Georgian and Ukrainian experiences.[19] In 2008 renewed political crisis befell Armenia when ten people were killed as post-electoral protests against President Serzh Sargsyan's victory were violently dispersed. Between stolen elections and fractious elites the Armenian–Azerbaijani peace process has consequently suffered, as Nina Caspersen observes, 'from the worst of two worlds: intense competition, especially in Armenia, but without the restraint and widened participation that democratisation can provide'.[20]

Mutual hybridity captures an important regime dynamic inhibiting the emergence of alternatives to rivalry. Yet the argument has two shortcomings. The first is the problem of equifinality – the idea that the same outcome may be reached by different or even contradictory means. If the Armenian–Azerbaijani rivalry is sustained by either too much or too little democratisation, then it follows that *either* more *or* less democratisation are valid responses.[21] By the first view, broadened participation could constitute a route to resolution by arming incumbents with clearer popular mandates with which to face down spoiler challenges. An alternative position entertains the insulation of authoritarian leaders to ease their path to agreement. By this view, as articulated by a diplomat close to the process in 2011, peace negotiations need to be 'kept as a tunnel, with the light at the end. The tunnel protects the negotiations. When we get to the end of the tunnel, then the NGOs can sell the agreement'.[22] This perspective reflects the 'presidents are ahead of their peoples' logic and is popular wisdom among senior policy-makers. This is problematic. Theoretically, it assumes that peace agreements arrived at by liberal and illiberal regimes are the same, whereas the kinds of politics that each entails are very different. These differences would likely be critical in the long and even more politically challenging implementation of any peace agreement. Empirically, the idea that authoritarian consolidation enhances conflict resolution is not supported by the Armenian–Azerbaijani experience. Consolidating authoritarianism in Azerbaijan has been accompanied by increasing escalation, not less.

A second shortcoming of the mutual hybridity argument is that the teleology of transition still lurks in the background when we qualify regimes as hybrids. Hybridity assumes the combination, or a halfway house, of democratic and authoritarian traits along which regimes are presumed to move. Thanks to the pervasive vision – if not reality – of transition, the democratic end of the spectrum is easily grasped: elections, human rights, plural civil and political societies, and so on. But the authoritarian end remains obscure. We consequently risk seeing Armenia and Azerbaijan as being hybrid in the same way, as the result of an absence of democracy rather than the presence of an alternative political logic. For example, defining Azerbaijan as a consolidated authoritarian regime and Armenia as a semi-consolidated authoritarian regime implies that it is only a matter of degree that differentiates them. But the study of post-Soviet authoritarianisms warns us that variations matter.[23] To understand more fully their interaction with rivalry maintenance, we need to see authoritarian regimes in Armenia and Azerbaijan as qualitative and path-dependent variations, rather than as gradations along an exogenously defined normative scale.

The Resilience of Networked Power

There is now a scholarly consensus on the primary importance of informal institutions and structures in post-Soviet regime dynamics. This consensus draws on a longer tradition in the study of authoritarianism to interpret post-Soviet politics beyond the 'transition' paradigm. Its primary contention is that the most important actors on the post-Soviet stage are neither formal institutions, such as the constitution, parliament, elections or political parties, nor ethnic groups, but 'extended and loosely hierarchical networks led informally by powerful patrons'.[24] A booming research tradition has yielded a proliferation of terms to describe these networks: patron-clientelism, neo-patrimonialism, patronal politics, *mafiya*, *vertikals* of authority and dual states to name but a few.[25] These concepts usefully home in on specific variations in the logic of practices often subsumed by catch-all terms such as 'corruption' or 'state capture'. Where all of these terms converge, however, is on the understanding that unlike abstracted communities such as the citizenry or nation, membership in such networks depends on chains of actual acquaintance and personalised exchange.[26] Post-Soviet networks in Armenia and Azerbaijan have their roots in the Soviet political class (*nomenklatura*) embedded during Leonid Brezhnev's era as Communist Party first secretary, and in the appearance of new network entrepreneurs in the perestroika and immediate post-Soviet periods.[27] Their subsequent trajectories were mediated by factors such as the unity or fragmentation of the political elite, economic resources and the outcomes of the 1992–4 war.

When referring in the following sections to the realm of written rules, the constitution and the formal institutions mandated by it, I use the terms constitutional rules and the constitutional state. When referring to unwritten rules, personalised norms of interaction and informal, extra-legal institutions or structures, I refer to networked power and networked regimes. At its most basic, this distinction captures the reality that it is not the formal institutions and rules as set out in the constitution that have ruled in post-Soviet Armenia and Azerbaijan, but the networked power of regimes operating through informal institutions. In both states, networked power provides the political logic that prevails over the fictive logic of democratisation. I now turn to the trajectories of networked power in each state.

Armenia: Competitive Authoritarianism and Informal Union with Nagorny Karabakh

The Karabakh movement of 1987–90 and victory in the subsequent war of 1992–4 bequeathed two mutually reinforcing legacies accounting for turbulence in Armenia's post-war regime politics. The first was the fracturing of the political elite in the perestroika era. In 1988–9 the Karabakh Committee rapidly became a 'second' or 'shadow government', eclipsing the discredited Communist Party elite. In legislative elections in May 1990 the Armenian Communist Party (ArmCP) won just over half of the votes, but many of its candidates sought to distance themselves from the party. Only 25 of its 136 deputies were able to form a faction in March 1991, one of several in a diverse parliament composed of communist, liberal democratic, nationalist, national democratic, Dashnaktsutyun and republican factions.[28] By 1990 the ArmCP was experiencing serious problems with personnel, recruiting its last two first secretaries from journalism and propaganda departments rather than the more politically reliable party bureaucracy; it did not even field a candidate in Armenia's first presidential election.[29]

The Karabakh Committee was institutionalised as the Pan-Armenian National Movement (PANM). Initially comprising a broad umbrella of revolutionary and oppositional forces, the PANM itself fractured in 1991 when Levon Ter-Petrossian became Armenia's first president. The erstwhile informal leader of the Karabakh Committee, Vazgen Manukyan, established the National Democratic Party as the primary opposition. Through to the end of the war with Azerbaijan in 1994 the PANM mobilised an effective consensus on the attainment of independence and sovereignty in Karabakh. But once these goals had been achieved it did not develop into a strong executive-oriented party organising networked patronage and loyalty.[30] The PANM suffered from continual defections, spawning rival political parties and political organisations.[31] The party never opened offices in Karabakh, and therefore never formed a single pyramid of power across both Armenia and Karabakh.[32] Tellingly, membership of the PANM was not the sole gateway to executive appointment. More than 90 per cent of all ministers appointed by Ter-Petrossian were not members of any political party: only a quarter of the regional governors (*marzpets*) appointed during his seven-year presidency were PANM members.[33] This may have reflected Ter-Petrossian's wish to avoid creating a single party of power[34] but also indicated preferences for experience over loyalty in what were times of sustained crisis. To be sure, some senior PANM figures, such as former Karabakh Committee member and Interior Minister Vano Siradeghian and Telman Ter-Petrossian (the brother of the president) headed corrupt networks.[35] But the PANM did not represent a unified party–state coalition maintaining continuity with the networks of the Soviet past. As a result, unlike republics that preserved ruling parties fused with the state at all levels, the PANM was not able to manage, and manufacture results for, elections in the republic.

A fractured political elite intersected with a legacy of the 1992–4 war: the emergence of a network of Karabakh war veterans encompassing both Armenia and Karabakh. Although relatively small, the veteran elite formed a cohesive entity, described by

Armenian political analyst Alexander Iskandaryan as 'a caste of men united by four years in the trenches, a soldierly brotherhood, a dearly bought victory and a feeling of uniqueness and deservedness'.[36] In Armenia it is the Yerkrapah veterans' corporation that represents this elite. Founded in 1993 on the basis of an earlier volunteer group dating back to 1990, Yerkrapah was the largest public organisation in Armenia for many years, with 10,000 members in 2008.[37] Its name translates as 'guardians of the land', a view resonant with its leadership's self-understanding as not only guardians but also father figures with a foundational – not representational – claim to rule. According to Manvel Grigorian, chairman of the Yerkrapah board in 2016: 'we founded this state, not knowing how it would turn out'.[38]

The combination of a relatively weak ruling party in the PANM and a powerful networked elite of veterans resulted in the latter's emergence as guardians not only of the land but also of regime security. Perestroika-era elite fracture bequeathed limited coalitions to post-Soviet Armenian presidents, who have only been able to win even fraudulent elections by the narrowest of margins. In contrast to Soviet successor states where the 'correct' results are manufactured through the fusion of party, state and electoral structures, Armenian presidential elections have been consistently close-run affairs characterised by second-round voting, or post-election protest against narrow incumbent wins. In the 1996 elections, Ter-Petrossian was declared the winner with 51.7 per cent over Vazgen Manukyan's 41.3 per cent. His successor Robert Kocharian was forced to a second-round vote in both 1998 and 2003, winning 39 per cent and 49.5 per cent in the first rounds respectively.[39] In 2008 Serzh Sargsyan secured election with only 52.8 per cent; in 2013 he was re-elected with 58 per cent. These are not the margins of secure autocrats. This created a need for ways to deal effectively with protest. Coercion, provided by security agencies in the hands of veteran networks, met this challenge. In 1996 fifty-nine people were injured as the army dispersed crowds protesting Ter-Petrossian's tainted re-election.[40] In April 2004 protestors calling for a referendum on public confidence in Robert Kocharian were violently dispersed and opposition parties and media offices raided.[41] In 2008, as noted above, ten people were killed as protestors were forcefully dispersed in Yerevan in the aftermath of Serzh Sargsyan's narrow win.

Networked power in Armenia was consequently the beneficiary of perestroika-era elite fracture and military victory. But it also owed its prevalence to the answers it provided to managing the problematic relationship between Armenia and the NKR in the context of a sovereign Armenian state. 'Augmented Armenia' was not only territorially incoherent with Armenia's constitutional state. It also entailed political, economic and (il)legal spaces in Karabakh and the occupied territories to which Armenia's constitutional rules, weak as they were, could not legitimately apply. 'Compliant Armenia' offered few answers to this problem, other than a downscaling of ambitions in the talks with Azerbaijan. This implied limiting the horizons for 'augmented Armenia' by admitting that an eventual political status less than sovereignty for the NKR was possible. Robert Kocharian, whose own migration from Stepanakert to Yerevan personified the informal union of Armenia and Karabakh, developed an alternative vision in order to sustain the vision of 'augmented Armenia'. Former advisor to Ter-Petrossian Gerard Libaridian observes that Kocharian's outlook was that of an engineer: 'Unity, for him, rested on mathematical calculations of the capabilities and potential of each component rather than on the politics of overcoming conflicts of principles, personalities, programs, or policies.'[42] Kocharian's state-building project indeed combined distinct yet intermeshing components in an unorthodox combination: a hollowed out and largely undemocratic constitutional state, a networked regime controlled by oligarchic power, and the nationalist space of 'augmented Armenia' that enjoyed popular legitimacy.[43] Networked power underpinned this structure, serving as the interface between 'compliant' and 'augmented' Armenias and allowing a unified political economy allocating resources such as the 'interstate loan' and off-ledger disbursements, sustaining the de facto republic in Nagorny Karabakh (see Chapter 8). Informal unification substituted for the elusive international recognition of the territorial unity of Armenia and Karabakh as a single homeland, and offered an alternative to compromise with Azerbaijan. Easily read as symptomatic of state weakness, this structurally incoherent configuration composed of disparate spaces, networks and territorial regimes proved surprisingly durable.

Under President Kocharian and his successor Serzh Sargsyan Armenia's networked regime both expanded and stagnated. Patrons from Kocharian's inner circle developed networks embracing Russia-oriented oligarchs and regional strongmen.[44] The Republican Party of Armenia (RPA) developed into a unified party of power, as executive appointments became increasingly synonymous with membership. Increasing through Kocharian's presidency, in Serzh Sargsyan's first term 2008–13, 80 per cent of ministerial and 70 per cent of regional governor appointments were RPA members.[45] In December 2015 a constitutional referendum was passed transforming Armenia into a parliamentary republic from 2018. A regime rather than popular initiative, the shift from a presidential to a parliamentary system sought to avoid a succession crisis at the end of Sargsyan's second term. The new constitution included a number of controversial measures, notably provisions aimed at ensuring the emergence of a 'sustainable majority' in run-off elections if no first-round majority was reached.[46] The embedding of a party of power offered a belated solution to the elite fragmentation inherited from the perestroika era, providing for a large and unified political elite.

These ambitions did not reckon, however, with the fact that networked power in Armenia was never as hegemonic as in some other post-Soviet states. It may have provided an informal solution to the legally challenging relationship between Armenia and the NKR, but lacked either the purchasing power or untrammelled coercion of regimes elsewhere in Eurasia. In the realm of constitutional party politics, opposition parties such as the PANM and the *Yelq* ('Way Out') alliance remained visible if numerically marginal advocates of constitutional rule represented in the National Assembly. Even within the networked elite of veterans of the Karabakh war, the mythology of the 'fraternity of the trenches' could not obscure a profound schism between those who had entered government to convert their symbolic capital into sinecures and monopolies, and those who retained a purist commitment to social justice. This schism grabbed the headlines in July 2016. A group of Karabakh war veterans, calling itself

Sasna Tsrer (meaning the 'daredevils of Sassoun', a reference to a medieval Armenian epic), seized a police station in a Yerevan suburb. They were calling for the release of their leader, Lebanese Armenian war veteran and oppositionist Jirair Sefilian, who had been arrested in June on charges of holding weapons. Several police officers were taken hostage, and two killed, before the group surrendered.[47] To the government's surprise, large-scale demonstrations in support of Sasna Tsrer quickly ensued embracing wider issues. Public protest had in fact become an increasingly regular feature of the Armenian political landscape, beginning with single-issue movements focused on issues such as fuel prices, but demonstrating rapid escalatory potential.[48]

Never high, public trust in President Sargsyan declined throughout his tenure. The 'four-day war' of 2–5 April 2016 ruptured the implicit contract between a networked regime that provided security and a society that tolerated poor governance. Revelations of corruption in the army in the aftermath shook belief in the previously vaunted Armenian armed forces (see Chapter 6). The real repercussions, however, came in April 2018. Reneging on an earlier commitment to the contrary, President Sargsyan's nomination as the RPA's candidate to fill the new post of prime minister proved a disastrous underestimation of public discontent. Under the charismatic but disciplined leadership of Nikol Pashinyan, a former newspaper editor and opposition parliamentarian (and former associate of Levon Ter-Petrossian), protests beginning on 12 April 2018 quickly escalated into a non-violent national uprising calling for political reform and social justice.[49] Eschewing geopolitically fraught branding as a 'colour revolution', Armenia's Velvet Revolution evoked an earlier tradition of post-communist emancipation. Sargsyan, after just one week in post as prime minister, resigned on 23 April 2018. Two weeks later Pashinyan took his place.

The early months of Pashinyan's premiership were marked by the public disgracing of many of the key arbiters of networked power in Armenia, including previously untouchable figures leading Yerkrapah. Two years after my interview with him, Manvel Grigorian was publicly disgraced after police raids of his properties in June 2018 discovered hoards of clothing, food, medicine and other items donated by citizens and diasporan Armenians to the army and population of Nagorny Karabakh at the time of the April 2016 violence.[50] Several mayors across the country were removed from power, and other members of the previous political and military elite were placed under investigation. But whether a long-term reconfiguration from networked power to the constitutional state ensues also depends on Pashinyan's capacity to reconcile 'compliant' and 'augmented' Armenias. The tension between these visions of Armenia has hitherto implicated Armenian regime politics in a continual networked power trap. On one hand, networked power is held to deliver 'augmented Armenia', but degrades the quality of government to such an extent as to lose legitimacy – and even threaten security as corruption, over time, inevitably pervades the army. On the other hand, to integrate and secure the unrecognised republic in Nagorny Karabakh, a space that is officially off-limits, there is little choice for Armenia's constitutional state but to tolerate informal networks and legal exceptionalism, subverting the basis of its own rule. The dynamics of this trap are not, of course, self-contained but depend on the interaction with networked power in Azerbaijan, caught in a trap of its own.

Azerbaijan: Hegemonic Authoritarianism and Credible Commitments

Contrasting with Armenia's more turbulent politics, networked power in Azerbaijan is noteworthy for its stability as well as resilience. This is attributable on the one hand to the preservation, despite the tumultuous early 1990s, of a large executive-oriented party of power uniting the elite. On the other, abundant oil wealth has enabled a political economy of persuasion, rather than outright coercion.

Perestroika-era Azerbaijan looked an unlikely case for subsequent executive stability. Serial interventions from Moscow could not salvage the Azerbaijani communist elite from its own inability and unwillingness to reform. Gorbachev's initial choreographing of leadership turnover appointed an unpopular outsider, Abdurahman Vezirov, as Azerbaijani first secretary in May 1988.[51] Vezirov's appointment fractured the communist elite, as several long-standing senior officials associated with outgoing First Secretary Kyamran Bagirov (and with Heydar Aliyev's network) lost their posts.[52] But Vezirov's inability to manage confrontation with the national-democratic forces of the Popular Front resulted in more crisis. Gorbachev intervened again by sending Soviet Interior Ministry forces into the streets of Baku in January 1990. At the cost of more than 130 lives, 'Black January' bought the beleaguered Communist Party structure in Azerbaijan a crucial reprieve, albeit as a discredited and illegitimate force. Believing he could go it alone, new First Secretary Ayaz Mutalibov then dissolved – rather than renamed – the Azerbaijani Communist Party on 14 September 1991.[53] Mutalibov lasted only six months without it, and the party structure's fate appeared to be sealed with the election of the Azerbaijani Popular Front counter-elite to power in 1992. It was the context of the Karabakh war, and the mutiny of Azerbaijani warlords against Abulfaz Elchibey's government, that revived the fortunes of the scattered party structure. Invited back to Baku in 1993 by a desperate Elchibey, Heydar Aliyev reconstituted networks dating back to the Brezhnev era as the New Azerbaijan Party (*Yeni Azərbaycan Partiyası*, YAP). A significant consequence was that Azerbaijan subsequently featured a large executive-oriented party, developing into a hegemonic presidential party interwoven with state structures. The political parties who had led Azerbaijan's brief experiment in democratisation in 1992–3, the APF and Musavat, went into opposition.

The shock of defeat in the 1992–4 war set the stage for Heydar Aliyev to revive communist era cadres and develop a 'watertight patronage machine that preserved the integrity of the elite'.[54] YAP fused with the state administration at every level and developed into an efficient machine delivering election results. In contrast to the tight margins by which Armenian presidents have scraped through, the lowest percentage of the vote ever secured by an Aliyev presidency is 77 per cent in 2003. Over time the manufacture of super-majority wins developed into an attractive alternative to reliance on crude fraud or coercive suppression of post-election protest. Contrasting with Armenia's political turbulence and intermittent violence, Azerbaijan's networked regime assumed a more hegemonic form. While coercion has certainly also been present, the smoother texture of Azerbaijan's hegemonic authoritarianism is also an effect of oil wealth.

Scholars concur on the relevance for Azerbaijan of the literature on the rentier state: states whose primary source of revenue comes from unearned 'rents', deriving from natural resources, foreign aid or transit rent. The core contentions of this literature – that rentier elites are freed from accountability to citizenries, are able to purchase loyalty through public spending, and can stunt the growth of autonomous civil society – hold true for Azerbaijan.[55] Oil wealth gave the Azerbaijani state purchasing power, lessening the need for direct coercion and allowing it to appear less predatory than lesser-endowed states. Although wealth distribution remains uneven, average monthly salaries in Azerbaijan rose continuously from the equivalent of $125 in 2005 to approximately $540 in 2013.[56] Azerbaijan kept a higher proportion of the citizenry in its direct employ than its South Caucasian neighbours.[57] Public sector employ paid consistently rising salaries on time, supplemented until the oil price slump of 2014 with informal cash bonuses drawing employees into the loyalty machine. Through the heyday of the oil boom in 2006–14, Ilham Aliyev secured elite loyalty and demonstrated the resource imbalance between himself and any alternative with increased expenditures.[58] Co-optation drew youth activism into the elite fold; the flagship policy of cash-free ASAN public service centres, introduced in 2012, reduced petty predatory bribery by significant margins.[59]

With a political economy of persuasion in place, contestation was relegated to the margins of Azerbaijani politics. Opposition parties continued to legally exist and operate, but under such marginalised conditions as only to affirm the futility of supporting them and lead to their own deskilling.[60] Organised mass protest, marking elections in 2003 and 2005, disappeared for the best part of a decade. While certainly dramatic, the reappearance of protest in the towns of Quba and Ismayilli in 2012–13 was quickly contained. It was also used to justify the arrest of leaders of new political parties appearing in the intervening period, such as the Republican Alternative party leader Ilgar Mammedov. A pliant justice system criminalised and imprisoned individual dissidents, or allowed them to leave. Online, the state effectively contained the prospects for oppositionally minded activism.[61] Moreover, the networked regime moulded Azerbaijan's constitutional state, already a strongly presidential system, in its own image. Successive constitutional referendums embedded prerogative powers not only in the office of the president but specifically in the person of Ilham Aliyev. In March 2009 a referendum approved the removal of term limits, which would have disqualified him from running for re-election in 2013. In 2016 another referendum extended presidential terms from five to seven years. These changes had several effects. They lengthened the regime cycle in Azerbaijan, reducing the impact of elections as scheduled fixtures for which oppositional forces could plan and prepare. They also removed uncertainty around the issue of succession and can be seen as a response to the succession election of 2003, the single pivotal moment of uncertainty in Azerbaijani politics since the mid-1990s.

The resulting stability in Azerbaijan's networked regime can be interpreted in two ways. In one view stability reflects secure autocracy, symbolised by the successful enactment of the former Soviet Union's first and to date sole dynastic succession, and Ilham Aliyev's consolidation of power since then. By this reading Azerbaijan can be parsed as having 'sultanistic' tendencies, a highly personalised regime type characterised by extreme development of the ruler's discretion.[62] An alternative reading explains Azerbaijan's stability in terms of an equilibrium among a small number of powerful factions, in which the president is leader by consensual default. Azerbaijan's informal factional politics are notoriously elusive, not only because of the opacity of the networks involved, but also because of their diverse origins, fluid boundaries and their inconsistency with any single principle of membership. For this reason, the terminology of 'clan' and 'clannishness' can confuse as much as it clarifies.[63]

The Azerbaijani term *yerbazlik* is usually translated as 'regionalism', but implies loyalty to one's place of origin and its associated network sufficiently compelling as to compete with national identity.[64] *Yerbazlik* featured in accounts of the 1990s, where a common understanding is that Heydar Aliyev relied on regional networks from his native Nakhichevan and among

Azerbaijanis from Armenia ('*Yeraz*') to regain and retain power. With the onset of the oil boom, the survival and wealth of different factions depended on their capacity, sometimes cemented by actual kinship, to leverage proximity to the president. Over Ilham Aliyev's first two presidential terms, three strata dominated the Azerbaijan's elite: the 'old guard' of holdovers from Heydar Aliyev's presidency and in many cases Soviet rule; the 'oligarchs', controlling business empires covering virtually all commodities; and the 'family', a cluster of factions rooted in the kinship networks of the president and First Lady Mehriban Aliyeva (née Pashayeva).[65] By the beginning of his fourth term in 2018, this tripartite structure had tipped in favour of the Pashayev network, as some formerly influential oligarchs fell from grace and by one informal estimate, Pashayev appointees accounted for two-thirds of all ministerial posts.[66]

The resilience of high-ranking personnel whose appointment pre-dated his rule suggests limits to understandings of Ilham Aliyev as a sultanistic ruler exercising unrestricted discretion to hire and fire. In 2010, seven years after he had become president, the same people who had served under his father occupied nine of thirteen senior posts in the all-powerful Presidential Administration and thirteen of sixteen posts in the Cabinet of Ministers; among the ministries and executive state committees, nearly half (eighteen of forty-one posts) were occupied by those who had served Heydar Aliyev.[67] In April 2018 Azerbaijan saw its first major government reshuffle in more than twenty years yet all core 'power ministries' remained as they were. By then the ministers of internal affairs, justice and emergency situations (the latter previously as head of the state customs committee) had served for twenty-four, eighteen and twenty-three years respectively.[68] Similarly enduring tenures are common in Azerbaijan's presidential administration and cabinet of ministers. Stability in elites is an indication of equilibrium among Azerbaijan's factions, and is suggestive of a 'strong–weak paradox' at the heart of Azerbaijan's networked regime. Ilham Aliyev stands at the apex of Azerbaijan's power pyramid, but does so as the embodiment of a delicate equilibrium amongst the country's factions. This equilibrium is so fragile, however, that no other individual can take his place. This extends to precluding keeping up appearances through devices such as the tandem arrangement by which Vladimir Putin ceded the Russian presidency for one term to Dmitry Medvedev. The sole example of delegated constitutional power, the Naxçivan (Nakhichevan) Autonomous Republic, is deeply woven into its networked regime as the native region of the Aliyev family and by direct kinship links (its leader Vasif Talibov is the son-in-law of Heydar Aliyev's niece).

Whether one puts the accent on the hyper-centralised or factionalised character of Azerbaijan's networked regime is an important question for understanding the country's elite politics. But the relevant aspect here is its aspiration to hegemony over Azerbaijan's constitutional state. In the politics of Azerbaijan's hegemonic authoritarianism, the only meaningful political pluralism lies in the plurality of factions contesting networked power. This matters for the continuation of the rivalry because Azerbaijan is the status quo challenger. Its position is predicated on overturning the status quo, to achieve a renewed coexistence of Armenians and Azerbaijanis in the same state. This vision of the peaceful end to the rivalry evokes a constitutional state capable of making credible commitments to the accommodation of a substantial political unit in Nagorny Karabakh endowed with delegated autonomous power. The fact that in twenty-five years Azerbaijan has never produced a concept or draft defining a constitutional status and rights for an autonomous Karabakh within its borders testifies to this prospect's disruptive potential. It can be argued that there are concerns over a domino effect inciting other minorities in Azerbaijan to similarly mobilise for autonomy.[69] But beyond demonstration effects, the revival of a constitutionalist discourse invoking rights, responsibilities and justice in and of itself challenges the hegemony of Azerbaijan's networked regime. There is consequently a fundamental incompatibility between Azerbaijan's preferred solution for a peaceful end to the rivalry, and the survival of its networked regime. Reviving Azerbaijan's constitutional state, a pre-condition for credible commitments under-writing any future cohabitation with Armenians within Azerbaijani borders, poses a greater threat to regime survival than continuation of the rivalry.

Rivalry as a Resource for Networked Regimes

In his farewell address to Congress on 19 April 1951 General MacArthur observed: 'War's very object is victory – not prolonged indecision. In war, indeed, there can be no substitute for victory.'[70] His comments came a few years after victories so total that they initiated the complete transformation of state and society in defeated Germany and Japan. The outcome of the Armenian–Azerbaijani war of 1992–4 could not be more different. The Armenian military victory in 1994 is extraordinary for its combination of tactical decisiveness and strategic inconclusiveness. There is perhaps a sense in which, like Israel in its confrontation with the Arab world, any Armenian military victory over Azerbaijan is destined to be tactical and local because of the latter's significantly greater resources.[71] In terms of the security it claimed to provide it was a victory of diminishing returns. This was one of Ter-Petrossian's core arguments as he exited the political stage in 1998. Whether he was right or wrong is today a question of perspective (in Chapter 6 I discuss the logic of counter-arguments against his position). But it was not only the looming power asymmetry, or international disapproval of occupation and the violation of territorial integrity, that qualified the Armenian victory. The sheer scale of the victory, spilling far beyond the original boundaries of the dispute, built into any future agreement a need for concessions challenging its architects and their interests. This set up a conflict between the original goals for which the war had been fought and 'concessions' needed to attain them through negotiation. Arkady Ghukasian, second de facto president of the NKR, captured this irony in 1997: 'In fact, Karabagh, *which won the war, is supposed to capitulate* ... It is not acceptable for us to become subordinate to Azerbaijan, to return the territories, along with the unilateral return of the Azeri refugees.'[72] Conceding war gains to secure original political goals would always be controversial; it would be ever more so with the passage of time. The nature of the 1994 victory thus established an ideological schism in Armenian politics – as in Israel – between territorial compromise and an alternative view that broaches no return of lands occupied in a defensive war. Strategic inconclusiveness and a victory that demanded too many concessions converged to generate precisely the prolonged indecision that General MacArthur warned against.[73]

Prolonged indecision has provided networked regimes with critical resources in three areas. First, it enables elites to homogenise political identities of the communities under their rule by portraying them as still vulnerable to external, indeed perpetual, threat. Second, through discourse and strategic language those standing outside (or overtly challenging) the homogenous communities thus conceived can be identified as an internal threat to their security. Finally, prolonged indecision justifies actions, including derogations from constitutional rules, to meet security threats. These tendencies combined can be called a *demobilisation effect*, whereby against the persistent backdrop (or anticipation) of violence, elites use the discourse of security and external threat to marginalise and silence dissent, and to portray alternative visions of political order as standing outside of legitimate political discourse.[74] It is important to note that the demobilisation effect does not imply pure elite manipulation or false consciousness. Post-Soviet Armenian and Azerbaijani elites inherited populations who not only had been mobilised around existentially threatened ethnic identities (see Chapter 1), but who had also experienced war and internalised affective identities of victor and victim.[75] Violence was already a deeply embedded experience delimiting identities conceived as homogenous and threatened. All elites had to do was to leverage this legacy to depict internal challengers to their rule as threats to the security of these identities.

Civil society activist Gevorg Ter-Gabrielyan captured the demobilisation effect in Armenia in 2015:

> Despite this regime's claims to speak for the nation, it has exploited the Karabakh issue to distort national identity in the interests of the few. The purpose is not only to keep this clique in power, but also to restrain the population, to limit its political repertoire to symbolic-ritualised activities, and to rely on highly simplified images to represent Armenian society to itself and the outer world.[76]

In the context of a strategically inconclusive victory, security became a creed that drew on the cumulative historical experiences and fears of Armenians and imposed a paramount perspective on all political and social issues. This tendency was actively cultivated in an outlook that reduced all socio-economic and political issues to an eternal Darwinian survival of the fittest between Armenians and 'Turks'. As the subsequently disgraced leader of Yerkrapah, Manvel Grigorian, explained: 'This is a millennial struggle, our fathers' and grandfathers' struggle ... The president has to defend the people, that is what we stand for: the leader defends the people . . .'.[77] In this reductive view of politics as ritual, policies, actors and institutions associated with security enjoy implicit legitimacy and intuitive public support. The army has consistently rated as the most or second most trusted institution in Armenia, rivalled only by the Armenian Apostolic Church. Violence solidifies this popularity: the level of trust in the army rose from 63 per cent in 2013 to 77 per cent in 2015, after a summer of heightened tensions and skirmishing in 2014.[78] By way of comparison, levels of trust in the parliament, political parties and president in 2015 stood at 11 per cent, 6 per cent and 16 per cent respectively. At least until 2016's 'four-day war' security also mediated popular support for Russia and Russian-led regional integration projects, even when these are perceived as inconsistent with Armenia's other interests. A demobilisation effect is visible, for instance, in the findings of a poll of 480 young people conducted by the NGO Peace Dialogue in 2014. This poll found that more than half (59.5 per cent) of respondents supporting Armenia's membership of the Russian-led Eurasian Economic Union (EAEU) nonetheless felt that Armenia's foreign policy was moving in the wrong direction.[79] Within this group's preferences, the perceived security benefits of joining the EAEU – a customs union – were almost twice as important as economic factors.[80]

Conversely, policies or people standing outside, or questioning, the homogenised community defined by security needs were marginalised and silenced under Republican Party rule. This demobilising effect concerned not only those who question security policy but any idea diverging from traditional norms:

This conflict is used to repress anyone who thinks differently in society, from peacebuilders, to feminists to homosexuals ... Anyone who diverges from this traditional Armenian norm, who tries to implement something new or raise new ideas, they will be faced by these ultranationalist ideas arguing that we are a country in conflict, we have threats, people like you who are raising these ideas are weakening the nation and making us more vulnerable.[81]

Human rights activists and journalists reporting on abuses and non-combat related deaths in the army faced official pressure not to publish their findings.[82] Those who did were branded as traitors and illegitimate outsiders: 'people without a homeland, without morals, without dignity'.[83] The ironies for the PANM were particularly sharp. Levon Zurabian, head of the party's parliamentary faction in 2015, lamented how the party that brought Armenia to independence and Karabakh to de facto sovereignty is now smeared as defeatist (*partvoghakan*) for publicly broaching territorial compromises.[84] At the level of formal institutions the prevailing ethos of security provided cover for the constitutional changes introduced by referendum in December 2015. President Sargsyan framed the most controversial aspect to Armenia's new parliamentary system, the provisions inducing a stable majority and limiting coalition politics, as a measure necessary for domestic and external security.[85] Securitisation is a bluff that can be called, however, if the elite fails to provide security against threats that it has consistently evoked. The vulnerabilities that the 'four-day war' of 2–5 April 2016 exposed in Armenian defences and security provisioning dealt a significant blow to the image of the incumbent elite in the one issue area where its claims to legitimacy were grudgingly acknowledged. This mitigated the demobilisation effect in advance of the crucial 2018 succession crisis and contributed to Sargsyan's downfall.

Ruling party stability and the political economy of persuasion have mitigated the challenge of mobilisation in Azerbaijan. But the demobilisation effect is still evident in homogenising Azerbaijan's nominally pluralist party politics, in depicting advocates of liberal democracy and constitutional protections as illegitimate, and in rationalising prolonged incumbency as a benefit to the citizenry.

Azerbaijan's story is indeed an example of how to turn defeat into an instrument of control.

After 1993 Azerbaijan was in the anomalous position, for a newly independent state, of featuring ex-Soviet conservatives in government and a nationalist opposition recently ejected from power. Nationalist parties could still mobilise substantial support, which could not be demobilised by being portrayed as outside the realm of legitimate political discourse. This challenge was met under Ilham Aliyev with discursive co-optation. Within two years of his accession, according to one of its authors, the official position had converged with that of the public consensus delimited in the Karabakh Charter.[86] An important consequence was the homogenisation of the ideological playing field on the conflict, which public opinion consistently lists as the number one problem facing Azerbaijan. As a result there was 'no real difference between the government and opposition' on the Karabakh issue.[87] Opposition party leaders could only differentiate themselves by committing to democratisation.[88] This opened the path for the regime to link democratisation to the risk of renewed insecurity and the possible return of the opposition to the prospect of definitively losing Karabakh.[89] With no choice but to retain the fractious and discredited opposition from Azerbaijan's democratic experiment in the early 1990s, the Aliyevs skilfully wrote this legacy into their own narrative, as a foil against which to tell a story about themselves and the dangers of democracy.

Rivalry subsequently provided the pretext and justification for constitutional changes embedding Ilham Aliyev's incumbency. The 2009 referendum abolishing presidential term limits specifies that this applies only in a 'state of war'. While this obviously referred to the situation in Karabakh, the Council of Europe's Venice Commission noted the vagueness of this definition and recommended a more stringent standard (such as a declaration of martial law or a state of emergency) to allow for the extension of terms.[90] The implication is that should Azerbaijan cease to be at war, the justification for extended terms would no longer exist. Rivalry and regime thus extend interlinked into an indefinite future. The rivalry also served as a pretext to silence advocates of liberal democracy remaining in civil society. While it would be an exaggeration to suggest that the charge of 'Armenian connections' has been used against every government critic, accusations against peacebuilding practitioners are more easily publicly accepted than those only working on human rights and democratisation.[91] Allegations of an Armenian connection have been used to remove some of the most vocal critics of government. Leyla and Arif Yunusov, authoritative figures in human rights activism, peacebuilding and scholarship on the Karabakh conflict, were among them.[92] Leyla Yunus describes the dynamic in terms of continuity with Soviet practices of denunciation:

> In Soviet times you were denounced as an imperialist stooge [*posobnik*], an enemy of the people. Today Ilham Aliyev uses the Karabakh conflict with Armenia to denounce those who criticise him in the same way. You are denounced as an Armenian stooge, an enemy of the people. If we look at the accusations that are made in the media, they focus on this issue: if you produce lists of political prisoners, it is because you work for Armenians; if you disseminate information about torture, it is because you work for Armenians; if you investigate non-combat related deaths in the army, it is because you work for Armenians.[93]

The Yunusovs faced several years of harassment and a series of attacks on their office, culminating in their arrest on 30 July 2014. Although convicted on charges of tax evasion and fraud a year later on 13 August 2015, Leyla Yunus was also initially charged with treason and espionage relating to her peacebuilding work. Sentenced to eight and a half and seven years' imprisonment respectively, Leyla and Arif were released to exile in December 2015 and now live in the Netherlands. Other activists accused of Armenian connections include three youth activists, Ruslan Bashirli, Said Nuri and Ramin Taghiyev in the Yeni Fikir group, arrested in August–September 2005 on charges of accepting funds from Armenian secret service agents in Tbilisi. The accused believed they had been meeting with civil society activists and the funds were for democratisation activities.[94] Prominent journalist Rauf Mirkadirov was also sentenced to six years' imprisonment for high treason on 28 December 2015.[95] He was accused of having been recruited by Leyla and Arif Yunusov for Armenian secret service agents and supplying them with state secrets; he was released with a suspended sentence in March 2016 and now lives in Switzerland.

The inconsistency with which charges of collaboration with Armenians are made – by no means all peacebuilders face such charges – indicates that the logic of these arrests lay elsewhere: in the accused's human rights and oppositional activities, or simply their critical views on government. Through accusations of an Armenian connection those advocating a different conception of political community in Azerbaijan – one based on liberal democracy and the formal rights as set out in the constitution – have been marginalised, silenced and removed from the political arena. More generally, an 'Armenian connection' is the reflex response of many Azerbaijani government officials when confronted with concerns about governance, corruption or human rights.[96]

Demobilisation requires the perception of threat and insecurity to work. Sustaining a plausible sense of risk is needed to justify derogations from constitutional rules and the homogenisation of the political field. In Azerbaijan, as the larger and more resource-rich rival, a sense of threat is harder to maintain. In a theatre of daily reminding, Armenia appears in televised Azerbaijani infomercials much like the fictive Eurasia on the telescreens of Oceania in George Orwell's novel *1984*: a malignant and omnipresent threat demanding vigilance. But demobilisation is at bottom a strategy involving the use of violence to homogenise and silence political communities. In this regard, civil society practitioners on both sides of the conflict are convinced that ceasefire violations are managed to this effect. In Azerbaijan Hillary Clinton's 2012 visit is frequently cited as an example where the prospect of a difficult dialogue on governance and human rights was deflected by an outbreak of violence claiming the lives of several soldiers.[97] In Armenia activists recall the distraction from the killing of protestors in Yerevan on 1 March 2008 by skirmishes around Mardakert in Karabakh in which at least five Azerbaijani soldiers were killed.[98]

It is difficult to prove the choreographing of Line of Contact violence. Yet the demobilising effects of this violence are clear.

In the aftermath of the escalation of violence in April 2016 the surge in security concerns in Armenia led opposition parties and politicians, independent experts and media normally critical of government to fall in line behind prescriptions for national unity. Independent journalists struggled with themselves how to report on casualties in the midst of the violence, perceiving a choice between being 'good journalists' or 'good citizens'.[99] In Azerbaijan a hegemonic narrative of the 'turning of the tide' took hold of media of all political orientations. The economic woes recently besetting the country – the sustained slump in the oil price since June 2014, a double devaluation taking 60 per cent off the value of the national currency, lay-offs and small-scale protests – were quickly sidelined.[100] As Azerbaijani activist Jasur Mammadov Sumerinli concludes:

> Whenever we see society consolidating the regime manages the societal mood with ceasefire violations. This is a very sensitive and emotional issue, because we are taught to believe and repeat that territorial integrity has to come first and all other issues should come later ... Every time that we see a European structure preparing to make a statement on democratic processes in Armenia or Azerbaijan, we see violence along the contact line. This is why we call for democratisation to come first, and conflict resolution later as otherwise the regimes exploit the conflict.[101]

In sum, in Armenian and Azerbaijani regime politics the idea of Karabakh shimmers elusively between democratic cause and autocratic ruse. In the late 1980s and early 1990s the archetypal images of the Armenian–Azerbaijani conflict were of crowds on squares, protest, disruption and subversion: in short, of contested politics. In later years the defining images changed to official symbols and depictions of elite-mediated power: new weaponry and frontline troops, the narrow huddle of presidential talks or the daily infomercials of oligarch-owned TV channels. Evading simple causalities, the Armenian–Azerbaijani conflict accounts for both the unleashing of short-lived democratic experiments across the divide, and renewed political closure restricting the ideals of popular sovereignty mobilised and fought for in 1988–94.

Over two and a half decades Armenian and Azerbaijani elites were caught in the trap of what I have termed mutual hybridity: regimes closed enough to contain democratic challenges, but not closed enough to be sure of subordinates' loyalties. Neither deepened legitimacy through democratisation, nor the autonomy of truly autocratic leadership, has been forthcoming as a route out of rivalry. This chapter has argued, however, that democratisation perspectives are insufficient to understand the institutional sources of the Armenian–Azerbaijani rivalry. Elites have in reality ruled instead through networked regimes, which although part of a broader post-Soviet phenomenon, were particular beneficiaries of the Armenian–Azerbaijani rivalry. In each state there was a two-level game at work, in which the institutionalised power fracture – between constitutional and networked principles and spaces of operation – generated additional constraints on the de-escalation of rivalry. Armenia's networked regime developed as both a product of the 1992–4 war and a solution to the spatial-political dilemmas bequeathed by its outcomes. The relationship of Azerbaijan's networked regime to the conflict is more opportunistic than existential. But its pervasive aspiration to hegemony contradicts the power-sharing premise of its own preferred vision for a peaceful outcome: autonomy in a reintegrated Karabakh.

Networked regimes found legitimacy through the rivalry's demobilising effects, providing a nationalist consensus smothering the absence of consensus on myriad other issues. Armenia's regime compensated for democratic decline with a narrative of military prowess and the informal attainment of 'augmented Armenia'; Azerbaijan's compensated for authoritarian consolidation with a narrative of economic prowess, political stability and the symbolic nationalism of 'wide Azerbaijanism'. Understandings of the conflict itself evolved as a consequence. What was once a policy problem, an issue that could be broken down into components, interests and trade-offs, became a litmus test, moral monopoly and roll call indefinitely mustering societies around the axis of conflict. The result has been a configuration of considerable stability. Elites cannot venture innovative policy but profit from persistent insecurity to demobilise dissent. Meanwhile, institutional capacities sufficient either to credibly meet the challenges of more effective negotiations or to restrain escalatory patterns remain stunted.

The perspectives presented in this chapter suggest that the fracture between constitutional and networked principles of power needs to be sutured within each society before sufficiently rooted constitutional states could credibly engage in the negotiation of a rule-bound solution. The fundamental problem, lying at the root of other problems, is one of formal political institutionalisation. Networked power can stand in when the constitutional state is *in extremis*, but its resilience over the *longue durée* has resulted in emaciated constitutions and an absence of cross-cutting institutions within each state. Simply put, where networks are strong, rules are weak. This does not translate automatically into weak *states* as conventionally understood. But it does mean the development of states that lack the kinds of institutionalisation generating cross-cutting restraints to the pursuit of rivalry or the capacity to adopt and sustain alternatives.

Armenia's Velvet Revolution warns, however, that demobilisation cannot stand in for political legitimacy indefinitely. More legitimate in his rule, Nikol Pashinyan may be able to face down spoilers and generate broad-based consent in ways that eluded his predecessors and make demobilisation unnecessary. Yet even if a democratic transition is sustained in Armenia, the rivalry will likely remain a mixed-regime dyad awaiting its first joint democratic opening. Such an opening, should it occur, will face significant risk of renewed violence, as threatened elites unrestrained by strong institutions could easily appeal to nationalism's emotive force. Some of Pashinyan's first gestures as prime minister were suggestive of these dynamics, as he burnished nationalist credentials his opponents had sought to discredit.[102] His first 'foreign' visit as leader took him to Stepanakert, where he reiterated a standard rhetorical line that the NKR should be represented at the talks with Azerbaijan. This followed a number of public speeches referring to Karabakh as an integral part of Armenia and as 'our homeland'.[103]

The appearance of new policy entrepreneurs may thus be understood as a necessary but not sufficient condition for the de-escalation of rivalry, certainly over the short to medium term. Yet the Armenian–Azerbaijani rivalry offers no empirical evidence that more authoritarian leaders insulated from public backlash can deliver. Rather, the 'tunnel' merely extends into an indeterminate future, as networked regimes hostile to reform reap the rewards of demobilisation. Without the positive-sum rationalities that democratisation might bring, it is through the prism of hard power that the rivals view their relations.

6 Truncated Asymmetry

Opening a new accommodation complex for displaced communities in May 2007, Azerbaijani President Ilham Aliyev declared that at $1 billion Azerbaijan's military expenditures now equalled – and would soon exceed – Armenia's entire state budget.[1] It was a portentous moment for Azerbaijan. Thirteen years after Aliyev's father had signed the 'contract of the century' with a consortium of international oil companies, and four since a nerve-wracking dynastic succession, the country had arrived on the global energy map. The previous year the first oil to be pumped through the recently inaugurated Baku–Tbilisi–Ceyhan pipeline had arrived at its terminus in Turkey. Azerbaijan had registered an astonishing 34.5 per cent in growth in 2006, nearly three times that of Armenia. Budgetary asymmetry between the two states quickly became a commonplace reiterated in countless speeches, articles and reports, at home and abroad. With it came the presumption of preponderance: the idea that by force of its size and strength Azerbaijan would eventually overpower a smaller and weaker Armenia. Nearly a decade later, this was how Azerbaijani Minister of Defence Zakir Hasanov foresaw the end of the rivalry. Speaking after the first demonstration of Azerbaijan's new military capability in April 2016, he claimed a rocket arsenal fifty times the size of Armenia's and said that Armenia was 'unable to keep up' with Azerbaijan.[2]

Hasanov's reckoning was rooted in a realist appreciation of power. When power and victory are positively correlated, the larger the ratio of forces favouring one actor over another, the more likely they are to win. It is a commonsense assumption, and a core tradition in the scholarship on war.[3] Preponderance offers one route out of an enduring rivalry by allowing one of the rivals to impose itself on the other. In the context of the Armenian–Azerbaijani rivalry, this perspective invites the question of why Azerbaijan, always the larger rival even without oil windfalls, has been unable to coerce Armenia into making concessions for more than a quarter of a century. How has Armenia, as a smaller and resource-poor state, managed to maintain a rivalry with a significantly larger and richer opponent? Routine reiterations of asymmetry point to answers in a crucial, but under-analysed, structural factor: the peculiar asymmetric power relations between the two rivals.

Asymmetric conflicts have long posed conceptual and practical challenges to scholars and policy-makers alike. Why do the strong sometimes lose wars to the weak?[4] Answers to this question have looked beyond power-based analysis to the higher stakes that weaker actors have in asymmetric conflicts, their ability to craft political victory out of military stalemate, and strategic interactions between strong and weak actors.[5] The concept of asymmetric conflict may at first glance appear at odds with that of enduring rivalry. Parity would appear to be a necessary condition for interstate rivalries to endure for the requisite two decades, while overwhelming preponderance would presumably deter weaker contenders from pursuing rivalries. But weaker states do sometimes attack stronger ones.[6] And contrary to a realist expectation that only broadly equal rivals can sustain long-term rivalry, some of the most notorious and longest-lasting rivalries of our times, such as the Arab–Israeli and Indian–Pakistani rivalries, are starkly asymmetric. These cases suggest that asymmetry is contextual, and that even within scenarios of deep disparity there can be mitigating power configurations that moderate the impact of asymmetry.

In this chapter I argue that the Armenian–Azerbaijani rivalry is both enduring and asymmetric, and that the peculiar power asymmetry that holds between the rivals is in fact critical to its persistence. On almost all aggregate indicators of material resources, such as size, demography, military capability and economic endowment, Azerbaijan is preponderant. But the power differential between the rivals is marked by a peculiar configuration of 'truncated asymmetry', meaning that while Azerbaijan's aggregate power capability is greater than Armenia's, several factors serve to reduce this disparity, especially in the local context of Nagorny Karabakh.[7] Local parity in the theatre of conflict, a deterrent strategic posture, and balancing with Russia have enabled Armenia to sustain the rivalry despite being materially weaker. This asymmetric structure makes compromise by either rival improbable in the short and medium terms. Materially preponderant Azerbaijan sees eventual victory in its larger size and aggregate capacity; there is, by this reasoning, no need to concede to a smaller and weaker rival. Yet from Armenia's standpoint the truncation of the power asymmetry has made the threat of outright coercion less credible and mitigated the considerable costs of maintaining the rivalry. Relying on time to embed the outcomes of the 1992–4 war has been a viable alternative.

This chapter proceeds by first considering Azerbaijan's preponderance across the parameters of economic wealth, military expenditures and demography. It then considers how Armenia truncates this asymmetry though parity in the conflict theatre of Nagorny Karabakh, a strategy of deterrence, and balancing with Russia. Several contradictions in the resulting dynamics are explored before finally considering the role of asymmetry in interests between the parties.

Azerbaijan's Aggregate Preponderance: Resources, Military Expenditure and Demography

Twenty years after independence, at the height of its oil boom, Azerbaijan enjoyed considerable preponderance over Armenia. Across diverse aggregated indicators the approximate differentials between Azerbaijan and Armenia were: size, 3:1; population, 3:1; GDP, 6.5:1; defence spending, 7.5:1; active military forces 2:1. Only for per capita income was the ratio between the two rivals closer.

Resources

After catastrophic economic collapse across the South Caucasus in the early 1990s, entailing falls of some 60 per cent in GDP, Armenia was the first to recover. Double-digit growth in 2001–7 briefly earned Armenia plaudits as a 'Caucasian Tiger', although foreign aid and diaspora investment played significant roles in the recovery.[8] In 2008 Armenia's growth was disrupted by the Russian–Georgian war in August, and more permanently by the global, and especially Russian, financial crisis. Armenia's economy shrank by 14.1 per cent and a decade later GDP had still to regain its pre-2008 levels. Over the next decade Armenia remained a low-middle-income country, in which around a third of the population was consistently below the poverty line.[9]

As Armenia contracted, Azerbaijan boomed. Although Caspian oil wealth was exaggerated in the early 1990s, Azerbaijan's proven oil reserves were still considerable for a state of its size at seven billion barrels, accounting for 0.4 per cent of the world's reserves. Its Shah Deniz gas field is the largest in the Caspian at 1.2 trillion cubic metres. With the opening of the Baku–Tbilisi–Ceyhan oil and Baku–Tbilisi–Erzurum gas pipelines in 2005–6 Azerbaijan emerged as the eastern hub of a trilateral regional axis connecting it with Georgia, Turkey and European energy markets. The pipelines circumvented Armenia, building asymmetry into development. Azerbaijan's national oil company, SOCAR, became a major investor in neighbouring states; in 2010 President Aliyev claimed that Azerbaijan's economy accounted for 75 per cent of economic activity in the South Caucasus.[10] Azerbaijani economic growth averaged 12.6 per cent per year between 2002 and 2013, driven by oil production, exports and a high oil price. For three years between 2005 and 2007 Azerbaijan was the fastest-growing economy in the world. Although qualified by uneven development and income gaps, the statistics of poverty reduction in Azerbaijan were dramatic. Poverty dropped from 49 per cent in 2001 to 6 per cent in 2012, as GDP per capita tripled and Azerbaijan became a middle-income country.[11] A State Oil Fund of Azerbaijan (SOFAZ) was established in 1999 with $271 million in assets; nearly twenty years later in 2017 SOFAZ reportedly held $36 billion.[12] A new narrative of development and stability became a mainstay of the country's brand, as city centres were transformed and a host of expensive international mega-events laid on in Baku.

The anticipation of economic preponderance was a recurrent theme in my first meetings with Azerbaijani politicians and activists in 2005. Most framed the coming boom as a motor of attraction, enabling Azerbaijan to draw Armenia and the Armenians of Nagorny Karabakh into an economically beneficial relationship. This was the rationale for ideas such as the 'peace road' linking central Azerbaijan, Karabakh, southern Armenia, Nakhichevan and Turkey floated by newly appointed Foreign Minister Elmar Mammadyarov in 2005.[13] After oil revenues from the Baku–Tbilisi–Ceyhan pipeline began to flow from 2006 the idea of using wealth for a conciliation strategy faded. In the years that followed policy-makers would sometimes express interest in ideas such as capital investment in Nagorny Karabakh or the establishment of a free economic zone in the territory.[14] But such schemes, or a wider concept or strategy within which they could be implemented, were never formalised. Instead Azerbaijan's political class increasingly linked the country's oil wealth to a more coercive bargaining strategy.

Military Expenditures

Oil windfalls enabled Azerbaijan to embark on an alternative strategy of power transition. This describes a scenario in which challenger Azerbaijan overtakes status quo power Armenia in terms of resources, capabilities and strength. Central to this strategy was an ambitious military modernisation programme, the scale of which became the dominant symbol of the asymmetry with Armenia. Azerbaijan's rearmament programme was aimed both at the purchase and eventual manufacture of weapons systems that would give it a numerical and technological edge over Armenia, and at pressuring Armenia through a spending war of attrition that as a small, resource-poor and blockaded state it could not win.

Twice in the first decade of Ilham Aliyev's presidency, in 2006 and 2011, Azerbaijan doubled its military expenditures. In 2011 the reported doubling of military budget to $3.1 billion (current USD), as pledged by the president in 2007, exceeded Armenia's state budget at $2.8 billion. Azerbaijan maintained this level of military expenditure through the next four years, out-spending Armenia at a ratio averaging 7.5:1. Azerbaijan progressed up the international league table of arms recipients from 53rd in 2002–6 to 19th in 2011–15, accounting for 1.5 per cent of all global arms transfers.[15] Azerbaijan's acquisitions included aviation, missile and surveillance systems, tanks and armoured combat vehicles. While Armenia's overall spending also increased, reported delivery volumes remained low. Among arms transfers recipients Armenia dropped from 71st place in 2002–6 to 125th place in 2011–15; in the 2011–15 period Azerbaijan's import volume of deliveries was a staggering 10,000 per cent higher than for Armenia in the same period.[16] In terms of the proportion of GDP spent on defence the proportions are more even, while as a share of overall government spending Armenia spends more. These calculations underpin assumptions that over the long term Armenia's capacity to maintain an arms race will be unsustainable.

Russia is the dominant supplier for both countries.[17] Russian supplies to Armenia enjoy a near-monopoly and have a contractual basis set out in the terms of bilateral agreements and Armenia's membership of the Collective Security Treaty Organization (CSTO). Russian supplies to Azerbaijan, which accounted for 65 per cent of all transfers to the country in 2013–17, have a commercial basis.[18] Azerbaijan has successfully lobbied against other prospective suppliers to Armenia, while diversifying its own suppliers.[19] From the 2010s Azerbaijan's earlier reliance on other post-Soviet suppliers in Russia, Ukraine and Belarus was increasingly supplemented with deals and negotiations with Israel (accounting for 29 per cent of all transfers to Azerbaijan in 2013–17), Turkey, South Africa and Pakistan. Both Armenia and Azerbaijan also established domestic arms production industries, aimed at joint production or limited production under licence of small and light weapons, munitions, vehicles and unmanned aerial vehicles (UAVs), with modest success.[20] With increasing deliveries, military balance indices indicated growing disparities in numbers of core categories of hardware, such as tanks, armoured combat vehicles, artillery and aviation.[21] While the principal technical base for both armies is still Soviet in origin, Azerbaijan purchases modern versions of hardware, while Armenian equipment is in some cases older. More importantly, the April 2016 escalation along the Line of Contact indicated that the Azerbaijani army was now capable of mounting and coordinating combined arms operations, albeit with limited objectives.

Numbers, of course, are malleable and expenditures are not the whole story. Three important qualifications to the military expenditure asymmetry need consideration. There is first the question of what gets counted. Behind the aggregated, totemic statistic of $3 billion lay profuse budgetary lines, many of them opaque, and some of which stretched the definition of 'military' to an all-inclusive concept of 'security'. Domestic monitors of Azerbaijan's defence sector in 2014 identified abundant structures incorporated into the military budget: the Ministries of Defence (including the Army Mobilisation Unit), Internal Affairs, National Security, Emergency Situations, and Defence Industry; the Military Prosecutor's Office; the Border Service; the penitentiary service within the Ministry of Justice; the Presidential Guard tasked with safeguarding the president and his family; and SOCAR's security detail tasked with safeguarding oil infrastructure.[22] Some of these have a tangential – if any – relation to scenarios of war in Karabakh. Hence, while the $3 billion figure expressed economic capability, it was diffused across a far wider range of bodies and institutions than likely to be directly engaged in any future conflict with Armenia.

Second, there is no simple equation between arms transfers and military capability.[23] Military capability depends on the integration of equipment and personnel through effective organisation, military doctrines and operability, and preparation for deployment conditions. Even after several years of substantial military spending, there was evidence that the endemic problems of the Azerbaijani army – the privileging of procurement over social provisioning for servicemen, low salaries, a lack of transparency, embedded informal networks, and the high incidence of non-combat related deaths – were deteriorating rather than improving.[24] Stagnating salaries cast doubt on widely publicised expenditures. Moreover, according to local monitors, more than 70 per cent of soldier deaths in 2003–13 were non-combat related; sharply increasing in 2011, non-combat related deaths outnumbered deaths due to enemy action by an average of five to one for the next two years, sparking public outcry.[25] Civil society monitors linked institutionalised negligence to stagnation of the army command structure. The Azerbaijani Ministry of Defence had been headed by Safar Abiyev for eighteen years, but not only had the minister and chief-of-staff remained in post for nearly two decades, division commanders were also found to hold tenure for stretches of twelve to eighteen years.[26] It was an open secret that preferential postings out of harm's way for conscripts and evasion of the draft altogether were available at a price.[27] On 27 October 2013 the Azerbaijani Ministry of Defence received a new minister, Zakir Hasanov, a former deputy minister of internal affairs.[28] Turnover of dozens of high-ranking personnel followed Hasanov's appointment as minister of defence, many of them in positions responsible for finance and supply.[29] At least thirty were arrested, although some senior staff, such as scandal-ridden former naval chief Shahin Sultanov, were released to house arrest.[30] Yet the fact that none of the Azerbaijani fatalities in April 2016 identified through social media were born in Baku, when the capital accounts for a fifth of the country's population, indicates that a culture of favours may take a long time to uproot.[31] A shady 'spy scandal' in May 2017, in which dozens of soldiers were reported to have been arrested on charges of spying for Armenia, several of whom then died in custody, served further notice of the limits to institutional reform of the Azerbaijani army.[32]

A third qualification of the impact of military expenditure asymmetry lies in the nature of the source of revenue. Petrodollars enable armament but depend overall on stability. They would be threatened by any long-term or serious conflict, and offer vulnerable targets to long-range, 'counter-value' missile strikes. Should oil and gas flows be disrupted, a core pillar of regime power in Azerbaijan would be compromised. Azerbaijan's rearmament programme is also vulnerable to vicissitudes of the relevant commodity prices. After the oil price slump of 2015, annual military expenditures in 2016–17 dropped by more than a third (while still remaining considerable, at $1.4–5 billion).[33] Of course, any state's military budget is subject to fluctuation, yet such sharp changes impede a long-term strategic perspective for military and operational planning. The resource power asymmetry between Armenia and Azerbaijan, while allowing the latter the resources to rearm, is a two-edged sword. It generates a constrained preponderance that can afford an expensive arms race, but which is averse to the risks of actual war for the source of its revenue.

Demography

A third area of consequential asymmetry for the Armenian–Azerbaijani rivalry is demography. Azerbaijan has always had a bigger population than Armenia, being twice as large in the last Soviet census of 1989. But this differential has deepened over the post-Soviet period. Trends indicate a shrinking or at best stagnant population in Armenia, with implications for the fundamental capacity to mobilise and maintain armed forces.

Three major trends are significant in understanding growth in the demographic imbalance. The first is mass migration. Estimates of the extent of migration inevitably vary, as statistics are scarce, contradictory and incomplete. Most sources agree that at least one million Armenians left Armenia in the first decade of independence.[34] In the second decade the rate of out-migration declined but remained considerable. Surveys indicate that between 2007 and 2013 an average of 35,000 people left Armenia annually.[35] By one estimate some 444,100 people left Armenia in 2000–16, bringing the total number of migrants from the country over its independence period to 1.5 million.[36] In comparison, Israel's population increased by almost the same number of immigrants (1.4 million) over its first twenty years as a sovereign state.[37] Migration from Armenia is overwhelmingly economically motivated.[38] Tellingly, the only three years in which Armenia experienced positive migration balance since independence corresponded with a period of growth and relative political stability in 2004–6. In Azerbaijan, demographic outflows are seen to contradict the state narrative of economic success and are exceedingly difficult to verify statistically.[39] Estimates for post-Soviet emigration from Azerbaijan reach as high as 1–1.5 million, but cannot be empirically demonstrated.[40] Substantial though these numbers are, confidence marks the Azerbaijani demographic outlook, with a significant ethnic consolidation of the domestic population compared with the Soviet era. Azerbaijanis also comprise the largest national minorities in neighbouring Georgia and Iran. A second trend is relative decline in fertility and rates of reproduction. Table 6.1 compares demographic indicators in Armenia and Azerbaijan over the 1990–2015 period. These show that while both states have experienced declines across core indicators such as birth and fertility rates and rates of natural increase, Azerbaijani demographic trends – possibly exaggerated in official data – have been more resilient. A final trend is the ageing of Armenia's population.

Table 6.1 Armenian and Azerbaijani demographic indicators compared, 1990–2015

Armenia	1990	2015
Registered population	3,514,900	3,010,600[a]
Population increase 1990–2015 (%)		–14.4
Birth rate (per 1,000)	20.5	13.6
Fertility rate	2.6	1.6
Natural increase (year)	57,889	12,509[b]
Population aged 65+ (%)	5.6	10.7
Azerbaijan		
Registered population	7,131,900	9,593,000
Population increase 1990–2015 (%)		34.5
Birth rate (per 1,000)	25.9	17.4
Fertility rate	2.8	2.1
Natural increase (year)	140,170	111,513
Population aged 65+ (%)	4.7	6.2

Source: Compiled from State Statistical Committee of the Republic of Azerbaijan <http://www.stat.gov.az>; National Statistical Service of the Republic of Armenia <http://www.armstat.am> (both last accessed 11 March 2019).
[a] This figure is the so-called de jure figure of officially registered residents. In the context of significant unregistered migration, the actual population is lower. Unofficial estimates put the real population of Armenia at a lower range of 2–2.5 million. Author's interviews, Armenia, March 2015.
[b] Garik Hayrapetyan, 'The Transition of Demographics and the Demographics of Transition', presentation to the conference Armenia: End of Transition – Shifting Focus, 10 April 2017, University of Southern California, <http://www.youtube.com/watch?v=2omhcOJ8haY> (last accessed 11 March 2019).

Between 1990 and 2016 the proportion of people over the age of 65 has almost doubled and is higher than the average for Eastern Europe and Central Asia; the corresponding proportion in Azerbaijan has moderately increased.[41]

These trends have long pointed in the direction of demographic crisis in Armenia. Already in 2007 the country's National Security Strategy identified 'a low national birthrate, disappointing indexes of health, mortality, life expectancy and the quality of life, unregulated and illegal migration, especially among the educational, scientific and cultural workforce, as demographic threats to national security'.[42] At constant 2017 fertility rates, the United Nations Population Fund (UNFPA) projected that by 2050 the population of Armenia will contract to just under 1.8 million.[43] Policy initiatives to address the crisis were scarce and belated, leaving it to civil society groups founded by repatriates to popularise the idea of repatriation among Armenia's diaspora.[44] Organisations such as Repat Armenia[45] and Birthright Armenia[46] have sought to learn from Israeli experience to create networks and infrastructure supporting Armenians to resettle in Armenia. But progress has been slow, with only an estimated 30,000–40,000 voluntary repatriations in the first two decades of independence.[47] Government inertia and reluctance to reduce prospective remittances, low economic prospects, cultural distance between repatriates and locals, and unrealistic expectations among repatriates have all contributed to low rates of sustained repatriation.[48]

Although requiring important qualifications, Azerbaijani preponderance is real. Notwithstanding fluctuations in commodity prices, aggregate economic dominance is set to continue. Azerbaijani numerical superiority across several weapon types is established, even if in the light of reducing oil revenues levels of military spending over the long term will not continue at their 2011–14 rates. Official population statistics in both states need to be viewed with caution, yet there is little doubt that at current growth rates Azerbaijan's differential with Armenia will continue to be in the region of 3:1 or more. This scale of asymmetry does not in itself preclude the maintenance of the rivalry. The population differential in the India–Pakistan rivalry, for example, is

6:1. But in conjunction with other factors growing demographic disparity will make the logic of asymmetric warfare more relevant over time. How then is Armenia, the weaker party on aggregate, able to sustain the rivalry?

How Armenia Truncates Asymmetry: Local Parity, Deterrence and Balancing

Three variables attenuate the disparities between Armenia and Azerbaijan, truncating the asymmetry between them and allowing the weaker protagonist to maintain the territorial status quo for a quarter of a century. These are local parity in the theatre of conflict, the strategy of deterrence, and balancing with Russia.

Local Parity

Although Azerbaijan is larger overall in terms of size, economy and military spending power and population, it is not overwhelmingly preponderant in the key theatre of conflict in Nagorny Karabakh itself. In Karabakh the factors of terrain, fortification and local armed forces deflect the impact of numerical preponderance, establishing a localised context of parity.

As the anthem of the de facto Nagorno-Karabakh Republic (NKR) points out, most of the territory under its control forms a natural fortress.[49] The terrain lends itself to the long-held wisdom that for asymmetric forces, the first condition for avoiding defeat is to refuse to confront the enemy on their own terms.[50] Comprising the eastern edge of Lesser Caucasus plateau, most of Karabakh's interior is mountainous and densely forested, with a rapid descent into some half-dozen river valleys to the west and south. In the north, some 70 kilometres of the Line of Contact follow the highest range in the Lesser Caucasus, the 3,300-metre high Murovdag (Mrav) mountain range. In the south, access is contained by the fact that Armenian-controlled territory directly abuts the Iranian border. The rest of the frontline is constituted of approximately 150 kilometres running from the north-east area of the River Terter valley to the extreme south on the

Iranian border. This exposed part of the Line of Contact has been heavily fortified since the 1994 ceasefire. An official Karabakh Armenian source describes the fortifications as 'a multi-layered defensive structure equipped for both breadth and depth, with both natural and man-made obstacles, systems of minefields and weapon emplacements capable ... of repelling a land and air attack by stronger forces ...'.[51] Historical examples considered in its construction were the Mannerheim, Maginot and 'Siegfried' lines in Finland, France and Germany. In Armenian calculations the resulting network of echelon-formation trenches, bunkers, minefields and parapets deflects numerical inferiority, risks significant losses for any attacking force and thus limits possibilities for an Azerbaijani blitzkrieg.[52]

There are weak points to the north–south stretch of the Line of Contact. Armenian positions along most of this line benefit from higher ground afforded by the Lesser Caucasus foothills, but others do not, opening up battle space where the numerical ratio of forces comes into play. That the Line of Contact is not impermeable was a core lesson from April 2016's 'four-day war', when Azerbaijani forces penetrated and to a limited extent reshaped the Line of Contact in the north-east and extreme south. But overall, even if Azerbaijan had preponderance in lowland areas, to take control over mountainous Karabakh would require a difficult offensive campaign in terrain linked to a nearby sanctuary and supply area in southern Armenia.[53] This is a last-resort scenario, however, because – as we will see – other aspects of Armenian strategy are aimed at precluding a prolonged war.

A second factor conditioning local parity is the presence of the NKR's armed forces, the self-styled Nagorno-Karabakh Defence Army (NKDA). Concerns to avoid the appearance of irredentism and to minimise Armenia's perceived role in the conflict motivate a traditional emphasis on the separation of the NKDA and Armenia's armed forces. Emerging from a collective of battalions and private brigades in early 1992 and institutionalised in 1994–5, the NKDA, like the NKR, is formally separate and operates in a distinct strategic context. In the 2000s, however, to all practical intents and purposes the NKDA and Armenia's army merged. Like the NKR and Armenia, the same individuals have often led both forces at different times in their careers. Karabakh Armenian servicemen are over-represented in both the NKDA and the Armenian military overall (relative to the population of the NKR), but the NKDA is nevertheless dependent on conscripted recruits as well as officer corps from Armenia.[54] The NKDA's own information is explicit about the context of asymmetry vis-à-vis Azerbaijani forces and stresses qualitative development of more compact, mobile and tactically versatile units in response.[55] Data on the capabilities of the NKDA is scant, but most assessments agree that some 18,000–20,000 combatants are deployed, along with a substantial ground force of tanks, armoured combat vehicles and artillery units.[56] When added to Armenia's armed forces the NKDA's capabilities narrow the Armenia–Azerbaijan asymmetry. Moreover, its deployment establishes a context of near-parity along the exposed parts of the Line of Contact, with two divisions and a total of some 20,000 troops deployed on each side.

Another important feature of the Line of Contact theatre is the disparity in the numbers of civilian populations on each side. On the Armenian side it is only in the area of Mardakert that there are settlements close to it. On the Azerbaijani side in the districts of Agdam and Fizuli, which are only partially occupied by Armenian forces, substantial communities live just metres from the Line of Contact. Some Karabakh Armenian politicians see the capacity to inflict a disproportionate humanitarian disaster upon Azerbaijan in the event of an attack as a kind of deterrent:

> We've got many advantages. Our population points are some distance away from the border [Line of Contact]. In Karabakh there is a population of around 150,000 spread across 12,000 square kilometres. On [the Azerbaijani side] side there are one million people living within range of our artillery. These people are [the enemy's] hostages, right in the line of fire.[57]

Some projections post-April 2016 indicated a possible mass displacement of 300,000 people on the Azerbaijani side in the event of large-scale warfare.[58]

As T. V. Paul observes, 'local power matters tremendously

in making an asymmetric rivalry enduring'.[59] In the context of Nagorny Karabakh, the factors of terrain, fortification and local capability combine to make the prospects of a swift and decisive Azerbaijani blitzkrieg improbable. Leaving aside the geopolitical constraints to a longer war of attrition, retaking Karabakh militarily evokes challenging scenarios of a protracted and costly land campaign and potentially asymmetric humanitarian crises.

The Strategy of Deterrence

Although Armenia's stance overall is politically revisionist, its strategic posture relative to the post-ceasefire situation in Nagorny Karabakh is defensive. Armenian security doctrine stresses defensive rather than offensive capabilities, and superiority in certain areas such as long-range precision weaponry, rather than overall superiority. This posture contrasts with Azerbaijan's increasingly offensive–defensive stance over time.

Armenia's defensive posture is reflected in a strategy of deterrence aiming to deter Azerbaijan from using its aggregate military superiority in a large-scale attack on Karabakh. The viability of a deterrent strategy in the Armenian–Azerbaijani context can certainly be questioned given the power asymmetry. The theory of deterrence essentially derives from the proposition that the more the military balance favours the deterrer, the more likely the deterrent is to be effective. Viewed through an aggregate lens, the Armenian–Azerbaijani rivalry inverts the classic relationship for successful deterrence: a preponderant defender deterring a weaker challenger. The Armenia–Azerbaijan rivalry is therefore a reverse image of the India–Pakistan rivalry, where despite being the weaker party on aggregate, Pakistan has been able through asymmetric warfare to continually challenge an adversary of several times its size and capability.[60] Yet even if the causal weight of deterrence in any context is notoriously difficult to pinpoint, it is clear that conventional deterrence held between Armenian and Azerbaijani forces until April 2016. Even then escalation to a full-scale war did not happen, indicating the presence of restraining factors.

A well-known distinction differentiates between two varieties of deterrent strategy, deterrence by punishment and deterrence by denial.[61] The Armenian deterrent features both components. In deterrence by punishment a defender threatens a sufficiently destructive retaliation as to shift a potential attacker's cost–benefit calculus away from attacking. Usually associated with nuclear weapons, in conventional contexts deterrence by punishment is associated with long-range missile systems capable of striking high-value targets such as industry and infrastructure. In Armenian calculations medium- and long-range missiles capable of striking targets deep in Azerbaijan, such as the *Iskander* surface-to-surface ballistic missile system, allow Yerevan to threaten counter-value strikes that would be prohibitively costly to Baku.[62] This kind of precision long-range weaponry is seen as an 'equaliser' countering military asymmetry and capable of hitting vulnerable oil and gas infrastructure central to Azerbaijan's political economy.[63]

Deterrence by denial involves the deployment of sufficient force and appropriate strategy to deny an opponent's objectives on the battlefield. In the Armenian–Azerbaijani context assessing the effectiveness of deterrence by denial comes down to whether Azerbaijani numerical advantage is offset by the quality of Armenian defensive capacity, and interpreting the interactions between the offensive and defensive strategies of the two armies. In quantitative terms Azerbaijani forces enjoy preponderance overall. This needs to be calibrated, however, with the traditional convention that attacking forces must outnumber defenders by 3:1 as a necessary, but not sufficient, condition of success.[64] The possibility of rapid mobilisation of the reserve in Nagorny Karabakh, 45,000 in contemporary Armenian estimates, could also offset numerical disadvantage during the critical opening stages of a conflict.[65] Azerbaijan's numerical advantage is therefore not sufficient to ensure a decisive advantage in a wider attrition war, although numbers are sufficient to allow concentrated attacks at one or more points along the Line of Contact.

For many years in Armenian and many international assessments there was a popular perception that the NKDA enjoys a qualitative edge over its Azerbaijani counterpart in experience (most senior officers are veterans of the 1992–4 war), morale and professionalism.[66] Such assessments need to be considered, however, in the light of a taboo in Karabakh on public discussion of problems in the military.[67] Due to a more open reporting environment in Armenia, as well as the stationing of citizens from Armenia in Nagorny Karabakh, endemic problems involving inadequate provisioning, hazing and non-combat related deaths have featured in media and NGO reporting.[68] Non-combat related deaths across both Armenian and NKDA forces could be as high as 100 per year over the first fifteen years of independence, but dropped significantly after public outcry in 2010.[69] In the mid-2000s most of the half-dozen or so Armenian soldiers inadvertently crossing the Line of Contact every year did so because they were fleeing hazing.[70] Corruption in the Armenian armed forces was spotlighted in the aftermath of the April 2016 violence.[71] Three senior Armenian army officials were sacked.[72] A longer-term problem for the NKDA is the ageing of some of its equipment. For example, despite modernisation the staple tank used by the NKDA, the T-72, compares poorly with its upgraded version, the T-90, acquired in substantial numbers by Azerbaijan.[73] But if complacency regarding the NKDA's capacities was certainly exposed in April 2016, its significance as an effective fighting force was also evident. Despite having the factor of strategic surprise working against it, NKDA forces recaptured within twenty-four hours a number of front posts lost in the initial attack and over the next three days inflicted equivalent casualties, including substantial numbers of Azerbaijani special forces servicemen.

Between terrain and local capability, the conditions in the theatre of conflict restrict the military options available to Azerbaijan. An Azerbaijani offensive would need to overrun the obstacle-ridden terrain of Nagorny Karabakh that restricts the movement of large armoured units necessary for an effective blitzkrieg. There is reason to believe that local armed forces, granted additional strategic depth by operating seamlessly with Armenia's army, could impose severe costs to such an offensive. Therefore even if Armenia's deterrence by punishment failed, the base condition of effective deterrence by denial is present in the theatre of conflict: the prospect of a long and costly attrition war. But in the context of the overall Armenian–Azerbaijani asymmetry, the dynamic does not end there. There is another risk for Armenia and the NKR. This is that in the event of a lengthy war of attrition, Azerbaijan's economic and demographic advantages would come into play. Meeting this risk is the third and most crucial factor truncating Armenian–Azerbaijani asymmetry: Armenia's balancing with Russia.

Balancing with Russia

Since the late 1980s balancing with Moscow has been a consistent strategy pursued by Armenians or Azerbaijanis in their conflict with each other. Azerbaijan was initially more successful in this strategy. In spring 1991 Azerbaijan exchanged loyalty to the continuation of the Soviet Union for a combined operation – Operation Ring – between Azerbaijani special forces units and Soviet 4th army units against Armenian irregulars around Karabakh (see Chapter 1). But in the decade after independence Azerbaijan prioritised Western-facing alignments with the United States, Europe and Turkey, before opting for a foreign policy eschewing formal alignments from the mid-2000s. In contrast Armenia, initially the anti-Soviet rebel, consistently deepened its alliance with Russia in tandem with its deepening asymmetry with oil-era Azerbaijan.

Russia's roles in the Armenian–Azerbaijani rivalry are plural and complex, and I will return to them in the next chapter. For the purposes of understanding how the Armenian–Russian alliance truncates the asymmetry with Azerbaijan, it is useful to distinguish three components to the alliance that have given Armenia 'borrowed power' and enabled it to maintain the rivalry. The first is the capability component. Russia has held a near-monopoly on arms supplies to Armenia, which has privileged access to the Russian arms markets and purchases weapons at discounted prices. Ad hoc loans and deliveries from Russia have also boosted Armenian arsenals in the absence of substantial military expenditures. In Armenian calculations this preferential access, combined with a defensive and deterrent posture, compensates for Azerbaijan's superior purchasing power. By this reckoning Armenia does not need the capability to win an offensive war against Azerbaijan, only sufficient capability to field a credible deterrent. Armenian capability is also boosted by the fact that Russian forces guard the country's border with Turkey. This eases the problem of maintaining two fronts and allows the main body of Armenian forces to be deployed along frontlines with Azerbaijan. Armenian analysis also emphasises that not all Russian deliveries are registered in international monitoring mechanisms.[74] Thus, even if international indexes record numerical disparities between Armenian and Azerbaijani forces, there is a certain 'shadow capability' represented by off-ledger Russian transfers. This is held to complicate Azerbaijan's calculation of the real military balance between the rivals.[75]

The second component of the Armenian–Russian alliance is the deterrent component, which covers numerous contractual obligations, formal alliances and joint military capabilities giving teeth to Armenia's deterrent. The principal deterrent effects arise from Armenia's direct bilateral agreements with Russia. Agreed in the late 1990s, these confer Russia's security guarantees on Armenia and following revision in August 2010, oblige Russia to provide Armenian armed forces with modern and effective weapons systems. Lending solidity to these guarantees is the substantial Russian military presence represented by the 102nd army base in Gyumri, established in 1994 on the basis of a previous Soviet motor-rifle division and upgraded in 2013, with a permanent force of some 5,000 men.[76] Together with an air squadron based at Erebuni, the Gyumri base is Russia's sole extant military installation in the South Caucasus outside of Abkhazia or South Ossetia, projecting Russian power into the region and 'loaning' it to Armenia. Armenia has also been a willing and loyal member of Russian-led multilateral security structures. It was a founder signatory of the 1992 Collective Security Treaty, subsequently becoming a founder member of the CSTO in 2002. CSTO membership allows preferential access to an internal arms market, but also confers the putative guarantee of the CSTO Charter's Article 4 committing member-states to treat an attack on one as an attack on all. The CSTO collective security guarantee has never been tested and remains ambiguous (see below). However, one dividend of CSTO membership is Armenia's incorporation into its regional air defence system. This is held to compensate for Armenia's limited air force capability, which is effectively outsourced to Russian aircraft and helicopter units stationed at the Erebuni air base.[77]

The third component to the Armenian–Russian alliance is the expectation that by aligning with a larger power averse to the outbreak of a new Armenian–Azerbaijani war, that power would take prompt action to stop any such war. As already noted, factors in the theatre of conflict make a rapid Azerbaijani victory unlikely. But in the light of the overall economic and demographic asymmetry with Azerbaijan, the scenario of a long attrition war also carries significant risks for Armenia and the NKR. Effective deterrence in this context therefore depends on *both* denying quick victory *and* precluding a lengthy attrition war. The Armenian calculation is that even if military factors in the theatre of conflict in Karabakh point to a protracted conflict, the political factor of great power intervention counters the risk of a longer war that could over time weaponise Azerbaijan's economic and demographic preponderance.[78] Balancing with Russia is therefore understood to buy an early curtain fall for any new outbreak, preventing sufficient time for Azerbaijan's aggregate superiority to come into play.

Balancing with Russia has afforded Armenia capability, deterrent and political resources truncating power asymmetries and sustaining the rivalry with Azerbaijan. But Armenia's embedding within Russian and Russian-led extended deterrence comes with several significant flaws. One issue is geography: without a common border with Russia or any other CSTO state the question of how rapidly alliance support could be mustered in the event of an attack on Armenia hangs over Russian-led extended deterrence. Another issue is the contradictions between the interests that Armenia seeks to secure by being a member of the CSTO and the political preferences of its other members. Several members of the CSTO have made plain their antipathy to secessionist movements. None recognise Russian revisions of de jure borders in Abkhazia, South Ossetia or Crimea, while some expressed political disapproval of 'augmented Armenia' by pointedly insisting that Armenia's accession to the Eurasian Economic Union should not encompass Nagorny Karabakh. A locally contained war in Karabakh would not activate the mutual security guarantee. Even symbolic solidarity has been elusive: in April 2016 Belarus issued statements supportive of Azerbaijan's position while fighting was still ongoing.[79] Russia's stance is less clear. While formal security guarantees do not extend to Karabakh, Russian officials from time to time make equivocal statements that appear to cast doubt on Russia's neutrality in the event of a longer war in Karabakh.

The latter point brings us to a third flaw that arises from Armenia's interactions with Russia's own balancing strategy between the rivals, and which affects the credibility of Armenia's deterrent. The Armenian–Russian alliance results in the meshing of two related but distinct deterrents – Armenian and Russian. The aims and target of the Armenian deterrent are clear: it seeks to deter an Azerbaijani attack on Karabakh or itself in the context of open and communicated enmity with Azerbaijan. While we will revisit Russian goals in the next chapter, here it is necessary only to observe that Russia also exercises a deterrent, one that aims to deter an Armenian–Azerbaijani war while retaining friendly relations with both parties. To be sure, both deterrents may be said to converge on the ultimate goal of preventing full-scale war and upholding the status quo. But the threats that they seek to diminish are subtly distinct and their targets are not identical. Armenia's reliance on Russia's extended deterrence depends on a clear commitment by an outside power to protect a protégé against an adversary. But Russia's strategy to prevent an all-out Armenian–Azerbaijani war depends on obscuring its real intentions in order to restrain *both* parties. The specific problem that their juxtaposition entails is the undermining of threats issued to define the Armenian deterrent by the more ambiguous threats and promises of the Russian deterrent. Put simply, if Armenia's deterrent relies on the certainty that Russia will act in a particular way in the event of war, Russia's deterrent relies on withholding any such certainty.

Russia's posture in the Armenian–Azerbaijani rivalry is an example of 'pivotal deterrence', when a third party or 'pivot' deters two adversaries from going to war.[80] Successful pivotal deterrence depends upon the pivot's ability to maintain sufficient flexibility to keep its targets uncertain of how it will act in the event of hostilities, and thereby to attach unacceptable risks to a calculus for war. The manner and means of pivotal deterrence consequently differ in several crucial ways from classical deterrence. Classical deterrence emphasises the need for certainty, publicly communicated threats and red lines, and clarity over intentions and commitments. These goals are pursued in regularly articulated threats by the Armenian and Karabakh Armenian political and military leadership and displays of weapons capability in military exercises and parades. Pivotal deterrence by contrast relies on the pivot's manipulation of threats and promises, the avoidance of firm commitments and the sowing of doubt in the minds of its targets, in order to restrain them from going to war.[81]

Russian pivotal deterrence is expressed in numerous contradictory policies and statements throwing uncertainty over the nature of Moscow's commitments (see Chapter 7). Most obviously, this concerns Russian arms sales to Azerbaijan: arming one's allies' enemies is hardly a conventional approach to extended deterrence. Others include the CSTO leadership's ambivalent public stance on whether and under what conditions the CSTO mutual security clause would be activated if Armenia were attacked.[82] Another example is the speculation as to Armenia's leeway to deploy its prized Iskander-M missile system free of Russian restraint.[83] Credibility is everything in deterrence. By borrowing Russian power, Armenia has also imported a Russian calculus over the threat and use of force that undermines the credibility of its own deterrent.

A final flaw in the Armenian–Russian alliance is that while the ruling out of a long attrition war reduces Armenia's asymmetric vulnerabilities, it also reduces the risks for Azerbaijan of operations with more limited aims. As an alternative to attrition or blitzkrieg strategies, the limited aims strategy uses surprise to take control over a limited area before the main forces of the defender are engaged. It assumes offensive thrusts followed by a rapid shift to a defensive posture to create a fait accompli situation generating political leverage, but falling far short of the complete defeat of the enemy. The limited aims strategy is risky when it might evolve into a protracted conflict. But with this eventuality ruled out, and a growing asymmetric advantage, this strategy is more attractive for Azerbaijan. This was the logic of the April 2016 operation, which was a textbook example of a limited aims operation: a quick offensive thrust that rapidly turned into a defence of newly acquired positions, under political conditions where escalation to a wider war could with some certainty be ruled out. That Azerbaijan is pursuing such a strategy presents the paradox of a stronger challenger using asymmetric warfare against a weaker defender, and is evidence of truncated asymmetry at work in the theatre of conflict.

Armenia's deterrent is a multilayered, spatially incoherent and ambiguous structure in which different commitments and threats apply to distinct levels and spaces. One could argue for all its faults that it has held fast in preventing a return to all-out war. The prospect of military subjugation cited by Armenian President Levon Ter-Petrossian when he resigned in 1998 as reason to consider compromise with Azerbaijan did not materialise. But this structure was not sufficient to prevent low-intensity strikes and raids, particularly in 2014–16. This threatens to take Armenia and Azerbaijan down the route of serial deterrence: iterated low-level conflict where each side uses violence to deter, but must maintain a reputation for not being cowed if it is to remain a viable actor.[84] Threats by either side no longer deter attacks or violence by the other, but only keep them within limits.

Interest Asymmetry

In his account of the 1992–4 Armenian–Azerbaijani war, reporter Thomas Goltz observed:

> The biggest difference between the Armenian and Azerbaijani approach to the Karabakh conflict was that while the former was marked by an eerie and admirable consensus that involved everyone in 'the good fight,' the latter was marked by the most open, appalling self-interest that I have ever seen.[85]

Goltz identifies a critical aspect to asymmetric conflicts that goes beyond material disparities: the asymmetry in interests between weaker and stronger actors. According to this argument, for weaker adversaries whose survival is at stake, war with a stronger opponent is 'total', demanding the dedication of the entire population and all resources. For stronger actors, whose survival is not threatened by weaker opponents, asymmetric conflicts are necessarily 'limited wars', and as such generate domestic constraints if they are prolonged and costly. Andrew Mack called this 'political vulnerability': the attrition of a stronger opponent's *political* capability to wage war and the emergence of dissent in society or among elites against its continuation.[86] This dynamic is central to the wider paradox of why the weak (sometimes) win wars. Goltz, living in Azerbaijan and eyewitness to successive implosions of its political elite during the early 1990s, over-estimates the degree of Armenian cohesion. Yet his observation aptly captures the dynamic that while for Armenians 'the good fight' was perceived as total, for Azerbaijanis it was seen as one among multiple interests and, consequently, limited.

The extent to which a quarter-century of Azerbaijani nation-building focused on the Karabakh issue has influenced the interest asymmetry that Goltz observed in the 1990s can only be a matter of conjecture. The real strength and ratio of interests, like morale or discipline, is revealed only after war has gone on for some time.[87] Across the conflict elite pronouncements and mass opinion polls alike frame the retention or restoration of Karabakh as a core national mission for both rivals. But two implications to Azerbaijan's preponderant posture bear consideration. Preponderance in and of itself assumes that the conflict is not a matter of survival. This is evident in Azerbaijan's standpoint that a military solution is an undesirable but possible last resort if negotiations fail. A war that one has to undertake if all other avenues are closed is by definition not a war for survival; there are other options. Moreover, Azerbaijan's petrodollar abundance and the development narrative of its elite undermine a conflict storyline credibly articulating the sense of an urgent and dangerous threat. There is an inherent contradiction in the project of mustering society around the axis of a conflict that leaders have framed as winnable through natural resource preponderance. Furthermore, a constant corollary of Azerbaijan's preponderant posture is a cognitive downsizing of Armenia as a poor, powerless and dependent state,[88] and a 'small and irrelevant territory'[89] that 'does not take its own decisions'.[90] Azerbaijani elite narratives of the Armenian–Azerbaijani conflict locate the real drivers of Armenian secessionism outside of Armenia, whether this is in the diaspora ('the Armenian lobby') or in Russian power politics, eliding the interests that motivate it in Armenia (and Karabakh itself).[91] At the same time Armenian secessionism is not even always framed as the most serious challenge that Azerbaijan faces compared, for instance, with Islamic militancy.[92] Whatever the Azerbaijani political leadership's real beliefs about Armenia, its reduction in status renders the idea of making concessions to it problematic. Ceding concessions to a weaker opponent that is 'on its knees' generates cognitive dissonance, as is clear in the following commentary:

> If Azerbaijan did not agree to variants [of a solution] that foresaw the separation of Karabakh when it was weak in 1993 or 1994, then to believe that it would agree now, when its economy is five or six times larger than Armenia's, when it has 20 times the financial capacity and the military balance is moving inexorably in its favour, is simply illusory.[93]

Azerbaijan's preponderant posture consequently constructs concessions as a humiliating climb-down – indeed a status reversal – attaching considerable domestic political costs for any leader choosing this path.

A second implication is that Azerbaijan's preponderant posture, combined with rising violence, has consolidated Armenian responses similarly hostile to concessions. This response has submerged earlier differences visible in the interests of Armenia and Karabakh. Karabakh Armenian officials frame their interest as existential, requiring the total mobilisation of the territory's population.[94] But in Armenia a case for moderation involving reciprocal concessions with Azerbaijan has been an intermittent if subdued thread in elite debates since the mid-1990s. Azerbaijan's preponderant posture, combined with escalating insecurity and demographic concerns, has withered the case for concessions. Instead, a 'total mobilisation posture', more characteristic of Karabakh, took root in Armenia that accepts and seeks to invert asymmetric disadvantage. After the April 2016 outbreak Armenian Defence Minister Vigen Sargsyan introduced the 'Nation Army' concept, aimed at the further integration of army and society, followed by a new universal tax to compensate families of soldiers seriously wounded or killed in action (see Chapter 9).[95] The total mobilisation posture chimes with a prominent thread in Armenian strategic culture that perceives Azerbaijan to be a 'soft state', ridden with internal problems and fractures and incapable of withstanding a determined opponent. Of course, it is impossible to know how Armenian and Azerbaijani strategic postures would play out in the event of prolonged war. As postures projecting interest and intent, however, they reinforce the overall truncation of the power asymmetry. The weaker defender sees survival at stake, while the stronger challenger sees a choice – not a necessity.

It is often said that both Armenia and Azerbaijan believe that time is on their side, and the structural factor of truncated asymmetry is an important reason why. It is a peculiar configuration of power that allows each side to believe that its preferred logic will prevail. Azerbaijan is unable to coerce Armenia into softening its position, but owing to the nature of its resources can pursue the rivalry without passing the cost on to society. The conflict is effectively compartmentalised in the domestic sphere, and there is very little that Armenia can do to impose costs on Azerbaijan for sustaining the rivalry. For Armenia the costs have been severe, and there are sunken costs of depopulation that are yet to be fully grappled with. Yet Russian under-writing of Armenia's capability and deterrent has made the cost of the rivalry bearable through a period of severe economic disparity with Azerbaijan. Truncated asymmetry serves as a cautionary perspective on aggregated power comparisons, emphasising instead the local and theatre-specific nuances in capabilities.

To the extent that truncated asymmetry validates the parties' preferred conflict strategies, it is a power configuration inimical to de-escalation of the rivalry. While there is little inducement to either party to concede, this is reinforced by the fact that in this rivalry it is the *challenger* that is preponderant. This is significant because the challenger's capacities matter more than those of the status quo power in mediating the persistence of rivalry.[96] In the Armenian–Azerbaijani rivalry there is no prospect that the status quo power will achieve overwhelming preponderance. Rather, it seems more likely that Armenia's response to increased Azerbaijani challenges would be to embed itself more deeply within Russian-led security structures. Within months of the April 2016 outbreak long-range *Iskander* missiles were displayed for the first time in Yerevan in September, and a Joint Group of Forces was established in December. The latter reinforces joint Armenian–Russian command structures for peacetime that potentially could be subordinated to Russia's Southern Military District in wartime.[97]

Truncated asymmetry is a power configuration not only inimical to peace, however, but also conducive to violence. The combination of terrain and alliance factors holds off possibilities of either a rapid and decisive Azerbaijani blitzkrieg or a protracted attrition war. But one of the consequences of Armenia's multilayered and spatially incoherent deterrent is a grey zone in Karabakh, where the cost for Azerbaijan of deterrence failure is ambiguous and bearable rather than certain and unbearable. In 2016 Azerbaijan demonstrated its willingness to precipitate a short-term crisis, anticipating that massive retaliation would be unlikely. Successive crises of this kind would have minimal strategic impact in terms of destroying Armenian armed forces and equipment, but would serve political aims in keeping the conflict internationally visible and encouraging war weariness in Armenia – or indeed quelling domestic dissent. Conversely, the defensive posture of Armenian forces, combined with the anticipated brevity of hostilities, results in limited capacity to mount punitive counter-offensives precluding further Azerbaijani challenges. Indeed, in the context of a defensive posture focused on Karabakh it is not clear what a decisive Armenian counter-offensive would look like. In short, there is ample scope for the parties to become mired in recursive, low-level and long-term violence. Deterrence might operate against all-out war, but not against a festering contest of inflicting and bearing pain in which neither side is willing to show it has reached its limit.

A final implication of truncated asymmetry is that internationalisation, in the form of balancing strategies with external powers in order to overcome asymmetric disadvantage, is integral to the rivalry. Truncating asymmetry necessitates borrowing power, bringing external agendas into the heart of the rivalry. It is to these agendas, and the international politics of the Armenian–Azerbaijani rivalry, that the next chapter turns.

7 An Exception in Eurasia

In the dominant Western script of contemporary Eurasian geopolitics, 'frozen conflicts' are contrived by Russia in order to counter a geopolitical tilt towards Europe by an elected, pro-Western elite. The normative conjuncture between a democratising, Westernising regime and the defence of territorial integrity cues Western support for parent states against secessionists, and Russia's counter-interventions. The Armenian–Azerbaijani rivalry deviates from this template. Here the parent state and defender of territorial integrity, Azerbaijan, preserves a normative distance from Euro-Atlantic structures on governance and democratisation, while it is the party violating territorial integrity, Armenia, which – while hardly democratic over its first quarter-century of independence – seeks a degree of convergence with Europe. The triggers of geopolitical competition elsewhere in Eurasia are correspondingly weak. Try as the belligerents might, this is not a rivalry easily scripted through the clashing spatial imaginaries of the 'free world' and its alternatives.

The Armenian–Azerbaijani rivalry, although certainly not immune to competitive external influence-seeking, is consequently a significant exception to Eurasia's competitive geopolitics. Readings of the rivalry in terms of great powers and client states are wide of the mark. It is precisely the ways in which the parties have *not* been able to make their claims resonate with – and truly become proxies for – great power agendas that distinguish this rivalry from other conflicts in Eurasia, and which need explanation. This chapter finds answers in the uniquely multidirectional patterning of international linkages, differentiating the rivalry from other conflicts in post-Soviet Eurasia.[1] Rather than reinforcing the conflict faultline, Armenian and Azerbaijani linkages are diffuse and cross-cutting. The antagonism between Armenia and Azerbaijan has consequently not mapped across the salient geopolitical divides in Eurasia today, and has not drawn in an over-arching Russian–Western polarity. Both rivals have remained stably peripheral actors in the wider drama of contested democratisation in Eurasia. Diffusion has also limited the alignment options available to Azerbaijan as the status quo challenger, and accounts for a degree of protective buffering from shocks in neighbouring theatres where geopolitical competition has been more intense. There is, in other words, a triple conjunction at work inhibiting movement in any direction: conflict resolution, escalation, or – at least until 2018 in Armenia – democratisation. The resulting structure has held the Armenian–Azerbaijani rivalry in a durable but precarious equilibrium, crowded both with geopolitical agendas and disincentives among outside actors to see their differences escalate out of control.

This chapter provides an account relating the rivalry's diffusion to its relative stability. Divided into three parts, the chapter examines first the emergence of Azerbaijan and Armenia as outsiders to the competitive bloc geopolitics of the Russian–European neighbourhood. It then briefly examines wider diffusions of the rivalry as a result of historical legacies, diaspora activism and diplomacy. It finishes with a discussion of the default outcome of this imperfectly yet surprisingly stable configuration: Russia's central but ambiguous role as a pivot deterring the rivals from going to war.

Geopolitical Outsiders

The exceptionality of the Armenian–Azerbaijani rivalry is rooted in the exceptional identities of each rival. With differing degrees of choice and compulsion, both Armenia and Azerbaijan emerged as outsiders in the competitive bloc politics of twenty-first-century Eurasia. In contrast, for example, to Georgia under Presidents Eduard Shevardnadze and Mikheil Saakashvili, affective affinities, symbolic debt and great power seduction had limited effects in structuring their relations with external powers. Their geopolitical trajectories were marked instead with growing isolation and autarchy respectively.

Azerbaijan and the Euro-Atlantic Powers: Linkage without Leverage

Commitments to the sovereignty of the South Caucasus, its nascent liberal-democratic regimes and its stability as NATO's south-east flank underpinned Euro-Atlantic perceptions of the region in the 1990s. But policy towards it was framed by two significant limitations: a lack of real levers in a new and unfamiliar space, and the balancing of this commitment with the prioritisation of the relationship with Russia. In the context of a sparse toolkit, the Euro-Atlantic policy agenda towards Azerbaijan became dominated by Caspian energy extraction and access. Although modest by global standards, Azerbaijan's oil and gas reservoirs came with an important geopolitical dividend: they offered an alternative to Russian and Iranian energy supplies. They became the basis for deep but undiversified linkages that led Western powers to default on the conditionality that – if weakly and inconsistently so – guided their engagement in post-communist Eurasia. For the United States, a narrative of Azerbaijan's strategic value was cemented by its position as a Western-friendly rampart bordering the pariah state of Iran and after 9/11, as a moderate, secular Muslim state 'essential' to the American-led alliance waging the War on Terror.[2]

Within six months of the ceasefire, the September 1994 'Contract of the Century' institutionalised a consortium of international stakes in Caspian oil production, and consequently in Azerbaijan's recovery. Midwife to the rebirth of a war-torn republic, the composition of the Azerbaijani International Operating Company reflected a privileged, but not exclusive, Western vector.[3] Collectively, American firms held the largest stake at 40 per cent; British Petroleum held the largest single international share with 17.1 per cent. The subsequent routing of Azerbaijan's oil pipelines reflected the same logic. The primary Baku–Tbilisi–Ceyhan pipeline, pushed through with heavy Western support, bypassed Russian soil. A secondary Northern Route Export Pipeline provided for Azerbaijani oil to be routed to the Russian Black Sea port of Novorossiysk. Russia's Lukoil (at least until it sold its share in 2002) reserved the right to export its share of the oil via the northern route. Subsequent routes of other energy and transportation infrastructure affirmed Azerbaijan's linkages with Western partners: the Baku–Tbilisi–Erzurum gas pipeline opened in 2006; the Baku–Tbilisi–Kars railway launched in October 2017; and Azerbaijan's participation in the Southern Gas Corridor to provide gas to Europe via the Trans-Anatolian Natural Gas Pipeline (TANAP) and Trans-Adriatic Pipeline (TAP). By 2015 the European Union (EU) accounted for nearly half of Azerbaijan's overall trade turnover (and 59 per cent of exports).[4] Turkey, the United Kingdom and Norway are Azerbaijan's top foreign investors.[5] Geo-economically, Azerbaijan was firmly rooted in a Euro-Atlantic vector. Geopolitically, however, its position was more ambiguous.

A Western foreign policy orientation was axiomatic in Heydar Aliyev's Azerbaijan, and was formally upheld by his son and successor, Ilham Aliyev. Ilham's early presidency, after a contested election and before the heyday of oil windfalls, constituted the high-water mark of Azerbaijani engagement with Euro-Atlantic structures. Although a membership perspective was never present, Azerbaijan followed up its 1999 Partnership and Cooperation Agreement with the EU with accession to the European Neighbourhood Policy (ENP) in 2004 and the signing of an Action Plan in 2006. The Action Plan's sparse set of governance actions indicated the narrowness of a joint EU–Azerbaijan agenda, confirmed in a Memorandum of Understanding in the same year limited to the field of energy. In 2003 Azerbaijan also volunteered to be a pilot country in the Extractive Industries Transparency Initiative (EITI), instituting the systematic disclosure, reconciliation and publication of extractive sector company payments to the government.

The advent of oil revenues, however, transformed the calculus of conditionality. A World Bank expert summarised the situation in 2006: 'Baku does not need a cent of World Bank money right now ... Conditionality is not an effective strategy for dealing with Azerbaijan.'[6] While Georgia and Moldova sought to accelerate their pro-European course, Azerbaijan's slowed down. From the mid-2000s oil windfalls lifted Azerbaijan out of categories mandating the presence of development agencies. Between 1992 and 2006 the EU gave €407 million to Azerbaijan in assistance, more than Armenia but less than Georgia.[7] By the mid-2000s foreign development agencies were cutting back their operations in Azerbaijan. The UK's Department for International Development ceased bilateral programming in Azerbaijan in 2002, while Sweden's Swedish International Development Cooperation Agency (SIDA) phased out its bilateral programmes from 2007, noting plaintively that the decision 'was received with a shrug from the Azeri side'.[8]

The US was the single largest donor to institutions promoting social change in the post-communist world. But Section 907 of the 1992 Freedom Support Act long hampered US assistance to Azerbaijan. Heavily lobbied by Armenian diaspora organisations, Congress attached Section 907 to the Act proscribing government-to-government aid for the reform of institutions 'until the [US] President determines, and so reports to the Congress, that the Government of Azerbaijan is taking demonstrable steps to cease all blockades and other offensive uses of force against Armenia and Nagorno-Karabakh'.[9] Circumvented by annual waiver after 2001, Section 907 politicised American aid by limiting it to the NGO sector, much of it staffed by former members of the Azerbaijani Popular Front now in opposition.[10] Overall, US democracy assistance in Azerbaijan per capita in 1990–2004 amounted to only a quarter of the corresponding figure for Armenia ($0.51 compared with $2.03; Georgia received twice as much at $1.24).[11] Aside from the affront to Azerbaijani national feeling, the practical impact of Section 907 should not be overstated: unrestricted aid to Armenia did not yield significantly better results. Yet without a normal assistance programme, the case for the relevance of democracy, human rights and economic reform was that much harder for US policy-makers to make.[12]

Successive rigged elections underlined a growing sense of normative autarchy in Azerbaijan. But unlike Belarus, punished by the EU with selective sanctions beginning in 2004, no actions were taken. Azerbaijan joined the Eastern Partnership in 2009, but negotiations on an association agreement foundered quickly.

After the election of a parliament lacking any oppositional representation in 2010, President Ilham Aliyev's election to a third term in 2013 and a visible contraction of space for independent political activity, the disjunctions between rhetoric and practice in the Western engagement of Azerbaijan became harder to ignore. ENP progress reports noted a disjunction between macro-economic achievements and 'regression in most areas of deep and sustainable democracy, human rights and fundamental freedoms'.[13] Policy dialogue decreased, and Azerbaijan progressively distanced itself from EU declarations.[14] Perceptions of corruption remained high, particularly at the level of the political elite.[15]

After popular protests had shaken the Arab world, Moscow and Kyiv in 2010–13 Azerbaijan took preventive action. In February 2014 legislative amendments imposed an abstruse process of registration for all foreign grants. Implementing foreign-funded grants evolved into a byzantine web of negotiation between five parties – the donor, the grantee, the Ministry of Justice, the notaries and the bank. New regulations and veto points, heated up with short deadlines and arbitrary tardiness in official responses, multiplied the difficulties of working with foreign grants.[16] Closures of numerous representations, and the activities they funded, later that year significantly weakened transnational civil society linkages. These included the Oslo-based Human Rights House Network in March; the National Democratic Institute in July; IREX (International Research and Exchanges Board) in September; Radio Liberty in December. In April Azerbaijan was also downgraded by EITI from 'compliant' to 'candidate' status on account of concerns regarding civil society's participation in extractive sector oversight; it later exited the organisation in March 2017.[17] In July 2015 the Project Coordinator's Office of the Organization for Security and Co-operation in Europe (OSCE) was closed. The United States Agency for International Development (USAID) remained active, giving more than $370 million in technical and humanitarian assistance by 2018, but from the mid-2010s programming had shifted towards development assistance and away from more politically sensitive rule of law activities.[18] Into this space a domestically funded civil society appeared. In 2007 a Council of State Support to NGOs (CSSN, known locally as the 'NGO Council') was established, which since 2008 has disbursed small grants (up to approximately $10,000 depending on exchange rates) to thousands of NGO projects.[19] Avoiding political issues, the NGO Council awards 'scattered, sporadic and small-scale grants which do not allow for sectoral strategic development, but which are useful for tactical co-optation'.[20]

Relations with the EU reached a low point with the passing of Resolution 2840 in the European Parliament on 10 September 2015.[21] The resolution condemned the crackdown in Azerbaijan in strong terms, called for negotiations on a Strategic Partnership Agreement to be put on hold and targeted sanctions to be considered, and called for corruption allegations against President Aliyev and members of his family to be investigated. On 16 December congressman Chris Smith proposed draft law HR 4264, known as the 'Azerbaijan Democracy Act', during a congressional hearing on persecuted former Radio Liberty journalist Khadija Ismayilova.[22] The Act proposed targeted sanctions and travel restrictions for senior politicians and family. Baku fired back with a public distancing of Azerbaijan from Western 'double standards' and 'disorder' in two tracts penned, in Russian, by powerful Head of the Presidential Administration Ramiz Mehtiyev.[23] Mehtiyev's accusations of Western double standards were entirely congruent with a Kremlin playlist condemning the 'colour revolutions' that had ousted vulnerable post-communist regimes elsewhere. But they also echoed revelations of the vulnerability of 'Western standards' to subversion from within. Presaging concerns at foreign meddling in liberal democracies that would dominate the coming decade, in 2012 revelations broke of how Azerbaijani lobbying had penetrated the Council of Europe. Famously dubbed 'caviar diplomacy' by the European Stability Initiative (ESI), these efforts neutralised Council of Europe criticisms of Azerbaijan's electoral and human rights records.[24] Azerbaijani lobbying targeted key posts and votes in the Council's decision-making processes. Monitors from the Council's Parliamentary Assembly found no fault in Azerbaijani elections deemed deeply flawed by the OSCE. Rapporteurs investigating human rights issues in Azerbaijan, such as political prisoners, found their access to the country barred and their motions in the Council vetoed down.

Subsequent investigations revealed the cultivation of a many-tentacled influence machine that had deeply penetrated European and American political establishments. This machine comprised three tiers of activity. There were first the activities of quasi-official, public advocacy groups such as the European Azerbaijani Society (TEAS) and Azerbaijan American Alliance (AAA). Links between these groups and the regime were intimate. Both were headed by the sons of ministers: TEAS was headed by Tale, son of Kamaleddin Heydarov, Minister for Emergency Situations and close associate of President Ilham Aliyev.[25] The AAA was headed by Anar, son of Ziya Mammadov, Azerbaijani minister for transport until 2017. At a second level, hired lobbyists targeted political institutions. In Europe, these focused on the Council of Europe; in member-states, groups such as the United Kingdom's Conservative Friends of Azerbaijan appeared. In the United States the AAA channelled millions of dollars into the recruitment of top-dollar PR firms such as the Podesta Group, Fabiani & Company, DCI Group and Roberti-White, and lobbied state legislatures for resolutions friendly to Azerbaijan.[26] As one US policy-maker put it in 2014: 'Azerbaijan has thrown money into local US politics. Hundreds of US senators have attended conferences in Baku. You see these guys from Mississippi showing up in Azerbaijan, with no idea about where they are, why they are there.'[27] Many returned home from these all-expenses-paid junkets replete with gifts and a positive narrative of Azerbaijan. The impacts of these exercises are difficult to assess, but resolutions acknowledging the February 1992 massacre of Azerbaijani civilians at Khojaly in Nagorny Karabakh were passed in several US states from 2010. At a third and more covert level, slush funds for lobbying and more direct financial interventions operated. In September 2017 the existence of what investigators dubbed the 'Azerbaijani Laundromat' was revealed after leaks to European media and the Organized Crime and Corruption Reporting Project (OCCRP). Nearly $3 billion were dispersed in more than 16,000 covert payments in a scheme centred on the United Kingdom.[28] Other investigations ruled that solicitors acting on behalf of members of the Aliyev family had failed to carry out money-laundering checks in the course of high-value real estate purchases in London.[29] In the US, indictments of disclosure failures issued from investigations by the Office of Congressional Ethics into the Houston-based Turquoise Council of Americans and Eurasians and the Assembly of Friends of Azerbaijan.[30]

There is nothing surprising in authoritarian lobbying and the conversion of natural into political resources. Wielding the conceits of 'youthful democracy' and the 'indispensable Eurasian state', where Azerbaijan stood out was its extraordinary success. As Gerard Knaus, ESI director and author of the caviar diplomacy moniker, observed, 'Few have achieved this much with so little real leverage.'[31] With skill and not inconsiderable resources, Azerbaijan had separated geopolitics and conditionality for three key audiences. For its Western partners, Azerbaijan had demonstrated that 'Western values' were negotiable in the light of other geopolitical interests, such as access to Caspian oil and gas or Azerbaijan's assistance with the routing of military supplies to Central Asia in support of the global 'war on terror'. Moreover, the very meaning of those values had proven vulnerable to challenge and obfuscation.[32] To the Azerbaijani democratic opposition, caviar diplomacy had demonstrated the corruptibility of the 'rotten West' and the futility of expectations that it would leverage its deep structural linkages in Azerbaijan in support of a democratic alternative. To Putin's Russia, Ilham Aliyev had demonstrated that he was a safe pair of hands in Eurasia's illiberal landscape. Azerbaijan had not only brushed off colour revolutionary phenomena with ease, but had taken the fight to Western capitals and proven their susceptibility to determined outside pressure.

After twenty-five years of independence, Azerbaijan's high linkage, low leverage profile had diminished external influence from any single direction. Resource autonomy, normative autarchy and rearmament defined a broader horizon of policy options than those facing Georgia, Moldova or, after 2014, Ukraine. But these outcomes also made Azerbaijan Eurasia's awkward parent state. Its membership of the Euro-Atlantic community was conceived on both sides of the relationship as transactional and negotiable, rather than civilisational. That negotiability attached to Western understandings of the country's territorial integrity, which was never seen as coextensive with 'Western values' in the same ways that framed Georgia and Ukraine as countries that 'mattered' to the West. Azerbaijani policy-makers interpreted this inconsistency as 'liberal hypocrisy'.[33] Yet the charge of inconsistency worked both ways. In its normative preferences Azerbaijan appeared a more likely candidate for regional cooperation rooted in authoritarian – not liberal – models of political order. But standing in the way of an Azerbaijani path to illiberal regionalism was Armenia's own participation in Russian-led regional schemes.

Armenia and Russia: Complementarity and Compulsion

In the previous chapter we saw how balancing with Russia is a core element in Armenia's strategy of truncating the power asymmetry with Azerbaijan. Balancing with Russia accounts for multiple strategic and security linkages constituting Armenia's interlinked deterrent against Azerbaijani military action to retake Nagorny Karabakh by force. Armenian policy-makers rationalised this part-willed, part-coerced enmeshing within Russian linkages through the doctrine of 'complementarity'.[34] This accepted the dominance of Russian linkages in the sphere of security, while seeking to activate linkages in other sectors in differing directions. Russian leverage has been sufficient, however, to block most of these efforts.

Armenia's trade patterns are complex. Russia is Armenia's single most important import and export partner, and completely dominates Armenia's trade with the Eurasian Economic Union (EAEU). Russia has also been by far the largest single foreign investor in Armenia, accounting for 40–50 per cent of its total foreign direct investment every year between 2009 and 2015.[35] As a bloc, however, the EU surpasses Russia as Armenia's primary export market. China, Iran and the United States also hold significant shares in Armenian trade. There is significant European investment in Armenia, notably from France, Cyprus and Germany, but the economy remains vulnerably import-dependent, especially in the energy sector where Russia also holds key assets.

Beyond strategic linkages and preponderance in Armenia's external trade, there are three other sources of deep structural linkage with Russia. The first is Russian ownership or majority stakes in several strategic sectors of the Armenian economy, including energy, telecommunications, transportation, mining, finance and insurance. Under Robert Kocharian's presidency, a succession of asset-for-debt agreements saw Armenia's debt to Russia waived in return for majority stakes or ownership of the republic's infrastructure for Russian firms, and for stable gas prices. These included acquisitions in 2002 of most of the Hrazdan thermal plant and several hydro-electric stations; control over the management of the Metsamor nuclear plant, supplying 40 per cent of Armenia's energy; acquisitions in 2004 of the Nairit chemical plant and a 70 per cent stake in the Armenian Savings Bank; acquisitions in 2006 and 2007 of mobile phone networks Armentel and Vivacell; Russian–Armenian joint venture ArmRosGazprom's acquisition of the Armenian sections of the Armenian–Iranian gas pipeline completed in 2008; and a thirty-year franchise to manage Armenia's railway network.[36] Although European and American firms have invested in the development of renewable energy, Russian supplies are essential given Armenia's exclusion from regional energy infrastructure. Russian energy giant Gazprom controls some 80 per cent of ArmRosGazprom and Armenia's energy deliveries. Recurrent government subsidising of gas prices during electoral cycles created a vicious circle of mounting debt and mortgaged assets.

Labour migration and the resulting remittance economy is a second source of deep structural linkage with Russia. Predominantly employed in construction and service sectors, migrant workers in Russia were able to earn salaries of $1,000 per month, more than twice the average national wage in Armenia, in the mid-2010s. Between three-quarters and 90 per cent of migrants make their way to Russia, which also accounts for virtually all seasonal labour migration from Armenia.[37] Until 2014 remittances stably accounted for around a fifth of Armenia's GDP, coming in at over $2 billion. Estimates vary over time, but around 70 per cent comes from Russia and the Russian remittance economy constitutes around a tenth of Armenia's GDP.[38] By the mid-2000s nearly 40 per cent of households were receiving remittance payments, in some cases accounting for the lion's share of household income.[39] These flows directly tie household incomes to the vicissitudes of Russia's economy. As the rouble depreciated in 2014–15 and Western sanctions in response to Russia's actions in Ukraine took hold, Armenia's remittance economy contracted from $2.3 billion in 2013 to $1.53 billion in 2016.[40] This bites directly into consumer spending and is reflected in declining retail sales. The legal regulation and profitability of employment in Russia are consequently sources of considerable concern in Armenia, and access to the Russian labour market is a powerful socio-economic rationale – and lever – for Armenia's membership of Russian-led regional organisations.

A third deep linkage is the Russian Armenian community. In the form of the 'Armenian lobby', Armenia's diaspora is often imagined as a force tying nationalist politics to political opportunity in Western states. This underestimates the growing role and influence of the Armenian community in Russia, the largest in the world. Some estimates of its size reach as high as three million, meaning that this population now rivals that of the homeland – of whose demographic decline it has been the main beneficiary.[41] In 1999 the Union of Armenians of Russia (UAR) was founded under the charismatic leadership of Ara Abrahamyan. The UAR has secured a dominant, even monopolistic, role in Armenian community life in Russia, within which the image of the 'integrated Armenian' is important.[42] Political loyalty is prominent among Russia's Armenians: the UAR has worked actively to marshal electoral support for President Putin within the community. The top-down institutionalisation of a wealthy and powerful Russian Armenian diaspora well connected to the Russian political elite also has legitimacy effects for Russian linkages more broadly in Armenia. Under President Sargsyan, moreover, the Armenian state sought to embed Russia's Armenian population – not traditionally considered part of the 'diaspora' – as the 'model diaspora community': loyal and 'constructive' in its relations with the homeland's regime, as opposed to more critical Armenian communities in Western states.[43]

These multiple, mutually reinforcing linkages gave Russia

sufficient leverage to define the scope of Armenia's relations with other partners. Prospects for increased energy independence by importing gas from Iran, for example, came to nought. Armenia conceded to Russian pressure to narrow the diameter of a pipeline completed in 2008, and did not take up subsequent Iranian offers of cheaper gas than Russia or investment in a possible second pipeline.[44] The most vivid display of Russian leverage, however, was Armenia's repudiation of an association agreement with the EU in September 2013. Over three years Armenia had concluded the negotiation of an association agreement, scheduled for signature alongside similar agreements with Ukraine, Georgia and Moldova, at an Eastern Partnership summit in Vilnius in November 2013. As the deadline approached, multiple Russian levers went into action: Moscow concluded a major arms deal with Azerbaijan in spring 2013, crowned with a state visit by Putin to Baku in August. The gas price rose in July, as subsidisation was touted as a benefit of EAEU membership. There were also threats to block Armenian remittance payments and to deport migrant workers; speculations on Russia's fulfilment of security guarantees; and threats of internal instability in Armenia if the association agreement was signed.[45] In June Armenian officials made European counterparts aware that 'some careful considerations' were still ongoing, and an unscheduled visit by EU Commissioner for Enlargement Stefan Füle was organised on 9 July to iron out the last details.[46] There was no indication at this meeting that the Armenian government would backtrack: 'we had the last dinner and the cognac, it was a done deal'.[47] But EU officials came back from their vacation to discover only three days before the 2 September announcement, by President Sargsyan during a visit to Moscow, that Armenia would instead join the EAEU.

Accession to the EAEU was quietly accepted by Armenia's political elite. Anecdotally, a working assumption within the elite appeared to be that the EAEU would eventually go the way of other Russian-led integration projects: with Armenia's needs covered in bilateral treaties, only lip-service would be required until the EAEU faded away of its own accord.[48] Uncertainty regarding Armenian capacities to meet the EU's normative regime, the socio-economic consequences for an already stretched populace and concomitant elite concerns regarding political stability also facilitated acceptance of the U-turn.[49] Public attitudes in Armenia towards Russia and its integration projects were in any case complex. Opinion polls before and after the announcement of Armenia's joining the EAEU indicate variable, yet always significant, attitudes favourable to Eurasian integration in the range of 40–60 per cent.[50] These suggest that more than just a foreign policy rubric, complementarity struck a chord with a deep bifurcation in Armenian attitudes towards the country's desired trajectory and a reluctance to polarize it. Buttressing Russia's coercive diplomacy were the hegemonic impacts of still resilient geopolitical rescue fantasies, Moscow's permissiveness of networked power, and the sheer depth of social linkage in a country where most families have a relative in Russia. But polls also indicated that *support* for membership did not necessarily correlate with *trust* in Russian-led regional organisations; this is suggestive of the demobilisation effect discussed in Chapter 5.[51]

In 2018 Armenia's Velvet Revolution confounded blithe analysis of Armenia as Russia's most submissive client. Nikol Pashinyan and his team assiduously avoided framing their endeavour as a geopolitically loaded 'colour revolution'. But the age and outlook of the leadership it installed carried clear implications, including a new foreign minister, Zohrab Mnatsakanyan, who had been the architect of Armenia's aborted association agreement with the EU. The Velvet Revolution confirmed what had already long been obvious: Armenia was not only the EAEU's least intuitive member in a geographical sense; from the varied perspectives of its other members, Armenia's European proclivities and commitment to territorial revisionism also made it the most politically suspect. For Moscow, the obviously transactional nature of this serially rebellious republic's membership of Russian-led regional schemes made Armenia an uncertain ally – an outsider on the inside.

Diffidence and Attraction: Azerbaijan and Russia, Armenia and Europe

Both Armenia and Azerbaijan emerged as outsiders, whether by choice or compulsion, within the framework of Eurasia's competitive geopolitics. Cross-cutting relations of attraction to other powers and geopolitical poles compound this sense of geopolitical ambiguity.

Parallels in the post-Soviet trajectories of Azerbaijan and Russia are unmistakeable. Democratic experiments in both states unravelled in the face of severe territorial challenges and the regrouping of power around former Soviet officials with backgrounds in security and intelligence. Both states enjoyed petro-dollar fuelled resurgence in the 2000s and converged on modernising authoritarianisms wary of democratic contagion. Subtlety and nuance in the relationship is also possible because Azerbaijan averted the leverage that Russia wields over other post-Soviet states still dependent on its energy supplies. Until the opening of the Atyrau–Alashankou oil pipeline running from Kazakhstan to China in 2009, Azerbaijan was the sole Caspian producer to avoid both energy and transit dependence on Russia. It remains the only one with a western route, and is less enmeshed within Russian energy infrastructure than any other. This containment of metropolitan linkages in the economic sphere was echoed in the military sphere. Azerbaijan's membership of the Commonwealth of Independent States (CIS) was purely symbolic, as Russian bases were withdrawn already under President Elchibey in 1993. In 2012 Azerbaijan evicted its last remaining Russian installation, the radar station at Qabala, when talks failed on renewing its lease.[52] Azerbaijani–Russian security linkages became commercial rather than structural as Russia became Azerbaijan's leading arms supplier.

Nevertheless, Russia retained linkages in several other areas viewed in Azerbaijan as potential sources of leverage. Russia remains the single largest importer of goods, accounting for 16 per cent of imports in 2015. Azerbaijan is also a significant investor in Russia's North Caucasus, home to an ethnic Azerbaijani minority numbering some 130,000 in the autonomous Republic of Dagestan. Minorities and migration provide for numerous kinds of social linkage between the two countries. Minority groups that straddle both states' borders are more of a concern. The possibility that Russia could 'activate' national minority tensions among Lezgins and Avars in northern Azerbaijan is taken seriously in Baku.[53] Russia has also been a destination for large if unverifiable numbers of Azerbaijani migrants. Studies in 2009–10 converged on estimates of some 1.1–1.3 million Azerbaijanis in Russia, of whom some 600,000–700,000 were thought to be Russian citizens.[54] Popular estimates, including those of Russian Azerbaijani community leaders, cite higher figures in the region of two million. Remittances sent by this community may not be significant as shares of Azerbaijan's economy overall (at 2–3 per cent of GDP in recent years), but have served as an important safety net covering basic social costs for families. Detentions of Azerbaijani migrant workers, delays of Azerbaijani agricultural produce supplying Azerbaijani-run markets, new work permit regulations, and the shutting down of Azerbaijani community organisations in Russia are all perceived in Azerbaijan as the leveraging of these social linkages.[55]

Russia has also long been a traditional destination for those exiled after losing out in intra-elite power struggles in Azerbaijan. These losers of factional struggles join a touchline watching the subsequent development of the political game in Baku, alongside interested spectators within Moscow's political establishment.[56] There are also numerous Russia-based, ethnically Azerbaijani oligarchs whose potential to influence events in the 'homeland' may curry favour in Moscow. The possibility of political conjunctures among disaffected former contenders on the touchline, the financial clout of Azerbaijani oligarchs based in Russia, an expanding migrant 'diaspora', and a Kremlin concerned that Azerbaijan's foreign policy is insufficiently accommodating to its interests are a continual source of disquiet in Baku. The establishment in 2012 of a new Union of Azerbaijani Organizations in Russia – dubbed the 'billionaires' union' – appeared to vindicate such fears, at a time when previously Russia-based oligarch Bidzina Ivanishvili had brought his Georgian Dream party to electoral success in Georgia.[57] Beyond the machinations of former and aspiring elite figures, cultural linkages through Russian-language media and education are gaining influence in Azerbaijan after prolonged decline.[58] But Russian motives to 'activate' these linkages into leverage have, on the whole, been few. This is because Azerbaijan's linkages with the West have, as we have seen, remained free of the kinds of value convergence that Moscow finds so threatening in other parts of its former periphery.

Diffidence and attraction also mark Armenia's relationship to Europe. As we have seen, the building of Euro-Atlantic linkages in Armenia stuttered fitfully in the face of deep and varied Russian linkages. Between 1992 and 2006 the EU disbursed €386 million in financial assistance to Armenia, less than to either Azerbaijan or Georgia. Armenia explicitly eschewed a membership perspective and across parameters such as trade volume and requests for Schengen visas, linkages remained comparatively low and leverage minimal. However, a combination of multiple crises in the year 2008 changed the leverage calculus: a domestic crisis caused by post-electoral violence in March, economic crisis wrought by the decline of the rouble from July, and the strategic vulnerability illustrated during the Russian–Georgian war in August. These developments coincided with the launch of a new template for relations with the EU, in the form of the association agreements of the Eastern Partnership, and increased EU presence with the opening of a delegation in Yerevan. Moreover, the association agreement and the negotiation of a Deep and Comprehensive Free Trade Area (DCFTA) were perceived in terms of 'long-term, low-politics cooperation on technical issues'.[59] Three years of 'silent Europeanisation' followed, during which Armenia made rapid if unsung progress in sectoral reform.

After the debacle of September 2013 the Armenian elite, privately split over the jettisoning of a European path, observed 'strategic silence' for a year and a half.[60] Far from killing complementarity, however, accession to the EAEU underscored its importance. Some civil society activists noted a warming of elite attitudes towards Western-funded NGOs as 'the anchors of Armenia's complementarity' in a Eurasian space.[61] In November 2014 the EU announced a new package of €140–170 million to support reforms.[62] Negotiations on a Comprehensive and Enhanced Partnership Agreement (CEPA) began in 2015, culminating in its signature on 24 November 2017. A scaled-down yet still ambitious document, the CEPA embraces a reduced scope of commitments and does not set up a free trade area as the DCFTA would have done.[63] Success depends on the interlinked

229

trajectories of the Velvet Revolution's domestic reform agenda and the nature of Armenia's Eurasian integration, and on Russian refrain from activating its bilateral leverage.

Complementarity 'does not enable a country to make many friends, but allows it to avoid making enemies'.[64] Whether conceived through the prisms of non-alignment or complementarity, and with differing degrees of success, Azerbaijani and Armenian foreign policies came to share a common founding principle: the avoidance of choice. While this evasive animus indeed succeeded in avoiding the making of new enemies, it also deprived the rivals of alignment options. The rivalry between them remained their own.

Wider Diffusions

The non-alignment of the Armenian–Azerbaijani rivalry with the standard templates of Eurasian geopolitics is reinforced by its wider diffusion. No other conflict in Eurasia implicates as diffuse and disparate a set of actors and interests. In necessarily brief form, this section surveys three vectors of diffusion: legacies of each rival's formative territorial politics, the Armenian diaspora factor, and Azerbaijan's multilateralist diplomacy.

The wider diffusion of the rivalry emerges first as a corollary of the historical truncation of both rivals' homeland spaces. Even under the best of circumstances the conflicted legacies of the fluctuating Armenian and Azerbaijani geo-bodies examined in Chapter 2 would quietly question the territorial parameters and founding myths of regional powers Turkey and Iran. Contemporary Armenian–Azerbaijani rivalry subsumes these legacies and gives them new life, implicating both neighbours. While Armenian–Turkish and Armenian–Azerbaijani conflicts are properly understood as quite distinct, Turkey is drawn into the Armenian–Azerbaijani rivalry by both the contested history of genocide and Armenian territorial claims in eastern Turkey, and a geopolitically intimate relationship with post-Soviet Azerbaijan. Although recognising Armenia's independence in December 1991, Turkey never opened diplomatic relations due to Armenian reluctance to formally relinquish the claims of genocide and possible territorial reparations.[65] Moreover, Turkey is one of the few states deploying punitive diplomacy towards Armenia. It shut down (already in practice highly limited) transit across its border with Armenia in April 1993 in protest at Armenian occupation of the Azerbaijani region of Kelbajar. Turkey also has a historical role as the formal guarantor of autonomy in Nakhichevan (with which it shares a short 12-kilometre border), as defined in the 1921 Treaties of Moscow and Kars. This role has arguably limited the scope of violence in and around Nakhichevan since the 1990s, but today contributes to an extended deterrent dynamic allowing Azerbaijan to concentrate armed forces in the exclave.[66]

Historically resonant and culturally intimate, the Azerbaijani–Turkish relationship was initially driven in the early 1990s by a euphoric sense of rediscovery, especially in Azerbaijan. This was echoed in Heydar Aliyev's famous aphorism in a speech to the Turkish parliament in 1995, 'one nation, two states', although already by then congruence of the two states' interests was no longer taken for granted. Over time, a diverse set of linkages developed around the core economic relationship in energy cooperation.[67] These subsume foreign direct investment, military cooperation, education, student exchanges, sponsoring of mosques, business operations and the spread of Turkish media in Azerbaijan. Azerbaijan's state oil company, SOCAR, is Turkey's largest single investor and its local subsidiary, SOCAR Turkey Enerji, is the second largest industrial company.[68] Although Turkey is sometimes framed as Azerbaijan's patron, the direction of influence is far from one-way. Through the oil boom Azerbaijani investment in Turkey nearly doubled Turkish investment in Azerbaijan.[69] Yet while Azerbaijani–Turkish linkages have proliferated in numerous sectors, several factors constrain more overt Turkish influence in support of Azerbaijan in its rivalry with Armenia. Turkey's higher-order geopolitical partnerships and priorities, including its membership of NATO, strategic partnership with Russia and aspirations to regional status, have complicated the development of a Turkish Caucasus policy. Repeated efforts to build economic ties into geopolitical influence, such as the Caucasus Stability and Cooperation Platform initiated in 2008, have quickly foundered.[70] In Turkey's domestic politics, distinct nationalist, liberal and Islamist ideological poles accord variable importance to the Caucasus and specifically to ethnic solidarity with Azerbaijan.[71] Most obviously, the absence of diplomatic relations with Armenia inhibits the roles that Turkey can play. These limitations were illustrated in the aborted attempt at normalising Turkish–Armenian relations in 2009–10.[72] Embedded within foreign minister Ahmet Davutoğlu's ambitious policy aiming at 'zero problems' with neighbours, and brokered by Switzerland and the United States, Azerbaijani resistance was central to its undoing. Implicated but not influential, Turkey remains an ambivalent bystander in the Armenian–Azerbaijani rivalry.

Legacies of twentieth-century territorial politics make Iran a second ambivalent bystander to the Armenian–Azerbaijani rivalry. By virtue of being a homeland to the world's largest single community of ethnic Azerbaijanis, Iran is more closely intertwined with the future trajectory of Azerbaijani statehood than any other state. Since ethnicity is not recorded in Iranian demographic data, their numbers are disputed and highly politicised.[73] This community's size, location, proximity to a kin-state in the Republic of Azerbaijan, and its own history of repeated twentieth-century revolt have sensitised Iranian nationalism to potentials for both secessionism within – and irredentism focused on – its Azerbaijani population.[74] This sensitivity is part of a wider dialectic between Iranian nationalism and 'ethnicist' movements for the greater expression of minority identities in Iran.[75] These movements were linked to unrest in various regions in 2006, including several cities in Iranian Azerbaijan, with uncertain numbers killed in an ensuing crackdown.[76] While the official ideology of Azerbaijanism defines itself as a counterpoint to irredentism, Baku's toleration of the presence of Iranian Azerbaijani activists has occasionally caused diplomatic infractions with Tehran.[77]

Coloured by memories of Abulfaz Elchibey's short-lived flirtation with irredentism, the existence of a thriving kin-state on the borders of its own Azerbaijani provinces has been an unsettling prospect for Iran. The Republic of Azerbaijan's pursuit of an avowedly secular nationalism and close relations with Turkey, the United States and, latterly, Israel, have compounded Iranian concerns. Conversely, in Azerbaijani geopolitical reasoning, the Armenian–Azerbaijani rivalry has been one lever, along with the contested delimitation of the Caspian Sea and alleged support of Islamic insurgent groups in Azerbaijan, with which Iran has reciprocated. Iran does not participate in the Turkish–Azerbaijani blockade of Armenia, providing the latter with an open southern border and an important resource overcoming the blockade.[78] The charge of Iranian complicity should not be over-stated: international sanctions have limited Armenian trade with Iran and imports from Turkey have exceeded those from Iran in many recent years. Yet while Iran's relations with Armenia are rhetorically warmer than with Azerbaijan, in practice deeper relations have continually confronted, as we have seen, the limits imposed by Russia's dominance of Armenia's strategic linkages and the wider impasse in Iran's relations with Euro-Atlantic powers.

The role of the Armenian diaspora represents a second vector of diffusion, rooting the politics of Armenian identity and territorial claims in the political systems of several major Western states. The global Armenian diaspora is an extremely diverse and fluid set of communities emerging from the variable 'contact and friction of traditional Armenian culture and the culture of the host-society'.[79] Although diasporic Armenian communities long preceded the twentieth century, the ideological foundation of the modern, post-genocide diaspora is encapsulated by the term *Hay Tad*. Meaning the 'Armenian cause', *Hay Tad* is a political creed concerned with genocide recognition and the claim to Western Armenia. One former adherent describes it critically as 'worshipping [at] the altar of Armenian nationalism in terms of a mythical, free, independent and united Armenia that had and has little connection to the reality of today's independent Armenian republic'.[80] Many diasporans had little conception of what, or even where, Nagorny Karabakh was when conflict broke out in 1988. Since then, through tropes of 'serial genocide' and 'victory for the victims', Karabakh has been incorporated into the prior over-arching frame of *Hay Tad*. Karabakh's 'restoration' to the homeland provided a second, rare moment of consensus after the genocide in the fractured politics of diaspora–homeland relations.

Diffusion across Armenian diaspora communities has had several effects embedding the Armenian–Azerbaijani rivalry. The diaspora constitutes first a transnational community of affect mobilising funds contributing to the sustainability of the de facto republic in Nagorny Karabakh (as well as Armenia itself). Diaspora funds, channelled through the All-Armenia Fund and its annual telethon in Los Angeles, have financed humanitarian and infrastructural initiatives in the territory (see Chapter 7). Nagorny Karabakh is also exceptional among post-Soviet de facto jurisdictions in securing financial aid from the United States government. Although the primary lobbying organisation in the US, the Armenian National Council of America (ANCA), initially failed to secure an amendment to the Foreign Policy Reform Act allowing direct assistance to the NKR in 1997, it successfully lobbied for $12 million to be disbursed in the following year via USAID.[81] Twenty years later former US ambassador to Armenia and congressman John Heffern put the total of US assistance to the NKR at $45 million, much of it directed towards demining and sanitation.[82]

Beyond humanitarian assistance and funds for infrastructure, where political systems allow for lobbying, diasporic organisations such as ANCA and the European Friends of Armenia (EUFOA) have become significant vehicles of advocacy. Armenian lobbying is most advanced in the United States, where as a US policy-maker puts it, 'by sheer virtue of population, Armenians have a say in US politics'.[83] Its main achievement was the securing of Section 907 to the 1992 Freedom Support Act described above. Since 2012, a series of resolutions have been passed by legislatures in Rhode Island, Massachusetts, Maine, Louisiana, California, Georgia, Hawaii, Michigan and Colorado in support of the NKR. These are not 'recognitions' per se. For example, Rhode Island's 17 May 2012 resolution 'encourages the Nagorno-Karabakh Republic's continuing efforts to develop as a free and independent nation in order to guarantee its citizens those rights inherent in a free and independent society' and 'respectfully urges the President and Congress of the United States of America to recognise the independence of the Nagorno-Karabakh Republic'.[84] This strategy emulates the precedent of securing sub-state resolutions recognising the Armenian genocide in order to create leverage on federal policy to do the same. The Australian state of New South Wales and the Basque Country in Spain passed similar resolutions in 2012 and 2014 respectively.

The proliferation of these resolutions has diffused the Armenian–Azerbaijani rivalry across *terra incognita* in the substate legislative politics of several major states. Advocates see them as a 'parade of recognitions' heralding progress towards increased international acceptance, *ex post*, of self-determination as secession. But they also raise a number of problems. The first is that this strategy is not synchronised with Yerevan's own policy and role as negotiating party in the official negotiations with Azerbaijan. The Armenian leadership has consistently stated its support for this process, whose aim is to negotiate Nagorny Karabakh's political status and whose outcome would therefore be pre-empted by any international recognition of the NKR. A second issue is that international resolutions elide the intractable issue of the NKR's borders, and, consequently, the legacy of ethnic cleansing on which maximalist borders are based. Finally, these resolutions are reciprocated in an equivalent effort by Azerbaijani lobbyists to mobilise resolutions mentioning the February 1992 massacre of Azerbaijani civilians in Khojaly. At the beginning of 2018 the campaigning site Justice for Khojaly reported thirteen states, including the Czech Republic, Pakistan, Mexico, Colombia and Honduras, and a dozen US legislatures, as having passed resolutions about the massacre, framed in Azerbaijani activism as 'recognitions of the Khojaly genocide'.[85]

Armenian diaspora activism is one area where the Armenian–Azerbaijani rivalry does connect with the affective, as well as material, funds of outside powers. Diaspora activism nests Armenian territorial claims within the democratic politics of several major Western states, narrates the campaign for secession as an expression of grass-roots democracy, and links claims in Karabakh to a meta-narrative of the Armenian genocide that is widely recognised in Western societies. But diaspora activism, with rare exceptions such as the imposition of Section 907 onto the US Freedom Support Act, does not decide foreign policy. Rather, the more significant impact of the Armenian diaspora has been a far-reaching softening of Armenia's authoritarian image and the reputational repercussions of being both a territorially revisionist actor on the global stage and a geopolitical partner to two pariah states, Putin's Russia and Iran. In Armenia itself, the impact on outsider perceptions of a small number of highly motivated, deeply skilled and articulate diasporans, fully conversant with the political cultures of Western states in which they were raised and often in outward-facing roles in government institutions, political parties and NGOs, cannot be over-estimated. If the 'Armenian lobby' is often exaggerated as an almost conspiratorial force, diaspora activism broadly understood exercises a significant soft power mitigating Armenia's isolation and attuning the territorial claim to Karabakh to an internationally resonant storyline of bottom-up, grass-roots politics.

A third vector of diffusion lies in Azerbaijan's multilateralist diplomacy, in many ways countering Armenia's soft diasporan power. In addition to its memberships of the United Nations, OSCE, Commonwealth of Independent States and Council of Europe, since 1992 Azerbaijan has been a member of the Organization of Islamic Cooperation and since 1997 of the GUAM (Georgia, Ukraine, Azerbaijan, Moldova) Organization for Democracy and Economic Development (now headquartered in Baku). In a significant departure from its early Western vector, Azerbaijan joined the Non-Aligned Movement in May 2011; it also took up observer status at the Shanghai Cooperation Organization in July 2015. Multiple memberships reflect plural identifications with different cultural and ideational worlds, echoed in the succession of high-profile sporting media spectacles framing Baku as the host city to both the first European Games in 2015 and Islamic Solidarity Games two years later in 2017. Within this wider multilateralist horizon, two strategic relationships stand out. Following in Turkish footsteps, Azerbaijan developed a strategic relationship with Israel.[86] Israel is drawn to Azerbaijan as a friendly state bordering Iran, and as a supplier of oil. Azerbaijan is home to a small Jewish community, and pride in the historical absence of anti-Semitism is a staple of the inter-cultural harmony underpinning the official ideology of Azerbaijanism. In 2011 Azerbaijan concluded a $1.6 billion arms contract with Israel (supplied without hindrance from European and OSCE-area embargoes), purchasing weapons systems including radar systems, multiple launch rocket systems and unmanned aerial vehicles (UAVs) – some of them deployed to deadly effect in April 2016.

Azerbaijan has likewise pursued a close relationship with Pakistan, one of the few states to unambiguously take sides in the Armenian–Azerbaijani rivalry by refusing to recognise Armenia as an independent state. Intensifying bilateral contacts between Baku and Islamabad signal Azerbaijani interest in procuring Pakistani weapons and plans for joint military production.[87] These meetings are accompanied by expressions of full, reciprocal solidarity on the issues of Karabakh and Kashmir, apparently without irony at the contrasting perceptions of irredentism in each country's respective cause. Armenia reciprocated by reportedly vetoing Pakistan's application for observer status within the CSTO in 2016 and sought to upgrade its relations with India.[88]

Among Eurasia's conflicts, the Armenian–Azerbaijani rivalry stands out in its capacity to draw in a series of meso-level actors beyond the protagonists and global powers. This propensity is often read as a source of risk through a possible 'domino effect'. But the multiplication of actors and agendas also has a stabilising and solidifying effect as the rivalry is woven into cross-cutting relations and higher-order priorities. In practice, this leads to a collective default among outside actors to the external power that has both the most extensive linkages and the widest bandwidth of policy attention dedicated to the rivalry. This brings us to one of the most frequently posed questions about the Armenian–Azerbaijani rivalry: what is the nature of Russia's role?

Russia: Patron, Baiter, Spoiler, Mediator?

The clustering of post-Soviet conflicts as the collective object of a coherent Russian policy – 'Putin's frozen conflicts' – underpins the popular script of Eurasian geopolitics opening this chapter. This streamlining accords with two prevailing narratives among Western and regional analysts and policy-makers interpreting

Russia's actions in its post-Soviet borderlands.[89] One sees Russia as an imperialist power carving out a sphere of influence or 'near abroad', a term that for liberal traditions both in the West and in the South Caucasus cues a retrograde and illegitimate understanding of geopolitics. A second rejects what it sees as wrongheaded liberalism to view Russia through a political realist lens as a rational 'great power'. By this interpretation Russia acts as any great power would: strategically maximising its own power and security at the expense of weaker neighbours. But whether out of ideological conviction or self-styled realist pragmatism, homogenising Russia's roles across Eurasian conflicts prevents a more nuanced understanding of its motives and capacities in the Armenian–Azerbaijani rivalry in particular.

It is worth recapping here some of the rivalry's distinctive features. As a recognised state and UN member, in pursuing territorial revisionism Armenia faces none of the limitations of the unrecognised republics contesting borders in Moldova, Georgia and Ukraine. The NKR is only indirectly part of Russia's 'geopolitical archipelago' of exceptional spaces.[90] Moreover, as this chapter has shown, the rivalry has spread across a highly diffuse set of linkages and relationships. Although Armenia and Azerbaijan are often dismissively referred to as a 'backyard', it is nonetheless a multi-facing one shaped by legacies and linkages older and deeper than a Russian presence. In terms of direct levers, Russia has neither an ethnic Russian population nor passportised 'compatriots' on the ground (with Armenian passports Karabakh Armenians have no need of Russian passports to travel). Russia is not contiguous to contested territory, and while present in Armenia, its own forces have no direct military involvement in the theatre of conflict. Finally, for reasons examined above, Armenia and Azerbaijan are borderlands largely free of the tripwires of Euro-Atlantic membership. Neither has declared intentions to join NATO or the EU.

These distinctive features combine to pose a unique dilemma for Russian policy-makers.[91] On the one hand, Russia seeks to dominate an internationalised peace process, whose successful conclusion would likely polarise relations with one of the rivals. On the other, it seeks to maintain friendly relations with both belligerents as part of its wider strategy to contain Euro-Atlantic encroachment and develop its own regional development projects. Put differently, Russia fields a number of incompatible goals: Armenia's loyalty, Azerbaijan's seduction, long-term Russian influence in the South Caucasus, and international buy-in for the outcome. This dilemma is complicated locally by the shift in power asymmetry in Azerbaijan's favour, with its threat of an all-out war that could force Russia's hand. Regionally it is complicated by competitive dynamics with Euro-Atlantic powers in the nearby theatres of Ukraine and Syria. Given the diversity of goals and the dynamism in and around the rivalry, Russian policy is best understood pluralistically. Table 7.1 identifies five distinct schemas that can explain Russian policy towards the Armenian–Azerbaijani rivalry.[92] They are not mutually exclusive and some blend into one another easily, but none is sufficient on its own to understand the full Russian policy spectrum, or indeed the different policy centres engaged with the Armenian–Azerbaijani rivalry. Russian policy is indeed sufficiently fluid and internally inconsistent that each schema has persuasive aspects (and adherents). I will argue, however, that the first three are flawed and that Russian policy is inconclusively suspended between the fourth and fifth schemas.

The first schema assumes congruence with Russia's roles in other conflicts in its borderlands to suggest that Russia supports the secessionist cause. Through an 'Armenia first' policy, Russia affirms the credibility of its security guarantees and the viability of the CSTO as a Russian-led security alliance. Borrowed Russian power, as Chapter 6 argued, is an integral component of Armenia's strategy for truncating the power asymmetry with Azerbaijan. Without Russian support, Armenia and Karabakh could still impose a costly military campaign on Azerbaijan, but whether they could sustain a decades-long rivalry is much more doubtful. But while several elements of Russian policy are consistent with an 'Armenia first' logic, others are not. Russian officials in the CSTO rarely refer to the organisation's security guarantees to Armenia as a factor in the conflict with Azerbaijan. Even in the aftermath of the April 2016 'four-day war', CSTO chief Nikolay Bordyuzha was less than publicly supportive of a member-state involved in conflict. More damning for an 'Armenia first' policy

Table 7.1 Schemas of Russian policy towards the Armenian–Azerbaijani rivalry

Schema	Logic	Main policy expressions
Armenia first	Support Armenia to maintain rivalry; validate Russian security guarantees and strengthen CSTO	Military alliance with Armenia including extended deterrent, discounted and off-ledger arms transfers and basing of Russian armed forces in-country
Bait and bleed	Enable and encourage low-level violence, fostering insecurity necessitating Russian intervention and draining both rivals of democratising potential	Arm challenger and signal parameters of 'acceptable' violence; leverage insecurity to dictate scope of foreign and domestic policies of both rivals
Resolution prevention	Maintain 'frozen conflict' to preserve Armenian dependence and maximise leverage over Azerbaijan	Strategic subversion of Minsk Group; unilateral initiatives and trilateral formats with Armenia and Azerbaijan; withhold leverage for resolution; enable rivals to maintain rivalry
Russia first	Secure peace agreement embedding long-term Russian presence in South Caucasus, including by preserving friendly relations with both rivals	High-level political attention to conflict; proposals for Russian-led peacekeeping operation and Eurasian infrastructural projects; using leverage to block Euro-Atlantic penetration of South Caucasus; symbolic affirmations of the Minsk Group
Pivotal deterrence	Prevent war and buy time without prejudicing future parameters of a solution	Manufactured ambiguity over terms and scope of deterrence and likely actions in the event of war; symmetric rearmament of rivals; negotiation within the Minsk Group framework as best holding mechanism

is Russia's arming of its ally's adversary. There is clearly a wider dynamic at play than simply supporting Armenia.

A second schema, 'Bait-and-bleed' could explain this dynamic.[93] The logic is simple: this strategy involves the enablement and encouragement of low-level violence that 'bleeds' the rivals dry and not only leaves the baiter's power intact, but could possibly justify a future intervention as peacekeeper. It assumes a serial policy of collusion, through arms transfers to the rivals (especially Azerbaijan as the challenger), and 'baiting' through tacit signalling of what constitutes violence 'acceptable' to Moscow. But unlike the original context for 'Bait-and-bleed' in great power rivalry, the imperative is not to bleed dry rivals who are proximate in size and capacity. Rather, the intention is to bleed Armenia and Azerbaijan 'dry' of any democratising potential by fostering a climate of generalised insecurity inhibiting democratic politics. 'Bait-and-bleed' can thus be read as a grand strategy for demobilisation in which Armenian and Azerbaijani networked regimes are themselves complicit.[94] This is a popular reading of Russian policy among more liberal circles in Armenia and especially Azerbaijan. But it is problematic on two principal counts. The first is that it is difficult to bait states into a militarised rivalry that they otherwise would not pursue.[95] As Russian policy-makers like to argue, if Azerbaijan did not buy arms from Russia, it would do so elsewhere with supposedly less Russian influence over the military balance.[96] Furthermore, Russia could hardly posture as neutral if it was arming only one of the rivals: exposés of Russian arms transfers to Armenia used to be a source of scandal in the Azerbaijani media in the 1990s.[97] A second problem with the 'Bait-and-bleed' schema is that it simplistically assumes that violence serves Russia's goals. Russia has of course used violence as a direct strategy in South Ossetia and Ukraine. In the Armenian–Azerbaijani rivalry, however, as the security guarantor of one of the rivals Russia's perspective is significantly different. One of the central ambiguities in Russia's role in this conflict is that it *is* a stakeholder in the collective effort to prevent war, and as the only state bearing treaty obligations in the event of interstate war, perhaps the most motivated to prevent this outcome. 'Bait-and-bleed' would thus be a high-risk strategy for

Russia, contingent on its ability to both rapidly and repeatedly negotiate ceasefires or face the collapse of the existing mediation structure that it informally leads and potentially even find itself fighting one of the rivals.

A third schema that could account both for Russia's support to Armenia and its rearming of Azerbaijan is 'Resolution prevention'. In this schema the status quo is Russia's best alternative to a negotiated settlement by both deterring large-scale war and maintaining the maximum possible leverage over both rivals. Arms transfers to the rivals, whether contractual or commercial, create strategic parity to preserve not only (relative) peace but also the logic of the rivalry itself. This schema assumes that Russia's role in the Minsk Process is largely cynical; its periodic establishment of unilateral initiatives and trilateral formats with Armenia and Azerbaijan, excluding the other co-Chairs, have been aimed at strategically subverting the Minsk Group. This is necessary because allowing the Minsk Group to succeed, at least within the parameters of the proposals on the table today, would potentially release Armenia from the need for strategic alliance with Russia. Conversely, Russia would lose the leverage over Baku granted by the possibility of using its influence to broker a solution favourable to Azerbaijan. Sustaining Armenian–Azerbaijani polarity – but not permitting war between them – is the basis for Russia's policy towards the rivalry. 'Frozen conflict' may therefore be a description of this *policy*, but not – as I argue in this book – an adequate *analysis* of the situation. By using 'frozen conflict' as a category of analysis, we ironically project what is arguably one of Russia's policy scenarios onto realities more complex.

'Resolution prevention' appears intuitively correct given the reality that indeed no resolution has been forthcoming. But this is not necessarily for want of Russian effort. Jarring with the 'Resolution prevention' schema are periodic Russian diplomatic initiatives that feed into, and consciously uphold, the Minsk Group. Three examples, to which I return in Chapter 9, are Foreign Minister Yevgeny Primakov's 1998 proposal for a 'common state', President Dmitri Medvedev's initiative in 2008–12, and Foreign Minister Sergey Lavrov's initiative in 2015–16. These initiatives are suggestive of a horizon of ambition for Russian diplomacy wider than 'Resolution prevention'. This could be termed a 'Russia first' strategy in which Russia does not see the status quo as the best possible outcome, carrying as it does significant risk. Rather, it seeks at least a partial resolution embedded within the broader policy horizons of Russia-centred security, infrastructure and development in Eurasia. As Russian foreign policy has become increasingly Eurasia-centric, the prospects for supportive moves in the Armenian–Azerbaijani rivalry have increased.[98] The founding of the EAEU and prospects for the bloc to trade with Turkey and Iran, the project for a north–south transport corridor connecting Russia, Azerbaijan and Iran, and the emergence of an informal Russian–Turkish–Iranian détente in the Middle East are all dynamic theatres of Russian foreign policy in Eurasia upon which the Armenian–Azerbaijani rivalry impinges. Securing progress in the Armenian–Azerbaijani negotiations coordinated with Russian agendas in these theatres could ensure that Russia itself is a major beneficiary of peace. By this view unilateral initiatives are not enacted to usurp the Minsk Group as such, but to lead it in the direction most useful to Russia. In doing so, and in contrast to its revisionist demarches in Georgia and Ukraine, Russia seeks collegiality and international recognition of its role. Symbolic affirmations of the Minsk Group consequently form part and parcel of a 'Russia first' strategy, which also chime with the premise of indispensability prominent in Russian strategic culture.[99]

'Russia first' may describe the *aspirational* logic of a strategic approach towards the rivalry of two small and peripheral powers on Russia's borders. But despite the periodic allocation of intense diplomatic energy and, in President Medvedev's case, considerable political capital of a sitting president, none of Russia's initiatives have yielded fruit. 'Russia first' is easily interpreted by the rivals as 'Russia only', a prospect triggering the sole moment of consensus among them: to prevent a Russian monopoly on managing the rivalry. In practice, Russian policy itself defaults to a fifth schema introduced in Chapter 6: 'Pivotal deterrence'. Recall that pivotal deterrence describes a situation where a third party or 'pivot' deters two adversaries from going to war. Unlike classical deterrence, pivotal deterrence relies on the avoidance of firm commitments and the sowing of doubt and uncertainty among its targets as to what the pivot would do in the event of war. This schema suggests that Russia's approach is essentially tactical, keeping the rivals in a holding pattern pending a strategically more opportune moment for 'Russia first'.

By virtue of its size and military capacity, Russia is a 'preponderant pivot', whose involvement in any future Armenian–Azerbaijani war is widely assumed to be decisive. The problem for a preponderant pivot is to convince its targets that its interests are sufficiently engaged in order for the leverage of its capabilities to be effective, but without making a firm commitment to act in a predictable way and thereby emboldening one side.[100] How has Russia solved this problem? It *has* made an alliance commitment, but with two important qualifications. First, Russia's alliance commitment is to the weaker rival that is also the status quo power with less interest in going to war. Through its alliance with Armenia Russia has signalled that significant interests, including reputation, security assets in Armenia and the viability of alliances of which it is the dominant power, are at stake. But the emboldening effect of this commitment reinforces rather than risks the status quo, by accruing to a weaker rival invested in a defensive-deterrent posture.

Yet by making an alliance commitment, Russia has also reduced the amount of uncertainty it is able to create and leverage over Armenia. This is in large part compensated for, as we have seen, by the depth of its other linkages in Armenia. But a second qualification to its alliance commitment is that it does not extend to Nagorny Karabakh, the survival of which is the vital security interest at stake for Armenia. This qualification breeds uncertainty over what Russia's policy would be in the event of war in Karabakh that did not extend to the territory of Armenia. This is uncertainty that is carefully cultivated by Russian officials. The CSTO's position is that its extended deterrent does not apply to Karabakh.[101] Yet in 2013 the commander of the Russian base at Gyumri suggested that the base could be deployed in defence of Karabakh in the event of a large-scale Azerbaijani offensive.[102] When asked by an Azerbaijani journalist in January 2017 whether Russia would 'look the other way' in the event of a 'counterterrorist operation' to retake Karabakh, Foreign Minister Sergey Lavrov's response caused dismay in Azerbaijan: 'This is no longer something abstract or related solely to Azerbaijan's internal affairs.'[103] In other words, Russia's neutrality in the event of a localised war – a *sine qua non* for an Azerbaijani campaign to retake Karabakh – cannot be assumed. Generating an uncertainty effect inducing caution in Azerbaijan's military calculus, Russia's strategic ambiguity generates an ingratiation effect in Armenia's broader geopolitical calculus (see Figure 7.1).[104] Armenia is thus deterred from foreign policy decisions, such as association with the EU, which Moscow sees as inimical to its interests. For this reason, I argue, the real centre of gravity of Russia's policy towards the Armenian–Azerbaijani rivalry lies between 'Russia first' and 'Pivotal deterrence'. Military and geopolitical threats and incentives entwine in pursuit of two fundamental goals, war denial to the rivals and area denial to Euro-Atlantic linkages.

Pivotal deterrence can be high statecraft. But in this case, it flows more from the multiplicity of incongruent Russian goals and policy interests. Russian-led regionalism, lucrative arms contracts, military force projection, transnational infrastructural projects, and bilateral interests with each rival compete to prevent the emergence of a coherent strategy. But while Chapter 6 argued that incoherence creates a credibility problem for Armenia's deterrent, for Russia it is – up to a point – a virtue. Russia's pivotal deterrence *depends* on ambiguity in order to generate uncertainty, which Russian officials diligently encourage. Pivotal deterrence also works best when its targets have few alignment options.[105] Armenian isolation and Azerbaijani autarchy consequently provide the basic enabling conditions for Russia's pivotal deterrence to be effective. It is essentially also the same tactic pursued by the other co-Chairs, justifying the collective default to Russia so long as it pursues the single consensual goal of war prevention. Yet pivotal deterrence is a serial tactic to do just that – prevent war. Tactical dexterity in averting war should not be confused with a strategy to resolve conflict. What emerges is not the rational calculation of a strategic arbiter – as the popular trope of 'Putin's frozen conflicts' has it – but the contingent and

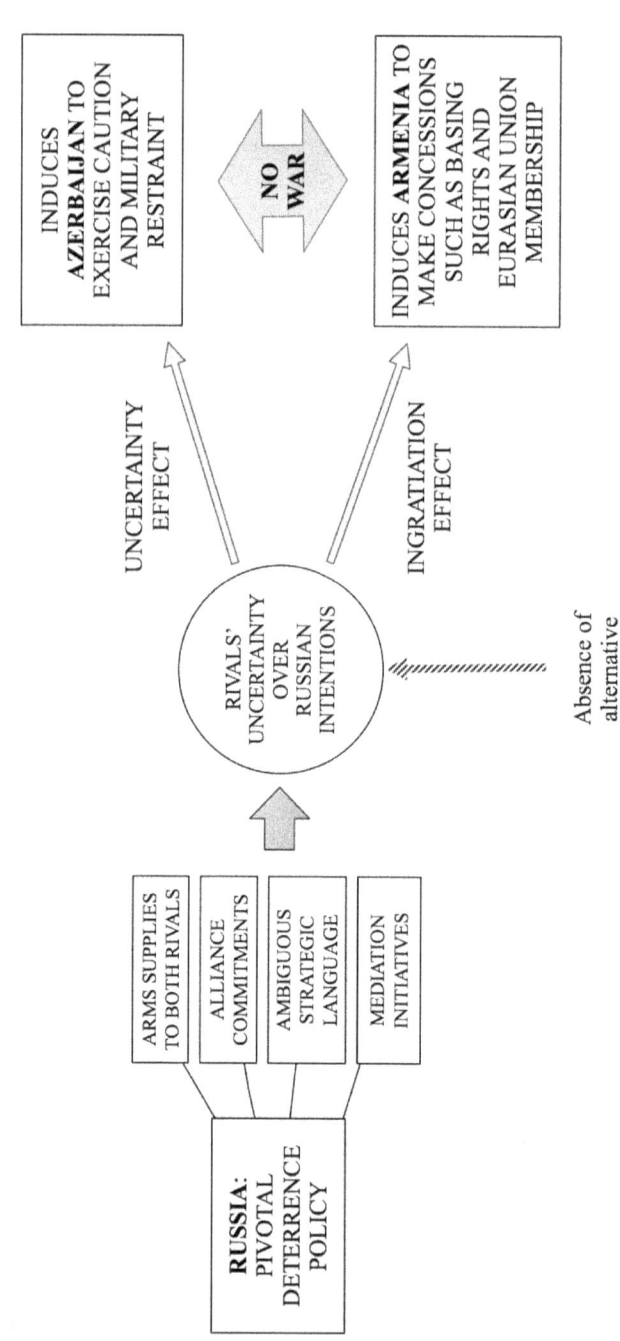

Figure 7.1 Russia's pivotal deterrence between Armenia and Azerbaijan. Adapted from *Pivotal Deterrence: Third Party Statecraft and the Pursuit of Peace*, by Timothy W. Crawford, p. 22. Copyright © 2003 by Cornell University. Used by permission of the publisher, Cornell University Press.

strategically contradictory responses of an outside power with considerable leverage but a medley of dissonant goals. Locked into an inflationary cycle of arms transfers and ambiguous commitments, Russia lacks the experience, institutional models or ideological appeal to offer an alternative. Whether Russia can become a strategic pivot using its leverage to extract concessions from the rivals that narrow the differences between them is a question for a future conjuncture, but it points to the fundamental role that Russia could play in a final settlement.

In sum, Armenia and Azerbaijan are outsiders pursuing a geopolitics of exception balancing between Euro-Atlantic, Eurasian and Middle Eastern worlds. Their memberships of blocs and alliances are consistently 'thin', sector-specific or largely performative, belying the absence of committed alignments. In this actor-rich but alignment-poor setting intractability is multi-vectored. First, multidirectional linkages limit the use of external conditionality in the direction of conflict resolution. Second, diffuse linkages limit Western leverage for reform, situating Armenia and Azerbaijan as stable outliers in the politics of democratisation in Eurasia over the rivalry's first two and a half decades. Third, scarce alignments also inhibit a calculus for escalation and make the rivals vulnerable to Russia's pivotal deterrence. Together, these factors account for the lack of connecting threads weaving the Armenian–Azerbaijani rivalry into familiar tableaux of Russian–Western confrontation in Eurasia's borderlands. This analysis should not be taken to trivialise the risk that the Armenian–Azerbaijani rivalry poses. Since it falls outside of the familiar script of Eurasian confrontations, we may not recognise risks of destabilisation when we see them. Over the last quarter-century the rivalry has become enmeshed within a bewildering matrix of interlinked interests that are almost always higher-order priorities among a crowded cast of outside actors. Contrary to the image of steadily mounting pressure, diffusion relieves some (if certainly not all) of these pressures. But there are immense dangers in the unpredictability of many multilateral interactions among several key and myriad secondary international actors in the event of crisis, and the contingency of responses filtered through higher-order policy interests.

In this and the preceding two chapters I have separated out, for the sake of analysis, three dynamics that are in reality inseparable and mutually constitutive. The resilience of networked regimes, the truncated power asymmetry that creates the opening for Russian penetration, and the dynamic of diffusion and collective default to Russia's pivotal deterrence together constitute the vicious circle in which Armenia and Azerbaijan have been locked since the 1990s. At the epicentre of this structure, yet often invisible in analysis of the rivalry, are the people whose political identity and status are its original cause: the Armenians of Nagorny Karabakh.

8 Unrecognised Reality

One of the least expected outcomes of the collapse of the Soviet Union was the emergence and sustainability of a group of political formations that came to be known collectively as 'de facto states'.[1] De facto states are secessionist entities that claim to be states, but which are not recognised as such by the international community. Violating the recognised borders of the parent state from which they have seceded, while imitating the appearance of a normal state of their own, they are paradoxically both transgressive and conformist. The premise behind the label de facto state, however, is that these entities have moved beyond mimicry. They may not exist de jure nor appear on the global map, but they feature permanent populations in fixed territories to which they provide goods and services and in which they have a monopoly on the legitimate use of force. In other words, they have achieved internal sovereignty. As such, they attract controversy as contenders for what is still seen as the ultimate – and indivisible – attribute of statehood.

There is no single issue today that divides Armenians and Azerbaijanis more than the existence of a de facto state in Nagorny Karabakh. Widely known as the Nagorno-Karabakh Republic (NKR), the entity formally renamed itself the Republic of Artsakh in 2017. There are no shades of grey in deeply polarised accounts of either a vibrant, self-determining young democracy, or the ethnically cleansed puppet state of an occupying power. The stakes in these competing perspectives are high: if Armenia is seen as responsible for the situation in the republic – as the European Court of Human Rights indicated in its judgment *Chiragov and Others v. Armenia* – then its existence as a separate polity is a fiction. This is Azerbaijan's reading of the situation in Karabakh today, evoking a collective duty of non-recognition among the international community. But if Karabakh Armenians are seen as having their own agency, then a case for recognition could more legitimately be made.

Conflicting visions of the NKR speak to a paradox characteristic of most de facto states: external dependence is a *sine qua non* of the formal independence that they claim.[2] Most de facto states survive only because of an external patron that finances and defends them and, in many cases, passportises their denizens into citizens. The relationship of dependency is nevertheless a fraught one for the aspirational sovereigns in de facto states that are already portrayed by parent states as 'marionettes' incapable of survival on their own. If integration becomes too deep, it may threaten the founding cause in whose name the de facto state was founded.[3] This is less of a problem for the NKR, however, because the Karabakh movement was founded on the idea of unification with Armenia. Therefore, although Karabakh may historically constitute a distinct geopolitical space within a wider Armenian archipelago, an intimate relationship with Armenia is the foundational premise of the jurisdiction in the area today. Today's ambiguous arrangement, where a recognised state is informally integrated with an unrecognised one claiming a separate sovereignty, is a contingent and unexpected outcome of the circumstances of Soviet collapse, the ensuing Armenian–Azerbaijani war, and the consolidation of a single networked elite across both spaces after 1998.

This chapter examines the unrecognised reality developing in Nagorny Karabakh since the 1994 ceasefire. What is the nature of this reality: is the NKR a state – or, if not, then what is it? Where should we place it on the spectrum between polarised perspectives of a 'self-determined young democracy' and 'puppet state of a foreign power'? What is the internal logic, beyond the geopolitical superstructure described in previous chapters, that drives it? Caricature aside, I acknowledge persuasive aspects to both portrayals of the NKR as a separate political society and a dependency without sovereignty of its own. Yet the normative judgements accompanying these contrasting portrayals tend to build in an all-or-nothing understanding of sovereignty missing the more nuanced politics of conditions between sovereignty and dependency. I argue that the NKR can more usefully be read as a political formation combining both tactical manifestations of sovereignty and strategic processes of integration with its patron state, Armenia. These variations represent a balancing act necessitated by the need for plausible deniability in the face of accusations of irredentism, and by the fact that for a movement premised on unification, de facto independence is not the optimum outcome. The NKR seeks neither a seamless integration with Armenia nor an absolute sovereignty of its own. The result is a fluid structure sometimes emphasising difference, sometimes unity. These ambiguities have coalesced over time into a significant political resource, in the form of malleable borders, for the nominally bifurcated elite ruling both spaces until 2018. Degrees of unity or separation between the two Armenian republics depend on the issue, theatre and audience, making for an ambivalent relationship in which borders between Karabakh and Armenia appear and disappear.

The chapter proceeds by considering first the domain where separateness is most visible: the establishment of separate political institutions and a state bureaucracy. Next I examine the domain where dependency is more obvious: the NKR's political economy. I then consider the impacts for the democratisation of the republic, before revisiting the question of borders and the emerging challenge of new human geographies within them. Researching these issues is complicated by the fact that for several years Azerbaijan has banned travel to the territory that it deems unauthorised. Baku has blacklisted, and in one highly publicised case even prosecuted, such visitors (see Chapter 9). The existence of an unrecognised republic in Nagorny Karabakh therefore faces a mutually reinforcing normative and analytical exclusion: neither is its existence recognised, nor can its material reality be visited without risk of diplomatic sanction. This account is premised on the principle that to seek understanding is not to condone or approve. While the dominant strategic interaction today is that between Armenia and Azerbaijan, any attempt to resolve the enduring rivalry between the two states cannot avoid engagement with the local reality in Nagorny Karabakh; it cannot be wished away. This reality plays a key role in the embeddedness of the rivalry and Armenia's motivations to maintain it. In the policy landscape, the unrecognised republic in Karabakh today may have become all but invisible, but in terms of the underlying causality driving rivalry it remains central.

A Tactical Sovereignty

Miatsum! – 'unification' in Armenian – was the rallying cry of the Karabakh movement in the late 1980s. Since its foundation, a pervasive duality between expressions of separateness and unity with Armenia has marked the construction of a republic in Nagorny Karabakh. Put simply, many who live in the republic see it as a temporary phenomenon, pending a more permissive climate for the movement's original goal, unification. But as that climate proves ever elusive, its temporariness has become permanent.

The founding of a separate republic was a result of the circumstances of the final weeks of 1991. The failure of the August putsch by Soviet hardliners obviated once and for all the centre's adjudication of the Armenian–Azerbaijani border dispute. With the dissolution of the Soviet state imminent, the issue of successor state borders became primary. Following Azerbaijan's declaration of independence on 30 August, the NKR was initially proclaimed on 2 September, incorporating both the Nagorno-Karabakh Autonomous Oblast (NKAO) and the Armenian-majority district of Shahumyan on its northern border. In November, the Azerbaijani parliament abolished the NKAO, creating an Armenian imperative to establish a successor entity that could embody the self-determination claim. What had been an internal matter of border revision was about to be transformed into an international situation easily readable as an irredentist campaign. The likelihood of global pressure on Armenia therefore also necessitated a bifurcation of sovereignty.[4]

The sovereignty of the NKR is consequently a tactical concession to the circumstances of its formation. Prime ministerial spokesman Artak Beglaryan frames the issue:

Independence is the intermediate goal but unification is the vision. But this does not mean that we *couldn't* be independent . . . Armenia is not seeking our unification, it seeks only our self-determination, then we can decide what we want.[5]

Hratchya Arzumanyan, an analyst at the NKR's Ministry of Foreign Affairs, concurs:

The NKR is only a temporary construct, one that international law requires us to build. It's an expensive luxury to have two Armenian states neighbouring each other, but international legal opinion doesn't allow us to unite immediately. It's a paradox, but we have to prove ourselves as an independent state in order to then come together. Like the two Germanys, one day our Helmut Kohl will appear . . . We are one nation, so of course we will unite.[6]

A tactical understanding of sovereignty explains the appearance and disappearance of borders between the NKR and Armenia. The NKR does not have a separate citizenship, physical border infrastructure (except for a checkpoint), or its own currency. The republic's legal base is Armenia's legislation; until and unless the parliament adopts legislation, it is Armenia's legislation that is the default law.[7] The NKR did not adopt its own constitution until December 2006, largely because of instability in Armenia's own constitutional framework. Nevertheless the NKR fields a complete state bureaucracy composed of executive, legislative and judicial branches, including seven standing parliamentary committees, eleven ministries and an ombudsman for a population of fewer than 150,000 – a generous estimate (see below). The dominant political parties are local parties that do not operate in Armenia; only one party, the Armenian Revolutionary Federation (ARF, or Dashnaktsutyun), operates in both spaces. The republic has its own Ministry of Foreign Affairs, which has a representative office in Yerevan, as well as representations in Moscow, Washington, Paris, Berlin, Beirut and Sydney. These popularise and advocate for the recognition of the NKR as a separate state-political unit. The Karabakh Armenian flag depicts these tensions through a fragment of the Armenian tricolor separated from the whole.

Popular attitudes towards unity or separation have ebbed and flowed in the territory over the three decades since the NKR was proclaimed. This appears to be a highly personal matter, overshadowed by an awareness that neither independence nor unification are likely as legally ratified outcomes for the foreseeable future. Moreover, the meaning of independence is often understood as independence *from* Azerbaijan (as conveyed by the term *anjatun*, 'separation'), a consensual position that does not prejudge status beyond that base condition. In the mid-2000s preference for an identity as a separate state was a subdued but audible tendency in Nagorny Karabakh, rooted not only in geography and socio-cultural difference (such as dialectal variation in the Armenian language), but also in an emancipated attitude towards the burdens of Armenian history. According to a senior de facto official, speaking in 2005: 'we suffer less from the victory complex: it is Armenia that needed the victory and indulges the triumphalism'.[8] In popular attitudes a substantial minority expresses preferences for the idea of an independent republic. In a 2002 poll 42.8 per cent favoured independence, compared with 49.1 per cent preferring unification.[9] A poll conducted more than a decade later in 2015 found 35.1 per cent in favour of independence, compared with 63.7 per cent for unification.[10] A survey in 2016 after April's 'four-day war', however, found increased support for independence at 48.9 per cent compared with 50.5 per cent favouring unification, noting that higher support for independence was correlated with youth who have grown up in the NKR.[11] For others, however, any long-term separation raises anxiety that distinct national identities, akin to Greece and Cyprus or Serbia and Montenegro, might be the undesirable result.[12] Beyond the caricatures of self-determined or puppet state, then, lies an undetermined political ethos, variably oriented towards separation or union, and accustomed to limbo. It can be safely assumed, however, that even the most ardent supporters of an independent status envisage very close ties with Armenia that would stretch a conventional understanding of independence or sovereignty.[13]

Beneath the formal institutions of separate sovereignty are the informal sinews binding the NKR into the wider Armenian body politic. In 1996 the NKR's first president, Robert Kocharian, took up the post of prime minister in Armenia; two years later he became Armenia's president. Kocharian's ascendance signified the eclipse of 'compliant Armenia', a geopolitical vision that saw the Armenia–Karabakh relationship as negotiable, by that of an 'augmented Armenia', a project assuming the unification of the two spaces (see Chapter 3). Since that time the politics of connectivity between Armenia and the NKR can be read in terms of the more fundamental division between networked regimes and constitutional states discussed in Chapter 5. For two decades in 1998–2018 Armenia and Karabakh formed a single networked space, overseen by a nominally bifurcated elite, which moved through and across this space easily. Especially in the Ministries of Defence and Internal Affairs and in the army, senior officials have circulated within a unified network. Karabakh Armenian ministers of defence have often previously served in high-ranking posts in the Armenian army, or go on to do so after their tenures in the Nagorno-Karabakh Defence Army (NKDA) have ended.

The formalisation and hardening of borders between Armenia and Karabakh is not only a tactical concession to international disapproval of irredentism, however. Borders also make tactical appearances in the context of sensitive domestic issues. One such area is in human rights. Citizens from Armenia who serve in the NKDA are not protected by Armenia's jurisdiction, and have no formal recourse in the event of human rights violations. But they cannot appeal to the NKR's jurisdiction either because, as Armenia-based human rights activist Edgar Khachatryan explains, 'it is not written down anywhere that conscripts are serving in Karabakh. They are officially volunteers, because there is not, and cannot be, an international agreement between Armenia and Karabakh that soldiers drafted in Armenia can serve in Karabakh.'[14] It is common knowledge that Armenians from Armenia are conscripted into the NKDA yet this remains an official taboo as an indicator of Armenia's extra-territorial jurisdiction in the NKR. This means, however, that if a citizen of Armenia is killed in a non-combat related death, relatives and human rights defenders in Armenia do not have the right to information because, in this instance, the NKR is considered another state. They can only petition the Armenian Ministry of Defence. As Khachatryan observes:

> It is very easy to manipulate when the situation is ambiguous. When the government needs it we are united, we are a single country. But if this is inconvenient, then we are different states. And as a citizen of this country [Armenia], you don't know whom to work with. If we are one state, then there should be a single legislative base, a single legal space and the same laws. If we are different states, then on what principle should we relate to one another, what is the relationship between our laws?[15]

More insurgent political challenges evoking a common constitutional space across Armenia and Karabakh, and seeking to mobilise support across it, also encounter borders – this time of a physical kind. In the run-up to the centennial of the Armenian genocide, Jirair Sefilian, a Lebanese-born veteran of the Karabakh war, led an oppositional movement calling itself the 'Founding Parliament'. Its programme was for regime change in Armenia in advance of the centennial. On 31 January 2015 a convoy bearing Sefilian and his supporters had just crossed into the NKR's de facto territory when police and other unidentified men stopped them and assaulted several of the protestors.[16] Their mission, to mobilise support in Karabakh, was thwarted. The incident, with its obvious implication that human rights violations impermissible in Armenia are less so in Karabakh (the convoy had progressed unimpeded up to the border with the NKR) and the subsequent silence from the NKR's parliament and ombudsman, caused outrage among Karabakh's civil society. According to Gegham Baghdasarian, director of the Stepanakert Press Club, the fiasco made a nonsense of the Karabakh Armenian elite's mantra of 'two Armenian states in the same legal plane'.[17]

Separateness, and the appearance of borders between Armenia and Karabakh, is consequently a contingent and variable phenomenon. The unified ethno-space of 'augmented Armenia' remains the hegemonic vision of the relationship between the two. But as a response to international disapproval of irredentism, or domestic challengers to networked power, a tactical sovereignty comes into play and borders – institutional, juridical or physical – appear. The result is a deeply ambivalent relationship. On the one hand, Karabakh is celebrated as an icon of Armenian democracy, yet on the other, it simultaneously appears as a dark space on the map of Armenian constitutional politics, a place to which Armenia's human rights defenders, insurgent protestors and citizens with human rights concerns have limited access. The ability to decide when, where and on what issue a border appears between Armenia and Karabakh became an important political resource. This becomes especially clear when we consider Nagorny Karabakh's political economy.

Monopoly Mediators

Political economy is a routinely under-studied aspect of unrecognised statehood. Outward-facing de facto officials, fluent in the rhetoric of self-determination, rarely welcome queries about what are almost always relations of economic dependence on external patrons. In Nagorny Karabakh's case this is mitigated by the emphasis on unification. Economic union with Armenia was an early symbolic step, with the NKAO being formally incorporated into the Armenian republican budget already on 9 January 1990. Moreover, the strategic context of being locked in a cul-de-sac framed by the Line of Contact to the north and east, and a closed border with Iran to the south, brought an end to historical patterns of economic interactions with the Azerbaijani plains to the east. Integration with Armenia was an economic as well as political imperative.

This context has resulted in a tripartite structure to the unrecognised republic's economy. Its economic backbone is the 'interstate credit' received annually from Armenia since 1993. The credit has in the past been parsed to outsiders as a loan. Officials reported to the International Crisis Group in 2005 that the credit is a loan with a ten-year repayment schedule at nominal interest, although there had been no repayments by 2005.[18] In 2014 the republic's Minister for Finance and the Economy indicated that was still the case, reporting instead that this was a rolling thirty- to fifty-year 'loan' without a formalised repayment schedule despite growing domestic revenues.[19] The interstate credit once accounted for as much as 70 per cent of the republic's revenues.[20] Official data indicate that it has stabilised at just over half of total expenditures (see Table 8.1). De facto officials are reticent on the mechanism through which the amount of the loan is determined. Officials in Yerevan indicate that the interstate credit varies in order to cover any deficit, confirmed in the fairly consistent correlation between the NKR's overall budget deficit and the amount of the interstate loan; the latter is usually enough to cover most of the deficits arising.[21] Over the decade from 2007 to 2016 the interstate credit has remained stable at accounting for between just over half to two-thirds of the republic's expenditures. This solidly reliable source of base revenue allows the NKR to consistently function with a substantial deficit, and explains why GDP per capita in the republic, at $3,227 according to official data for 2016, compares favourably with Armenia ($3,605 according to World Bank open data) despite a much smaller economy.

Diaspora fundraising provides a second source of revenue, ranging between $10 million and $37 million annually over the NKR's first two decades.[22] The main vehicle for these flows is the annual telethon, organised by the Armenia Fund, an American affiliate of the Hayastan All-Armenia fund. Diaspora funding has been instrumental in humanitarian projects and the construction of hospitals, schools and roads. The humanitarian segues silently into the geopolitical through diaspora financing of major new highway constructions overturning Nagorny Karabakh's enclave geography. Diasporic contributions to the post-war connective highways from Goris to Stepanakert via Lachin, the north–south highway within the territory, and most recently the highway connecting Vardenis with Mardakert via Kelbajar, are flagged by roadside poster-boards. Framed as 'lifelines', these infrastructural entrenchments also embed the NKR's post-war geography, elide the fact of occupation and, ultimately, constrain the parameters of a future solution.

The third source of revenues is domestic extraction. In the Soviet period agriculture accounted for 70 per cent of the NKAO's domestic production. Most of the sector, much of it war-damaged,

Table 8.1 Domestic income, expenditure and interstate credits in the de facto Nagorno-Karabakh Republic, 2007–16 (in current US dollars)

Year	Total domestic incomes	Total expenditures	Budget deficit	Interstate credit	Interstate credit as % of GDP	Interstate credit as % of expenditures
2007	34,029,200	90,146,450	56,117,300	60,139,750	29.1	66.7
2008	65,077,300	163,658,850	98,582,550	87,926,250	30.9	53.7
2009	58,495,400	151,665,350	93,169,900	91,221,600	32.4	60.1
2010	63,716,050	166,418,850	102,702,800	88,815,200	28.1	53.4
2011	69,146,550	180,882,700	111,736,150	94,923,100	26.1	52.5
2012	74,340,370	174,100,460	99,760,090	92,923,140	24	53.4
2013	68,658,520	171,215,820	102,557,300	96,630,430	23.3	56.4
2014	77,149,300	191,434,910	114,285,610	104,806,790	22.7	54.8
2015	72,233,080	174,325,000	102,092,000	95,479,090	21.7	54.8
2016	68,974,120	173,238,670	104,264,550	96,709,770	20.6	55.8

Source: Author's calculations based on the statistical yearbooks of the National Statistical Service of the NKR, 2007–16.

remains unmodernised with dramatically reduced levels of production. Only in the areas of fruit, conserves and alcohol production has the agricultural sector been modernised, with Artsakhfrukt being the major producer. The republic's largest single employer after the state is Base Metals, part of the Liechtenstein-registered Vallex Group responsible for mining operations at Drmbon and in Mardakert region. Energy has emerged as a growth area: the republic is 80 per cent energy self-sufficient, with a 25-megawatt hydroelectric power station at the territory's largest reservoir, Sarsang, and up to ten other smaller stations.[23] Two investment funds disburse business loans to encourage the formation of small and medium-sized businesses. From 2007 the Village and Agricultural Fund issued low-interest loans for land development, animal husbandry and equipment.[24] Founded in 2008, the Artsakh Development Fund by 2014 had an annual budget of $10 million, and had supported some 600 small and medium-sized businesses.[25] Several sectors enjoy income and value-added tax relief, even as a newly professionalised State Taxation Service doubled the republic's (modest) taxation revenues.[26]

Taken together, these developments construct a positive narrative of domestic revenue growth and growing self-sufficiency documented in the republic's official news agency, Artsakhpress, and its own reports. But even de facto officials do not seem to believe the hype of self-sufficiency. Many interviews that begin with the requisite affirmations of self-determination and state-building later reveal a modus operandi adapted to – and content with – dependency. According to Parliamentary Speaker Ashot Gulyan, for example, Karabakh's economy is too small to be attractive on its own and will be more viable if integrated with Armenia.[27] Asked about the need or desire for self-sufficiency, Prime Minister Araik Harutyunyan noted with satisfaction growth in the interstate credit, symbolic of the republic's dependency, as well as local revenues. The fact that the interstate credit stabilised at 50–55 per cent of expenditures indicates that self-sufficiency remains aspirational. Clarifying his commitment to the independence of the NKR, Harutyunyan explained: 'Independence is relative. We can unite with Armenia but have our own special status. This is also possible, but with self-government. We cannot enter

Armenia as ordinary Armenian provinces [*marz*] ...'.²⁸ Officials within economic structures, perhaps less trained in the rhetorical performance of self-determination, make little effort to disguise an economic integration with Armenia that they see as normal, logical and desirable. Where the political economy of the NKR is concerned, then, borders between Karabakh, Armenia and the wider Armenian diasporic world fade away. The aspiration to genuine self-sufficiency, and a separate sovereignty, is more performance than practice.

Does this make the NKR, as its detractors have it, a 'puppet state'? Such a view captures only one direction of the flows between Armenia and Nagorny Karabakh. Flowing in the other direction are the colossal leverage and influence that Karabakh has over the wider political field in Armenia, reanchored since the 1990s around the hegemonic geopolitical vision of 'augmented Armenia' in which developments in Karabakh are of foundational importance. This allows us to reconceptualise the role of the NKR's political elite. Neither sovereigns of a self-determining republic intent on separation, nor clients completely dependent on outside support, they are 'monopoly mediators' controlling monopolies on economic flows coming into the de facto republic, and on the symbolic influence that – as the cornerstone of contemporary Armenian national identity and geopolitical culture – Karabakh projects across the wider Armenian political field.²⁹ This puts the idea of recognition as an independent state in a different light. If the NKR were to become a legalised space, citizen access to a wide range of international linkages and public goods currently withheld due to non-recognition would expand. The nodal gateway between de jure and de facto spaces that its political elite currently monopolises would diversify – and face competition. Monopoly mediation and the rents it yields, such as the interstate credit, therefore depend on preserving the distance between metropole and periphery. This is evident in Araik Harutyunyan's discursive positioning of Karabakh as a 'special region' of Armenia even if one day formally integrated. It is also detectable in concern among those outside government that rent-seeking opportunity has overtaken popular goals: 'we have to remember that we are not creating institutions and self-government for the sake of it, there is a higher goal and that is unity and continuity. As things are, we risk mistaking the instrument for the goal . . .'.[30]

Polarised stereotypes of self-determining or marionette regimes do little justice to the subtleties of the political logic underpinning the NKR. The republic is a more complex formation – tactically sovereign and strategically dependent – than an all-or-nothing understanding of sovereignty allows for. As Giorgio Comai argues for post-Soviet de facto states more generally, the republic is better conceived as a small dependent jurisdiction seeking to pool aspects of its sovereignty with Armenia in ways that its inhabitants see as both normal and desirable.[31] Tropes of separation or union also obscure the value of ambiguity between the two for those positioned at the nodal gateways between the two Armenian spaces. Even those who indicate that their preference is independence for the republic, such as Prime Minister Harutyunyan in 2014, appear to conceive that status in ways that would challenge a traditional view of sovereignty. In sum, the NKR has been effectively run as an informal region of the wider Armenian state, heavily subsidised through the extraction of rents from the wider Armenian political field, while anchoring the legitimacy of Armenia's political elite and fielding a complete bureaucracy symbolising separate sovereignty for international audiences. Isolated and fearful, Karabakh Armenian society has had few levers to rein in bureaucrats well versed in using the rhetoric of security to demobilise the participatory politics in whose name the republic was founded. This raises the question of how democratic the NKR is, and indeed can be, under the circumstances.

A Democratic Republic?

On 22 March 2000 the NKR's de facto president Arkady Ghukasian was the target of a botched assassination attempt. The republic's former defence minister and commander-in-chief, Samvel Babayan, was tried for the crime and sentenced to fourteen years' imprisonment. Babayan, a former car mechanic, had demonstrated military genius during the Karabakh war. But in a struggle characteristic of de facto states, the lingering influence of what some Karabakh residents call 'self-made Napoleons' can be a matter of life or death, not just for civil leaders but for the entire state-building project.[32] As Ghukasian puts it:

> [Babayan] tried to establish a military dictatorship here, to subordinate everything to his will and lay down the law using the army. We either had to stop this process or to forget about independence. If we have any chance of being recognised by the outside world, it is as a democratic state and not a military junta or dictatorship. In this sense, it was a question of life or death.[33]

Ghukasian's emphasis on recognition reflects the evolution of the self-determination claim that took place while he was president. Nina Caspersen likens de facto states to Alice in Wonderland, forever chasing the white rabbit that is the global community of states in the quest for recognition.[34] They are engaged in a constant process of tailoring the appeal of their sovereignty claim to the norms and expectations of the outside world. By the turn of the millennium it was clear that while the outside world had accepted the collapse of the Soviet Union as dissolution, the fragmentation of Soviet successor states was seen differently as secession, activating the protection of territorial integrity. The *uti possidetis juris* ('as you possess') legal norm defending the territorial integrity of successor states took precedence, indicating the limits to nationalist grievance and a corresponding self-determination claim based on identity. The quest for legitimacy consequently moved on.

Catalysed by 'colour revolutions' in Georgia and Ukraine, the first decade of the new millennium saw the peak of Western enthusiasm and receptivity to democratisation in the post-Soviet space. In the region's de facto states nationalist grievance gave way to an emphasis on proven institution-building and democratic progress. In 1998 Freedom House, the Washington-based NGO rating democratic performance across the world, included Nagorny Karabakh for the first time in its Freedom in the World Index. This allowed direct comparison between de facto and parent states. Rated 'partly free' in 2003, Nagorny Karabakh edged ahead of Azerbaijan, rated as 'not free', enabling a justification of secession based on values as well as identity. A rift in values with Azerbaijan, so this argument goes, both precludes reintegration into an authoritarian Azerbaijani state and merits recognition by the outside world. The image of democratic pluralism is consequently 'crucial to the republic's foreign policy'.[35] This is also a depiction of reality that accords with the mass origins of the Karabakh movement:

> The Karabakh movement was first and foremost a political-liberationist movement, headed by politicians and not by field commanders. They only came into politics later ... We are not a failed state like every Western project except Kosovo. This context has proved itself, there is an institutionalised reality here that is worth supporting.[36]

The NKR was founded in 1991 as a parliamentary republic, with an eighty-one-seat legislature dominated by the ARF. Within six months an Azerbaijani offensive had taken control of much of the territory it claimed, precipitating a centralisation of power in August 1992 under a State Defence Committee headed by Robert Kocharian. After the ceasefire in May 1994, the parliament was reduced to a thirty-three-member body and a semi-presidential system. Initially Kocharian was elected president by parliamentary franchise only; in November 1996 he became the republic's first popularly elected president with 89 per cent of the vote. After his transfer to Yerevan, the republic's foreign minister, Arkady Ghukasian, succeeded him as president in 1997, also with 89 per cent of the vote.

By the early 2000s there was evidence of public demand for democratic reform. In a 2002 poll, half of the population (48.7 per cent) believed that the republic was not democratic.[37] Especially for a de facto state founded as a popular movement, legitimacy is a crucial aspect of internal sovereignty. Without this the prevention of disengagement and emigration, and the continual mobilisation of the population necessary to defend the polity, become harder to achieve.[38] Yet what happened came as a shock to authorities and populace alike. According to a local activist in 2005, 'having declared the need for an opposition, the elite lost control of this discourse'.[39] Shortly before municipal elections in August 2004 a new opposition party was founded, Movement-88. In alliance with the ARF, party leader and parliamentarian Eduard Agabekyan won the second round of the mayoral election in Stepanakert with 55.3 per cent of the vote on 22 August 2004. Agabekyan's success would be short-lived: he was accused of embezzlement, hounded by prosecutors and eventually forced to retire from politics for health reasons.[40] He later returned to politics as a campaign manager for oppositional presidential candidates.

Agabekyan's unexpected victory at the municipal level, however, had no analogue at the level of presidential or parliamentary elections. The NKR is in many ways a rather typical example of a post-Soviet 'competitive authoritarian' regime, in which opposition candidates can freely run and campaign, but in which the odds are unfairly stacked against them.[41] As an *unrecognised* competitive authoritarian regime, however, the choreographing of pluralism is seen as an essential component of elections in the republic.[42] The NKR's presidential elections have featured regime-approved local candidates drawn from the networked regime spanning both Yerevan and Stepanakert, who are then 'validated' by the electorate. In 2007 and 2012 this candidate was Bako Sahakyan, a former minister of interior and from 2001 head of the NKR's national security service. Sahakyan enjoyed the same 'administrative resources' – the mobilisation of state employees and premises, and state-controlled media coverage – used by incumbents across the post-Soviet space.[43]

Nevertheless, actors within society have been able to mobilise significant support for candidates beyond the anonymous 'also-rans' required for choreographed pluralism. In 2007 former Deputy Foreign Minister Masis Mayilian decided at the last minute to run for president out of dissatisfaction with the authorities' 'plan for the election'.[44] Mobilising a cross-section of support in a wide campaign, Mayilian secured 12.5 per cent of the vote. More importantly to him, Nagorny Karabakh continued to secure the coveted status of 'partly free' in the Freedom in the World Index.[45] In 2010, however, the absence of opposition in parliamentary elections caused the territory to drop to 'not free'.

Mayilian persuaded Karabakh war veteran Vitaliy Balasanyan to run for president in 2012 in order 'to correct this mistake' and ran his media campaign.[46] Balasanyan secured a substantial 31.5 per cent of the vote, a high oppositional showing for presidential contests in the post-Soviet South Caucasus. Mayilian's and Balasanyan's experiences demonstrate the risks to power of political choreography. Karabakh's formally democratic structures – like the ethno-federal institutions of the Soviet Union before them – have the potential to become subversive institutions challenging networked power. Yet the concept of pluralism that these candidates espouse is not necessarily the same as that of many outside observers. According to Mayilian: 'I don't consider myself an oppositionist so much as an alternative.'[47] Balasanyan is more forthright: 'Armenians should have one party, maximum two. Today there's a hundred-plus parties across Armenia and Karabakh and that's wrong.'[48] These views reflect an ingrained tendency in the NKR towards being a 'garrison state' formally run by a civilian elite but preoccupied with external threats and security. Under less insecure conditions more genuine pluralism would undoubtedly emerge, as it has in other de facto states when security threats have been lifted.[49]

In the NKR's political party system there is a similar dynamic between choreographed pluralism, political conformism and a subdued yet sustained demand for public participation. Party politics is structured by the practical reality that sustaining a party without access to state resources is an option open only to the ARF. This is the only party operating in both Armenia and Karabakh, and is networked with efficient fundraising structures in the Armenian diaspora, a wider connectivity emphasised by its local chapter in Karabakh: 'we should not distinguish Armenia, Nagorny Karabakh and the diaspora: this is one living organism'.[50] Consequently when the ARF is in opposition a certain bipolarity can result between it and the pro-regime party in the NKR's domestic politics. It was through alliance with the ARF that the oppositional Movement-88 was able to win the Stepanakert mayoralty in 2004, and three seats in parliament in 2005–10.[51] But its external connections also make the ARF vulnerable to accusations that it represents 'outside agendas' when in opposition;

moreover, its access to sources of fundraising in the diaspora makes it a highly attractive partner to incumbents.[52] In 2007 the ARF entered a ruling coalition with two local parties associated with elite factions, the Democratic Party of Artsakh (led by Parliamentary Speaker Ashot Gulyan) and Free Motherland (led by Prime Minister Araik Harutyunyan). The stagnation of this set-up led to the absence of opposition in the 2010 parliamentary elections and the loss of the territory's 'partly free' status. This situation was 'rectified' in the 2015 election, in which small opposition parties Movement-88 and Revival secured three mandates.[53]

Civic life in the republic is also severely circumscribed by a near-total absence of resources. There are approximately a hundred NGOs registered in the territory, but informed local estimates suggest that fewer than ten are active. Normative sensitivities result in donor reluctance to fund activities bringing Armenia- and Karabakh-based civil societies together. For Yerevan-based NGOs, it 'is easier to fundraise $1,000 to bring a European here than $300 to bring a Karabakh Armenian'.[54] Six hours away by car from Yerevan, Karabakh civil society remains small and isolated with limited exposure to the constitutional politics of the wider Armenian political field. Isolated even from Yerevan, NGOs in Karabakh are able to secure funding only from the de facto authorities, who in 2014 had a limited budget in the region of $180,000, the diaspora or through internationally funded peacebuilding programmes conceived in terms of conflict resolution.[55] Local media operate without censorship (with the exception of conditions in the army), but have little influence. According to a local journalist:

> You can write what you want, but no one in the elite cares and you cannot change anything. The elite has no fear of moral rebuke or sanction from society. Their attitude, as an old saying has it, is that a dog can bark and the caravan moves on.[56]

Increasing insecurity widened the latitude for the NKR's political elite to diverge from the script of democratisation. Across the post-Soviet space incumbents, including in Armenia and Azerbaijan, have often used the introduction of new constitutions to 'reset', that is prolong, their terms in power. In 2006, nine years into his presidency, Ghukasian introduced the republic's first constitution. Critical speculation that he would use the occasion to extend his presidency was rife.[57] Ghukasian took public measures to distance himself from the idea, giving a press conference on 11 October 2006 and publishing an open letter denying any such intent.[58] A decade later Bako Sahakyan did not face the same limitations. His leadership coincided with Azerbaijan's much-publicised rearmament and a gradient of low-level violence along the Line of Contact escalating sharply in 2014 and culminating in April 2016's 'four-day war'. Similar to Armenia and Azerbaijan, a demobilisation effect was at work: 'there is strong self-censorship here: people know that for one critical comment they could lose their only source of income'.[59] In a February 2017 referendum 87 per cent of the populace approved a new constitution introducing a fully presidential system, and allowing for a largely unremarked continuation of Sahakyan's presidency during a transition period until 2020. He was re-elected through a parliamentary vote (with the approval of twenty-eight of the thirty-two parliamentarians present), opposed by former mayor Eduard Agabekyan.[60]

In sum, over three decades the NKR developed a limited kind of competitive politics finely calibrated to have the necessary impact on international opinion, but never to lead to the possibility of instability. Pluralism was an essential aspect of the NKR's international brand, and public frustration with a corrupt elite could be registered and expressed without hindrance in surprisingly high protest votes. Yet the territory's central role in legitimating Armenia's wider networked regime, in addition to the prevailing conditions of insecurity, constrained local expressions of democracy. In 2018, however, the repercussions of Armenia's Velvet Revolution were not long in reaching Karabakh. Just over a month after the fall of President Sargsyan in Armenia, several senior NKR officials, including former Prime Minister and now State Minister Araik Harutyunyan, resigned after large-scale demonstrations were sparked by a violent incident involving security personnel.[61] Relieving Karabakh of its twenty-year role as the anchor of the Yerevan elite's legitimacy, the Velvet Revolution may remove some of the domestic constraints to the practice – as opposed to mere performance – of pluralism. This may allow the unrecognised republic to reconnect with the popular roots of the movement that brought it into being. In the short to medium term the prevailing security trends will be key. In the longer term, however, desecuritising the NKR's domestic politics confronts the problem of its layered territorial regimes.

New Frontiers, New Communities

The renaming of the republic in 2017 as the Republic of Artsakh removed the ideologically awkward Turco-Persian compound 'Karabakh' from its formal title. It also submerged lingering ambiguities regarding the borders of the NKR. As a result of a series of accretions since the early 1990s, what was once the 4,400 square kilometres of the NKAO in 1988 expanded into the 11,500 square kilometres claimed by the NKR today.[62] The internal rebordering of the NKR has led to a situation where three geographies compete to define Nagorny Karabakh (see Table 8.2). An Azerbaijani geography covers over the boundaries of the former NKAO, while leaving the surrounding occupied regions within their pre-occupation configurations. The fluid and evolving geography of 'augmented Armenia' has submerged both the NKAO and the surrounding occupied regions into the NKR, now renamed Artsakh. Suspended between these rival geographies is an uncertain international geography evoking, by default, Soviet boundaries. International discourse about the conflict refers to the seven occupied regions surrounding Karabakh, and by implication remains committed to the boundaries of the NKAO. The subdued geography of 'compliant Armenia' conforms to this vision, depicting Armenia without Karabakh, but is visible only in negated form in Nagorny Karabakh itself (see Figure 8.1).

Nagorny Karabakh's cartographic absorption of occupied territories has not been matched by a demographic incorporation. As for all of the de facto states in the South Caucasus, population is a hotly contested and largely unverifiable issue. Official data for the overall population, 146,100 in 2016, undoubtedly exaggerate the number of people in the territory by continuing to record the

Table 8.2 Traditions and territorialisations of Nagorny Karabakh, 1991–present

Tradition	Time period	Spatial extent	Political narrative	Associated with
Nagorno-Karabakh Autonomous Oblast (NKAO)	1923–91	Armenian-populated highland areas	Resolution of prior Armenian–Azerbaijani conflict, 1918–20	Soviet Union, 1921–3
Yuxarı Qarabağ (Upper Karabakh)	1991–present	Five districts (*rayonu*): Terter, Kelbajar, Khojaly, Shusha and Khojavend covering highland area	Integral Azerbaijani space	Azerbaijan Republic
Nagorno-Karabakh Republic (NKR; 1991 borders)	1991–4	NKAO plus Shahumyan region to north	Self-determination through democratic referendum	Karabakh movement 1987–91
NKR (1994 borders)	1994–2006	NKAO plus Shahumyan plus seven districts (Lachin, Kelbajar, Qubatly, Cebrayil, Zangilan, Agdam, Fizuli)	Defensible borders behind negotiable 'security zone'	1992–4 Armenian–Azerbaijani war
NKR (2006 borders)	2006–present	All territory behind Line of Contact, rebordered into seven regions (*shrjan*): Shushi, Shahumyan, Mardakert, Askeran, Martuni, Hadrut, Kashatagh; also includes Azerbaijani-controlled Shahumyan and 'fingers' on other side of Line of Contact	De facto statehood	NKR Constitution, 2006
Artsakh	Post-Soviet revival of pre-Christian and medieval geography	Unclear; largely covered by NKR (2006 borders)?	Original Armenian ownership (*prior tempore, prior jure* claim)	Armenian nationalist consensus; Republic of Artsakh Constitution of 2017

Figure 8.1 Rejecting 'compliant Armenia': school classroom wall, Lachin, 2014. Author photo.

registration (*propiska* in Russian) of individuals who in reality live in Armenia or Russia. Local informal estimates of numbers in the territory range from 90,000 to 130,000. Diaspora settlement to Karabakh has been negligible; the much-publicised movement of Syrian Armenians fleeing civil war in the Middle East had by 2014 resulted in the settlement of some thirty families to the territory.[63] De facto officials have few qualms in conceding that in the context of a wider Armenian demographic crisis, the desired level of settlement has not been achieved.

Much has been made in political rhetoric of the incentives extended to settlers willing to locate to the territories occupied during the 1992–4 war.[64] In 2005 a fact-finding mission for the Organization for Security and Co-operation in Europe (OSCE) estimated a total settler population of around 10,000–12,000, most of it concentrated in the regions of Lachin and Kelbajar.[65] As the regions inter-positioned between Armenia and Karabakh, these are critical to a geopolitical project of submerging Karabakh's enclave geography. Within the republic's de facto boundaries they form parts of two larger regions, Kashatagh and Shahumyan respectively. In Kelbajar the OSCE mission came to the conclusion that the authorities 'are unable to proactively create the physical and administrative conditions that would allow for the rapid growth of settlements'.[66] A different situation obtained in Lachin, where a more coherent effort extended incentives to settlers and for them to establish large families. In the mid-2000s settlers in

Lachin reportedly received a start-up disbursement of 25,000 Armenian drams per couple (approximately $70), and a monthly payment of 5,000 Armenian drams (approximately $15) per child.[67] These are hardly generous sums given overall conditions of hardship; local residents also complain that benefits can be difficult to procure, or that child benefits are 'prematurely cut'.[68] Exaggerated for political effect on both sides of the Armenian–Azerbaijani rivalry, settler benefits appear less appealing close up. Demographic consolidation has consequently been elusive. A second OSCE fact-finding mission in 2010 never published its full results, but an executive summary roughly estimated the population of the territories occupied in 1992–4 at 14,000, with 'no significant growth' since 2005.[69] In the early 2010s the official demography of the republic indicated declining or stagnating populations in Shahumyan (stagnant at just under 3,000) and Kashatagh (declining from 9,700 in 2006 to 8,500 in 2012), and extremely low population densities (two and three persons per square kilometre for Shahumyan and Kashatagh regions respectively).[70] In 2016 official data recorded a population just under 14,000 for these two regions.[71]

The overall absence of large-scale settler movements does not mean, however, that significant processes of change are not happening in the occupied territories. Armenian political analyst Alexander Iskandaryan captures the dynamic:

> There were always a few individuals in these territories, homeless people who started scavenging metal fittings or masonry from the ruins there and took them away. Over time this changes to using the land, which they start sowing. Then, for instance in Kelbajar, or Karvajar as the Armenians call it, they are building a road. If there's a road, then there can be tourism. There are several sites in that area that people started to visit, such as the Dadivank monastery, a very ancient Christian site. Then along that road they ship ore that they are mining. If there is a road, then there appears infrastructure along it, and with that comes a sense of Armenian ownership ... The longer it goes on, the more the claim shifts from the metaphysical – this land is Armenian because ancient ancestors lived here – to the physical: this land is Armenian because it's mine, my house stands

on it, I've sown these fields, these are my children and there is their school ...⁷²

Many of those living in these territories are Armenians displaced from other parts of Azerbaijan in 1988–94. Ethnic cleansing has in this way constituted the de facto jurisdiction in Nagorny Karabakh in two ways: its Azerbaijani population, and the Azerbaijani population living in surrounding areas, was ethnically cleansed; its own depleted population was augmented by Armenians ethnically cleansed from metropolitan Azerbaijan.

While communities remain small, they are growing to establish new frontiers within a fluid, aggrandised NKR. According to locals in Lachin, the first human rights organisation in the republic outside of Stepanakert was established here. While older locals still use the Azerbaijani name of Lachin, a new identity as the people of Kashatagh – *kashataghtsi* – is taking hold. According to a local activist:

> This is like a mini-Armenia, everyone comes from somewhere else, from Syria, from Iraq, from Azerbaijan. We have a new beginning here. *Kashataghtsi* is a new identity that can integrate Armenians from across the Middle East. Our children already bear this identity, and our Kashatagh honey is already a brand [in Armenia]. It's a welcoming identity: we can integrate others and be integrated ourselves.[73]

In the less populated Kelbajar development has been slower. Settlers there nevertheless describe a tipping point reached in the late 2000s with increasing numbers of children being born. Numbers remain low: plausible local estimates put the total number of people in Kelbajar in 2013 at 3,000, with 700 in Kelbajar town.[74] The completion of the Vardenis–Mardakert highway that runs across Kelbajar region in 2015 may accelerate development. These communities live a reality far removed from the negotiable categories of the formal peace negotiations. Responses to queries about the possibility of territorial concessions are met – at best – with bemusement. According to another settler: 'For a long time we lived with the belief that we would give back these lands in exchange for some kind of security guarantee.

But it gradually dawned on us that there is no better guarantee than the lands themselves.'[75]

Such views are the norm in the occupied territories, the wild frontier of Armenian nationalism. But over the last decade, the mental incorporation of these territories as inalienable parts of a single augmented Armenian geo-body has accelerated and broadened. In Nagorny Karabakh itself, a growing attachment to the territories as non-negotiable pillars of security and identity has been clear since the mid-2000s. According to Masis Mayilian: 'territorial concessions might make rational or theoretical sense from an armchair in Europe, but when you are in Nagorny Karabakh and you live this reality, it looks and feels very different'.[76] A survey conducted in the republic in 2011 illustrated the popularity of a territorially maximalist definition of the NKR as embracing all areas under Armenian control, in addition to those areas included in the NKR of September 1991 but remaining under Azerbaijani control as of the ceasefire. More than 60 per cent of respondents understood the NKR in these terms; less than 15 per cent saw the Soviet-era boundaries of the NKAO as legitimate.[77] Polls in 2015–16 indicate that 95–96 per cent of respondents in Nagorny Karabakh are opposed to the return of territories to Azerbaijani jurisdiction.[78] But in Armenia in the mid-2000s significant numbers of people could still conceive of the return of occupied territories to Azerbaijani jurisdiction in exchange for a desirable status for Nagorny Karabakh. In a 2004 poll two-thirds of the population of Armenia was willing to envisage territorial concessions as part of an overall deal if Azerbaijan would recognise the NKR (itself a hypothetical outcome, of course). That negotiability was a major casualty of the increased violence along the Line of Contact from 2014. In polls conducted in 2017 this figure had dropped to 8.2 per cent. Conversely, 86.4 per cent were opposed to territorial concessions under any circumstances and supported recognition of Nagorny Karabakh in today's de facto borders.[79]

The NKR is a fluid and in many ways paradoxical entity, juxtaposing tactical sovereignty and the appearance of a separate state with a growing material and symbolic entrenchment within a single Armenian geopolitical space. Its elusiveness also lies, however, in the inability of outsiders to recognise alternatives to a traditional all-or-nothing understanding of sovereignty. The animus driving the republic over its first quarter-century of existence lies somewhere between a self-effacing irredentism and self-determining statehood: a pooled sovereignty with a patron-state that the local population sees as its natural ethno-political home. De facto state-political institutions originally envisaged as temporary have over time solidified into traditions of their own that seek less than full sovereignty but more than unqualified 'annexation'.

If the NKR does indeed seek less than the absolute sovereignty that the de facto state moniker implies, this could point in the direction of creative institutional solutions allowing for more limited expressions of sovereignty. The progressive securitisation of the context surrounding the NKR since the late 2000s led, unfortunately, in the opposite direction: the rallying of frustrated and fearful populations around the strongman politics of networked power and sovereign posturing. Over time attitudes across Nagorny Karabakh and Armenia towards the different territorial regimes that make up the NKR have increasingly converged into non-negotiable commitments to maximalist borders. Inside the republic new forms of nationalism may in the future rival the performative pluralism that has at times conceded heavily to the movement's original demand for public participation. Endowed with the legitimacy of having settled land in a geopolitical culture preoccupied with its loss, it is quite possible that over time settler communities will emerge as significant players in the wider Armenian political field out of all proportion to their size. These incremental, hard-to-trace changes work against the release of the NKR's long-term democratic prospects from the illegitimacy and insecurity associated with occupation. They also have ominous implications for the already nearly three decades-long quest to negotiate an Armenian–Azerbaijani peace, to which the next and final chapter turns.

9 'Land for Peace'

'Can you think of a conflict where the winning party has given up land for a promissory note?' I was in Washington, in the hubbub following the close of an event at a downtown thinktank in 2014. My interlocutor was an activist in one of the Armenian lobbying groups active in the US capital. Her question conceded too much to a victor's outlook, but captured the elusiveness of the 'land for peace' formula widely seen as the key to an Armenian–Azerbaijani peace. Nearly thirty years of diplomacy mediated by the Organization for Security and Co-operation in Europe (OSCE) has yielded only two documents signed by Armenian and Azerbaijani leaders, both brokered by Russia. These are the 12 May 1994 ceasefire, known as the Bishkek Protocol, and the Moscow Declaration of 20 November 2008, a symbolic commitment to a peaceful resolution that subsequent events proved meaningless. Despite continuous dialogue, plentiful peace proposals and intermittent high-level attention from global leaders, the Armenian–Azerbaijani conflict still awaits its peace conference.

Why has mediation failed? The deep dynamics of rivalry explored in previous chapters offer a range of explanations, from overlapping and indivisible geopolitical visions, to the dynamics of hybrid regimes, the strategic parity of truncated asymmetry, the diffusion of international leverage, and the congealing of de facto realities in the territory at the heart of the rivalry. This chapter considers three sets of factors that can loosely be considered intrinsic to the process of mediation itself. They trace a broadly chronological arc from the earliest mediation efforts while hostilities were still ongoing in the 1990s to the present day. The first is the impact of mediator rivalries. The domination of the OSCE's mediation body, the Minsk Group, by three global powers, France, Russia and the United States, which also represent three poles in today's competitive Eurasian geopolitics, accounts for the popularity of geopolitical perspectives in explaining mediation failure, especially in Azerbaijan. As Azerbaijani Deputy Foreign Minister Araz Azimov contends, 'the Minsk Group is an institution that has been used and abused for geopolitical purposes'.[1] Geopolitical perspectives also account for one of the most frequently asked questions about the peace process: whether other mediators could achieve more. There is ample evidence of mediator rivalries hampering early efforts. Yet after the mid-1990s the nexus of external interests in averting another Armenian–Azerbaijani war has resulted in what one former mediator calls 'shockingly good' cooperation between Russian and Western counterparts.[2]

Superseding mediator rivalries from the late 1990s were problems relating to the structure and sequencing of the negotiating agenda. This agenda, already confronting the contradiction between territorial integrity and self-determination, was overlaid by the dramatic outcomes of the 1992–4 war. Most obviously, the occupation by Armenian forces of seven districts surrounding Nagorny Karabakh gave rise to a working distinction between the 'consequences' and 'causes' of conflict. This distinction yields the 'land for peace' formula. Simply put, this proposes that the occupied territories return to Azerbaijani jurisdiction in exchange for an agreed determination of status for Nagorny Karabakh. Between 1997 and 2004 a succession of proposals attempted to manage this equation in a variety of different ways. None succeeded. On the Armenian side a more demanding alternative, 'land for *status*', vies with 'land for peace'. This ties the return of occupied territories to an explicit recognition of Karabakh's secession from Azerbaijan, casting the territories as bargaining chips in a game of geopolitical extortion. This approach never overcame Azerbaijani resistance to territorial fragmentation, and increasingly confronts deepening Armenian attachments over time to 'augmented Armenia' and perceptions of the territories as more existential than collateral in significance.

On the Azerbaijani side, 'land for peace' has been understood in a different way, where 'peace' implies a renewed contract between the Azerbaijani state and the Armenians of Karabakh within the preserved framework of territorial integrity. In the 1990s this accorded with the global hegemony of what is known as the 'liberal peace': an ambitious, interventionist approach seeking to resolve armed conflict across the world through negotiations, third-party mediation, elections and democratisation, the rule of law, protections for human, gender and minority rights, and liberalised market development.[3] Territorial integrity, so this thinking went, would be preserved but qualified by the introduction of a new constitutional settlement including new institutions, such as genuine self-rule for minorities. In other words, for the 'land for peace' equation to work for Azerbaijan, the formula implied 'land for a *liberal* peace'. What appeared to be a statist stance upholding the territorial integrity norm in fact presumed a far-reaching transformation of parent states in accordance with the heady, post-Cold War expectations of a 'third wave' of democratisation and the prescriptions of post-socialist transitology.

The normative assumptions of the liberal peace underpin OSCE mediation to this day. From the late 2000s, however, these assumptions were increasingly overtaken by a third set of problems in the form of illiberal strategies pursued by the parties dissolving the social, cultural and political basis for a liberal Armenian–Azerbaijani peace. Sophisticated formulas attempting to finesse the 'land for peace' equation were eclipsed by the devaluation of liberal-democratic norms and practices in Armenia and Azerbaijan, the accumulated effects of networked regime-building, and the revival of violence. The salience of these strategies transformed the meaning of mediation. Constrained from resolving and not mandated to directly arbitrate, mediation devolved to conflict management. Put simply, mediation became mitigation. Mediation 'failure' is therefore relative: while no agreement has indeed been signed, the process has inhibited violence and maintained a continuous dialogue between Armenia and Azerbaijan.[4]

Fractured Mediations (1991–6)

Mediation initiatives long preceded the termination of hostilities. Interventions by Russian and Kazakh presidents Boris Yeltsin and Nursultan Nazarbayev in September 1991 and by Iran in May 1992 generated commitments by the parties (the Zheleznovodsk and Tehran Communiqués respectively), but were almost immediately overtaken by escalating violence. These initiatives failed because they preceded escalation to war perceived as sufficiently costly for the parties to see mediation as an alternative.

In January and March 1992 respectively Armenia and Azerbaijan acceded to the Conference for Security and Co-operation in Europe (CSCE) and United Nations. After fact-finding missions to the South Caucasus, on 24 March 1992 a special meeting of the CSCE's Council of Ministers mandated a conference to serve as a platform for a negotiated settlement of the Armenian–Azerbaijani conflict, to be held, at the suggestion of the delegate from Belarus, in Minsk. The UN declared its support for the CSCE's initiative, which was historic as the first mediation effort undertaken by a new regional security organisation growing out of the end of the Cold War. Untested, inclusive and founded on the equality of participating states, the CSCE was seen as a credible mediator. It brought both impartiality and ignorance to its mission: as American ambassador to the CSCE John Maresca observed, Western diplomats 'could hardly even discuss [the Armenian–Azerbaijani conflict] because it was so obscure to them'.[5]

The foreign ministers who mandated the Minsk conference in March 1992 did so believing that it would be 'a question of months' before the conference would begin work.[6] Yet military action, unclear interests, rotating chairs and institutional unwieldiness resulted in its indefinite postponement. Armenian–Azerbaijani talks in Rome, Geneva and Stockholm in 1992–3 made little headway; CSCE ceasefire plans fell through in December 1992 and summer 1993.[7] Parallel and competitive Russian efforts, notably those led by Minister of Defence Pavel Grachev, undermined these multilateral initiatives. Wryly depicting himself as a poor relation to Richard Holbrooke, US envoy to the conflict in Bosnia in the 1990s, Maresca recalls:

> I couldn't get the high-level attention from the Russians I wanted, and there was a lot of confusion because there was no single Russia policy. There were two or three policies, depending on whether you were dealing with the Ministry of Defence or the Ministry of Foreign Affairs. I would have meetings with Ministry of Defence people and the Russian co-Chair, my negotiating partner, wasn't allowed in the room because he represented a different policy.[8]

Russia's policies oscillated between pushing for a Russian-led peacekeeping operation under the formal aegis of the Commonwealth of Independent States (CIS) – similar to that introduced into Abkhazia, Georgia – and support for a multilateral CSCE operation. Yet although the Bishkek Protocol, brokered by veteran Russian diplomat Vladimir Kazimirov, commits the parties to 'suggest Parliaments of the CIS member-states to discuss the initiative ... on creating a CIS peacekeeping force', this was never acted upon, largely due to Azerbaijani resistance. The Armenian–Azerbaijani ceasefire of 12 May 1994 emerged as self-regulating, overseen by neither a CSCE-led multilateral nor a Russian-led CIS peacekeeping force. It consequently owed its durability to belligerent exhaustion, not international oversight.

The CSCE's Budapest summit of 5–6 December 1994 solidified the mediation structure. At the summit, the CSCE transformed itself into the Organization for Security and Co-operation in Europe, an ambitious jump in scope and purpose. With regard to the Armenian–Azerbaijani conflict, the summit mandated 'a single coordinated effort' to consist of newly appointed co-Chairs of the still pending Minsk Conference, who would chair the Minsk Group, the collective of states originally designated as participants to the conference, and report to the OSCE's Chairman-in-Office (CiO).[9] The summit also mandated the establishment of a High-Level Planning Group (HLPG), 'to make recommendations on, inter alia, the size and characteristics of the [peacekeeping] force, command and control, logistics, allocation of units and resources, rules of engagement and arrangements with contributing States'.[10]

The co-Chair system replaced the earlier rotating single chair, initially held by Italy then Sweden. A dual system was introduced whereby Russia had a permanent chair and a rotating chair was held by a 'neutral' state (Sweden in 1994, then Finland in 1995–6).[11] This arrangement acknowledged Russia's role while embedding it within a multilateral format. Russian acquiescence reflected a newfound commitment to the OSCE as a regional mechanism balancing the perceived encroachment of Western-led structures, such as NATO's Partnership for Peace, into the post-Soviet space.[12] The addition in 1995 of the onerously titled Personal Representative of the Chairperson-in-Office on the Conflict Dealt with by the OSCE Minsk Conference (PRCiO) completed the OSCE's mediation structure. Since July 1996 Ambassador Andrzej Kasprzyk, of Polish origin, has filled the post of PRCiO; together with five field assistants, he is the OSCE's only field presence.[13] The PRCiO is responsible for monitoring the ceasefire with pre-arranged, bi-monthly inspections, and has played a critical role in, inter alia, crisis communication, prisoner exchanges and facilitating the exchange of human remains in the aftermath of April 2016's 'four-day war'.

The consolidation of the Minsk Group relieved but did not resolve the problem of fractured mediations. Under the Finnish–Russian co-Chairmanship in 1995–6, the Minsk Group held regular meetings. Concurrently a backchannel was opened between presidential envoys Gerard Libaridian and Vafa Guluzade, articulate negotiators with a good personal rapport. At the same time in February 1996 the new Russian Foreign Minister Yevgeny Primakov also circulated a blueprint proposing loose confederal relations monitored by Russian-led peacekeeping operations.[14] Parallel international initiatives were finally reined in through the introduction in January 1997 of a permanent troika of Minsk Group co-Chairs, consisting of Russia, as before, in addition to France and the United States.[15] Carey Cavanaugh, former US co-Chair of the Minsk Group in 1999–2001, explains the virtues of this approach:

> Many countries would dream of having such a negotiating structure. You've got all the major powers at the table . . . If you have a solution,

no single party could implement it on their own: Russia has to be there, it is the only power with the local presence to provide security. But Russia doesn't have the finances nor the international influence with financial organisations like the International Monetary Fund, international NGOs, the donors ... that's where the US comes in, we could provide that. And you need Europe too, that's a geographic and political inevitability, that's where these countries are ultimately headed. So you have the political, military and economic backing for a settlement, and what's more, the endorsement of three members of the United Nations Security Council. You don't get much better than that.[16]

Not all actors see the Minsk Group troika in such a positive light. John Maresca observes that the arrangement 'brought the interests of the co-Chair nations into the mechanism. There were built-in incentives to bring geopolitical interests to the table, and it created disincentives to change the mechanism.'[17] Yet the finalisation of the troika also preceded the most productive era of the Armenian–Azerbaijani peace process. Mediator rivalries faded into the background of an equally complex set of challenges posed by the nature of the negotiations agenda.

Structure and Sequence (1997–2004)

Between 1997 and 2004 Armenian and Azerbaijani leaders discussed a succession of concepts for peace within the framework of the Minsk Group. In variable – sometimes diametrically contrasting – ways, all grappled with a set of problems associated with the structure of the conflict, the issues at stake, and possible sequences of their resolution. None found viable solutions.

A first problem was the structure of the conflict. The Armenian–Azerbaijani conflict confronts all mediation efforts with the contested primacy of territorial integrity and self-determination, and the presence of a non-state actor in the form of the unrecognised Nagorno-Karabakh Republic (NKR). Unlike the four resolutions issued by the United Nations Security Council in 1993, all of which had explicitly highlighted territorial integrity, in its early deliberations the CSCE, then OSCE, had fudged this issue.[18] The 1992 mandate for the Minsk Conference stipulated the participation of 'elected and other representatives' of Nagorny Karabakh as 'interested parties'.[19] This ostensibly covered both the Armenians of Karabakh, and the Karabakh Azerbaijani minority displaced from the territory. However, by 1996 the proliferation of secessionist claims in the former Yugoslavia, heightened international perceptions of the brutality accompanying secessionism, and the transformation of the CSCE into an organisation composed of ethnically diverse states, several of which confronted separatism or outright secessionism, resulted – in combination with an Azerbaijani diplomatic offensive – in a more statist vision of European security at the OSCE's 2–3 December 1996 Lisbon summit. The principle of territorial integrity was explicitly affirmed for Georgia and Moldova.[20] Owing to Armenia's exercise of its veto, a similar commitment to Azerbaijan was relegated to a separate statement by the chairman affirming the territorial integrity of both Armenia and Azerbaijan, self-rule for Karabakh within Azerbaijani borders, and security guarantees for the 'whole population' of Karabakh as the parameters for a solution to the Armenian–Azerbaijani conflict.[21] Azerbaijan considered the Lisbon summit a diplomatic triumph and validation of its position. Its statist emphasis confronted Karabakh Armenians with the prospect that military victory might result in less than independence.[22] But this also flagged the problem of a state-based negotiation of a conflict in which a non-state actor – the NKR – was central.

A second problem was the structure of the issues comprising the negotiation agenda. Negotiators in the mid-1990s defined two agendas: 'military-technical issues', interpreted as addressing the consequences of conflict, and the 'status issue', interpreted as its original cause and concerned with determining the status and rights of Karabakh Armenians.[23] In addition to humanitarian issues shared by all parties, for Azerbaijan the salient consequences of the conflict included the occupation, in whole or in part, of the Azerbaijani regions of Agdam, Fizuli, Jebrayil, Zangelan, Qubatly, Lachin and Kelbajar surrounding the former autonomous oblast. For Armenians, the salient consequences were the blockades maintained by Azerbaijan and Turkey, and the persisting insecurity confronting the NKR as an unrecognised entity in an international environment privileging territorial integrity. An implicit assumption accompanied this division of the negotiation agenda. This was that since Azerbaijan's losses had been greater in terms of territory and internal displacement, its fundamental interests were driven more by consequences than causes, suggesting that it would be tractable on causes in order to undo the consequences of conflict. This assumption underpinned the alternative formula of 'land for status', a hardline variation on 'land for peace'.

This division of the negotiation agenda generated in turn a third problem, namely whether consequences and causes of conflict should be dealt with simultaneously or sequentially. In the parlance of the Armenian–Azerbaijani negotiations, these distinct approaches are popularly labelled 'package' and 'step-by-step' respectively. The package approach implies a one-step, comprehensive agreement on all issues.[24] In theory, this enables trade-offs in which parties 'win' or 'concede' according to the variable importance they accord to individual issues in an over-arching grand bargain. This assumes, however, that the negotiating parties do not privilege the same issue as the most important. The package approach also introduces the element of conditionality, since agreement on one negotiation agenda is contingent on agreement of all. Conversely, the step-by-step approach reduces conditionality by delinking agendas and allowing progress on one independently of agreement on the other. The logic of this approach is that the most intractable issues are 'kicked down the road', allowing trust and confidence to build up through the resolution of lesser issues. The problem here is that implementation of the earlier steps has a direct causal impact on the shape and form that resolution of the more critical issues will eventually take. In the context of the Armenian–Azerbaijani negotiations the critical distinction between these approaches is whether to 'frontload' or 'backload' the issue of Nagorny Karabakh's status.

Three Package Proposals and a Step-by-Step Alternative

Between 1997 and 2001 Armenian and Azerbaijani leaders discussed what were essentially three package plans that – even if vaguely – specified the contours of a final status solution, and one step-by-step concept that only committed the parties to a deferred negotiation of status at a future, unspecified date (see Table 9.1). The three package proposals are the 'package' proposal of May–June 1997, the Russian-inspired 'common state' proposal of November 1998, and the 'territorial swap' concept discussed by Presidents Heydar Aliyev and Robert Kocharian in 1999–2001. These three concepts can loosely be interpreted as resolving the status issue through autonomy, confederalism and secession respectively. Each had a distinct political genealogy.

The Minsk Group co-Chairs elaborated the first package proposal through the early months of 1997, and presented it to the parties in May–June. There is some ambiguity over the labelling of this proposal as a package deal. US diplomat Philip Remler clarifies that the Armenian and Azerbaijani leaderships always understood the proposal as a phased negotiation, in which Agreement I on security issues would be adopted before the negotiation of Agreement II on status issues began.[25] Nevertheless, even if understood as a phased negotiation, the proposal followed closely in the wake of the Lisbon summit and reflected its emphasis on territorial integrity in prescribing a final status for Karabakh. The published text of Agreement II defined Nagorny Karabakh as 'a statal and territorial formation, within the borders of Azerbaijan'.[26] The proposal listed an extensive set of rights consistent with self-government for Nagorny Karabakh and free mobility and migration to Armenia, yet the envisaged status was less than independence. Karabakh Armenians would elect representatives to the Azerbaijani parliament, and hold Azerbaijani passports – albeit specially annotated – and their holders would not be considered foreigners in Armenia. This was, in effect, 'land for a liberal peace', additionally qualified by the fact that as per Agreement II, Armenia would only recognise Azerbaijan's territorial integrity once Karabakh's status had been mutually agreed.[27] Within its 1988 borders, Karabakh would be linked to Armenia

Table 9.1 Armenian–Azerbaijani peace proposals discussed by the Minsk Group, 1997–present

	Period	Approach	Associated with	Status mechanism
Package approach				
Package	May–June 1997	Divide issues into security and status clusters and agree guidelines for both	Minsk Group; back-channel between Vafa Guluzade and Gerard Libaridian	Self-government for Karabakh within Azerbaijan, to be negotiated at a later date after progress on Agreement I
Common state	1998	Confederal	Yevgeny Primakov	Karabakh becomes equal state-forming unit in horizontal arrangement
Territorial swap				
I.	1999	Exchange of territories in grand bargain	Paul Goble; Heydar Aliyev; Robert Kocharian	Karabakh plus corridor transferred to Armenia in exchange for Meghri corridor
II.	2001		Aliyev-Kocharian talks at Key West	Karabakh plus corridor transferred to Armenia in exchange for sovereign right of use of corridor linking mainland Azerbaijan and Nakhichevan
Phased approach				
Step-by-step	September 1997	Address consequences of conflict and defer status	Guluzade-Libaridian; Levon Ter-Petrossian	Deferred until progress on other issues has impact
Hybrid approach				
Madrid (Basic) Principles	2007–present	Agree framework first then comprehensive peace agreement	Prague Process; Elmar Mammadyarov, Vartan Oskanian	Agree status mechanism as part of framework, but defer implementation; interim status until then

via a corridor crossing Lachin, to be leased by Azerbaijan to the OSCE; the other occupied regions would return to Azerbaijani jurisdiction. While Yerevan and Baku conditionally accepted the plan as a basis for negotiations, its guarantees were insufficient to persuade the Karabakh Armenians to accept it.

The second package proposal was the 'common state' plan developed by Russian Foreign Minister Yevgeny Primakov and presented in November 1998. This proposal was not individually tailored for the Armenian–Azerbaijani conflict, but reflected a wider vision of Russian-led conflict management and geopolitical influence in post-Soviet Eurasia:

> Taking into consideration that [globally] two thousand nationalities and peoples live in more than 150 states, one can conclude that the general policy should be to ensure the rights of national minorities in multinational states. This became Russia's guideline. We . . . advanced concrete proposals to safeguard the territorial integrity of Georgia, Azerbaijan, and Moldova while providing wide-ranging rights to such national formations as Abkhazia, Southern Ossetia, Nagorno-Karabakh, and Pridnestrovie within the framework of those states.[28]

The concept had its roots in the short-lived Russian plan of 1996, and before that in the Russian Ministry of Defence's deliberations on wide deployments of Russian-led peacekeeping forces in post-Soviet conflicts. It proposed a loose, confederal arrangement of horizontal relations between two equal state-forming units, Azerbaijan and Nagorny Karabakh. Although emulating the language of earlier Minsk Group proposals, the powers accruing to Nagorny Karabakh were significantly wider, including direct foreign relations and participation with a vague veto power on some issues in Azerbaijan's foreign policy. Azerbaijan was quick to reject the proposal, as 'a recognition of statehood in Karabakh . . . a violation of our territorial integrity and too much of a compromise'.[29]

There is some irony in the fact that the third package proposal, admitting secession as a route to resolution, was that developed by Armenian and Azerbaijani leaders on their own. President Robert Kocharian acceded to the Armenian presidency in 1998, bringing about a situation where a Karabakh native occupied Armenia's top political post and negotiated on behalf of Armenia and Karabakh. President Heydar Aliyev, his health in decline and political succession on his mind, sought to simplify the conflict's legacy to his son. Over sixteen meetings in a two-year period, working 'often alone', the presidents elaborated the Aliyev–Kocharian plan.[30] The evolution of their plan and its details are still shrouded in secrecy and controversy. Unlike previous and later peace plans, no document exists today in the public domain: it was a 'two-man solution' never submitted to wider scrutiny.

The idea of a territorial exchange as a solution had circulated since the beginning of the Armenian–Azerbaijani conflict in 1988. Several external observers, including US State Department analyst Paul Goble, Nobel Prize winner Andrey Sakharov and Turkish President Turgut Özal, had all ventured ideas of this kind.[31] The idea's attractiveness lay in its potential to simultaneously resolve the territorial problems posed by Nagorny Karabakh's enclave and Nakhichevan's exclave status, two geopolitical 'islands' seeking access to their 'mainlands'. Aliyev and Kocharian developed a concept that accepted the post-war status quo, but also saw in it a historic opportunity to permanently disentangle Armenian and Azerbaijani geo-bodies. They discussed the transfer of Nagorny Karabakh to Armenian jurisdiction in exchange for the ceding of a corridor across Armenia's southernmost Meghri region to Azerbaijan. For Azerbaijan, a coveted corridor to Nakhichevan was the quid pro quo for losing Karabakh. No longer divided into mainland and exclave, Azerbaijan would have lost one form of territorial integrity, but gained another. For Armenia, a lost border with Iran was the corresponding quid pro quo for finally legalising possession of Karabakh. The underlying logic was 'land for status', but with a radical twist that included the ceding of de jure Armenian territory as part of the deal. It was the ultimate geopolitical solution, taking a transactional attitude to territorial integrity in quest of a cartographic fix.

An initial iteration of this plan failed due to the shocked reactions of elites when the presidents revealed their plan, and to the devastating impact of political assassinations whose connection to the proposal remains the subject of febrile speculation.

On the Azerbaijani side, three senior Azerbaijani officials, firstly presidential advisor Vafa Guluzade and then Foreign Minister Tofik Zulfuqarov and Presidential Secretary Eldar Namazov, resigned in October 1999 in protest at the ideas under discussion. Guluzade's response, on learning of the plan, was to tell Aliyev: 'You are not a landlord to give away our lands.'[32] Three days later, terrorism interceded when former journalist and political extremist Nairi Hunanyan, his brother and three others broke into the Armenian parliament on 27 October 1999 and shot dead Armenian Prime Minister Vazgen Sargsyan, Parliamentary Speaker Karen Demirchian and six other senior officials. The link between the assassinations and the peace process is much conjectured but unproven. It hinges on the assumption that the assent of war hero and networked strongman Vazgen Sargsyan was crucial to overcoming likely domestic resistance to the plan. Yet there is no evidence that the assassins could have known of his disposition towards the plan, on which accounts in any case vary.[33] Domestic political motives, rather than bringing down a peace plan, may account better for the assassinations, yet the impact was the same: the peace process halted for a year.

The territorial swap plan was revived in 2001 in a second iteration that offered Azerbaijan less. Former Foreign Minister of Armenia Vartan Oskanian explains what was under discussion:

> Karabakh with Lachin was being given to Armenian sovereignty. Paragraph 2 was clear on this point ... and what we were giving in return was sovereign use of the corridor through Armenian territory to link Azerbaijan and Nakhichevan. [There] was the difference between the two sovereignties: sovereign use meant that [Azerbaijani citizens] will cross the Armenian border without any border control, no one could stop them on that road to Nakhichevan ... But you cannot put a gas station on that road because it is not your territory, you just have sovereign use.[34]

These ideas were discussed at talks in Key West, Florida, in April 2001. But no breakthrough ensued, and the peace process lapsed into desuetude. Even without the destabilising effects of political murder, domestic resistance to territorial swap concept

Figure 9.1 Poster-board, Meghri, Armenia, 2015. The legend reads: 'Armenians, Meghri is the door to your home!' Author photo.

was critical. From an Azerbaijani perspective, what was discussed at Key West 'was not even a territorial swap, because we were getting only a corridor'.[35] Even Oskanian concedes that the formula seemed uneven, and expectations that Azerbaijan would withdraw were high. On the Armenian side the conceding of the border with Iran was widely seen as prohibitively costly. Seventeen years later poster-boards in the town of Meghri still declared the region to be the 'door to Armenia' (see Figure 9.1).

The three package proposals are striking in their coverage of the full spectrum of possible outcomes. The logic of the first package proposal, in essence, was a solution consistent with Azerbaijani territorial integrity that compensated Armenians with wide-ranging rights and veto-points precluding – in theory – the imposition of a status not to their satisfaction. Conversely, the territorial swap proposal essentially accorded with the Armenian position and compensated Azerbaijanis with access to Nakhichevan. The common state proposal sought an ambiguous third path of horizontal relations. That none of these three plans were accepted is an indication of the limitations of the package approach, and its promise of trade-offs, when the conflict parties privilege the same issue – the status of Nagorny Karabakh – as the most important. Each package plan demanded of one party or another concessions on this issue that they were not willing to make, which even generously conceived compensation could not indemnify, and which outside powers could not compel them to agree to.

What, then, of the phased approach? After the rejection of the first package plan in August 1997, the Minsk Group held further consultations and presented an updated, 'step-by-step' proposal in September. The essential difference from the first package proposal was the omission of Agreement II issues. Rather than a specified commitment to a status solution, Paragraph XI only committed the parties to further negotiation of the status of Nagorny Karabakh. Several sensitive issues previously explicit in Agreement I of the package proposal, such as the Lachin corridor and displaced community return to Shusha and Shahumyan, were also included in this basket of deferred issues. The plan consequently provided for the return of occupied territories and demilitarisation without an explicit determination of the crucial status issue. This was 'land for a peace subject to further negotiation'. With reservations, Baku accepted the concept. Armenian President Ter-Petrossian's advocacy of this plan, articulated in his article 'War or Peace? Time for Reflection', was rejected by Prime Minister Kocharian and his supporters, who then forced Ter-Petrossian's resignation in February 1998.[36]

The step-by-step proposal is remembered today as a significant moment when Armenian and Azerbaijani leaderships aligned around the same plan as a basis for negotiations, but did little to prepare or advocate for it. It failed for several reasons. First, it still had the shadow of the Lisbon summit hanging over it. The plan was closely associated with – indeed an outgrowth of – the package plan of only a few months before that had offered Karabakh Armenians a status less than independence. Second, the plan effectively entrusted the fate of the Karabakh Armenians to Yerevan, and consequently to President Levon

Ter-Petrossian. His and the Pan-Armenian National Movement's vision of a 'compliant Armenia' was ambivalent on the role of Nagorny Karabakh in a sovereign Armenian state. Moreover, his hold on power had been weakened by allegations of fraud and post-electoral violence at his re-election as president in 1996, accumulating discontent over the economy and corruption, and his own dependence on Kocharian's nationalist legitimacy to stay in power. But perhaps most significantly, the step-by-step plan failed because of the 'promissory note' problem identified at the beginning of this chapter. The NKR leadership saw no reason to concede to a vague 'land for peace' formula – which they saw as leading back to autonomy – when 'land for status' was within reach.[37] The plan contradicted a strategic calculus that Azerbaijan had more to gain from reversing the consequences of the conflict than it had to lose from being tractable on its cause: the status of Karabakh. As Heydar Aliyev's apparent pliability in 1999–2001 subsequently showed, this was not an outlandish calculation. But it proved ultimately untenable because of the under-estimation of the power behind the narratives constituting Azerbaijani geopolitical culture examined in Chapter 2, and an Azerbaijani calculus that the coming power asymmetry with Armenia made concessions on status unnecessary.

Towards a Hybrid Approach: From Proposals to Principles

Following the discarding of the territorial swap concept, talks resumed in the 'Prague Process' from 2002 between presidential envoys, Deputy Foreign Ministers Araz Azimov and Tatul Markaryan. In 2004 Foreign Ministers Vartan Oskanian and Elmar Mammadyarov took up the process and engaged in new ideas. First, they sought to reconcile the package and step-by-step conundrum through a hybrid approach. This envisaged agreement on the mechanism for deciding the final status of Karabakh, but the deferral of its implementation until after the return of the occupied territories and settling of security issues.[38] In other words, the strategy was to frontload agreement on the status determination mechanism, but backload its deployment in the process. Second, rather than setting out elaborated proposals, the foreign ministers sought to agree a framework agreement of basic principles on the basis of which a comprehensive peace agreement would then be developed.

The result of these negotiations was the Basic Principles (informally referred to as the 'Madrid Principles'), presented by the Minsk Group co-Chairs in the Spanish capital in November 2007. The document presented in Madrid constituted a set of fourteen bullet points over two sides of A4, which remain the basis for negotiations to this day.[39] They provide for withdrawals of Armenian forces from the occupied territories (with a distinct timetable for the region of Kelbajar), a corridor 'of an agreed width' between Karabakh and Armenia, a right of return for all displaced persons and the deployment of an international peacekeeping force. Two of the Principles provide for a two-step solution to the question of status. Nagorny Karabakh would receive an interim status, effectively codifying its de facto status of today, until its final legal status is determined in a plebiscite at a time to be further negotiated. Vartan Oskanian explains:

> Interim status plus the prospect of a referendum sometime down the road, for us, was almost tantamount to independence. You have interim [status] until the referendum, and you know the result of the referendum because it is clearly stated that the proportion [of Armenian and Azerbaijani voters respectively] cannot be more than 80:20, so that was guaranteed. We know how the Armenians would vote, so you have interim status which is almost independence and the prospect for self-determination expression through the referendum, the combination was for us independence. That was our face-saving.[40]

In this vision, the Madrid Principles essentially offer an alternative route to consensual secession that the territorial swap proposal had made imaginable, but with a 'softer landing'. The face-saving element for Azerbaijan was that at the moment of signing a framework agreement, the plebiscite would only be a future commitment; territorial integrity, for the moment, would remain intact as other territories returned to Azerbaijani jurisdiction. This is not, however, a vision shared in Azerbaijan, where officials are less sanguine on the face-saving potential of the Madrid Principles. They highlight the problem of signing twice: the Madrid document commits leaders to signing off on the framework, and the subsequent negotiation of a comprehensive agreement within six months. This has significant political implications, as noted by Araz Azimov:

> The adoption of the Madrid Principles as a text would be lauded as a breakthrough, but there is no agreement in the Principles, it would be in a spiral coming out of them. The same problems would extend into the negotiation of a comprehensive peace agreement, they wouldn't end with a framework agreement. The practical effect of accepting the Basic Principles would thus be zero, you wouldn't get territories coming back or people returning to them straight away. But the political impact would be devastating.[41]

Given that the Madrid document stipulates the boundaries, electorate and unlimited nature of status options to be offered in the future plebiscite, its outcome can indeed be seen as a foregone conclusion. Unsurprisingly, there have been multiple working versions of the Principles circulating at different times, or even concurrently, with language suiting one side or the other. What are sometimes referred to as 'updated' Principles refer not to a plebiscite, for example, but to a 'mutually agreed and legally binding expression of will'. The Azerbaijani vision of this vote contrasts sharply with that elucidated above by Vartan Oskanian. As Azimov explains:

> Yes, there will be a vote on status at the end of the process . . . We see interim status as the recognition of [Karabakh Armenians'] status until the determination of their final status within the framework of territorial integrity. It means the legitimation of a local authority, of economic relations, of tourism and so on. Karabakh Azerbaijanis would have the same legal rights, so they too would have some kind of interim status . . . [Karabakh Armenians] have to agree to interim status with police forces, demobilisation of the army they have there, legal security forces. They have to become legalised within our system, not Armenia's.[42]

These perspectives indicate a growing divergence between an Armenian reading of the Madrid Principles in which the referendum is the first principle on which all the others hang, and an Azerbaijani reading in which the referendum is the last principle, the need for which is obviated by the successful enactment of the others.[43] The hybridity of the Madrid Principles thus did not overcome the essential problems of the structure and sequencing of the negotiating agenda:

> We ended up in a situation where there is no document on the table, and what we are arguing today is not the substance of one particular document, but we are arguing about which document should be the basis of our talks.[44]

A determined effort by President Dmitri Medvedev in 2009–12 generated the last occasion when a breakthrough was plausibly anticipated, at a summit in the Russian city of Kazan in June 2011, but was insufficient to secure an agreement on the Principles.[45]

Among mediators there is a sense of inevitability to the ideas contained in the Madrid Principles. As US co-Chair James Warlick noted in a speech at the Carnegie Endowment for International Peace in 2014, 'after each failed round [of negotiations], the building blocks of the next "big idea" were similar to the last time'.[46] This is underscored by the sheer longevity of the Madrid Principles. While other proposals have come and gone in a matter of months, they have lain on the negotiating table for twelve years. Over that extended period, however, the conceptual refinement of the Madrid Principles was gradually eclipsed by a new political logic undermining the very assumptions on which they were based.

Liberal Assumptions, Illiberal Practices

The Madrid Principles, in their provisions for rights, electoral mechanisms, inclusivity and participation, represent a liberal model of conflict resolution. They reflect the core principles of the Helsinki Final Act, and the OSCE's foundational purpose as a regional security organisation in post-Cold War Eurasia. The measures they envisage are increasingly at odds with a normative context evolving over their lifespan, both regionally and globally, challenging liberal norms and practices. Globally, the management of internal conflicts has become a key area of contestation as the United Nations Security Council has been repeatedly deadlocked over appropriate responses to conflicts in Sri Lanka, Sudan, Kosovo, Libya, Syria and Ukraine. The hegemony of the liberal peace as a model 'exporting' conflict resolution norms through democratisation, human rights and liberal governance, has been challenged both theoretically and empirically.[47] Regional hegemons, including Russia and China, openly reject international liberal norms and manage their own internal conflicts through authoritarian alternatives. While the threshold of recognition for new states remains high, the fracturing of global opinion on the secessions of Kosovo and Crimea in particular undermined prior assumptions of a unified, law-bound approach to internal conflicts in Eurasia. These factors have constrained the OSCE's peacebuilding impact.[48] Several of its mediation structures have never in fact been activated, while consensual decision-making has held the organisation hostage. In 2017 the OSCE conceded the closure of its field office in Armenia, its last ground presence in the South Caucasus, due to Azerbaijani objections to its support of demining activities in Armenia.[49]

Beyond these issues, however, the OSCE's commitments to liberal norms of conflict resolution are increasingly at odds with the challenge of non-liberal approaches to conflict. In the 1990s the liberal peace was conceived, like democratisation, as diffusing across a global normative periphery. As was the case for democratic transition, this vision was rapidly understood to be overambitious. Alternative conceptions of 'post-liberal' or 'hybrid' peace subsequently emerged that allowed for combinations of liberal international and local political norms in addressing conflict.[50] Over time, however, it became clear that the liberal peace confronted more than the residual resistance of non-liberal actors. Rather, the problem was the development of a coherent, illiberal alternative that did not seek to adapt, hybridise or cohabit with the norms and practices of a liberal peace, but to manage conflict in ways consistent with the preservation of authoritarian rule. This alternative entails the suppression of armed rebellion through an array of political, social and economic policies, and has been termed 'illiberal peace' or 'authoritarian conflict management'.[51]

In the context of the Armenian–Azerbaijani rivalry this alternative might be called the 'authoritarian conflict strategies' of the parties. These are premised on the idea that liberal peacebuilding cannot arrive at resolutions of the conflict compatible with the continued rule of networked regimes. Authoritarian conflict strategies do not seek to de-escalate or terminate rivalry, but rather to exploit it as a domain for the development, experimentation and deployment of practices embedding existing power hierarchies. They entail the homogenising of political space, the legitimation of the state to the detriment of other actors, and the strengthening of illiberal political and security controls diminishing accountability. Their impact on mediation, and the solutions envisaged in the Madrid Principles in particular, is to dissolve the basis for liberal norms to govern measures such as interim status, the return of displaced communities, inclusive governance and electoral mechanisms, or credible security guarantees. Authoritarian conflict strategies are Janus-faced in that they seek both to contain conflict without recourse to liberal norms, and to exploit it in order to embed illiberal norms in the wider governance of the state. They channel the generalised insecurity of enduring rivalry into a resource for political domination.

This argument comes with important caveats. First, authoritarian conflict strategies do not imply a normative association only with authoritarian regimes. They define a set of practices enacted within specific policy domains related to conflict, and as such can also be enacted by ostensibly democratic states.[52] Israel and Sri Lanka in 2006–8 offer examples of formally democratic states enacting authoritarian practices in specific, conflict-related spaces or issue areas. Such zones of exception beyond democratic oversight are typically unsustainable, however, as they ultimately undermine the wider democratic order. A second caveat is that the underlying logic of authoritarian conflict strategies may vary. In Azerbaijan's case, such strategies are congruent with the wider practices of a hegemonic authoritarian regime. In Armenia's case, they can also be seen as instruments aimed at the consolidation of military victory as an alternative to a peace agreement. The nature of the victory, involving substantial territorial overspill and the growing power asymmetry with Azerbaijan, builds in a dependence on authoritarian conflict strategies in order to sustain a tenuous victor's peace. Finally, I am not arguing that those negotiating on behalf of Armenia and Azerbaijan since the mid-2000s, often with great skill and sophistication, have done so cynically. Indeed, most of their labour has been undone by the impacts of these strategies, which generally serve the interests of the networked regimes to which foreign ministers are not traditionally close.

I examine here three aspects to authoritarian conflict strategies. The first concerns a strategy of control that disables the voice and representation of significant constituencies affected by conflict, prevents dialogue, and produces a singular, hegemonic discourse about the conflict. The second defines a process that I call the communalisation of the narratives, issues at stake, and essence of the conflict, binding people into homogenised, ascriptive identities and silencing other political agendas and conceptions of identity. The third involves the deployment of coercion that transforms the political arena through violence and justifies the strengthening of authoritarian political and security controls.

Control

Liberal models of conflict resolution seek to open up peace processes to diverse stakeholders and, by acknowledging and reconciling opposed views, to legitimate peace through inclusivity. These are the principles on which the OSCE defines its approach to mediation.[53] Authoritarian conflict strategies conversely seek to limit the expression of differing views and the agency of other actors, and to promote a single hegemonic narrative that exclusively legitimates the state.[54]

The strategy of control has been visible first in the narrowing of the negotiating table in the Minsk Group itself. The original mandate for the Minsk Conference, as already noted, specified the participation of 'elected and other representatives' from

Nagorny Karabakh as interested parties. Early Minsk Group talks in 1992–6 took place in this wider format. This not only created concerns for Azerbaijan regarding the tacit recognition of the NKR, but admitted an official platform where Karabakh Armenian grievances could be legitimately raised and expressed. Azerbaijan sought to preclude this through the elaboration of a discursive and political equivalence between the 'two communities of Karabakh', with equal claims to self-determination:

> Our vision is of two communities equally footed, equally provided for and engaged in self-rule, whether bi-communally or separately. I would prefer it to be bi-communally in shared institutions, but if that is not possible then separately. But both should have equal status.[55]

Rancorous argument regarding the status of delegations from Karabakh ensued. Maresca recalls of the Minsk Group's first meeting in 1992: 'after a day of wrangling we found a solution by agreeing that the representatives of the two ethnic population groups from Nagorno Karabakh would be associated with the delegations of Armenia or Azerbaijan'.[56] This wider format ended in 1997 as Azerbaijan successfully leveraged the more statist emphasis of the Lisbon summit, and as former NKR leader Robert Kocharian acceded to the Armenian presidency and negotiated for both Armenia and Karabakh from 1998. Since then the Minsk Group has narrowed to become the near-exclusive preserve of presidents and foreign ministers: 'the presidents refuse any translation by their own staff. We work in English with Aliyev and in Russian with Sargsyan and there are no local interpreters involved. Overall, there are not more than five people involved from both sides.'[57] This format affirms the exclusive legitimacy of the heads of state, emphasises the interstate dimension of the conflict and denies agency to other actors. One Azerbaijani official likens dialogue between Armenians and Azerbaijanis of Karabakh on status and security to talks between Presidents Aliyev and Sargsyan on nuclear disarmament: 'They simply cannot decide on such matters because it is beyond their remit.'[58] According to another Azerbaijani official: 'of course the two communities in Karabakh do not decide anything'.[59] Articulated in this way, the 'communities approach' unravels the initial inclusivity of the Minsk Conference mandate, and deprives constituencies on both sides of a voice in matters relating directly to their own status and security.

Azerbaijan has also sought to delegitimate Karabakh Armenian claims by portraying the conflict solely through the framework of occupation. Official Azerbaijani discourses reject interpretations of the conflict in terms of 'civil war', 'inter-communal violence' or 'self-determination'. Emphasis on Armenia as an occupying power excludes the idea that there are legitimate local grievances in Nagorny Karabakh. By this reading, as several Azerbaijani policy-makers have impressed upon me over the years, there *is* no conflict in Nagorny Karabakh. There are only interfering geopolitical forces, to which only securitised responses are appropriate. Azerbaijan has also sought to map the conflict onto the discourse of the global 'war on terror'. Addressing the United Nations Security Council on 4 May 2012 during Azerbaijan's non-permanent accession to that body, President Ilham Aliyev argued that 'Areas affected by armed conflict – especially territories under foreign military occupation – create conditions conducive to networking between terrorists and those acting in such territories.'[60] Securitising external powers as the source of conflict justifies colossal military spending, the secrecy that enshrouds these flows, and precludes attempts to initiate more liberal policies that could acknowledge local dynamics.

Armenians similarly depict Karabakh Azerbaijanis as illegitimate interlocutors, with whom dialogue is 'a waste of time. We maybe could have discussed this in the 1990s but not now.'[61] In a symmetry of exclusion, de facto officials depict Karabakh Azerbaijanis in much the same way as they are themselves depicted in official Azerbaijani discourse, as an instrument of hostile state power rather than a community with legitimate concerns, grievances and rights: 'we exercise statehood, but Karabakh Azerbaijanis are merely appointees'.[62] When posturing for international audiences, official Karabakh Armenian discourses admit the possibility of Azerbaijani displaced community return. In reality, a strong taboo on any interactions in a 'bi-communal' format reinforces the gradual effacing of the historical presence of Azerbaijanis in Nagorny Karabakh. The liberalism of the Karabakh Armenian self-determination claim thus gazes exclusively outwards. This also entails a denial of the claim of the larger Azerbaijani population internally displaced from the occupied territories surrounding the former oblast. Return to these areas, according to this logic, must be symmetric with the return of Armenian refugees to other parts of Azerbaijan.[63] Through such discursive deflection, displaced populations and the spaces from which they were displaced are homogenised in the service of a chilling equation dictating that all displaced persons must return, or none will.

Authoritarian actors also seek to control the media environment surrounding a conflict, and to suppress alternative sources of information and interpretation contradicting official lines. Since the late 2000s, Azerbaijan has compiled a 'black list' of foreign citizens deemed to have visited Nagorny Karabakh illegally.[64] Since 2010 between 50 and 100 people have been added to the list every year; by February 2018, 707 people appeared on it. Analysis of the professions of those visiting the territory indicates that the list is a highly targeted instrument driven by an awareness of the importance of narrative. Journalists, including bloggers, writers and other media professionals, accounted for just over 30 per cent (215 people). Foreign parliamentarians and those visiting the territory in the capacity of observers of its de facto elections are also a particular focus. The denial of access to seceded territories is a characteristic element of counter-secession strategies, allowing for the ongoing expression of the parent state's claim to the territory. But in 2017 the blacklist hit the headlines when Azerbaijan prosecuted blacklisted Israeli–Russian blogger Aleksandr Lapshin for having visited Nagorny Karabakh, after securing his extradition from Belarus.[65] In what was the first prosecution of its kind, Lapshin was sentenced to three years' imprisonment (he was released three months later).

The blacklist polarises the transmission of alternative narratives about life in Nagorny Karabakh, by leaving it in the hands of those already committed to the territory's Armenian identity or who have little to lose in their relationship with Azerbaijan. The main casualty of this situation is the field of independent knowledge about the territory, and the possibility of triangulating the hegemonic narratives disseminated by the parties with observations from the field. Censorship, moreover, has not been limited to contested territory in Nagorny Karabakh. In 2011 US Ambassador Matthew Bryza to Azerbaijan was denied access to the site of an ancient Armenian cemetery deliberately destroyed at Julfa (Jugha) in Nakhichevan in 2005.[66]

Communalisation

Nationalism has of course been present in different forms since on the onset of the Armenian–Azerbaijani conflict. Communalisation describes a more specific process aimed at homogenising political identities through ahistorical story-telling centred on ethnic identities unqualified by time, place or circumstance:

> The enemy here is mythical, it's not about real people or real agendas. If you look back at the original demands, they were to do with textbooks and TV towers, not this zero sum fight to the death. It's a fight with an imagined enemy, sustained by historical memories.[67]

As we saw in Chapter 5, communalisation is central to demobilisation by framing other kinds of identity positioning as illegitimate.

In Armenia, a communal narrative structured around eternal images of the self and 'the Turk' has vied with a legal-political discourse of self-determination since the onset of the conflict. Militarism, considered by many necessary in order to mobilise sufficient resources in the context of an asymmetric conflict, competed with liberal discourses focused on rights, emancipation and harmonisation with global democratic norms. Growing Line of Contact violence, and April 2016's 'four-day war' in particular, strengthened the hand of the former. In the aftermath of the 'four-day war' figures in Karabakh condemned premature institution-building efforts, calling for an exclusive emphasis on the military.[68] In Armenia, this emphasis took the form of the 'Nation-Army' concept announced by Minister of Defence Vigen Sargsyan in October 2016. According to Sargsyan, the concept envisaged that the 'entire population, not just those who serve in the armed forces, should have many scientific, economic, industrial or other projects related to the army'.[69] Initially manifested as a 1,000-dram levy (around $2.30) on monthly salaries, the concept extended to new recruitment programmes, amendments to arrangements for draft deferral among students, and directing financial and human resources towards the domestic defence industry. Public demand for the eradication of corruption in the army, heightened by Armenian losses in April 2016, was genuine. However, the Nation-Army concept spread into the sphere of 'military-patriotic education', identifying, inter alia, 'the existence of citizens reluctant to protect the country' and the 'tendency to communicate foreign cultural values' as internal threats. This signified for Armenian liberals a wider project in communalised militarism, taking Armenia in the direction of a 'garrison state' peopled by soldiers bound by duty, not citizens endowed with rights.[70] That most Armenian citizens did not share this vision was vividly demonstrated less than two years later in April 2018's Velvet Revolution.

In Azerbaijan, the shift to communalisation was starkly illustrated by the case of Ramil Safarov, an Azerbaijani military officer convicted of the gruesome murder of an Armenian counterpart, Gurgen Markaryan, with an axe at a NATO training seminar in Budapest on 19 February 2004. Sentenced to life imprisonment by a Hungarian court, he was extradited to Azerbaijan in August 2012 where he received a hero's welcome, a presidential pardon and promotion, and financial reward.[71] The Safarov case caused a furore in Armenia; in Azerbaijan, it marked a significant transition from the late 1980s, when those killing Armenians in communal violence were depicted as circumstantial hooligans. In the aftermath of Safarov's return, in January 2013 former parliamentarian and celebrated novelist Akram Aylisli released a draft novella, entitled *Stone Dreams*, set against the backdrop of the anti-Armenian pogrom in Baku in January 1990.[72] Depicting Armenians in an empathetic light, Aylisli was publicly condemned, his books burnt in the street, and a bounty placed on his ear by a member of parliament.[73] Azerbaijani arguments highlighted Safarov's origins in the occupied city of Jebrayil, and the fact that Armenian political culture has similarly lionised terrorists operating in groups such as the Armenian Secret Army for the Liberation of Armenia. Whataboutism is ubiquitous in Armenian–Azerbaijani rhetorics, but in this case ignores the fact that it is Azerbaijanis and not Armenians who seek a future cohabitation. The tragic irony of the Safarov case is the convergence it signified with a much-quoted and criticised comment by Armenian President Robert Kocharian claiming a fundamental 'ethnic incompatibility' between the two nations.[74] Since the late 2000s Azerbaijan has effectively implemented this axiom as policy through a near-total ban on entry into Azerbaijan by any ethnic Armenian – whatever their citizenship – with extremely rare and choreographed exceptions usually relating to political or sporting events. Others, such as Turkish citizen and professional pianist Burak Bedikyan, scheduled to perform at the tenth anniversary party of mobile phone company Azercell in 2006, or Estonian citizen Karina Oganesyan, a local government official in Tallinn and delegation member to a conference in Baku in March 2018, are deported on arrival.[75]

Coercion

A third aspect to Armenian and Azerbaijani authoritarian conflict strategies is coercion. This is a long-term trend with roots in the dynamism of evolving power asymmetry, accelerating in 2014–15 and culminating in the 'four-day war' of April 2016. These destabilising years saw the intensifying collision of two strategies of coercion: the embedding of Armenian deterrence and a gradual shift in Azerbaijan's policy from strategic patience to compellence. Increased Line of Contact violence in 2014–16 effectively suggested 'land for security', a strategy aimed at Armenian territorial concessions in return for basic security, along a revised Line of Contact. This reading of 'land for peace' makes it easy to portray Azerbaijan as the party driving the coercive turn. As Sergey Minasyan observes, 'Deterrence is typically a strategy of preservation, while compellence is a strategy for change.'[76] Yet both deterrence and compellence are strategies of coercion, and indeed the occupation of territory has long been seen as part of an Armenian calculus compelling Azerbaijan to submit to secession.

It can be argued, as many Armenian commentators have, that compellence is unlikely to succeed as a *military* strategy. The dynamic of truncated asymmetry discussed in Chapter 6 offers some support to this view. Yet this conclusion under-estimates the political utility of violence to authoritarian elites confronting domestic political challenges and popular mobilisation. Violence enacted at such times can be targeted just as much against the society in whose name it is committed, as it is against its direct victims.[77] Where such violence succeeds in demobilising domestic challengers and homogenising political space, military objectives may be secondary. The coercive turn culminating in April 2016's explosion of violence gave political cover to a wide range of illiberal outcomes in its aftermath. These included referendums that in different ways secured and prolonged the rule of incumbents in Azerbaijan and Nagorny Karabakh. New military doctrines and legislation were introduced, such as Armenia's Nation-Army concept discussed above, and an Azerbaijani law strengthening presidential authority over other units with men-at-arms, such as the internal ministry troops, border guards and civil defence units under the Ministry of Emergency Situations.[78] Despite slow growth, continual public protest on socio-economic issues and continuing exposés of elite corruption, in 2017 both states increased their military budgets. In Armenia the overhanging security threat was taken to give cover to Serzh Sargsyan's reneging of a prior commitment not to assume the country's 'new' lead post of prime minister. This was a landmark in Armenia's steady regression from its early democratic promise, and was swiftly punished by an outraged citizenry in April 2018.

Authoritarian conflict strategies have provided networked regimes with cover for the indefinite deferral of democratic transition. It is telling that the solution on which Armenian and Azerbaijani leaders have come closest to agreement, the plans for a territorial swap of 1999–2001, avoided any need for transitions to new institutions or power-sharing arrangements challenging the flows of networked power. Authoritarian conflict strategies have also supplied leaders with otherwise scarce connective tissue with reservoirs of genuine popular sentiment, committed to the status quo in the case of Armenians, and unreconciled to it in the case of Azerbaijanis. In this sense, these strategies are hardly 'authoritarian', but benefit from broad-based popular support for illiberal approaches to conflict. In Armenia, the 2018 Velvet Revolution demonstrated the limits to their effectiveness in deflecting the citizen's gaze from the domestic encroachments of an authoritarian state. Yet a central problem confronting the new Armenian leadership was whether Armenia could be liberalised while still upholding the practices of an illiberal peace, or whether only a limited variety of 'garrison democracy', undermined by continued reliance on islands of authoritarian practice to sustain rivalry, was possible.

In conclusion, despite uninterrupted dialogue, myriad peace proposals, the efforts of highly skilled negotiators, the intermittent attention of global leaders, the diversion of economic resources, and the continuing loss of life along the Line of Contact, the parties' positions a quarter-century after the ceasefire on the core issue at stake – Karabakh's political status – remain as implacably opposed today as they were in 1988. This is all the more remarkable given that the same basic components of a solution have been discussed for at least a decade, sometimes two. The Madrid Principles linger on the negotiating table, neither accepted nor rejected, a meta-proposal for peace that serves the sole – if still important – purpose of justifying continued dialogue. This outcome is often interpreted in terms of absence and insufficiency: of political will, preparation of societies, statesmanship, peacebuilding impact, and so on. In this chapter I have argued that mediation failure should be understood not only in terms of the absence of enabling conditions, but in terms of actively pursued strategies dissolving the basis for the liberal peace on which the current mediation approach is based. Rather than the convergence between a liberal peace and democratic transitions that informed thinking about conflict resolution in the 1990s, a dynamic emerged in Armenia and Azerbaijan that was more or less its opposite: stably non-democratic regimes developing in a co-constitutive dynamic with strategies harnessing the context of rivalry to authoritarian power. Control, communalisation and coercion form a coherent model completely at odds with the normative assumptions of a liberal peace based, inter alia, on inclusive negotiations, the acknowledgement and expression of grievances, electoral mechanisms, power-sharing arrangements, and the desecuritisation of politics. They substitute the political earthquakes of compromise with a mythology of irreconcilable difference.

Afterword: Rivalry Unending?

I began thinking about this project in 2013 convinced of the inadequacy of 'frozen conflict' as an analysis of the Armenian–Azerbaijani conflict. Over the following three years a new dynamic of violence, culminating in the major escalation of April 2016, confirmed that conviction. To meet the analytical challenge of this evolving context, this book has argued for a new reading of Armenian–Azerbaijani conflict as an enduring rivalry. While it shares several formative aspects with other conflicts in the former Soviet Union, the Armenian–Azerbaijani rivalry has increasingly more in common with long-term militarised and violence-prone rivalries elsewhere in the world. It shares with the India–Pakistan and Arab–Israeli rivalries features such as territorial contestation, inconclusive strategic interactions, diffusion across fractured regional environments, the involvement of great powers, and nation- and state-building processes under conditions of long-term, competitive militarisation. A key implication is that the Armenian–Azerbaijani enduring rivalry cannot be understood through single-factor analysis. Rather, its persistence needs to be explained by the convergence of international, strategic, domestic and leadership factors.

At the international level, the enduring rivalry framework questions explanations of post-Soviet conflicts extrapolating causalities from the wider state of Eurasian geopolitics. Since their emergence in the early 1990s, understandings of the nature of these conflicts, and the terminology used to describe them, have taken their cues from over-arching scripts of geopolitics in Eurasia. An evolving terminology described conflicts first as residual ('ancient hatreds', 'post-Soviet conflicts') in the aftermath of

Afterword

the Soviet collapse, then as inactive ('frozen conflicts', 'no war, no peace') through the period of relative détente to 2008, and more recently as instrumental ('Putin's frozen conflicts') in the era of confrontation that followed. This study acknowledges the roles of outside actors, above all Russia, in lending Armenia the necessary power to maintain the rivalry despite the growing power asymmetry with Azerbaijan. But the problem with geopolitical and great power-centred explanations is that the Armenian–Azerbaijani rivalry has outlasted several distinct geopolitical conjunctures and regional shocks, including Russian–Western rapprochement in the 1990s, 9/11 and the global 'war on terror', uprisings and civil war in the Middle East from 2011, the Georgian and Ukrainian crises of 2008 and 2014 respectively, and the Russian–Turkish crisis of 2014–16. None of these has been sufficient to alter the configuration of rivalry between Armenia and Azerbaijan.

To explain this, this study has argued that an instrumental or competitive attitude towards the rivalry among outside actors is less important than the peculiar balance of power that it sustains among them. Among Eurasia's conflicts it remains unique in the scale of its diffusion across both regional and global contexts, and as a post-Soviet theatre where an external consensus on preventing escalation has remained solid. Russia, an aspiring regional hegemon and a global entrepreneur of authoritarian conflict management, is embedded within the deep structure of the rivalry because of the power asymmetry. As the only external state with treaty obligations in the event of all-out war, however, Russia is also a key stakeholder in the tactical consensus with Euro-Atlantic partners on deterring renewed Armenian–Azerbaijani war. Yet that consensus appears incapable of conversion into a strategic partnership to bring about positive peace, and would surely be tested if Armenian–Azerbaijani negotiations were to move in the direction of a negotiated agreement – particularly one taking liberal form. The prospects of this are dim, however, owing to the fracturing of the global policy landscape dealing with internal conflicts, and the emergence of authoritarian models of conflict management as a rival to the liberal peace. The liberal peace is in retreat across the world, and across post-communist Eurasia in particular. The Armenian–Azerbaijani rivalry is consequently embedded within a wider regional context where liberal schools of conflict resolution are likely to recede further. The OSCE's Minsk Group, for now, quietly works around these contradictions.

The regional policy landscape towards territorial conflict is highly fractured. There are inconsistent approaches by both Russia, which recognises some – but not other – de facto states as independent states, and the Euro-Atlantic powers, which enact sanctions in support of some parent states – but not others. This inconsistency intersects with the quite distinct projects in hegemonic regionalism pursued by the European Union and the Eurasian Union (EAEU), neither of which appears likely to offer inclusive regional ties capable of influencing the Armenian–Azerbaijani rivalry in the foreseeable future. Europeanisation, once considered plausible as a route to resolving Eurasian conflicts,[1] confronts both a lack of appetite for membership perspectives in either rival and the wider retreat of the liberal peace. The EAEU, meanwhile, comprises a security community of illiberal states invested in authoritarian models of managing conflict that is deeply unsympathetic to territorial revisionism. There is consequently no meta-region or security community bridging the security and normative priorities of both rivals within which the rivalry could be embedded and de-escalated.

Also at the regional level, the absence of connective infrastructure and the truncated power asymmetry are central to the rivalry's persistence. Economic interdependence is a commonly cited variable in reducing conflict between states, by establishing common interests in peace, cross-border flows and stability. The absence of economic relations between Armenia and Azerbaijan is a direct result of the fracturing impacts of the rivalry. Owing to its oil and gas reserves, Azerbaijan enjoys a high level of structural autarchy. Armenia's isolation from regional projects and opportunities for development have in turn driven alternative strategies of dependency on Russia and on remittance communities, again overwhelmingly located in Russia. Yet isolation has never been sufficient to force Armenia to accept the opening of communications and borders as a substitute for its desired political status for Karabakh. Conversely, there are few grounds to convince

Azerbaijan that Armenia would become more politically tractable should its economic isolation lessen. Across the rivalry alternatives to regional trade, whether in the form of petro-dollars, diasporic funds or interstate credits, have been effective in supporting regimes while bypassing societies. This inhibits economic diversification and the development of socio-economic classes and interests autonomously from the state. There is consequently no basis for interdependencies to develop among plural and diversified actors and groups across the rivalry.

The truncated power asymmetry across the rivalry is a critical factor in its persistence. As the parties both understand, especially after April 2016's 'four-day war' did not escalate into a wider conflagration, this dynamic makes the chances of a major war slim. The low-intensity conflict over recent years indicates instead the presence of a stability–instability paradox, whereby major war is unlikely but there is increasing frequency of minor skirmishes and contained escalations. These take place, however, in a context marked by multiple and overlapping deterrents – Armenian and Russian – that have distinct strategic goals and targets. The risks of recursive, low-level violence in this context are high. Yet because of the truncated power asymmetry, neither rival has a logic for concessions. Armenia has developed what is certainly an uneven and unpredictable but still functional deterrent against an Azerbaijani blitzkrieg, diminishing the prospect of an existentially threatening war. Azerbaijan meanwhile continues to see its resource profile and development prospects as leading eventually to an overwhelming preponderance. The truncated asymmetry dynamic has two important implications. The first is Russia's strategic insertion into the rivalry, underscoring the fact that Russia's greatest single source of leverage over Armenia and Azerbaijan is the rivalry between them. The second is that while Azerbaijan's capacity to coerce Armenia outright is limited, for as long as Armenia must devote a substantial share of its resources to the rivalry and shape its geopolitical alliances accordingly, Azerbaijan effectively holds significant veto power over its future.[2]

At the domestic level, it needs to be constantly stated and restated that Armenian–Azerbaijani rivalry is not enduring because of fundamental cultural – still less religious – differences between

Armenians and Azerbaijanis. Rather, this study has sought to contextualise the Armenian–Azerbaijani rivalry against the contingency of the territorial homelands inherited from imperial and Soviet rule. In their Soviet templates Armenian and Azerbaijani homelands generated compelling perceptions of incompleteness that first cultural, then political elites found to be irresistible sources of social capital and power. Territorial unity became a compelling icon of national identity in both Armenian and Azerbaijani geopolitical cultures. But while irredentist ideas were more marginal in Azerbaijani geopolitical culture, they became hegemonic in its Armenian counterpart. The component of irredentism, hardwired into Armenia's political culture by the advent of sovereignty, military victory and the post-war migration of leadership from Nagorny Karabakh to Armenia, embedded a political elite defined by the idea of unification. This entrenched an irredentist ideology within Armenia's domestic politics to an unparalleled degree in any post-Soviet conflict. An imaginary parallel would be the capture of the Russian presidency by natives of Crimea for twenty years. Conversely, rather than the unity of the ethnic nation, it was the integrity of the territorial state that came to define resistance to Armenian irredentism in Azerbaijan.

Historically, states pursuing irredentism as a geopolitical creed have often been punished. For some scholars, indeed, irredentism and self-destructive behaviour go hand in hand.[3] Within Armenian geopolitical culture, however, affective commitments to territorial revisionism are perceived as positive and worthy ideals: the aspiration to self-rule, the right to self-determine, the obligation to prevent genocide, and the desire to overcome the burdens of an exceptionally traumatic twentieth-century history. The unrecognised Nagorno-Karabakh Republic (NKR) is the geopolitical embodiment of these ideals. But as is the case elsewhere in the post-Soviet space, the pursuit of these ideals has also been a 'will-to-power disguised as virtue'.[4] The NKR, particularly in its maximalist boundaries, silently incorporates the same practices of ethnic cleansing and exclusion to which it is also a response. An alternative project, which I have termed 'compliant Armenia', to normalise Armenian geopolitical culture – including through an interrogation of irredentist ideas – was a significant casualty of this will-to-power. In the process Armenia conceded wider concerns over statehood, relations with neighbours and the country's place in the international state system to the politics of sovereignty over a peripheral and contested borderland. Over a quarter-century of rivalry with Azerbaijan deprived Armenia of its early democratic promise, much-needed development as resources were diverted into defence, and the human material of nationhood itself, by exacerbating demographic decline due to migration.

Yet assessments of Armenian irredentism as self-destructive can hardly ignore how Azerbaijan's responses have been a central factor legitimating the continued vitality of 'augmented Armenia' as a construct in Armenian geopolitical culture. The abolition of autonomy in Nagorny Karabakh in November 1991, the serious consideration given by the Azerbaijani leadership to conceding its secession a decade later, the failure to specify an alternative vision of status within Azerbaijani borders, and since the mid-2010s the coercive strategy of compellence have denied conditions of possibility for the Armenian–Azerbaijani cohabitation on which Azerbaijan's formal position rests. These strategies have only consolidated 'augmented Armenia' as a security imperative as well as geopolitical cause. Abundant oil and gas reserves have enabled Azerbaijan to present the façade of a developmental state to the outside world and its own population. Yet having developed as a state that distributes, rather than extracts, resources, Azerbaijan's institutional capacity to accommodate contested politics remains extremely limited. In the medium to long term, as oil and gas reserves decline, the limits to hegemonic authoritarianism at home and compellence as a strategy towards Armenia and Nagorny Karabakh will be reached. A visionary elite and autonomous civil society will be essential if Azerbaijan is to successfully transform itself into a state that can institutionalise political pluralism and an effective peace strategy as a route out of rivalry.

Obstructing these possibilities is the fact that Azerbaijani geopolitical culture has imbibed its adversary's preoccupations with territorial palimpsests, insurgent cartographies and the rhetoric of maps. 'Wide Azerbaijanism' flexes the Azerbaijani geo-body across its Armenian counterpart in its entirety, a retroactive irredentism reciprocating Armenian practices similarly construing

Azerbaijan as a recent and artificial construct. Geopolitical cultures across the rivalry have converged on the ubiquitous conceit of 'lost lands' effaced by an alien geo-body. This relentless and uncritical imagining of places past and present as homogenous ethno-space entails its own effacements, and fails to account for the commingling of Armenian and Azerbaijani communities throughout history. Reproduced in political rhetoric, poetic mythscapes and school textbooks, these ideas belie the emancipatory promise of the territorial paradigm. They drive instead the continuing dominance of a partitioning politics that fails to acknowledge – and reconcile – the mutual embeddedness of Armenian and Azerbaijani spaces and human experiences.

Scripted in the vocabulary of sovereignty and statehood, these ideas provide powerful discourses of nationhood and community driving Armenia's irredentism, Nagorny Karabakh's secessionism and Azerbaijan's counter-irredentism, and legitimate the use of force in pursuing these goals. The question is why elites committed to these incompatible policies were able to capture the policy-making process for so long. This study has argued that domestic institutions, rather than geopolitical forces, provide answers. Authoritarian and hybrid regimes are more likely to escalate symbolic politics, and can more easily manipulate geopolitical cultures and inculcate particular narratives and suppress others among their populations. While there is no single explanation for the durability of authoritarian regimes, rivalry has been a crucial resource in shaping the political arena in ways that constrain proponents of change. It has allowed political elites to diverge from, and then discard, the ideals of increased political participation that many Armenians and Azerbaijanis aspired to, and mobilised for, in the final years of the Soviet Union. Securitised territorial nationalism, fed by the shifting power asymmetry and militarisation, has stood in for other kinds of legitimacy made redundant by the sheer longevity of incumbency. Political elites leveraged compelling storylines, such as the restoration of territorial integrity, the prevention of another genocide, and the empowerment of the army to achieve these goals, that resonated with most citizens – or which many found it difficult to question or refuse – and securitised alternatives.

Afterword

Leadership is thus central to the enduring rivalry framework. This is significant because, unlike Warren Zimmerman's description of the Balkan wars of the 1990s, the Armenian–Azerbaijani *conflict* of 1988–94 is not easily told as 'a story with villains'.[5] But in answering the question of why the Armenian–Azerbaijani *rivalry* has not ended, the role of leadership is much more central. Rivalry is no longer limited to the territorial issues at stake, but also expresses an elite strategy to define the political arena in ways that secure power. Pervasive geopolitical framing, securitised politics and the exploiting of rivalry to quell dissent are witness to the failure of genuine public spaces – real civic *agora* – to emerge as responses to demands for political participation expressed in the late 1980s. Recurrent efforts in the 2010s to reclaim the street as a space for public contestation – even as regimes sought to mobilise ever-increasing numbers of citizens into the disciplining confines of the army – bore witness to this frustrated demand. It is telling that with the exception of demonstrations in the immediate aftermath of the April 2016 violence, Armenian and Azerbaijani protests were not related to the conflict. Their agendas overwhelmingly concerned political participation, social and economic well-being and the protection of rights from the encroachments of networked power. Swept to power by the Armenian street, Nikol Pashinyan's accession to the Armenian leadership in 2018 indicated that the politics of securitisation has limits. In the face of institutional degradation and visible policy failures, it is corrupt officials indefinitely wielding the rhetoric of insecurity that ultimately come to be seen as the gravest threat to public security.

This argument is not to caricature rivalry as an elite fabrication. On the contrary, Armenian and Azerbaijani elites over the last twenty-five years have tapped into deep reservoirs of popular sentiment with considerable success. There is little doubt that the official narrative depicting Armenia as the real source of conflict resonates more powerfully with most Azerbaijanis than a liberal conception of conflict resolution based on territorial autonomy addressing Karabakh Armenian grievances. In Armenia and Karabakh, intergenerational hatred towards 'Turks' to be passed from father to son remains a powerful and ubiquitous cultural schema. But it is an argument that seeks to interrogate the instrumentality of rivalry. With an eye more on incumbency than legacy, the authoritarian conflict strategies of Armenian and Azerbaijani leaderships have committed to the cycle of conflict, and to the principle of personalised, networked power that is ultimately the greatest long-term threat to secure sovereignty and statehood in both states. Especially in Azerbaijan, an ageing networked regime, entering its third continuous decade in office with declining purchasing power, is likely to find growing temptation in rivalry as a strategy of demobilisation. Can democratisation, then, lead to a route out of rivalry? As political scientists warn, democratisation is not a panacea. Transitions to more democratic rule will be fraught as rival factions within each state could attempt to outbid one another as the best defender of ethnic interests. Unilateral, partial, stop-start and hybrid-democratic dynamics, involving an unforeseeable number of variables, could see tensions become more acute. In the long term, however, democratisation offers the prospect that coercion will no longer be seen as a legitimate means to resolve Armenian–Azerbaijani differences. Under those conditions a re-evaluation of possible means to achieving the underlying goals currently pursued through the strategy of coercion will be possible.

The enduring rivalry framework in some ways offers a pessimistic outlook. Neither frozen nor pliable, by the standards of some enduring rivalries, the Armenian–Azerbaijani rivalry may still be relatively 'young'. Yet its apparent imperviousness to surrounding change and resistance to coercive termination also underscore the poverty of interventionist geopolitics and militarism as approaches to its resolution. This points ultimately to the necessity of change from within, enacted through the agency of human communities and creative leadership. The only certainty is that for as long as Armenians and Azerbaijanis do not find a way to rebuild their relations, they will remain vulnerable to the thrall of expansive geopolitical visions, the strongmen who come to control them, and the narrowing of identities and liberties that inevitably follows.

Notes

Introduction

1. The total casualties for the Armenian–Azerbaijani escalation of April 2016 remain a matter of speculation as Azerbaijan treats this data as a state secret. Independent estimates by Azerbaijani media and researchers reach as high as more than ninety. For Armenian figures see *The Armenian Weekly*, 'Report: 165 Armenian Servicemen Died in 2016', 12 January 2017, <https://armenianweekly.com/2017/01/12/report-165-armenian-servicemen-died-in-2016/> (last accessed 3 July 2018). The 'four-day war' is covered in detail in Laurence Broers, *The Nagorny Karabakh Conflict: Defaulting to War* (London: Royal Institute for International Affairs, 2016).
2. This trope headlined an op-ed on an earlier round of Armenian–Azerbaijani skirmishing in August 2014. Brenda Shaffer, 'Russia's Next Land Grab', *The New York Times*, 9 September 2014, <https://www.nytimes.com/2014/09/10/opinion/russias-next-land-grab.html> (last accessed 11 August 2018).
3. Christoph Zürcher, *The Post-Soviet Wars: Rebellion, Ethnic Conflict, and Nationhood in the Caucasus* (New York and London: New York University Press, 2007); Cory D. Welt, 'Explaining Ethnic Conflict in the South Caucasus: Mountainous Karabagh, Abkhazia, and South Ossetia' (PhD dissertation, Massachusetts Institute of Technology, 2004); Georgi M. Derluguian, *Bourdieu's Secret Admirer in the Caucasus* (Chicago and London: University of Chicago Press, 2005); Vicken Cheterian, *War and Peace in the Caucasus: Russia's Troubled Frontier* (London: Hurst, 2008); Emil Souleimanov, *Understanding Ethnopolitical Conflict: Karabakh,*

South Ossetia, and Abkhazia Wars Reconsidered (Basingstoke: Palgrave Macmillan, 2013).
4. Zürcher, *Post-Soviet Wars*, p. 7.
5. The Russian term 'near abroad' (*blizhnee zarubezh'e*) refers to formerly Soviet and now sovereign territories where many Russians feel there is a justified claim for Russia's continued interests and influence. See Gerard Toal, *Near Abroad: Putin, the West and the Contest over Ukraine and the Caucasus* (Oxford: Oxford University Press, 2017), p. 3; Licínia Simão, *The EU's Neighbourhood Policy towards the South Caucasus: Expanding the European Security Community* (New York: Palgrave Macmillan, 2017).
6. Robert Orttung and Christopher Walker, 'Putin's Frozen Conflicts', *Foreign Policy*, 13 February 2015, <http://foreignpolicy.com/2015/02/13/putins-frozen-conflicts/> (last accessed 3 July 2018).
7. Svante E. Cornell, *Small Nations and Great Powers: A Study of Ethnopolitical Conflict in the Caucasus* (London: Curzon, 2001); Jeffrey Mankoff, *Russian Foreign Policy: The Return of Great Power Politics*, 2nd edn (Lanham: Rowman & Littlefield, 2011); Agnia Grigas, *Beyond Crimea: The New Russian Empire* (New Haven and London: Yale University Press, 2016); James J. Coyle, *Russia's Border Wars and Frozen Conflicts* (New York: Palgrave Macmillan, 2017); Emil Aslan Souleimanov, Eduard Abrahamyan and Huseyn Aliyev, 'Unrecognised States as a Means of Coercive Diplomacy? Assessing the Role of Abkhazia and South Ossetia in Russia's Foreign Policy in the South Caucasus', *Southeast European and Black Sea Studies* 18: 1, 2018, pp. 73–86.
8. See, for example, Mark Beissinger, *Nationalist Mobilization and the Collapse of the Soviet State* (Cambridge: Cambridge University Press, 2002), pp. 132–3. Agnia Grigas argues the opposite position to my own when she states: 'Too often each of the post-Soviet frozen conflicts has been treated as a singular case and a product of unique circumstances, with insufficient attention awarded to their similarities and common origins in Russian policies . . .'. Grigas nevertheless concedes that the Armenian–Azerbaijani conflict is an exception to what she terms Russia's 'reimperialization' project. Grigas, *Beyond Crimea*, p. 253.
9. Svante E. Cornell, 'The Armenian–Azerbaijani Conflict and Eurasian Security', in Svante E. Cornell (ed.), *The International Politics of the Armenian–Azerbaijani Conflict: The Original*

'Frozen Conflict' and European Security (New York: Palgrave Macmillan, 2017), p. 16.
10. Gearóid Ó Tuathail, *Critical Geopolitics: The Politics of Writing Global Space* (London: Routledge, 1996); John Agnew, *Geopolitics: Re-visioning World Politics* (London: Routledge, 1998); Klaus Dodds, *Global Geopolitics: A Critical Introduction* (Harlow: Pearson Education, 2005); Gearóid Ó Tuathail, Simon Dalby and Paul Routledge (eds), *The Geopolitics Reader*, 2nd edn (London and New York: Routledge, 2006).
11. Gearóid Ó Tuathail, 'Geopolitical Structures and Geopolitical Cultures: Towards Conceptual Clarity in the Critical Study of Geopolitics', in Lasha Tchantouridze (ed.), *Geopolitical Perspectives on World Politics*, Bison Paper 4 (Winnipeg: Centre for Defence and Security Studies, November 2003), pp. 75–102.
12. Klaus Dodds and David Atkinson (eds), *Geopolitical Traditions: A Century of Geopolitical Thought* (London and New York: Routledge, 2000).
13. Paul F. Diehl and Gary Goertz, *War and Peace in International Rivalry* (Ann Arbor: University of Michigan Press, 2000), p. 44. These authors stipulate six or more militarised disputes over a twenty-year period as the criteria for a rivalry to be considered enduring.
14. Zeev Maoz and Ben D. Mor, *Bound by Struggle: The Strategic Evolution of Enduring International Rivalries* (Ann Arbor: University of Michigan Press, 2002), p. 4; emphasis in original.
15. Laura Weisskopf Bleill, 'Enduring Rivalries', *LASNews*, Fall/Winter 2005–6, <http://www.las.illinois.edu/alumni/magazine/articles/2005/enduringrivalries/> (last accessed 3 July 2018).
16. Diehl and Goertz, *War and Peace*, pp. 50–61.
17. Douglas M. Stinnet and Paul F. Diehl, 'The Path(s) to Rivalry: Behavioral and Structural Explanations of Rivalry Development', *Journal of Politics* 63: 3, 2001, pp. 717–40, p. 718.
18. Stuart Bremer, 'Dangerous Dyads: Conditions Affecting the Likelihood of Interstate War, 1816–1965', *Journal of Conflict Resolution* 36: 2, 1992, pp. 309–41.
19. Jaroslav Tir and Paul F. Diehl, 'Geographic Dimensions of Enduring Rivalries', *Political Geography* 21, 2002, pp. 263–86.
20. Ibid., p. 275.
21. John W. Garver, *Protracted Contest: Sino-Indian Rivalry in the Twentieth Century* (Seattle and London: University of Washington Press, 2001), ch. 3.

22. Agnia Grigas, *Frozen Conflicts: A Toolkit for US Policymakers* (Washington DC: The Atlantic Council, 2016).
23. Many feature in the three documentary films of the *Parts of a Circle* series, and are cited with reference to the relevant film in the notes. Where I have drawn on interview material that does not appear in the films, I refer to the *Parts of a Circle* interview archive. Work to make this archive more widely available is in progress.

Chapter I

1. These quotes come from three prominent accounts of Soviet nationalities policy, respectively: Yuri Slezkine, 'The USSR as a Communal Apartment, or How a Socialist State Promoted Ethnic Particularism', in Geoffrey Eley and Ronald Grigor Suny (eds), *Becoming National* (Oxford: Oxford University Press, 1996), pp. 203–38; Terry Martin, *The Affirmative Action Empire: Nations and Nationalism in the Soviet Union, 1923–1939* (Ithaca and London: Cornell University Press, 2001); Francine Hirsch, *Empire of Nations: Ethnographic Knowledge and the Making of the Soviet Union* (Ithaca: Cornell University Press, 2005).
2. Scholarship on Soviet nationalities policy refers to the group for which a territory was named as its 'titular' nationality, which enjoyed privileged rights within that territory. Hence, Kazakhs were the titular nationality in Kazakhstan, Moldovans in Moldova, and so on.
3. Sabrina P. Ramet, *Nationalism and Federalism in Yugoslavia, 1962–1991*, 2nd edn (Bloomington and Indianapolis: Indiana University Press, 1992), pp. 51–3.
4. Svante E. Cornell, 'Autonomy as a Source of Conflict: Caucasian Conflicts in Theoretical Perspective', *World Politics* 54: 2, 2002, pp. 245–76.
5. Tadeusz Swietochowski, *Russia and Azerbaijan: A Borderland in Transition* (New York: Columbia University Press, 1995), p. vii.
6. Transcaucasia is the translation of the Russian term *Zakavkaz'e*, literally meaning 'on the other side of the Caucasus' and thereby reflecting a Russian gaze upon the Caucasus. I use this term for the period up to 1991, after which I use the less geopolitically loaded term 'South Caucasus'.
7. Vartan Gregorian, 'Minorities of Isfahan: The Armenian

Community of Isfahan', *Iranian Studies* 7: 3–4, 1974, pp. 652–80, pp. 664–5. See also Ina Baghdiantz McCabe, *The Shah's Silk for Europe's Silver: The Eurasian Trade of the Julfa Armenians in Safavid Iran and India (1530–1750)* (Atlanta: Scholars Press, 1999), ch. 2.
8. Audrey L. Altstadt, *The Azerbaijani Turks: Power and Identity under Russian Rule* (Stanford: Hoover Institution Press, 1992), ch. 3; Aydin Balayev, *Azerbaydzhanskaya Natsiya: osnovnye etapy stanovleniya na rubezhe XIX–XX vv.* (Moscow: Tirazhi.Ru, 2012), pp. 110–30.
9. Tadeusz Swietochowski, *Russian Azerbaijan, 1905–1920: The Shaping of National Identity in a Muslim Community* (Cambridge: Cambridge University Press, 1985), pp. 38–45; Leslie Sargent, 'The "Armeno-Tatar War" in the South Caucasus, 1905–1906: Multiple Causes, Interpreted Meanings', *Ab Imperio* 4, 2010, pp. 143–69.
10. Ronald Grigor Suny, *The Baku Commune, 1917–1918: Class and Nationality in the Russian Revolution* (Princeton: Princeton University Press, 1972).
11. Swietochowski, *Russian Azerbaijan*, pp. 112–40; Michael G. Smith, 'Power and Violence in the Russian Revolution: The March Events and Baku Commune of 1918', *Russian History* 41, 2014, pp. 197–210. For local perspectives see Hranush Kharatyan, 'Opyt Proshlogo', in Grisha Oganezov and Hranush Kharatyan, *Samooborona armyan Kirovabada v 1988–1989 gg. glazami ochevidtsev* (Yerevan: Gitutyun, 2014), pp. 53–80; Solmaz Rustamova-Togidi, *Mart 1918 g. Baku. Azerbaydzhanskie pogromy v dokumentakh* (Baku: Ministry of National Security, 2009); Aydin Balayev, *Azerbaydzhanskoe Natsional'noe Dvizhenie v 1917–1918 gg.* (Baku: Elm, 1998), pp. 163–81.
12. Numbers are contested between Armenian and Azerbaijani historians. Contemporary Armenian sources put the number of victims at around 3,000; contemporary Azerbaijani sources and post-Soviet Azerbaijani scholarship estimate 12,000. See the discussion in Kharatyan, 'Opyt proshlogo', p. 58, and Smith, reporting on recent Azerbaijani scholarship, 'Power and Violence', pp. 204–5.
13. The memory of early twentieth-century violence was preserved in contemporary texts occluded from Soviet historiography. Many enjoyed a new lease of life in the aftermath of 1990s violence. They include Zare Melik-Shahnazarov, *Zapiski Karabakhskogo Soldata* (Moscow: n.p., 1995); Mammad Said Ordubadi, *Years of Blood*,

republished by the European Azerbaijani Society (Reading: Ithaca Press, 2011); Bakhshi Ishkhanian, *Velikie uzhasy goroda Baku* (Tiflis: n.p., 1920).

14. Jamil Hasanli, *The Sovietization of Azerbaijan: The South Caucasus in the Triangle of Russia, Turkey, and Iran, 1920–1922* (Salt Lake City: University of Utah Press, 2018), ch. 5.
15. According to the 1926 census, Azerbaijanis (referred to as *tyurki*) comprised 8.7 per cent of the ArmSSR's population. Armenians comprised 12.4 per cent of the AzSSR's population; Russians would outnumber them for most of the following decades until the late 1970s, when Armenians again became Azerbaijan's largest minority by a small margin.
16. Arsène Saparov, *From Conflict to Autonomy in the Caucasus: The Soviet Union and the Making of Abkhazia, South Ossetia and Nagorno Karabakh* (London and New York: Routledge, 2015), ch. 4.
17. Ibid., p. 173. For a different view see Hasanli, *Sovietization of Azerbaijan*, pp. 146–57.
18. Saparov, *From Conflict to Autonomy*, p. 123.
19. See Gerard Libaridian (ed.), *The Karabagh File: Documents and Facts on the Question of Mountainous Karabagh 1918–1988* (Cambridge: Zoryan Institute, 1988).
20. Cory Welt makes this argument, highlighting that unusually among smaller autonomous groups in the Soviet Union, Karabakh Armenians and Abkhazians were 'status losers': they had had, or had at one point been promised by Soviet founders, a more valuable status. Cory D. Welt, 'Explaining Ethnic Conflict in the South Caucasus: Mountainous Karabagh, Abkhazia and South Ossetia' (PhD dissertation, Massachusetts Institute of Technology, 2004), pp. 247–8.
21. Several Soviet autonomies, such as the autonomous republics of Dagestan (Russia) and Crimea (Ukraine), and the autonomous oblast of Gorno-Badakhshan (Tajikistan), connoted geographic rather than ethnographic spaces.
22. Saparov, *From Conflict to Autonomy*, p. 162.
23. *Zakon Azerbaydzhanskoy Sovetskoy Sotsialisticheskoy Respubliki o Nagorno-Karabakhskoy Avtonomnoy Oblasti* (Baku: Azerbaijan State Publishing House, 1981), pp. 49–50.
24. Saparov, *From Conflict to Autonomy*, p. 158.
25. V. B. Arutyunyan, *Sobytiya v Nagornom Karabakhe. Khronika, Chast' 1* (Yerevan: Armenian Academy of Sciences, 1990), p. 26.

26. Ibid.
27. Mark Beissinger, *Nationalist Mobilization and the Collapse of the Soviet State* (Cambridge: Cambridge University Press, 2002), pp. 27–34.
28. One is alleged to have been killed by an Azerbaijani policeman, rather than local Armenians. Thomas de Waal, *Black Garden: Armenia and Azerbaijan through Peace and War*, 2nd edn (New York: New York University Press, 2013), p. 16; Tatul Hakobyan, *Karabakh Diary: Green and Black* (Antelias: n.p., 2010), pp. 27–8.
29. De Waal, *Black Garden*, pp. 68–73.
30. The politically charged atmosphere inside the court rooms during the Sumgait trials is captured in a chronicle of a Moscow trial written by a Russian Armenian translator: Pavel Gevorkyan, *Diary of Court Trial: The Case of the Crimes Committed against the Armenian Population in Sumgait (Azerbaijan)* (Yerevan: VMV Print, 2013).
31. On these see Mark Malkasian, *'Gha-ra-bagh!' The Emergence of the National Democratic Movement in Armenia* (Detroit: Wayne State University Press, 1996); Rasim Agaev and Zardusht Alizade, *Azerbaydzhan. Konets Vtoroy Respubliki* (Moscow: Granitsa, 2006).
32. Christoph Zürcher, *The Post-Soviet Wars: Rebellion, Ethnic Conflict, and Nationhood in the Caucasus* (New York and London: New York University Press, 2007), pp. 3, 171.
33. De Waal, *Black Garden*, pp. 108–24; Hakobyan, *Karabakh Diary*, pp. 93–9.
34. Barry R. Posen, 'The Security Dilemma and Ethnic Conflict', *Survival* 35: 1, 1993, pp. 27–47.
35. Karabakh Armenians note that the NKAO had in fact ceased to meaningfully exist considerably earlier with the imposition of direct rule from Moscow from mid-1988.
36. Stuart J. Kaufman, *Modern Hatreds: The Symbolic Politics of Ethnic War* (Ithaca and London: Cornell University Press, 2001), p. 9.
37. Aleksandr Lebed', *Za derzhavu obidno* (Moscow: Moskovskaya Pravda, 1995), p. 219.
38. Ibid., p. 218.
39. Samuel Shahmuratian (ed.), *The Sumgait Tragedy*, vol. 1 (New Rochelle and Cambridge, MA: Aristide Caratzas and the Zoryan Institute, 1990), pp. 146, 156, 164, 166, 169, 188, 199, 223–5, 247, 278.

40. Ibid.; Arif Yunusov, 'Pogromy v Armenii v 1988–1989 godakh', *Ekspress Khronika* 9, 26 February 1991, p. 5.
41. Oganezov and Kharatyan, *Samooborona armyan Kirovabada*, p. 7.
42. De Waal, *Black Garden*, p. 157.
43. Kaufman, *Modern Hatreds*, p. 82.
44. Agaev and Alizade, *Konets Vtoroy Respubliki*, p. 271.
45. Ibid., pp. 92–3.
46. Ibid., pp. 113–17.
47. Today the official Azerbaijani death toll at Khojaly is 613. Contemporary international media reporting and human rights reports on the massacre are collated in Taleh Baghiyev, Taleh Heydarov, Fiona Maclachlan and Ian Peart (eds), *Khojaly Witness of a War Crime: Armenia in the Dock* (Reading: Ithaca Press, 2014). Reporter Thomas Goltz arrived in Khojaly within hours of the massacre and provides a vivid account in *Azerbaijan Diary: A Rogue Reporter's Adventures in an Oil-Rich, War-Torn, Post-Soviet Republic* (Armonk, NY and London: M.E. Sharpe, 1998), pp. 117–30.
48. Goltz, *Azerbaijan Diary*, pp. 132–9.
49. Ibid., pp. 356–65.
50. Armenian occupation of Agdam and Fizuli is partial: three-quarters of Agdam and around a third of Fizuli are under Armenian control. See the calculations in de Waal, *Black Garden*, p. 328.
51. See ibid., pp. 250–1.
52. In January 2014, the Azerbaijani authorities released the first official but still incomplete data on combatant deaths in the 1991–4 war, listing 11,557 fatalities. The Armenian figures stand at approximately 7,000 combatant and 1,260 civilian deaths. In December 2015 the International Committee of the Red Cross (ICRC) presented an updated list of 4,496 persons reported missing during the conflict by its delegations in Armenia, Azerbaijan and Nagorny Karabakh. These figures indicate that an overall death count of 25,000 is a broadly accurate if probably conservative figure, as Azerbaijani civilian deaths are uncertain and combatant data is incomplete. *Azatutyun.am*, 'Baku Reports Karabakh Death Toll', 13 January 2014, <http://www.azatutyun.am/a/25228960.html> (last accessed 3 July 2018); ICRC, 'Nagorny Karabakh: ICRC Submits Updated List of Missing Persons', press release, 15 December 2015, <http://www.icrc.org/en/document/nagorny-k

arabakh-icrc-submits-updated-list-missing-persons> (last accessed 3 July 2018).
53. Zürcher, *Post-Soviet Wars*, p. 167.
54. As argued in a compelling account by V. P. Gagnon Jr., *The Myth of Ethnic War: Serbia and Croatia in the 1990s* (Ithaca and London: Cornell University Press, 2004).
55. Robert D. Kaplan, *Balkan Ghosts: A Journey through History* (New York: St. Martin's Press, 1993).
56. Viktor A. Shnirelman, *The Value of the Past: Myths, Identity and Politics in Transcaucasia*, Senri Ethnological Studies 57 (Osaka: National Museum of Ethnology, 2001).
57. Martin, *Affirmative Action Empire*, p. 461.
58. Shnirelman, *Value of the Past*, p. 12.
59. De Waal, *Black Garden*, pp. 156–7.
60. Kaufman, *Modern Hatreds*, p. 32.
61. De Waal, *Black Garden*, pp. 312–16.
62. See Nora Dudwick, 'Memory, Identity and Politics in Armenia' (PhD dissertation, University of Pennsylvania, 1994), pp. 345–66; Joseph Harrison King, 'The (Un)making of Soviet Kirovabad: Pogroms and the End of the "Friendship of Peoples" in Azerbaijan' (MA thesis, Central European University, 2015), pp. 44–50; Kharatyan, 'Opyt Proshlogo', pp. 44–5.
63. The Armenian word Ֆեդայի (*fedayi*) derives from the Arabic فدائيون† (*fidā'īyīn*), and literally means 'those who sacrifice'. The adjectival form is Ֆեդային (*fedayin*). In Armenian the term has positive connotations proximate to those conveyed by the English term 'freedom fighter'; the term could also be translated as 'militant', 'militia' or 'guerrilla'. Personal communication, Sossie Kasbarian, December 2017.
64. Rauf Garagezov, *Kollektivnaya Pamyat': kak sozdayutsya, sokhranyayutsya i vosproizvodyatsya kollektivnye predstavleniya o proshlom* (Baku: Elm, 2013), pp. 157–65.
65. As recounted by Adalet Tahirzade, *Meydan: 4 il 4 ay* (Baku: Ay-Ulduz, 1997).
66. Gerard Toal (Gearóid Ó Tuathail) and Carl T. Dahlman, *Bosnia Remade: Ethnic Cleansing and its Reversal* (Oxford: Oxford University Press, 2011), p. 38.
67. Oganezov and Kharatyan, *Samooborona armyan Kirovabada*, p. 27.
68. Author's field observations, Armenia and Azerbaijan, 2013–15.
69. Oganezov and Kharatyan, *Samooborona armyan Kirovabada*, p. 109.

70. Beissinger, *Nationalist Mobilization*, pp. 21, 451–7.
71. Lee Ann Fujii, *Killing Neighbors: Webs of Violence in Rwanda* (Ithaca and London: Cornell University Press, 2009), p. 19.
72. King, 'The (Un)making of Soviet Kirovabad', p. 71.
73. Ibid., p. 29.

Chapter 2

1. 'Zayavlyayu vo vseuslyshanie: unichtozheniya ili nasil'stvennogo vyseleniya armyan v Artsakhe ne budet. My ne dopustim novogo Genotsida – Serzh Sargsyan', *Tert.am*, 24 April 2016, <http://www.tert.am/ru/news/2016/04/24/serj-sargsyan/1999856> (last accessed 4 July 2018).
2. Author's interview, Baku, 20 February 2015.
3. Ernest Gellner, *Nations and Nationalism* (Oxford: Blackwell, 1983), p. 1.
4. Thongchai Winichakul, *Siam Mapped: A History of the Geo-body of a Nation* (Chiang Mai: Silkworm Books, 1994), p. 17.
5. Tadeusz Swietochowski, *Russia and Azerbaijan: A Borderland in Transition* (New York: Columbia University Press, 1995), pp. 53–4.
6. On these see Tadeusz Swietochowski, *Russian Azerbaijan, 1905–1920: The Shaping of National Identity in a Muslim Community* (Cambridge: Cambridge University Press, 1985), pp. 56–75; Brenda Shaffer, *Borders and Brethren: Iran and the Challenge of Azerbaijani Identity* (Cambridge, MA and London: MIT Press, 2002), ch. 1; Aydin Balayev, *Azerbaydzhanskaya Natsiya: osnovnye etapy stanovleniya na rubezhe XIX–XX vv.* (Moscow: Tirazhi.Ru, 2012), ch. 3; Jamil Hasanli, *Ali Mardan-bek Topchibashev: Zhizn' za ideyu* (Moscow: Flint/Nauka, 2014).
7. Aydin Balayev, *Azerbaydzhanskoe natsional'noe dvizhenie v 1917–1918 gg.* (Baku: Elm, 1998), ch. 2; Balayev, *Azerbaydzhanskaya Natsiya*, p. 307; Swietochowski, *Russian Azerbaijan*, p. 93.
8. Aydin Balayev, *Mamed Emin Rasulzade 1884–1955: Politicheskiy Portret* (Baku: KitabKlubu.org, 2014).
9. The first articulations of a cultural Azerbaijani identity are usually attributed to articles published in the local *Kaspiy* and *Kashkul* newspapers in 1891, but Audrey Altstadt finds an earlier reference to the 'Tatar-Azerbaijani language' dating from 1861. Over subsequent decades the local vernacular was increasingly referred to

as 'Türki-Azerbaijan'. See Balayev, *Azerbaydzhanskaya Natsiya*, pp. 161–3; Audrey L. Altstadt, *The Politics of Culture in Soviet Azerbaijan, 1920–40* (London and New York: Routledge, 2016), pp. 13–14.
10. Swietochowski, *Russian Azerbaijan*, p. 155.
11. Swietochowski, *Russia and Azerbaijan*, p. 69; Balayev, *Azerbaydzhanskaya natsiya*, pp. 337–8.
12. Harun Yilmaz, 'The Soviet Union and the Construction of Azerbaijani National Identity in the 1930s', *Iranian Studies* 46: 4, 2013, pp. 511–33, p. 515.
13. According to senior Azerbaijani communist Sultan Majid Afandiyev, speaking at the Congress of the Peoples of the East on 2 September 1920. John Riddell (ed.), *To See the Dawn: Baku, 1920 – First Congress of the Peoples of the East* (New York: Pathfinder, 1993), p. 99.
14. Altstadt, *Politics of Culture*, pp. 72–7.
15. Azerbaijani and Armenian historiographies offer divergent narratives of this period in Karabakh and in particular the nature of the agreement reached with the Karabakh Armenian population. See Jamil Hasanli, 'Azerbaijani Diplomacy and Karabakh: From the Kurekchay Treaty to the Bolshevik Occupation', *Istoriya Diplomatii Azerbaydzhanskoy Respubliki*, vol. II (Moscow: Flinta/Nauka, 2013), pp. 169–76; V. A. Mikaelyan, *Nagornyy Karabakh v 1918–1923 gg.* (Yerevan: Armenian Academy of Sciences, 1992).
16. According to Azerbaijani historian Jamil Hasanli, the territories of the ADR constituted 97,298 square kilometres. This expanded to 113,896 square kilometres if wider Azerbaijani territorial claims were included. The AzSSR covered 86,600 square kilometres. Hasanli, *Istoriya Diplomatii Azerbaydzhanskoy Respubliki*, p. 177.
17. Tadeusz Swietochowski estimates that 29,000 of 70,000 fatalities in Azerbaijan's Great Terror were intelligentsia members, charged with pan-Turkism, pan-Islamism and Musavatism. Swietochowski, *Russia and Azerbaijan*, p. 127.
18. Yilmaz, 'Soviet Union and the Construction of Azerbaijani National Identity', pp. 528–9.
19. On the Soviet Union's wider deployment of the 'Piedmont principle' see Terry Martin, *The Affirmative Action Empire: Nations and Nationalism in the Soviet Union, 1923–1939* (Ithaca and London: Cornell University Press, 2001), pp. 8–9.

20. Yilmaz, 'Soviet Union and the Construction of Azerbaijani National Identity', pp. 517–21.
21. On Azerbaijani language reforms and their impacts over the twentieth century see Aydin Balayev, *Etnoyazykovye protsessy v Azerbaydzhane v XIX–XX vv.* (Baku: Nurlar, 2005); Lynley Hatcher, 'Script Change in Azerbaijan: Acts of Identity', *International Journal of the Sociology of Language* 192, 2008, pp. 105–16; Altstadt, *Politics of Culture*, pp. 64–72, 85–8.
22. On *kasraviyya* and expressions of integrative nationalism in Pahlavi Iran see Ervand Abrahamian, *Iran between Two Revolutions* (Princeton: Princeton University Press, 1982) pp. 125, 218–20; Shaffer, *Borders and Brethren*, pp. 50–2; Touraj Atabaki, *Azerbaijan: Ethnicity and Autonomy in Twentieth-Century Iran* (London and New York: British Academic Press, 1993), pp. 55–85.
23. Charles King, *The Moldovans: Romania, Russia, and the Politics of Culture* (Stanford: Hoover Institution Press, 2000), p. 91.
24. Azerbaijani historian Jamil Hasanli emphasises the role of indigenous factors in his *SSSR-Iran: Azerbaydzhanskiy krizis i nachalo kholodnoy voyny (1941–1946 gg.)* (Moscow: Geroy Otechestva, 2006). For an account stressing the non-indigenous character of the PGA see Atabaki, *Azerbaijan: Ethnicity and Autonomy*. Louise Fawcett reviews the key contested issues in the light of new research, including Soviet archival sources, in 'Revisiting the Iranian Crisis of 1946: How Much More Do We Know?', *Iranian Studies* 47: 3, 2014, pp. 379–99.
25. Swietochowski, *Russia and Azerbaijan*, p. 162.
26. Hasanli, *SSSR-Iran: Azerbaydzhanskiy krizis*, pp. 23–6.
27. Shaffer, *Borders and Brethren*, pp. 104–9.
28. On this process in Azerbaijan see Viktor A. Shnirelman, *The Value of the Past: Myths, Identity and Politics in Transcaucasia*, Senri Ethnological Studies 57 (Osaka: National Museum of Ethnology, 2001), chs 10–12.
29. Ibid., pp. 116–71.
30. Ibid., pp. 127–46.
31. Author's interview with Adalet Tahirzade, former deputy minister for education 1992–3 and press secretary to Abulfaz Elchibey, Baku, 1 June 2014.
32. Abulfaz Elchibey, 'Beşinci söhbət. Bütöv Azərbaycanla baghli düşüncələr', in Adalet Tahirzade, *Qurtuluş və Bütövük Yolu* (Baku: Elçibəy kitabxanası nəşriyyatı, 2003), pp. 186–7.
33. Interview Tahirzade.

34. Balayev, *Etnoyazykovye protsessy*, pp. 232–3.
35. Shaffer, *Borders and Brethren*, p. 201.
36. Ibid., pp. 178–9; Gilles Riaux, 'La radicalisation, une résultante de strategies de demarcation: la cause azerbaïdjanaise en Iran dans les années 2000', *Lien social et Politiques* 68, 2012, pp. 231–46.
37. On these fissures see David Laitin's 'most favoured lord' model of elite incorporation. David Laitin, *Identity in Formation: The Russian-Speaking Populations in the Near Abroad* (Ithaca and London: Cornell University Press, 1998), pp. 60–1.
38. Shaffer, *Borders and Brethren*, p. 202.
39. Cameron S. Brown, 'Wanting to Have Their Cake and Their Neighbor's Too: Azerbaijani Attitudes towards Karabakh and Iranian Azerbaijan', *Middle East Journal* 58: 4, 2004, pp. 576–96, pp. 590–2.
40. Razmik Panossian, *The Armenians: From Kings and Priests to Merchants and Commissars* (London: Hurst, 2006), pp. 130–1.
41. Ibid., ch. 4.
42. Ronald Grigor Suny, *'They Can Live in the Desert but Nowhere Else': A History of the Armenian Genocide* (Princeton: Princeton University Press, 2015), pp. 37–40.
43. On this contrast see Gerard J. Libaridian, 'What Was Revolutionary about Armenian Revolutionary Parties in the Ottoman Empire?', in Ronald Grigor Suny and Fatma Müge Göçek (eds), *A Question of Genocide: Armenians and Turks at the End of the Ottoman Empire* (Oxford: Oxford University Press, 2011), pp. 94–5.
44. On the problem of Ottoman demography vis-à-vis the Armenians see Raymond Kévorkian, *The Armenian Genocide: A Complete History* (London and New York: I.B. Tauris, 2011), pp. 265–78; Fuat Dündar, *Crime of Numbers: The Role of Statistics in the Armenian Question (1878–1918)* (New Brunswick and London: Transaction, 2010).
45. Suny, *'They Can Live in the Desert'*, pp. 187–8, 269.
46. Plans for autonomy in Ottoman Armenia, with varying extents of participation by the great powers, were a constant through the last decades of Ottoman rule. On the plan of Patriarch Nerses Varjabedian see Libaridian, 'What Was Revolutionary', p. 90; on Russia's 1914 'Mandel'shtam plan' see Suny, *'They Can Live in the Desert'*, p. 200, and Peter Holquist, 'The Politics and Practice of the Russian Occupation of Armenia, 1915–February 1917', in Suny and Göçek, *A Question of Genocide*, p. 153.

47. On the *millet* system see Suny, *'They Can Live in the Desert'*, pp. 11–12, 43–50.
48. Panossian, *The Armenians*, p. 152; emphasis in original.
49. George A. Bournoutian, *The Khanate of Erevan under Qajar Rule 1795–1828* (Costa Mesa and New York: Mazda Publishers, 1992).
50. Panossian, *The Armenians*, pp. 142–7.
51. On these see Libaridian, 'What Was Revolutionary'.
52. I do not rehearse here familiar arguments regarding the applicability, attribution or legality of the term genocide, since my argument encompasses only its historicity and not its legal implications. The mainstream of reputable scholarship concurs that genocide is an appropriate historical understanding of the fate that befell the Ottoman Armenians in 1915–16. For examples from a substantial literature see Taner Akçam, *A Shameful Act: The Armenian Genocide and the Question of Turkish Responsibility* (London: Constable, 2007); Donald Bloxham, *The Great Game of Genocide: Imperialism, Nationalism, and the Destruction of the Ottoman Armenians* (Oxford: Oxford University Press, 2005); Fatma Müge Göçek, *Denial of Violence: Ottoman Past, Turkish Present and Collective Violence against the Armenians, 1789–2009* (New York: Oxford University Press, 2015); Kévorkian, *Armenian Genocide*; Michael Mann, *The Dark Side of Democracy: Explaining Ethnic Cleansing* (Cambridge: Cambridge University Press, 2005); Donald E. Miller and Lorna Touryan Miller, *Survivors: An Oral History of the Armenian Genocide* (Berkeley: University of California Press, 1993); Suny, *'They Can Live in the Desert'*; Suny and Göçek, *A Question of Genocide*; Ugur Ümit Üngör, *The Making of Modern Turkey: Nation and State in Eastern Anatolia 1913–1950* (Oxford: Oxford University Press, 2011).
53. Suny, *'They Can Live in the Desert'*, ch. 10; Panossian, *The Armenians*, p. 240.
54. George A. Bournoutian, *A Concise History of the Armenian People (From Ancient Times to the Present)*, 2nd edn (Costa Mesa, CA: Mazda Publishers, 2003), p. 297.
55. See Richard G. Hovannisian's comprehensive *The Republic of Armenia*, 3 vols (Berkeley: University of California Press, 1971–96).
56. Ara Papian's commentary to a reproduction of President Wilson's report notes that the territory allocated under the award was

less than half of the 279,718 square kilometres covered by the six *vilayets* of eastern Anatolia under Ottoman rule. Ara Papian (ed.), *Arbitral Award of the President of the United States of America Woodrow Wilson: Full Report of the Committee upon the Arbitration of the Boundary between Turkey and Armenia, Washington, November 22nd, 1920* (Yerevan: Asoghik, 2011), p. iv.
57. The Committee authoring President Wilson's arbitral award estimated that the territory covered by their delimitation of an Armenian state held a pre-war population of 3.75 million, with 49 per cent Muslims and 40 per cent Armenians. Assuming the repatriation of Armenian refugees and the migration of part of the Muslim participation, they calculated that after a year the new state would reverse these proportions to have a population of three million, 50 per cent Armenian and 40 per cent Muslim. They expected the Armenian proportion to rise in subsequent years. Ibid., pp. 69–73.
58. On these see Thomas de Waal, *Great Catastrophe: Armenians and Turks in the Shadow of Genocide* (Oxford: Oxford University Press, 2015), ch. 7; Vicken Cheterian, *Open Wounds: Armenians, Turks and a Century of Genocide* (London: Hurst, 2015), ch. 5.
59. Monte Melkonian, 'Melkonian Responds to Bagdassarian', in Markar Melkonian (ed.), *The Right to Struggle: Selected Writings of Monte Melkonian on the Armenian National Question*, 2nd edn (San Francisco: Sardarabad Collective, 1993), p. 13; emphasis in original.
60. Ronald Grigor Suny, *Looking towards Ararat: Armenia in Modern History* (Bloomington and Indianapolis: Indiana University Press, 1993), ch. 10.
61. Maike Lehmann, 'A Different Kind of Brothers: Exclusion and Partial Integration after Repatriation to a Soviet "Homeland"', *Ab Imperio* 3, 2012, pp. 171–211.
62. Ibid., p. 172.
63. Panossian, *The Armenians*, p. 365.
64. Lehmann, 'A Different Kind of Brothers', pp. 203–5.
65. Atakhan Pashayev (ed.), *Deportatsiya azerbaydzhantsev iz Armyanskoy SSR (1948–1953 gg.)* (Baku: Directorate of the Azerbaijani National Archive, 2013), p. 37.
66. Ibid., pp. 46–8.
67. Ibid., p. 56. Soviet census data for the numbers of Azerbaijanis in the ArmSSR in 1939 and 1959 support this figure, rather than the

100,000 often cited in Azerbaijani sources today. In 1939 there were 130,900 Azerbaijanis in Armenia, constituting 10.2 per cent of the population; in 1959 there were 107,800, or 6.1 per cent of the population.
68. Ibid., p. 60.
69. Ibid., p. 56.
70. Vahakn Dadrian, 'An Appraisal of the Communist Formula "National in Form, Socialist in Content" with Particular Reference to Soviet Armenia', *Armenian Review* 16: 3, 1963, pp. 3–14, p. 9.
71. Maike Lehmann, 'Apricot Socialism: The National Past, the Soviet Project, and the Imagining of Community in Late Soviet Armenia', *Slavic Review* 74: 1, 2015, pp. 9–31, pp. 15–16.
72. Panossian, *The Armenians*, p. 322.
73. Ibid., pp. 333–42.
74. Dadrian, 'An Appraisal', p. 12.
75. Javakheti is known in Armenian sources as Javakhk, and is sometimes referred to as Akhalkalak, meaning 'new town' in Georgian.
76. Panossian, *The Armenians*, pp. 323–7.
77. Suny, *Looking towards Ararat*, p. 187; Alexander Iskandaryan, Hrant Mikaelian and Sergey Minasyan, *War, Business and Politics: Informal Networks and Formal Institutions in Armenia* (Yerevan: Caucasus Institute, 2016), pp. 32–3.
78. See Shnirelman, *Value of the Past*, pp. 57–78.
79. Lori Khatchadourian, 'Making Nations from the Ground Up: Traditions of Classical Archaeology in the South Caucasus', *American Journal of Archaeology* 112, 2008, pp. 247–78.
80. Lehmann, 'Apricot Socialism', pp. 18–21.
81. Maike Lehmann, 'The Local Reinvention of the Soviet Project Nation and Socialism in the Republic of Armenia after 1945', *Jahrbücher für Geschichte Osteuropas* 59: 4, 2011, pp. 481–508.
82. De Waal, *Great Catastrophe*, pp. 140–5.
83. Richard Hovannisian, 'Armenia's Road to Independence', in Richard Hovannisian (ed.), *The Armenian People from Ancient to Modern Times*, vol. II: *Foreign Domination to Statehood: The Fifteenth Century to the Twentieth Century* (New York: St. Martin's Press, 1997), p. 301.
84. Panossian, *The Armenians*, pp. 365–76; de Waal, *Great Catastrophe*, p. 102.
85. Gerard J. Libaridian, *The Challenge of Statehood: Armenian Political Thinking since Independence* (Watertown, MA: Blue Crane Books, 1999), p. 124.

86. Ibid.
87. Monte Melkonian, 'Why Soviet Armenia Does Not Currently Constitute a Total Response to Our National Aspirations', in Melkonian (ed.), *Right to Struggle*, pp. 175–81, p. 180.
88. Nora Dudwick, 'Memory, Identity and Politics in Armenia' (PhD dissertation, University of Pennsylvania, 1994), p. 66.
89. Author's interview with Hranush Kharatyan, Institute of Archaeology and Ethnography, Yerevan, 17 March 2015.
90. Author's conversations in Armenia, 2005–15; Sen Oganisyan, *Armeniya Nakhichevan Genotsid* (Yerevan: Naapet, 2016).
91. Martin Dodge, Rob Kitchin and Chris Perkins, *Rethinking Maps* (London and New York: Routledge, 2009), p. 9.

Chapter 3

1. Anatoliy Yamskov, 'Traditsionnoe zemlepolzovanie kochevnikov istoricheskogo Karabakha i sovrcmcnnyy armyano-azerbaydzhanskogo etnoterritorial'nyy konflikt', in M. Olcott and A. Malashenko (eds), *Faktor etno-konfessional'noy samobytnosti v postsovetskom obshchestve* (Moscow: Moscow Carnegie Centre, 1998), pp. 168–97.
2. Johann Schiltberger, *The Bondage and Travels of Johann Schiltberger, A Native of Bavaria, in Europe, Asia, and Africa, 1396–1427*, trans. J. Buchan Telfer, with notes by P. Bruun (London: Hakluyt Society, 1879), p. 86.
3. Robert Hewsen dispels the idea that the term Karabakh is a translation of Artsakh, although he cites a proximate Armenian etymology for Artsakh meaning 'black field'. Robert H. Hewsen, 'The Meliks of Eastern Armenia: A Preliminary Study', *Revue des Études Arméniennes* IX, 1972, pp. 285–329, p. 288, note 14.
4. Robert H. Hewsen, 'The Kingdom of Arc'ax', in Thomas J. Samuelian and Michael E. Stone (eds), *Medieval Armenian Culture* (Chico, CA: Scholars Press, 1984), pp. 42–68, p. 44.
5. Hewsen, 'Meliks of Eastern Armenia'.
6. On this period see the chronicles of Mirza Jamal Javanshir, vizier to the last khan of Karabakh, and Mira Adigözal Beg, son of a local tribal chieftain who pursued a career in the service of the Russian tsar, reproduced in George A. Bournoutian, *Two Chronicles on the History of Karabagh* (Costa Mesa: Mazda, 2004); see also Muriel

Atkin, 'The Strange Death of Ibrahim Khalil Khan of Qarabagh', *Iranian Studies* 12: 1–2, 1979, pp. 79–107.

7. Gertjan Dijkink, *National Identity and Geopolitical Visions: Maps of Pride and Pain* (London and New York: Routledge, 1996).
8. Raffi (Hagob Melik Hagobian), *The Five Melikdoms of Karabagh (1600–1827)*, trans. Ara Stepan Melkonian (London: Taderon Press, 2010).
9. Mark Malkasian, *'Gha-ra-bagh!' The Emergence of the National Democratic Movement in Armenia* (Detroit: Wayne State University Press, 1996), p. 4; Gerard J. Libaridian, *The Challenge of Statehood: Armenian Political Thinking since Independence* (Watertown, MA: Blue Crane Books, 1999), p. 26.
10. See the essays by various Russian intellectuals in S. T. Zolyan and G. K. Mirzoyan, *Nagornyy Karabakh i vokrug nego glazami nezavisimykh nablyudateley. Sbornik dokumentov* (Yerevan: Luis, 1991).
11. Author's interview with Igor Muradyan, former activist, Yerevan, 1 April 2015.
12. See Thomas de Waal's account of his interview with Muradyan in *Black Garden: Armenia and Azerbaijan through Peace and War*, 2nd edn (New York: New York University Press, 2013), pp. 17–19.
13. See the discussion in Tatul Hakobyan, *Karabakh Diary: Green and Black* (Antelias: n.p., 2010), pp. 56–60; interview with Vazgen Manukyan, former Karabakh Committee member, *Parts of a Circle*, Film One: The Road to War, documentary film (London: Conciliation Resources, 2013).
14. Hakobyan, *Karabakh Diary*, p. 75.
15. Ibid., p. 55; Rasim Agaev and Zardusht Alizade, *Azerbaydzhan. Konets Vtoroy Respubliki* (Moscow: Granitsa, 2006), pp. 142–3.
16. G. A. Galoyan and K. S. Khudaverdyan (eds), *Nagornyy Karabakh. Istoricheskaya Spravka* (Yerevan: Armenian Academy of Sciences, 1988), p. 9.
17. See the discussion in Robert H. Hewsen, *Armenia: A Historical Atlas* (Chicago and London: University of Chicago Press, 2001), pp. 119–20 and maps 100–3 at p. 123; the first official atlas of the NKR declares that the de facto republic is established on the 'main part of historical Artsakh'. Manuk Vardanyan (ed.), *Atlas Nagorno-Karabakhskoy Respubliki* (Yerevan: Centre for Geodesy and Cartography, 2009), p. 7.

18. See, for example, Galoyan and Khudaverdyan, *Nagornyy Karabakh*, pp. 37–44.
19. Meaning 'as you possess' in Latin, the *uti possidetis* principle validates former internal administrative boundaries (such as those of the former union republics in the Soviet Union) as the legitimate borders of sovereign successor states.
20. See the collection of essays, interviews and speeches collected in Gerard Libaridian (ed.), *Armenia at the Crossroads: Democracy and Nationhood in the Post-Soviet Era* (Watertown, MA: Blue Crane Books, 1991), especially Rafael Ishkhanyan, 'The Law of Excluding the Third Force', pp. 9–38, and Vazgen Manukyan, 'It Is Time to Jump Off the Train', pp. 51–86.
21. See Gerard Libaridian, 'Democracy, Diaspora, and the National Agenda', in Libaridian, *Armenia at the Crossroads*, pp. 157–70.
22. Declaration on Armenia's Independence by the Parliament of Armenia, in Libaridian, *Armenia at the Crossroads*, pp. 107–10. Libaridian notes that this was more a declaration on, than of, independence that left many issues open.
23. Turnout was 82.2 per cent (108,736) of a registered electorate of 132,328. Data from the official website of the Nagorno-Karabakh (Artsakh) Republic Central Election Commission, <http://cecnkr.am> (last accessed 14 March 2019).
24. Ibid.
25. In 1991 Shahumyan (Shaumyan in Russian) district featured a population of some 17,000 Armenians, 3,000 Azerbaijanis and 1,000 Russians. On 26 July 1989 the district assembly in Shahumyan voted for unification with the NKAO, but on 15 January 1991 the district was dissolved by the Azerbaijani Supreme Soviet and merged with the neighbouring Kasum-Ismayilli district, creating a new Azerbaijani-majority district, Goranboy. In April several villages saw their populations deported during the course of 'Operation Ring'; violence resumed in the aftermath of the August coup attempt in Moscow, leading on 2 September to a joint declaration by legislative councils of the NKAO and Shahumyan on the formation of the NKR, covering both areas. Azerbaijani forces overran Shahumyan in June 1992, and the district remained under Azerbaijani control at the end of the war. See 'Verishen: napryazhennost' sokhranyaetsya', *Ekspress-Khronika* 35, 27 August 1991; de Waal, *Black Garden*, pp. 121–2; Hakobyan, *Karabakh Diary*, pp. 167–9; Vardanyan, *Atlas*, p. 7.

26. Author's conversations with Armenian journalists, Yerevan, 2011–12.
27. Thomas de Waal, *The Karabakh Trap: Dangers and Dilemmas of the Nagorny Karabakh Conflict* (London: Conciliation Resources, 2008), p. 7.
28. Cartographic exhibitionism may be understood as the desire within Armenian geopolitical culture to project and display enlarged national territorial images. See Laurence Broers and Gerard Toal, 'Cartographic Exhibitionism? Visualizing the Territory of Armenia and Karabakh', *Problems of Post-Communism* 60: 3, 2013, pp. 16–35.
29. The de facto National Assembly approved the territorial delimitation of the NKR as a polity defined by its post-war boundaries on 26 June 1998. This expansive definition of the republic was affirmed in the constitution of 2006, whose Article 142 read: 'Till the restoration of the state territorial integrity of the Nagorno Karabakh Republic and the adjustment of its borders public authority is exercised on the territory under factual jurisdiction of the Republic of Nagorno Karabakh.'
30. Author's field notes, Nagorny Karabakh, 2008–13; author's conversations with settlers in Kelbajar, June 2013.
31. Author's interviews, Nagorny Karabakh, September 2014.
32. See, for example, Shagen Mkrtchyan, *Istoriko-Arkhitekturnye Pamyatniki Nagornogo Karabakha* (Yerevan: Ayastan, 1988); Jean-Michel Thierry, *Eglises et couvents du Karabagh* (Antelias: Armenian Catholicos of Cilicia, 1991).
33. Gerard Toal and John O'Loughlin, 'Land for Peace in Nagorny Karabakh? Political Geographies and Public Attitudes Inside a Contested De Facto State', *Territory, Politics, Governance* 1: 2, 2013, pp. 158–82, p. 170.
34. See the RAA's website at <http://www.raa-am.com/raa/public/home.php?first=1> (last accessed 13 August 2018).
35. Samvel Karapetyan, *Pamyatniki Armyanskoy Kul'tury v Zone Nagornogo Karabakha* (Yerevan: Gitutyun, 2000).
36. Samvel Karapetyan, *Northern Artsakh* (Yerevan: Gitutiun, 2007). This volume is roughly twice the length of that dedicated to Nagorny Karabakh itself.
37. See the Birthright Armenia website at <https://www.birthrightarmenia.org/en/> (last accessed 13 August 2018).
38. Rik Adriaans, 'The Humanitarian Road to Nagorno-Karabakh: Media, Morality and Infrastructural Promise in the Armenian

Diaspora', *Identities: Global Studies in Culture and Power*, 3 August 2017, <http://www.tandfonline.com/doi/abs/10.1080/1070289X.2017.1358004> (last accessed 13 August 2018).
39. See, for example, 'Otkrytoe pis'mo molodezhnykh organizatsiy Artsakha prezidentu RA Serzhu Sargsyanu', *Demo*, 16 December 2008, p. 11.
40. Toal and O'Loughlin, 'Land for Peace', p. 174.
41. Personal conversation, senior Armenian official, Yerevan, March 2011.
42. Author's interview with David Harutyunyan, Minister-in-Chief of the Government Staff and Chairman of the Standing Committee on State and Legal Affairs at the National Assembly, Yerevan, 7 April 2015.
43. Senior de facto official from the NKR, speaking under the Chatham House rule in London, 2012.
44. Agaev and Alizade, *Konets Vtoroy Respubliki*, p. 103.
45. Viktor Shnirelman, *Who Gets the Past? Competition for Ancestors among Non-Russian Intellectuals in Russia* (Washington DC: Woodrow Wilson Center Press, and Baltimore and London: Johns Hopkins University Press, 1996), pp. 25–6.
46. Hewsen, *Armenia: A Historical Atlas*, p. 119. Greco-Roman tradition referred to Albania; Armenian tradition to Agvank or Aluank; Arab tradition to al-Ran and later, Arran.
47. Farida Mamedova, *Kavkazskaya Albaniya i Albany* (Baku: Centre for the Study of Caucasian Albania, 2005); Farida Mamedova, *Politicheskaya Istoriya i Istoricheskaya Geografiya Kavkazskoy Albanii* (Baku: Elm, 1986); Z. M. Buniyatov (ed.), *Istoricheskaya Geografiya Azerbaydzhana* (Baku: Elm, 1987).
48. These debates are meticulously traced in Viktor A. Shnirelman, *The Value of the Past: Myths, Identity and Politics in Transcaucasia*, Senri Ethnological Studies 57 (Osaka: National Museum of Ethnology, 2001), ch. 13.
49. Azerbaijani Voluntary Association for the Preservation of Historical and Cultural Monuments, *Karta Drevnykh i Srednevekovykh Pamyatnikov Zodchestva Azerbaydzhanskoy SSR* (Moscow: Glavnoe Upravlenie Geodezii i Kartografii pri Sovete Ministrov SSSR, 1980).
50. Later research establishes the early eighth century as the point when Albania ceased to have its own ruling dynasty. Mamedova, *Politicheskaya Istoriya*, pp. 208–13.
51. Mark Saroyan, 'The "Karabakh Syndrome" and Azerbaijani

Politics', *Problems of Communism*, September–October 1990, pp. 14–29.
52. Agaev and Alizade, *Konets Vtoroy Respubliki*, pp. 68–9.
53. See Rafik Mamedov, *Sobytiya v Nagornom Karabakhe i vokrug ego. Po stranitsam gazet*, 3 vols (Baku: Azerbaijani Communist Party Central Committee Press Centre, 1988–9).
54. Agaev and Alizade, *Konets Vtoroy Respubliki*, p. 226.
55. De Waal, *Black Garden*, p. 114.
56. Nora Dudwick, 'The Case of the Caucasian Albanians: Ethnohistory and Ethnic Politics', *Cahiers du monde russe et soviétique* 31: 2–3, 1990, pp. 377–83.
57. Igrar Aliyev, *Nagornyy Karabakh: Istoriya, fakty, sobytiya* (Baku: Elm, 1989), pp. 74–5.
58. On the former see Gerard Toal (Gearóid Ó Tuathail) and Carl T. Dahlman, *Bosnia Remade: Ethnic Cleansing and its Reversal* (Oxford: Oxford University Press, 2011), ch. 2; on the latter see Kevin Tuite, 'The Rise and Fall and Revival of the Ibero-Caucasian Hypothesis', *Historiographia Linguistica* 35: 1–2, 2008, pp. 23–82, pp. 60–5.
59. Aliyev, *Nagornyy Karabakh*, p. 101.
60. Zardusht Alizade narrates these events in Agaev and Alizade, *Konets Vtoroy Respubliki*, pp. 377–81.
61. Ibid., p. 598.
62. De Waal, *Black Garden*, p. 328.
63. For different perspectives on Azerbaijanism see Ramiz Mehdiyev, 'Azerbaijanism as an Example of National Ideology' (in Azerbaijani), *Azərbaycan*, 9 November 2007, <http://www.azerbaycanli.org/az/page55.html> (last accessed 4 July 2018); Aydin Balayev, *Etnoyazykovye protsessy v Azerbaydzhane v XIX–XX vv.* (Baku: Nurlar, 2005), pp. 234–6; Svante E. Cornell, Halil Karaveli and Boris Ajeganov, *Azerbaijan's Formula: Secular Governance and Civic Nationhood* (Washington DC: Central Asia-Caucasus Institute and Silk Road Studies Program, 2016); Laurence Broers and Ceyhun Mahmudlu, 'Civic Dominion: Nation-Building in Post-Soviet Azerbaijan', in Peter Rutland (ed.), *Nations and States in the Post-Soviet Space* (Oxford: Oxford University Press, forthcoming).
64. Author's interview with Farida Mamedova, Baku, 3 July 2014.
65. Ibid.
66. The KLO was founded in 1993 as an organisation for veterans and refugees. Discredited by alleged involvement in a 1996 coup

attempt led by Rovshan Javadov (popularly referred to as the 'Turkish coup' owing to Turkey's alleged involvement), the KLO was rehabilitated in 1998. Author's interview with Akif Nagi, KLO leader, Baku, 20 June 2014.
67. Fuad Akhundov, *Unichtozhenie Erivani, kak chast' bol'shogo plana* (Baku: n.p., 2015).
68. On Babak see Touraj Atabaki, 'Iranian History in Transition: Recasting the Symbolic Identity of Babak Khorramdin', in Abbas Amanat and Farzin Vejdani (eds), *Iran Facing Others: Identity Boundaries in a Historical Perspective* (New York: Palgrave Macmillan, 2012), pp. 63–76.
69. Tadeusz Swietochowski, *Russia and Azerbaijan: A Borderland in Transition* (New York: Columbia University Press, 1995), p. 2.
70. Y. M. Mahmudov, *Azərbaycan Tarixi Atlası* (Baku: Baku Cartographic Factory, 2011), p. 32; Y. M. Mahmudlu, N. I. Məmmədova, I. X. Zeynalov, M. Q. Abdullayev, K. H. Məmmədov and N. K. Ilyasova, *Tarix* (Baku: Tələbə qəbulu üzrə Dövlət Komissiyası – Abituriyent, 2013), pp. 344–66.
71. Zemfira Gadzhieva, *Garabagskoe Khanstvo: sotsial'no-ekonomicheskie otnoshcheniya i gosudarstvennoe ustroystvo* (Baku: Taxsil, 2008).
72. Sabir Asadov, *Istoricheskaya Geografiya Zapadnogo Azerbaydzhana* (Baku: Azerbaydzhan Publishing House, 1998).
73. Yagub Makhmudov (ed.), *Irevanskoe Khanstvo. Rossiyskoe zavoevanie i pereselenie armyan na zemli Severnogo Azerbaydzhana* (Baku: A. A. Bakikhanov Institute of History at the Azerbaijani Academy of Sciences, 2010), p. 18.
74. George A. Bournoutian, *The Khanate of Erevan Under Qajar Rule 1795–1828* (Costa Mesa and New York: Mazda Publishers, 1992), pp. 48–57.
75. Aziz Alakbarli, *The Monuments of Western Azerbaijan* (Baku: Ministry of Culture and Tourism of the Azerbaijani Republic, 2007).
76. See President Aliyev's speech at the opening of a memorial in Quba, 26 September 2013, <http://en.president.az/articles/9397> (last accessed 4 July 2018).
77. 'Il'kham Aliyev nazval strategicheskoy tselyu azerbaydzhantsev "vozvrashchenie" Erevana', Interfax, 8 February 2018, <http://www.interfax.ru/world/599092> (last accessed 4 July 2018); 'Vlasti Armenii vosmutilis slovami Alieva ob istoricheskikh zemlyakh Azerbaydzhana', *Kavkazskiy Uzel*, 9 February 2018,

<https://www.kavkaz-uzel.eu/articles/316333/> (last accessed 4 July 2018).
78. Franck Billé, 'Territorial Phantom Pains (and Other Cartographic Anxieties)', *Environment and Planning D: Society and Space* 32: 1, 2014, pp. 163–78.
79. Mahmudlu et al., *Tarix*, p. 614.
80. See Yair Wallach's insightful article on uncannily similar Israeli and Palestinian 'mirror-maps', on which this paragraph draws. Yair Wallach, 'Trapped in Mirror-Images: The Rhetoric of Maps in Israel/Palestine', *Political Geography* 30, 2011, pp. 358–69.

Chapter 4

1. Elmira's story is told in the short film *All Films about Love*, directed by Lusine Musaelyan and Levon Kalantar. The film can be found in *Dialogue through Film: A Handbook* (London: Conciliation Resources, 2012), and online at <https://vimeo.com/channels/dialoguethroughfilm/12366582> (last accessed 18 July 2018).
2. On the difficulties of defining who 'counts' as a member of a stigmatised nationality in a post-conflict setting see Sevil Huseynova, '"Ya znala, chto nigde ne smogu zhit." Iz issledovaniya povsednevnykh praktik bakinskikh armyan', *Azerbaijan in the World* 1: 3, 2006, pp. 143–52.
3. Armenians assert an international border between Nagorny Karabakh and Azerbaijan by describing those who have crossed it as 'refugees', while Azerbaijan and the international community describe them as 'internally displaced persons'.
4. These flows were externally displaced in the sense that they crossed over to another republic of the Soviet Union. At the time, these were of course internal movements within the same state; sovereignty transformed internally displaced persons into refugees.
5. Arif Yunusov, *Migration Processes in Azerbaijan* (Baku: Adiloglu, 2009), pp. 27–8. This figure includes some 40,000 Armenians displaced in 1992 from the areas to the north of the NKAO (the former Khanlar and Shahumyan districts).
6. State Migration Service, 'The Number of the Armenian Population in the Main Cities and Regions of Azerbaijan SSR', 18 April 2014, <http://www.smsmta.am/?menu_id=87> (last accessed 11 July 2018).
7. Yunusov, *Migration Processes*, p. 22. In 1996 UNHCR registered

233,000 refugees in Azerbaijan, a figure including Meskhetian Turks displaced from Central Asia. UNHCR, *Refugees and Others of Concern to UNHCR* (Geneva: UNHCR, 1998), Table 2.
8. Laura Baghdasarian and Arif Yunusov, 'War, Social Change and "No War, No Peace" Syndromes in Azerbaijani and Armenian Societies', in Laurence Broers (ed.), *The Limits of Leadership: Elites and Societies in the Nagorny Karabakh Peace Process*, Accord 17 (London: Conciliation Resources, 2005), p. 53; UNHCR, *Refugees and Others of Concern*, Table 1.
9. Nagorno-Karabakh Republic/Artsakh, *Statebuilding: Progress towards Freedom, Democracy and Economic Development* (Washington DC: Office of the NKR in the USA, 2005), p. 57.
10. Yunusov, *Migration Processes*, p. 25; UNHCR, *Refugees and Others of Concern*, Table 1.
11. The dating of the first forced displacements and communal violence is the subject of bitter Armenian–Azerbaijani polemics. De Waal offers eyewitness testimony of movements of Azerbaijanis from the southern Armenian area of Kapan in November 1987. Azerbaijani historian Arif Yunusov witnessed arrivals of Azerbaijanis from Armenia to Baku in January 1988 (personal communication with Arif Yunusov, May 2012). Armenian scholars argue, however, that no displacements took place from Armenia until February 1988. See Thomas de Waal, *Black Garden: Armenia and Azerbaijan through Peace and War*, 2nd edn (New York: New York University Press, 2013), pp. 19–20; Grisha Oganezov and Hranush Kharatyan, *Samooborona armyan Kirovabada v 1988–1989 gg. glazami ochevidtsev* (Yerevan: Gitutyun, 2014), p. 94, fn. 85; Tatul Hakobyan, *Karabakh Diary: Green and Black* (Antelias: n.p., 2010), pp. 39–44.
12. Gerard Toal (Gearóid Ó Tuathail) and Carl T. Dahlman, *Bosnia Remade: Ethnic Cleansing and its Reversal* (Oxford: Oxford University Press, 2011), p. 13.
13. Out of thirty-one assailants that Lyudmila identified, four were Azerbaijanis from Kapan in Armenia. Samuel Shahmuratian (ed.), *The Sumgait Tragedy*, vol. 1 (New Rochelle and Cambridge, MA: Aristide Caratzas and the Zoryan Institute, 1990), p. 139.
14. Huseynova, '"Ya znala, chto nigde"'; Irina Mosesova, *Armyane Baku: Bytie i iskhod* (Yerevan: Ayastan, 1998), pp. 83, 140–1; interview with Mariya Sarkisova, former Baku resident, *Parts of a Circle*, Film One: The Road to War, documentary film (London:

Conciliation Resources, 2013); Aleksandr Lebed', *Za derzhavu obidno* (Moscow: Moskovskaya Pravda, 1995), p. 242–3.
15. Arif Yunusov, 'Pogromy v Armenii v 1988–1989 godakh', *Ekspress Khronika* 9, 26 February 1991, p. 5. In Kapan the local party boss's wife instructed local Azerbaijanis to leave. Interview with Mehman and Ofelia, former residents of Kapan, *Parts of a Circle*, Film One: The Road to War, documentary film (London: Conciliation Resources, 2013).
16. Thomas Goltz, *Azerbaijan Diary: A Rogue Reporter's Adventures in an Oil-Rich, War-Torn, Post-Soviet Republic* (Armonk, NY and London: M.E. Sharpe, 1998), p. 78.
17. On these perspectives see Donald Horowitz, *Ethnic Groups in Conflict* (Berkeley: University of California Press, 1985), chs 4 and 5; Stephanie H. M. van Goozen, Nanne E. Van de Poll and Joseph A. Sergeant (eds), *Emotions: Essays on Emotion Theory* (Hillsdale, NJ and Hove: Lawrence Erlbaum Associates, 1994); Ronald Grigor Suny, *Why We Hate You: The Passions of National Identity and Ethnic Violence* (Berkeley: Berkeley Program in Soviet and Post-Soviet Studies Working Paper Series, 2004); Roger D. Petersen, *Understanding Ethnic Violence: Fear, Hatred and Resentment in Twentieth-Century Eastern Europe* (Cambridge: Cambridge University Press, 2002).
18. Petersen, *Understanding Ethnic Violence*, p. 21.
19. On the vicissitudes in the Russian–Armenian relationship in the Russian Empire see Ronald Grigor Suny, *Looking towards Ararat: Armenia in Modern History* (Bloomington and Indianapolis: Indiana University Press, 1993), pp. 31–51.
20. Hranush Kharatyan, 'Opyt Proshlogo', in Oganezov and Kharatyan, *Samooborona armyan Kirovabada*, pp. 42–3.
21. Terry Martin, *The Affirmative Action Empire: Nations and Nationalism in the Soviet Union, 1923–1939* (Ithaca and London: Cornell University Press, 2001), pp. 23–4, 126–9.
22. Lee Ann Fujii, *Killing Neighbors: Webs of Violence in Rwanda* (Ithaca and London: Cornell University Press, 2009), p. 12.
23. For a discussion of how emotion can substitute for leadership in collective violence see Petersen, *Understanding Ethnic Violence*, pp. 4–5.
24. Matthew Lange, *Killing Others: A Natural History of Ethnic Violence* (Ithaca and London: Cornell University Press, 2017).
25. Yunusov, *Migration Processes*, p. 13.

26. Yu. A. Polyakov (ed.), *Vsesoyuznaya perepis' naseleniya 1939 goda: Osnovnye Itogi* (Moscow: Nauka, 1992), Table 56. Similarly, within the technical sector ethnic Azerbaijanis accounted for 61.3 per cent of agronomists but only 9.6 per cent of more prestigious construction technician roles.
27. Grey Hodnett, *Leadership in the Soviet National Republics* (Oakville, Ontario: Mosaic Press, 1978), p. 103. Their share of the overall population in 1959 was 67.5 per cent.
28. Bruce Grant, 'Cosmopolitan Baku', *Ethnos* 75: 2, 2010, pp. 123–47.
29. Author's interview with Armenian refugee and former Baku resident, Yerevan, 7 March 2015.
30. Eyewitness account of Aleksandr Mikhailovich Gukasian, in Shahmuratian, *Sumgait Tragedy*, p. 288.
31. Shahmuratian, *Sumgait Tragedy*, p. 177.
32. Ibid., p. 284.
33. Lebed', *Za derzhavu obidno*, p. 232.
34. Ibid., p. 258.
35. Interview with Mariya Sarkisova, former Baku resident, *Parts of a Circle* interview archive.
36. Humiliation through cruelty is one of the most unambiguous ways to demonstrate domination over others. Nico Frijda, 'The Lex Talionis: On Vengeance', in van Goozen et al., *Emotions: Essays on Emotion Theory*, p. 280. On the role of public humiliation see James C. Scott, *Hidden Transcripts: Domination and the Arts of Resistance* (New Haven and London: Yale University Press, 1990), pp. 214–15.
37. Author's interview with Larisa Alaverdyan, former ombudsman, Yerevan, 17 April 2015.
38. Interview Sarkisova.
39. Interview with Arif Yunusov, Azerbaijani scholar, *Parts of a Circle*, Film One: The Road to War, documentary film (London: Conciliation Resources, 2013).
40. Mosesova, *Armyane Baku*, pp. 183–4.
41. Nora Dudwick, 'Memory, Identity and Politics in Armenia' (PhD dissertation, University of Pennsylvania, 1994), pp. 69–70.
42. A. N. Yamskov, 'Ethnic Conflict in the Transcaucasus: The Case of Nagorno-Karabakh', *Theory and Society* 20: 5, 1991, pp. 631–60, p. 645.
43. Dudwick, 'Memory, Identity and Politics', p. 70.
44. See de Waal, *Black Garden*, p. 310; Razmik Panossian, *The*

Armenians: From Kings and Priests to Merchants and Commissars (London: Hurst, 2006), pp. 281–2.
45. Yunusov, 'Pogromy v Armenii'; Mane Papyan, 'Sobytiya v Gugarke. Kak gromili azerbaydzhantsev v Armenii', *epress.am*, 29 April 2015, <http://www.epress.am/ru/2015/04/29/события-в-гугарке-как-громили-азербай.html> (last accessed 5 July 2018).
46. Petersen, *Understanding Ethnic Violence*, p. 64.
47. Dudwick, 'Memory, Identity and Politics', chs 2 and 3.
48. Ibid., pp. 76–99.
49. Harutyun Marutyan, *Iconography of Armenian Identity Volume 1: The Memory of Genocide and the Karabagh Movement* (Yerevan: Gitutyun, 2009), ch. 3.
50. *Zerkalo*, 23 July 2002; the relevant excerpt is cited in Arsène Saparov, *From Conflict to Autonomy in the Caucasus: The Soviet Union and the Making of Abkhazia, South Ossetia and Nagorno Karabakh* (London and New York: Routledge, 2015), p. 164.
51. Personal communication with Tabib Huseynov, 12 November 2018.
52. Author's interview with former Karabakh movement activist, Stepanakert, 16 September 2014.
53. 'Khodzhalu', *Ekspress Khronika* 45, 6 November 1988.
54. Mark Malkasian, *'Gha-ra-bagh!' The Emergence of the National Democratic Movement in Armenia* (Detroit: Wayne State University Press, 1996), pp. 142–6.
55. The official census figure did not include Armenians from Sumgait, Baku and other cities displaced to the NKAO after communal violence had begun in February 1988, but who were still legally registered at their former residences in January 1989 when the census was conducted.
56. See Shahmuratian, *Sumgait Tragedy*, p. 286, and the recollections of Soviet official Grigory Kharchenko in de Waal, *Black Garden*, p. 40. Sumgait survivor Karine Melkumyan recalls: 'When we were already in the party building, everyone said they wanted to go to Russia, to the last one. No one wanted to go to Armenia.' Interview with Karine Melkumyan, former Sumgait resident, *Parts of a Circle* interview archive.
57. According to Ramiz Melikov, deputy press secretary of the Azerbaijani Ministry of Defence, interviewed by Human Rights Watch in 1992. Human Rights Watch/Helsinki, *Bloodshed in the Caucasus: Escalation of the Armed Conflict in Nagorno Karabakh* (Washington DC: Human Rights Watch, 1992), p. 6.

58. Stef Jansen, '*Refuchess*: Locating Bosniac Repatriates after the War in Bosnia-Herzegovina', *Population, Space and Place* 17, 2011, pp. 140–52.
59. See Chapter 1, note 33.
60. Human Rights Watch/Helsinki, *Bloodshed in the Caucasus*, p. 8.
61. See Human Rights Watch/Helsinki, *Seven Years of Conflict in Nagorno-Karabakh* (New York: Human Rights Watch, 1994).
62. De Waal, *Black Garden*, p. 116.
63. Tabib Huseynov, 'Return and its Alternatives: A Case Study on the Armenian–Azerbaijani Conflict', in Conciliation Resources, *Forced Displacement in the Nagorny Karabakh Conflict: Return and its Alternatives* (London: Conciliation Resources, 2011), pp. 33–46, p. 35.
64. Author's notes, meeting with Ali Hasanov, Head of the State Committee for Refugees and Internally Displaced Persons, Baku, 13 September 2007.
65. Amnesty International, *Azerbaijan: Displaced then Discriminated Against – The Plight of the Internally Displaced Population*, EUR 55/010/2007 (London: Amnesty International, 2007), p. 26. I was the principal researcher and author of this report.
66. Author's conversation with a settler in Lachin, September 2014.
67. Author's interview with Ashot Gulyan, de facto Speaker of Parliament, Stepanakert, 22 September 2014.
68. Nagorno-Karabakh Republic/Artsakh, *Statebuilding*, p. 57.
69. Author's conversations with Shusha residents, March 2005.
70. Author's conversations with Shusha residents, 2005–14.
71. Gerard Toal, 'Return and its Alternatives: International Law, Norms and Practices, and Dilemmas of Ethnocratic Power', in Conciliation Resources, *Forced Displacement in the Nagorny Karabakh Conflict*, pp. 7–21, p. 10.
72. European Court of Human Rights (ECtHR), *Case of Sargsyan v. Azerbaijan* (Application No. 40167/06), 16 June 2015, Paragraph 83, <http://hudoc.echr.coe.int/eng?i=001-155662> (last accessed 5 July 2018).
73. See Artak Ayunts, 'Return and its Alternatives: Perspectives from Armenia', in Conciliation Resources, *Forced Displacement in the Nagorny Karabakh Conflict*, pp. 23–31; Y. Ghazaryan, 'Obstacles to the Integration and Naturalization of Refugees: A Case Study of Ethnic Armenian Refugees in Armenia', unpublished manuscript, American University of Armenia, no date, <http://www.nispa.sk/news/ghazaryan.rtf> (last accessed 5 July 2018).

74. Author's interview with Armenian refugees from Baku, Yerevan, 7 March 2015.
75. Interview Hasanov.
76. Amnesty International, *Displaced then Discriminated Against*.
77. World Bank, *Azerbaijan Living Conditions Assessment Report*, Report No. 52801-AZ (Washington DC: World Bank, 2010), p. 35.
78. Huseynov, 'Return and its Alternatives', p. 45.
79. Ibid., p. 44.
80. Aram Arkun, 'Exclusive: President Sahakyan Declares Azerbaijani Refugees Can Live Peacefully in Artsakh Republic', *The Armenian Mirror-Spectator*, 28 March 2018, <https://mirrorspectator.com/2018/03/28/exclusive-president-sahakyan-declares-azerbaijani-refugees-can-live-peacefully-in-artsakh-republic/> (last accessed 5 July 2018).
81. Author's notes, meeting with Nizami Bakhmanov, then Shusha community leader-in-exile, Baku, 7 July 2005.
82. Author's interview with Sergey Shahverdyan, Director, Department of Tourism, Stepanakert, 19 September 2014. This is a reading upheld in the territory's tourist brochures, such as Research on Armenian Architecture, *The Islamic Monuments of the Armenian Architecture of Artsakh* (Yerevan: Ministry of Culture of the Republic of Armenia, 2010).
83. John O'Loughlin, Vladimir Kolossov and Gerard Toal, 'Inside the Post-Soviet De Facto States: A Comparison of Attitudes in Abkhazia, Nagorny Karabakh, South Ossetia and Transnistria', *Eurasian Geography and Economics* 55: 5, 2014, pp. 423–56, p. 447.
84. This remarkable story is told in Sevil Huseynova, Arsen Hakobyan and Sergey Rumyantsev, *Beyond the Karabakh Conflict: The Story of Village Exchange* (Tbilisi: Heinrich Böll Foundation South Caucasus Regional Office, 2012).
85. Dissenting judges, however, suggested the court was watering down evidentiary standards in defining extra-territorial jurisdiction. See the partly dissenting and dissenting opinions of Judges Ziemele (pp. 86–92) and Pinto de Albuquerque (pp. 125–59, at pp. 147–9), in ECtHR, *Case of Chiragov and Others v. Armenia* (Application No. 13216/05), 16 June 2015, <http://hudoc.echr.coe.int/eng?i=001-155353> (last accessed 5 July 2018).
86. Concurring opinion of Judge Yudkivska, ECtHR, *Sarsgyan v. Azerbaijan*, at pp. 85–9.

Notes

87. ECtHR, *Chiragov and Others v. Armenia*, Paragraph 199; ECtHR, *Sargsyan v. Azerbaijan*, Paragraph 238.
88. ECtHR, *Sargsyan v. Azerbaijan*, Paragraph 171.

Chapter 5

1. See, for example, Bruce Russett and John R. Oneal, *Triangulating Peace: Democracy, Interdependence, and International Organizations* (New York: Norton, 2001).
2. Paul R. Hensel, Gary Goertz and Paul F. Diehl, 'The Democratic Peace and Rivalries', *Journal of Politics* 62 (2000): 1173–88.
3. Paul F. Diehl and Gary Goertz, *War and Peace in International Rivalry* (Ann Arbor: University of Michigan Press, 2000), pp. 120–1.
4. On Israeli democracy see the essays collected under the heading 'A Democracy?', in Eliezer Ben-Rafael, Julius H. Schoeps, Yitzhak Sternberg and Olaf Glöckner (eds), *Handbook of Israel: Major Debates*, vol. 2 (Berlin and Boston: Walter de Gruyter, 2016), pp. 639–773.
5. Edward D. Mansfield and Jack Snyder, *Electing to Fight: Why Emerging Democracies Go to War* (Cambridge, MA and London: MIT Press, 2005); Jack Snyder, *From Voting to Violence: Democratisation and Nationalist Conflict* (New York: Norton, 2000).
6. Mansfield and Snyder, *Electing to Fight*, pp. 230–3.
7. Paul F. Diehl, Gary Goertz and Daniel Saeedi, 'Theoretical Specifications of Enduring Rivalries: Applications to the India–Pakistan Case', in T. V. Paul (ed.), *The India–Pakistan Conflict: An Enduring Rivalry* (Cambridge: Cambridge University Press, 2005), p. 50.
8. Jonathan Wheatley and Christoph Zürcher, 'On the Origin and Consolidation of Hybrid Regimes: The State of Democracy in the Caucasus', *Taiwan Journal of Democracy* 4: 1, 2008, pp. 1–31; Steven Levitsky and Lucan A. Way, *Competitive Authoritarianism: Hybrid Regimes after the Cold War* (Cambridge: Cambridge University Press, 2010); Henry E. Hale, *Patronal Politics: Eurasian Regime Dynamics in Comparative Perspective* (Cambridge: Cambridge University Press, 2015).
9. The mutual hybridity argument (although she does not refer to it as such) is set out in Nina Caspersen, 'Regimes and Peace Processes:

Democratic (Non)development in Armenia and Azerbaijan and its Impact on the Nagorno-Karabakh Conflict', *Communist and Post-Communist Studies* 45, 2012, pp. 131–9. I draw heavily on Caspersen's analysis in this section.

10. The Freedom Rating is derived by averaging two scores, one for political rights and the other for civil liberties, based on twenty-five indicators surveyed for each country. Freedom House, *Freedom in the World*, <https://freedomhouse.org/report-types/freedom-world> (last accessed 5 July 2018).
11. For a comprehensive overview of elections in Azerbaijan 1995–2013 see Audrey L. Altstadt, *Frustrated Democracy in Post-Soviet Azerbaijan* (Washington DC and New York: Woodrow Wilson Center Press and Columbia University Press, 2017), ch. 3.
12. OSCE/ODIHR, *Republic of Armenia, Parliamentary Election, 30 May 1999: Final Report* (Warsaw: OSCE/ODIHR, 1999), p. 1; OSCE/ODIHR, *Republic of Armenia, Parliamentary Elections, 12 May 2007: OSCE/ODIHR Election Observation Mission Report* (Warsaw: OSCE/ODIHR, 2007), p. 1.
13. Levitsky and Way, *Competitive Authoritarianism*, pp. 207–13. Levitsky and Way coded Azerbaijan as a full authoritarian regime (p. 34) but acknowledged its borderline status.
14. 'Voice and Accountability', <https://info.worldbank.org/governance/wgi/pdf/va.pdf> (last accessed 14 March 2019).
15. This phrase is from Robert Packenham, *Liberal America and the Third World* (Princeton: Princeton University Press, 1973), cited in Mansfield and Snyder, *Electing to Fight*, p. 2.
16. Gerard J. Libaridian, former advisor to Ter-Petrossian, provides a sympathetic analysis of the latter's resignation in *The Challenge of Statehood: Armenian Political Thinking since Independence* (Watertown, MA: Blue Crane Books, 1999), pp. 47–68. For another view see Stephan H. Astourian, *From Ter-Petrosian to Kocharian: Leadership Change in Armenia* (Berkeley: Berkeley Program in Soviet and Post-Soviet Studies, 2000).
17. Author's notes, meeting with Karabakh Charter author, Baku, February 2005. The text of the Charter is published in Avaz Hasanov (ed.), *Karabakh Obsuzhdaetsya* (Baku: Society for Humanitarian Research and Conciliation Resources, 2006), p. 59. It called for a solution based on territorial integrity, the return of displaced persons and delegated self-government for Armenian and Azerbaijani communities in Nagorny Karabakh. The Charter called for the use of force in the event of the failure of negotiations.

18. Rasim Musabayov, 'The Karabakh Conflict and Democratisation', in Laurence Broers (ed.), *The Limits of Leadership: Elites and Societies in the Nagorny Karabakh Peace Process*, Accord 17 (London: Conciliation Resources, 2005), p. 63.
19. On these see Mikayel Zolyan, 'Armenia', in Donnacha Ó Beacháin and Abel Polese (eds), *The Colour Revolutions in the Former Soviet Republics* (London and New York: Routledge, 2010), pp. 83–100; Anar M. Valiyev, 'Parliamentary Elections in Azerbaijan: A Failed Revolution', *Problems of Post-Communism* 53: 3, 2006, pp. 17–35.
20. Caspersen, 'Regimes and Peace Processes', p. 132.
21. Ibid., p. 131.
22. Personal conversation, Western diplomat, May 2011.
23. On this point see the persuasive arguments set out in Eric McGlinchey, *Chaos, Violence, Dynasty: Politics and Islam in Central Asia* (Pittsburgh: Pittsburgh University Press, 2011).
24. Hale, *Patronal Politics*, p. 95.
25. Ibid., pp. 23–8.
26. Ibid., pp. 9–10.
27. On Soviet-era patronage structures see Ronald Grigor Suny, *Looking towards Ararat: Armenia in Modern History* (Bloomington and Indianapolis: Indiana University Press, 1993), pp. 182–3, 196–7; Rasim Agaev and Zardusht Alizade, *Azerbaydzhan. Konets Vtoroy Respubliki* (Moscow: Granitsa, 2006), pp. 10–25.
28. Alexander Iskandaryan, Hrant Mikaelian and Sergey Minasyan, *War, Business and Politics: Informal Networks and Formal Institutions in Armenia* (Yerevan: Caucasus Institute, 2016), p. 43.
29. Ibid., pp. 44–6.
30. On the importance of a unified executive-oriented party as a legacy to post-Soviet regimes see McGlinchey, *Chaos, Violence, Dynasty*, pp. 9–11.
31. Libaridian, *Challenge of Statehood*, p. 23.
32. Ibid., p. 92.
33. AREG (Scientific Youth Cultural Association), *The Political Elite of Post-Independence Armenia: Characteristics and Patterns of Formation* (Yerevan: Edit Print, 2014), p. 32.
34. Gerard J. Libaridian, *Modern Armenia: People, Nation, State* (New Brunswick and London: Transaction Publishers, 2004), pp. 213–14.
35. David Petrosyan, 'Oligarchy in Armenia', *Caucasus Analytical*

Digest 53–4, July 2013, p. 14; Astourian, *From Ter-Petrosian to Kocharian*, pp. 16–17.

36. Alexander Iskandaryan, 'From Totalitarianism via Elitist Pluralism: Whither Armenia?', in Mikko Palonkorpi and Alexander Iskandaryan (eds), *Armenia's Foreign and Domestic Politics: Development Trends* (Yerevan: Caucasus Institute and Aleksanteri Institute, 2013), pp. 48–54, p. 51.
37. Iskandaryan et al., *War, Business and Politics*, pp. 113–17. For a critical perspective on Yerkrapah see Mikael Danielyan, 'The People with Guns', *WarReport* 57, December 1997–January 1998, p. 18.
38. Author's interview with Manvel Grigorian, Chairman of the Board of Yerkrapah, Yerevan, 8 June 2016.
39. These first-round results were obtained in elections deemed neither free nor fair by the OSCE's ODIHR. See ODIHR/OSCE, *Republic of Armenia, Presidential Election, March 16 and 30, 1998: Final Report* (Warsaw: OSCE/ODIHR, 1998) and *Republic of Armenia, Presidential Election, 19 February and 5 March 2003: Final Report* (Warsaw: OSCE/ODIHR, 2003).
40. Boris Navasardian, 'Bitter Victory in Yerevan', *WarReport* 46, October 1996, pp. 18–19.
41. Zolyan, 'Armenia', p. 94.
42. Libaridian, *Challenge of Statehood*, p. 98.
43. For this argument see David Lewis, 'The Contested State in Post-Soviet Armenia', in John Heathershaw and Edward Schatz (eds), *Paradox of Power: The Logics of State Weakness in Eurasia* (Pittsburgh: Pittsburgh University Press, 2017), pp. 120–35.
44. Author's interviews with Richard Giragosian, Director, Regional Studies Center, Yerevan, 8 April 2015 and Artur Sakunts, Director, Helsinki Citizens' Assembly Vanadzor, Vanadzor, 5 March 2015.
45. AREG, *Political Elite of Post-Independence Armenia*, p. 33.
46. Artak Galyan, 'Gearing towards Consensualism or Unrestrained Majoritarianism? Constitutional Reform in Armenia and its Comparative Implications', *Constitutionnet*, 23 October 2015, <http://www.constitutionnet.org/news/gearing-towards-consensualism-or-unrestrained-majoritarianism-constitutional-reform-armenia> (last accessed 5 July 2018).
47. Thomas de Waal, 'Armenia's Crisis and the Legacy of Victory', Open Democracy, 3 August 2016, <https://www.opendemocracy.net/od-russia/thomas-de-waal/armenia-s-crisis-and-legacy-of-victory> (last accessed 17 July 2018).

48. Zhanna Andreasyan and Georgi Derluguian, 'Fuel Protests in Armenia', *New Left Review* 95, September–October 2015, pp. 29–48; Armine Ishkanian, 'Self-Determined Citizens? New Forms of Civic Activism and Citizenship in Armenia', *Europe-Asia Studies* 67: 8, 2015, pp. 1203–27.
49. Emil Sanamyan, 'Saint Nick of Armenia: How Protest Leader Nikol Pashinyan "Rescued" Armenia and Made it Merry', *Open Democracy*, 5 May 2018, <https://www.opendemocracy.net/od-russia/emil-sanamyan/saint-nick-of-armenia-how-nikol-pashinyan-rescued-armenia-and-made-it-merry> (last accessed 5 July 2018).
50. Radio Free Europe/Radio Liberty, 'Armenian Lawmakers Strip Retired General of Immunity after Security Raid', 19 June 2018, <https://www.rferl.org/a/armenia-lawmakers-strip-retired-general-of-immunity-after-security-raid/29305045.html> (last accessed 17 June 2018).
51. On Abdurahman Vezirov's background and appointment see Agaev and Alizade, *Konets Vtoroy Respubliki*, pp. 89–94; Agaev offers a sympathetic assessment of Vezirov's time in office at p. 177.
52. Ibid., pp. 92–3.
53. Ibid., pp. 290–6.
54. Author's notes, Azerbaijani intellectual, Baku, February 2005.
55. Anja Franke, Andrea Gawrich and Gurban Alakbarov, 'Kazakhstan and Azerbaijan as Post-Soviet Rentier States: Resource Incomes and Autocracy as a Double "Curse" in Post-Soviet Regimes', *Europe-Asia Studies* 61: 1, 2009, pp. 109–40; Andreas Heinrich and Heiko Pleines (eds), *Challenges of the Caspian Resource Boom: Domestic Elites and Policy-Making* (Basingstoke and New York: Palgrave Macmillan, 2012); Andrea Kendall-Taylor, 'Purchasing Power: Oil, Elections and Regime Durability in Azerbaijan and Kazakhstan', *Europe-Asia Studies* 64: 4, 2012, pp. 737–60.
56. World Bank Group, *Azerbaijan Systematic Country Diagnostic* (Washington DC: World Bank, 2015), p. 41.
57. Farid Guliyev, 'Political Elites in Azerbaijan', in Heinrich and Pleines (eds), *Challenges of the Caspian Resource Boom*, pp. 120–1.
58. Kendall-Taylor, 'Purchasing Power', p. 738.
59. Six ASAN public service centres were opened in 2012, comprising 'one-stop shops' initially for up to forty, and now hundreds, everyday legal services (such as registration and receipt of identity documents, taxpayer status and so on), <http://www.asan.gov.az/

az> (last accessed 14 March 2019). See Transparency Azerbaijan, *National Integrity System Assessment Azerbaijan* (Baku: Transparency Azerbaijan, 2014), p. 25. More critical perspectives see the ASAN centres as 'a parallel system that only compensates for the failures of the state'. Author's interview with civil society activist, Baku, May 2014.

60. Jody LaPorte, 'Hidden in Plain Sight: Political Opposition and Hegemonic Authoritarianism in Azerbaijan', *Post-Soviet Affairs* 31: 4, 2013, pp. 339–66.
61. Katy E. Pearce and Sarah Kendzior, 'Networked Authoritarianism and Social Media in Azerbaijan', *Journal of Communication* 62: 2, 2012, pp. 283–98.
62. On sultanism see Houchang E. Chehabi and Juan J. Linz, 'A Theory of Sultanism 1: A Type of Nondemocratic Rule', in H. E. Chehabi and Juan J. Linz (eds), *Sultanistic Regimes* (Baltimore and London: Johns Hopkins University Press, 1998), pp. 3–25. By their definition a sultanistic ruler commands loyalty not only by the distribution of patronage but by 'a mixture of fear and rewards to his collaborators' (p. 7). Farid Guliyev introduces the concept to the Azerbaijani context in 'Post-Soviet Azerbaijan: Transition to Sultanistic Semiauthoritarianism? An Attempt at Conceptualization', *Demokratizatsiya* 13: 3, 2005, pp. 393–435.
63. Bahodir Sidikov, 'New or Traditional? "Clans", Regional Groupings, and the State in Post-Soviet Azerbaijan', *Berliner Osteuropa Info* 21, 2004, pp. 68–74.
64. Altstadt, *Frustrated Democracy*, p. 72.
65. For this schema see Guliyev, 'Political Elites in Azerbaijan'.
66. Personal communication, Azerbaijani activist, September 2018.
67. Author's calculations from *Azərbaycanda Kim Kimdir?* (Baku: Azerbaijan State Encyclopedia Publishing House, 2001) and *Azərbaycanda Kim Kimdir* (Baku: Çıraq, 2010).
68. 'Il'kham Aliev sformiroval novyy sostav pravitel'stvo', Turan, 21 April 2018, <http://www.contact.az/ext/news/2018/4/free/politics%20news/ru/70797.htm> (last accessed 19 July 2018).
69. Author's notes, Azerbaijani intellectual, Baku, 13 March 2009.
70. Transcript of General Douglas MacArthur's Address to Congress, 19 April 1951, available on the website of the Harry S. Truman Presidential Library and Museum at <http://www.trumanlibrary.org/whistlestop/study_collections/koreanwar/documents/index.php?documentid=ma-2-18&pagenumber=1> (last accessed 5 July 2018).

71. See the discussion in Alon Pinkas, 'Garrison Democracy: The Impact of the 1967 Occupation of Territories on Institutional Democracy in Israel', in Edy Kaufman, Shukri B. Abed and Robert L. Rothstein (eds), *Democracy, Peace, and the Israeli–Palestinian Conflict* (Boulder and London: Lynne Rienner Publishers, 1993), pp. 61–83, p. 66.
72. Aragil Electronic News, 'Stepanakert Will Never Be Subordinate to Bakou [sic]: Interview with Newly Elected President Arkady Ghoukasian', *Aragil Events of the Week*, 8–15 September 1997, cited in Astourian, *From Ter-Petrosian to Kocharian*, p. 53; emphasis added.
73. See Pinkas, 'Garrison Democracy', pp. 68–9, for a discussion of the impacts of what he calls 'protracted temporariness' in the Israeli–Palestinian context.
74. In a study of Serbia and Croatia in the 1990s, V. P. Gagnon defines demobilisation as 'a process by which people who had previously been politically mobilised, or who were in the process of being mobilised, become silenced, marginalised, and excluded from the public realm' through violence. My use of demobilisation in the Armenian–Azerbaijani context differs from the Serbian and Croatian scenarios examined by Gagnon. Although some Azerbaijani readings of the early stages of the conflict do essentially describe a demobilisation thesis, as I argued in Chapter 1 the questionable extent of elite control over violence in the late 1980s and early 1990s makes the demobilisation theory problematic for that period. Rather, demobilisation in the Armenian–Azerbaijani context is a *post*-war strategy that instrumentalises the legacies of conflict while also tapping into popular grievance. For this reason, I refer to a demobilisation effect rather than the process *tout court*. V. P. Gagnon Jr., *The Myth of Ethnic War: Serbia and Croatia in the 1990s* (Ithaca and London: Cornell University Press, 2004), p. xviii.
75. Laura Baghdasarian and Arif Yunusov, *Armenia and Azerbaijan on the Crossroad of 'Neither Peace Nor War'* (Yerevan: Research Center Region of Investigative Journalists, 2005).
76. Author's interview with Gevorg Ter-Gabrielyan, Director, Eurasia Partnership Foundation, Yerevan, 8 April 2015.
77. Interview Grigorian.
78. Data derived from the Caucasus Barometer time-series dataset for Armenia, <http://caucasusbarometer.org/en/cb-am/codebook/> (last accessed 5 July 2018).

79. Diana Ter-Stepanyan and Edgar Khachatryan, *Between Freedom and Security: Research Analysis* (Vanadzor: Peace Dialogue, 2015), p. 28.
80. Ibid., p. 32.
81. Author's interview with Lara Aharonyan, Director, Women's Resource Center, Yerevan, 6 March 2015.
82. Author interview with Edgar Khachatryan, Director, Peace Dialogue, Vanadzor, 5 March 2015.
83. Interview with Deputy Minister Vladimir Gasparyan on the Zinuzh (Army Forces) TV programme, cited in Naira Hayrumyan, 'Army Deaths: "Suicides" in the Ranks Renew Calls for Military Reform', *ArmeniaNow.com*, 17 October 2011, <https://www.armenianow.com/social/human_rights/32429/army_deaths_armenia> (last accessed 5 July 2018).
84. Author's interview with Levon Zurabian, head of the Armenian National Congress parliamentary faction, Yerevan, 28 April 2015.
85. Arshaluis Mghdesyan, 'Armenia's Contested Political Reforms', Institute for War and Peace Reporting, 7 August 2015, <https://iwpr.net/global-voices/armenia%E2%80%99s-contested-political-reforms> (last accessed 5 July 2018).
86. Author's notes, meeting with former senior Azerbaijani official, Baku, February 2005.
87. Author's notes, meeting with Isa Gambar, Musavat Party leader, Baku, February 2005.
88. Author's notes, meeting with Fuad Mustafayev, Popular Front of Azerbaijan Party representative, Baku, February 2005.
89. Author's notes, meetings with Azerbaijani intellectuals, Baku, February and July 2005.
90. European Commission for Democracy Through Law (Venice Commission), Opinion on the Draft Amendments to the Constitution of the Republic of Azerbaijan, adopted 13–14 March 2009, p. 6, <http://www.venice.coe.int/webforms/documents/default.aspx?pdffile=CDL-AD(2009)010-e> (last accessed 11 July 2018).
91. Author's interview with civil society activist, Baku, June 2014.
92. Thomas de Waal, 'A Free Thinker Loses His Freedom in Azerbaijan', *Open Democracy*, 9 January 2015, <https://www.opendemocracy.net/od-russia/thomas-de-waal/freethinker-loses-his-freedom-in-azerbaijan> (last accessed 5 July 2018).
93. Author's interview with Leyla Yunus, Director, Institute for Peace and Democracy, Baku, 20 June 2014.

94. Human Rights Watch, 'Azerbaijan: Opposition Youth Activists on Trial', 30 March 2006, <https://www.hrw.org/news/2006/03/30/azerbaijan-opposition-youth-activists-trial> (last accessed 5 July 2018).
95. Radio Free Europe/Radio Liberty, 'Prominent Azerbaijani Journalist Jailed for Six Years', 28 December 2015, <https://www.rferl.org/amp/prominent-azeri-journalist-jailed-for-six-years/27453794.html> (last accessed 5 July 2018).
96. See the official responses to the 'Azerbaijani Laundromat' money-laundering scandal of September documented in Arzu Geybullayeva, 'Azerbaijan Runs $2.9 billion "Laundromat" but Soros and the "Armenian Lobby" Are to Blame', Global Voices, 9 September 2017, <https://globalvoices.org/2017/09/09/azerbaijan-runs-2-9-billion-laundromat-but-soros-and-the-armenian-lobby-are-to-blame/> (last accessed 5 July 2018).
97. Author's interviews with Azerbaijani civil society activists, May–June 2014.
98. Author's interviews with Armenian civil society activists, March–June 2015.
99. Author's interview with Tatul Hakobyan, journalist and political analyst, Yerevan, 1 June 2016.
100. See Laurence Broers, *The Nagorny Karabakh Conflict: Defaulting to War* (London: Royal Institute for International Affairs, 2016), pp. 13, 17–18.
101. Author's interview with Jasur Mammadov Sumerinli, Director, Doktrina NGO, Baku, 29 May 2014.
102. In an eight-hour parliamentary session on 1 May 2018, parliamentarians aligned with the former ruling party considering Pashinyan's candidacy as prime minister continually cited his unsuitability as commander-in-chief and guarantor of Armenia's security. See the session broadcast by CivilNet, 'Live. With English Interpretation. – Will Nikol Pashinyan Be Prime Minister?', 1 May 2018, <https://www.youtube.com/watch?v=E2NSImJQtlc> (last accessed 17 July 2018).
103. BBC Russian Service, 'Nikol Pashinyan: so storony Armenii otnoshcheniyam s Rossiey nichego ne grozit', 29 April 2018, <https://www.bbc.com/russian/features-43940532> (last accessed 17 July 2018); Eduard Abrahamyan, 'Pashinyan Stiffens Armenia's Posture toward Karabakh', *Eurasia Daily Monitor* 15: 72, 10 May 2018, <https://jamestown.org/program/pashinyan-stiffens-armenias-posture-toward-karabakh/> (last accessed 17 July 2018).

Chapter 6

1. Speech in Ramana, Sabuncu district, 4 May 2007, available at the website of the State Committee for Affairs of Refugees and Internally Displaced Persons, <http://www.refugees-idps-committee.gov.az/en/pages/37.html> (last accessed 9 July 2018).
2. Ria Novosti, 'Zakir Gasanov: peregovory po Nagornomu Karabakhu slishkom zatyanulis', 13 July 2017, <https://ria.ru/amp/interview/20170713/1498376245.html> (last accessed 9 July 2018).
3. John A. Vasquez, *The War Puzzle* (Cambridge: Cambridge University Press, 1993), pp. 93–111.
4. Ivan Arreguín-Toft, *How the Weak Win Wars: A Theory of Asymmetric Conflict* (Cambridge: Cambridge University Press, 2005).
5. Ibid.; Andrew J. Mack, 'Why Big Nations Lose Small Wars: The Politics of Asymmetric Conflict', *World Politics* 27: 2, 1975, pp. 175–200.
6. T. V. Paul, *Asymmetric Conflicts: War Initiation by Weaker Powers* (Cambridge: Cambridge University Press, 1994).
7. The term 'truncated asymmetry' is T. V. Paul's. He devised it to describe the asymmetric rivalry between Pakistan and India and in particular how Pakistan has mitigated Indian preponderance. T. V. Paul, 'Why Has the India–Pakistan Rivalry Been So Enduring? Power Asymmetry and an Intractable Conflict', *Security Studies* 15: 4, 2006, pp. 600–30.
8. Saumya Mitra, Douglas Andrew, Gohar Gyulumyan, Paul Holden, Bart Kaminski, Yevgeny Kuzentsov and Ekaterine Vashakmadze, *The Caucasian Tiger: Sustaining Economic Growth in Armenia* (Washington DC: World Bank, 2007), p. 3.
9. National Statistical Service of Armenia, Ministry of Health and ICF International, *Armenia: Demographic and Health Survey 2010*, p. 1, <http://dhsprogram.com/pubs/pdf/FR252/FR252.pdf> (last accessed 9 July 2018); International Monetary Fund (IMF), *Republic of Armenia: Selected Issues*, IMF Country Report No. 17/227, 7 June 2017.
10. As reported in International Crisis Group, *Armenia and Azerbaijan: Preventing War*, Briefing No. 60, 8 February 2011, p. 6.
11. World Bank Group, *Azerbaijan Systematic Country Diagnostic* (Washington DC: World Bank, 2015), p. 15. For a critical

perspective on poverty reduction and social spending see Audrey L. Altstadt, *Frustrated Democracy in Post-Soviet Azerbaijan* (Washington DC and New York: Woodrow Wilson Center Press and Columbia University Press, 2017), pp. 102–8.

12. *Azernews*, 'SOFAZ Reveals its All-Time Revenues', 25 December 2017, <https://www.azernews.az/oil_and_gas/124536.html> (last accessed 9 July 2018).
13. Elmar Mammadyarov, 'Towards Peace in the Nagorny Karabakh Region of the Republic of Azerbaijan through Reintegration and Cooperation', in Laurence Broers (ed.), *The Limits of Leadership: Elites and Societies in the Nagorny Karabakh Peace Process*, Accord 17 (London: Conciliation Resources, 2005), pp. 18–19.
14. Author's notes from meetings with Azerbaijani Ministry of Foreign Affairs and Presidential Administration officials, 2008–12.
15. Stockholm International Peace Research Institute, *SIPRI Yearbook 2016: Armaments, Disarmament and International Security* (Oxford and Solna: Oxford University Press, 2016), p. 580.
16. Ibid., p. 585.
17. Both Azerbaijan and Armenia are subjects of a voluntary arms embargo in the Organization for Security and Co-operation in Europe (OSCE). A majority of licence applications to European Union member-states to supply arms to either country are rejected. Paul Holtom, 'Arms Transfers to Armenia and Azerbaijan, 2007–11', in Stockholm International Peace Research Institute, *SIPRI Yearbook 2012: Armaments, Disarmament and International Security* (Oxford: Oxford University Press, 2012), pp. 286–92.
18. Pieter D. Wezeman, Aude Fleurant, Alexandra Kuimova, Nan Tian and Siemon T. Wezeman, 'Trends in International Arms Transfers', *SIPRI Fact Sheet*, March 2018, p. 10.
19. Holtom, 'Arms Transfers to Armenia and Azerbaijan', pp. 289–90.
20. Zaur Shiriyev, 'Azerbaijan Looks to Greater Reliance on Domestically Produced Weapons', *Eurasianet*, 14 October 2016, <http://www.eurasianet.org/node/80891> (last accessed 9 July 2018). Armenian security analyst Sergey Minasyan assessed the Armenian domestic arms industry as 'an expensive luxury', highlighting that it is still cheaper to buy equipment in Russia and import it than to assemble it under licence in Armenia. Author's interview with Sergey Minasyan, Deputy Director of the Caucasus Institute, Yerevan, 9 March 2015.
21. See the successive entries of *The Military Balance*, compiled by the

International Institute for Strategic Studies, <http://www.tandfonline.com/loi/tmib20> (last accessed 9 July 2018).
22. Author's interview with Jasur Sumerinli, Director of Doktrina, Baku, 29 May 2014.
23. Cassady Craft, *Weapons for Peace, Weapons for War: The Effect of Arms Transfers on War Outbreak, Involvement, and Outcomes* (London and New York: Routledge, 1999).
24. Interview Sumerinli; Jasur Sumerinli, 'Armiyu neobkhodimo obespechit' kvartirami i vysokimi zarplatami', *Zerkalo*, 19 October 2012, <http://www.zerkalo.az/2012/armiyu-neobhodimo-obespechit-kvartirami-i-vyisokimi-zarplatami> (last accessed 19 July 2017); Jasur Sumerinli, 'Reformy v armii provedeny na bumage', *Zerkalo*, 17 May 2013, <http://www.zerkalo.az/2013/reformyi-v-armii-provedenyi-na-bumage> (last accessed 19 July 2017). On corruption in procurement see the series of articles written by Afgan Muhtarli and published on the Germany-based oppositional website Meydan TV; for example, 'Bidding Secrets of the Armed Forces Part 1: Purchases without Tenders', Meydan TV, 16 October 2014, <https://www.meydan.tv/en/site/politics/3402/Bidding-Secrets-of-the-Armed-Forces-Part-1-Purchases-without-tenders.htm> (last accessed 9 July 2018).
25. Interview Sumerinli; Idrak Abbasov, 'Azeri Anger Roused by Soldier's Death', Institute for War and Peace Reporting, 18 January 2013, <http://iwpr.net/report-news/azeri-anger-roused-soldiers-death> (last accessed 9 July 2018).
26. Sumerinli, 'Reformy v armii provedeny na bumage'.
27. Author's conversations in Azerbaijan, May–June 2014.
28. Jasur Sumerinli, 'Izmeneniya v Ministerstve oborony', *Zerkalo*, 29 November 2013, <http://www.zerkalo.az/2013/izmeneniya-v-ministerstve-oboronyi> (last accessed 19 July 2017).
29. Interview Sumerinli.
30. APA, 'Shahin Sultanov: I Thank President Ilham Aliyev for My Release', 25 December 2014, <http://en.apa.az/azerbaijan-politics/domestic-news/shahin-sultanov-i-thank-president-ilham-aliyev-for-my-release.html> (last accessed 9 July 2018).
31. Emil Sanamyan, 'The New Karabakh War: Who Is Fighting and Who Is Dying', presentation to the conference 'Armenia: End of Transition – Shifting Focus', Institute of Armenian Studies at the University of Southern California, 10 April 2017, <http://www.youtube.com/watch?v=2omhcOJ8haY> (last accessed 9 July 2018).

32. Ron Synovitz, 'Azerbaijani Spy Scandal Leaves Trail of Dead Suspects', *RFE/RL* report, 16 June 2017, <https://www.rferl.org/a/azerbaijani-spy-scandal-dead-suspects/28558844.html> (last accessed 4 December 2018).
33. SIPRI Military Expenditure Database 1988–2017, <http://www.sipri.org/databases/milex> (accessed 9 July 2018).
34. Gevorg Poghosyan, *Armenian Migration* (Yerevan: National Academy of Sciences, 2014), pp. 30–1.
35. International Organization for Migration (IOM), *Report on Household Survey on Migration in Armenia* (Yerevan: IOM, 2014), p. 63.
36. Garik Hayrapetyan, 'The Transition of Demographics and the Demographics of Transition', presentation to the conference 'Armenia: End of Transition – Shifting Focus', Institute of Armenian Studies at the University of Southern California, 10 April 2017, <http://www.youtube.com/watch?v=2omhcOJ8haY> (last accessed 9 July 2018).
37. James L. Gelvin, *The Israel–Palestine Conflict* (Cambridge: Cambridge University Press, 2005), p. 168.
38. IOM, *Report on Household Survey*, p. 59.
39. Arif Yunusov, *Migration Processes in Azerbaijan* (Baku: Adiloglu, 2009), pp. 106–7; Sergey Rumyansev, 'A New Immigration Policy in Azerbaijan', in Anna Bara, Anna Di Bartolomeo, Zuzanna Brunarska, Shushanik Makaryan, Sergo Mananashvili and Agnieszka Weinar (eds), *Regional Migration Report: South Caucasus* (Florence: European University Institute, 2013), pp. 82–3.
40. Sergey Rumyansev, 'General Trends of Migration Processes and Policy in Post-Soviet Azerbaijan (Immigration and Emigration)', in Bara et al., *Regional Migration Report*, p. 88.
41. For regional averages see UNFPA, *State of the World's Population 2016*, <https://www.unfpa.org/sites/default/files/pub-pdf/The_State_of_World_Population_2016_-_English.pdf> (last accessed 10 July 2018).
42. *Republic of Armenia National Security Strategy*, 26 January 2007, available at the website of the Ministry of Defence, <https://www.mfa.am/en/security-and-defense/> (last accessed 10 July 2018).
43. Alternative optimistic, pessimistic and realistic projections indicated populations of 3,122,009, 1,668,111 and 2,054,200 respectively. The United Nations' *World Population Prospects* median projections for the populations of Armenia and Azerbaijan in

2050 are 2,700,000 and 11,039,000 respectively. Hayrapetyan, 'Transition of Demographics' and United Nations, *World Population Prospects 2017 Revision. Volume II: Demographic Profiles* (New York: United Nations, 2017), pp. 71, 87.
44. 'Serzh Sargsyan: By 2040 the Population of Armenia Should Reach 4 million', Arminfo, 19 May 2017, <http://arminfo.info/full_news.php?id=25830&lang=3> (last accessed 10 July 2018).
45. Repat Armenia <http://repatarmenia.org> is a foundation established in 2012 to advance the repatriation of Armenians, by advocating for repatriation in the diaspora and supporting repatriates with finding employment and establishing businesses once in Armenia. In 2015 it had a network of up to 700 repatriated Armenians. Author's interview with Vartan Marashlyan, Director, Repat Armenia, Yerevan, 31 March 2015.
46. Modelled on Birthright Israel, Birthright Armenia was founded in 2003 to support three-month home stays and internships for diasporan Armenians between the ages of 20 and 32, including Armenian language and culture tuition. By 2015, 1,000 Armenians, two-thirds from North America, had passed through the programme. Author's interview with Sevan Kabakyan, Director of Birthright Armenia, 2 April 2015.
47. Interview Marashlyan.
48. Ibid. Thirty per cent of repatriates do not stay.
49. The republic's anthem enjoins citizens to 'build Artsakh like a fortress' that for centuries has been an 'impregnable stronghold'.
50. Mack, 'Why Big Nations Lose Small Wars', p. 176.
51. Senor Hasratian, *Defense Army of the Republic of Nagorno-Karabakh* (Yerevan: Tigran Mets, 2013), p. 195.
52. Sergey Minasyan, *Sderzhivanie v Karabakhskom Konflikte* (Yerevan: Caucasus Institute, 2016), pp. 142–52.
53. The assumption that the total ethnic cleansing of civilian populations would accompany renewed war means that traditional guerrilla warfare can be largely written off as a possibility.
54. Personal communication with Emil Sanamyan, 15 October 2018.
55. Hasratian, *Defense Army*, pp. 199–201.
56. For a quantification of the forces deployed across Azerbaijan, Armenia and Nagorny Karabakh as of January 2016 see Minasyan, *Sderzhivanie*, pp. 266–9. For other sources on the figure of 18,000–20,000 see International Crisis Group, *Nagorno-Karabakh: Viewing the Conflict from the Ground*, Europe Report No. 166, 14 September 2005, p. 9.

57. Author's interview with Vitaly Balasanyan, veteran and former presidential candidate, Stepanakert, 12 September 2014.
58. Personal communication, international humanitarian organisation official based in the South Caucasus, July 2017.
59. Paul, 'Why Has the India–Pakistan Rivalry Been So Enduring?', p. 628.
60. T. V. Paul (ed.), *The India–Pakistan Conflict: An Enduring Rivalry* (Cambridge: Cambridge University Press, 2005).
61. On this distinction see John J. Mearsheimer, *Conventional Deterrence* (Ithaca and London: Cornell University Press, 1983), pp. 14–15.
62. The *Iskander* is considerably more advanced than older *Scud*, *Typhoon* or *Tochka-U* missiles, being capable of accurately hitting targets 280–500 kilometres away depending on specification, and overcoming most missile defence systems.
63. Minasyan, *Sderzhivanie*, pp. 107–8.
64. Mearsheimer, *Conventional Deterrence*, p. 47.
65. Minasyan, *Sderzhivanie*, p. 136. Estimates of the reserve in the mid-2000s were lower at 20,000–30,000. International Crisis Group, *Nagorno-Karabakh*, p. 9.
66. See, for example, Wayne Merry, 'Karabakh: Is War Inevitable?', Open Democracy, 22 May 2009, <https://www.opendemocracy.net/article/email/karabakh-is-war-inevitable> (last accessed 10 July 2018).
67. Author's conversations with journalists in Nagorny Karabakh, 2012–14.
68. See Safe Soldiers for a Safe Armenia, <http://safesoldiers.am/en/>, implemented by the Vanadzor-based NGO Peace Dialogue.
69. Interview Minasyan; Gayane Abrahamian, 'Armenia: New Army Killings Raise Non-Combat Death Toll to 15 since July', *Eurasianet*, 22 November 2010, <http://www.eurasianet.org/node/62425> (last accessed 10 July 2018).
70. Author's notes, Armenian human rights activist, 4 April 2006.
71. Sara Khojoyan, 'Money for Army: Anti-corruption Sentiments Grow in Armenia Amid Karabakh Escalation', *ArmeniaNow.com*, 15 April 2016, <https://www.armenianow.com/en/society/2016/04/15/armenia-panama-papers-offshore-scandal-mihran-po ghosyan-karabakh/1067/> (last accessed 10 July 2018).
72. 'Senior Armenian Military Officials Sacked', *Azatutyun.am*, 26 April 2016, <https://www.azatutyun.am/a/27699843.html> (last accessed 10 July 2018); 'Melsik Chilingaryan osvobozhden ot

dolzhnosti nachal'nika upravleniya vooruzheniy VS Armenii', *Panarmenian.net*, 23 May 2016, <http://www.panarmenian.net/rus/news/212951/> (last accessed 10 July 2018).
73. Minasyan, *Sderzhivanie*, p. 141.
74. Ibid., p. 132.
75. Interview Minasyan.
76. Also deployed at the base are several hundred tanks, artillery units and armoured combat vehicles, S-300 *Favorit* surface-to-air and *Smerch* missiles, and two squadrons of MiG-29 fighter jets and Mi-24/Mi-8 helicopters. Richard Giragosian, *Cause for Concern: The Shifting Balance of Power in the South Caucasus* (Yerevan: Regional Studies Center, 2013), p. 2; Minasyan, *Sderzhivanie*, p. 107. Initially lasting twenty-five years, the base's lease was extended in 2010 until 2044.
77. Minasyan, *Sderzhivanie*, p. 127.
78. Ibid., p. 151. See also Mearsheimer, *Conventional Deterrence*, p. 208.
79. Belarus News, 'Belarus Advocates for Peaceful Settlement of Nagorny Karabakh Conflict', 4 April 2016, <http://eng.belta.by/politics/view/belarus-advocates-for-peaceful-settlement-of-nagorny-karabakh-conflict-90198-2016/> (last accessed 10 July 2018).
80. Timothy W. Crawford, *Pivotal Deterrence: Third-Party Statecraft and the Pursuit of Peace* (Ithaca and London: Cornell University Press, 2003).
81. Ibid., pp. 9–12.
82. Siranush Ghazanchyan, 'Armenia Will Get Assistance from CSTO Partners if Necessary: Nikolay Bordyuzha', *Public Radio of Armenia*, 18 June 2015, <http://www.armradio.am/en/2015/06/18/armenia-will-get-assistance-from-csto-partners-if-necessary-nikolay-bordyuzha/> (last accessed 10 July 2018).
83. Eduard Abrahamyan, 'Armenia's New Ballistic Missiles Will Shake Up the Neighbourhood', *The National Interest*, 12 October 2016.
84. On serial deterrence see Patrick M. Morgan, *Deterrence Now* (Cambridge: Cambridge University Press, 2003), pp. 266–7.
85. Thomas Goltz, *Azerbaijan Diary: A Rogue Reporter's Adventures in an Oil-Rich, War-Torn, Post-Soviet Republic* (Armonk, NY and London: M.E. Sharpe, 1998), p. xxiv.
86. Mack, 'Why Big Nations Lose Small Wars', pp. 177–81.
87. Arreguín-Toft, *How the Weak Win Wars*, pp. 26–7.

Notes

88. These tropes feature regularly, for example, in President Ilham Aliyev's Twitterfeed (@presidentaz).
89. Senior Azerbaijani official, speaking at the Azerbaijani Diplomatic Academy, Baku, June 2014.
90. Author's notes, meeting with Ali Hasanov, Head of Department for Public Political Issues, Presidential Administration, Baku, 24 February 2015.
91. On Azerbaijani elite views reflecting these perspectives see Ceylan Tokluoglu, 'The Political Discourse of the Azerbaijani Elite on the Nagorno Karabakh Conflict 1991–2009', *Europe-Asia Studies* 63: 7, 2011, pp. 1223–52.
92. Author's interview with Deputy Foreign Minister Araz Azimov, Baku, 20 February 2015.
93. Author's interview with Rasim Musabekov, Member of Parliament, Baku, 29 May 2014.
94. Author's interview with Senor Hasratian, Press Officer of the NKDA, Stepanakert, 15 September 2014.
95. See Gayane Abrahamyan, 'Armenia: Nation-Army Plan Raises Concerns about Society's Militarization', *Eurasianet*, 14 June 2017, <http://www.eurasianet.org/node/83991> (last accessed 10 July 2018).
96. Paul, 'Why Has the India–Pakistan Rivalry Been So Enduring?', p. 629.
97. Emil Sanamyan, '"Joint" Armenian-Russian Force: What it Is and What it Isn't', *Focus on Karabakh*, 1 December 2016, <http://armenian.usc.edu/focus-on-karabakh/analysis/new-agreement-defines-joint-armenian-russian-military-grouping/> (last accessed 10 July 2018).

Chapter 7

1. The arguments in this chapter are grounded in the work of Steven Levitsky and Lucan Way, 'Linkage versus Leverage. Rethinking the International Dimension of Regime Change', *Comparative Politics* 38: 4, 2006, pp. 379–400. Some of them appeared in earlier form in Laurence Broers, 'Diffusion and Default: A Linkage and Leverage Perspective on the Nagorny Karabakh Conflict', *East European Politics* 32: 3, 2016, pp. 378–99.
2. Richard, D. Kauzlarich, *Time for Change? U.S. Policy in the Transcaucasus* (New York: The Century Foundation, 2001), p. 71.

3. The original eleven-strong consortium was composed of firms from Britain, the US, Russia, Norway, Turkey and Saudi Arabia. In the latest iteration of the AIOC, as of September 2017, British Petroleum has the largest single share at 30.37 per cent. For the full composition in 2017 see BP Global, 'The Azerbaijan Government and Co-venturers Sign Amended and Restated Azeri-Chirag-Deepwater Gunashli PSA', 14 September 2017, <https://www.bp.com/en/global/corporate/media/press-releases/the-azerbaijan-government-and-co-venturers-sign-amended-and-restated-azeri-chirag-deepwater-gunashli-psa.html> (last accessed 11 July 2018).
4. Data derived from turnover and trade by country tables on the website of the State Statistical Committee of the Republic of Azerbaijan <http://www.stat.gov.az> (last accessed 18 March 2019).
5. International Monetary Fund's Coordinated Direct Investment Survey (CDIS) database, <http://data.imf.org/?sk=40313609-F037-48C1-84B1-E1F1CE54D6D5&sId=1482331048410> (last accessed 11 July 2018).
6. Personal conversation, World Bank expert, Washington DC, 27 March 2006.
7. For aid data see Gwendolyn Sasse, 'Linkages and the Promotion of Democracy: The EU's Eastern Neighbourhood', *Democratization* 20: 4, 2013, pp. 553–91.
8. SIDA, *Armenia and Azerbaijan: Sida Country Report 2007*, p. 4, <https://www.sida.se/English/publications/113599/armenia-and-azerbaijan/> (last accessed 11 July 2018).
9. The full text can be found at S.2532 FREEDOM Support Act, 24 October 1992, <http://www.congress.gov/bill/102nd-congress/senate-bill/2532/text> (last accessed 11 July 2018).
10. For a trenchant perspective on the effects of Section 907 in Azerbaijan see Thomas Goltz, 'Oil and Civil Society Don't Mix', *WarReport* 45, September 1996, pp. 41–3.
11. Valerie J. Bunce and Sharon L. Wolchik, *Defeating Authoritarian Leaders in Postcommunist Countries* (Cambridge: Cambridge University Press, 2011), p. 234.
12. Kauzlarich, *Time for Change?*, p. 27.
13. European Commission, *Implementation of the European Neighbourhood Policy in Azerbaijan: Progress in 2014 and Recommendations for Actions*, p. 3, <https://library.euneighbours.eu/content/implementation-european-neighbourhood-policy-azer

baijan-progress-2014-and-recommendations-ac> (last accessed 11 July 2018).
14. In 2014 Azerbaijan did not align itself with any of the EU's Common Foreign and Security Policy (CFSP) Declarations, while in 2013 it aligned with only seven of thirty-two CFSP declarations it was invited to support. Ibid., p. 8.
15. Group of States Against Corruption (GRECO), *Fourth Evaluation Round (Corruption Prevention in Respect of Members of Parliament, Judges and Prosecutors)*, Evaluation Report – Azerbaijan, 2 April 2015, <https://www.coe.int/en/web/greco/evaluations/round-4> (last accessed 11 July 2018).
16. Author's conversations with Azerbaijani civil society activists, May–June 2014.
17. Thomas de Waal, 'Azerbaijan's Lost Transparency', Carnegie Europe, 20 March 2017, <http://carnegieeurope.eu/strategiceurope/68332> (last accessed 11 July 2018).
18. Author's conversations with USAID and Commission on Security and Cooperation in Europe employees, Baku and Washington DC, December 2014–September 2015. Aid figure from USAID's mission to Azerbaijan website, <https://www.usaid.gov/azerbaijan/history> (last accessed 11 July 2018).
19. See the official website of the CSSN, <http://www.cssn.gov.az/index.php?lang=en> (last accessed 11 July 2018).
20. Author's conversation with Azerbaijani civil society activist, Baku, June 2015.
21. European Parliament Resolution on Azerbaijan 2015/2840, 10 September 2015, <http://www.europarl.europa.eu/sides/getDoc.do?pubRef=-//EP//TEXT+TA+P8-TA-2015-0316+0+DOC+XML+V0//EN> (last accessed 11 July 2018).
22. Radio Liberty/Radio Free Europe, 'U.S. Bill Seeks Sanctions on Azerbaijani Officials for "Appalling" Human Rights Record', 16 December 2015, <https://www.rferl.org/a/us-bill-seeks-sanctions-on-azeri-officials-for-appalling-rights-record/27432171.html> (last accessed 10 July 2018).
23. Ramiz Mehtiyev, 'Miroporyadok dvoynykh standartov i sovremennyy Azerbaydzhan', *Day.Az*, 3 December 2014, <http://news.day.az/politics/539699.html> (last accessed 11 July 2018); 'Ot mirovogo poryadka k "besporyadku"', *1News.Az*, 22 October 2015, <www.1news.az/politics/20151022101657526.html> (last accessed 11 July 2018).
24. ESI, *Caviar Diplomacy. How Azerbaijan Silenced the Council*

of Europe, 24 May 2012, <https://www.esiweb.org/index.php?lang=en&id=156&document_ID=131> (last accessed 11 July 2018).
25. Although TEAS claims independence from the Azerbaijani government, its representatives told me in London in March 2007 that the organisation was funded by Gilan Holding, the conglomerate owned by Minister of Emergency Situations Kamaleddin Heydarov, and 'companies in Baku'.
26. Michael Weiss, 'The Corleones of the Caspian', *Foreign Policy*, 10 June 2014, <http://foreignpolicy.com/2014/06/10/the-corleones-of-the-caspian/> (last accessed 11 July 2018).
27. Personal conversation, US policy-maker, Washington DC, 16 December 2014.
28. Luke Harding, Cailainn Barr and Dina Nagapetyants, 'UK at Centre of Secret $3bn Azerbaijani Money Laundering and Lobbying Scheme', *The Guardian*, 4 September 2017, <https://www.theguardian.com/world/2017/sep/04/uk-at-centre-of-secret-3bn-azerbaijani-money-laundering-and-lobbying-scheme> (last accessed 11 July 2018).
29. Luke Harding, 'Azerbaijan Leader's Daughters Tried to Buy £60m London Home with Offshore Funds', *The Guardian*, 21 December 2018, <https://www.theguardian.com/uk-news/2018/dec/21/azerbaijan-leaders-daughters-tried-to-buy-60m-london-home-with-offshore-funds> (last accessed 21 December 2018).
30. OCCRP, 'Ethics Report Reveals Azerbaijan Secretly Bankrolled Trip for US Lawmakers', 14 May 2015, <https://www.occrp.org/en/daily/3950-ethics-report-reveals-azerbaijan-secretly-bankrolled-trip-for-us-lawmakers> (last accessed 11 July 2018); United States Department of Justice, 'Former Non-Profit President Pleads Guilty to Scheme to Conceal Foreign Funding of 2013 Congressional Trip', press release, 10 December 2018, <https://www.justice.gov/opa/pr/former-non-profit-president-pleads-guilty-scheme-conceal-foreign-funding-2013-congressional> (last accessed 19 December 2018).
31. Gerald Knaus, 'Europe and Azerbaijan: The End of Shame', *Journal of Democracy* 26: 3, 2015, pp. 5–18, p. 7.
32. One tactic used at the Council of Europe was to challenge resolutions on political prisoners by asserting the absence of an agreed definition of the term. Ibid., p. 13.
33. Farid Shafiyev, 'Liberal Hypocrisy on Post-Soviet Separatism', *The National Interest*, 13 June 2016, <http://nationalinterest.

org/feature/liberal-hypocrisy-post-soviet-separatism-16575> (last accessed 11 July 2018).
34. Alexander Iskandaryan, 'Armenia's Foreign Policy: Where Values Meet Constraints', in Mikko Palonkorpi and Alexander Iskandaryan (eds), *Armenia's Foreign and Domestic Politics: Development Trends* (Yerevan: Caucasus Institute and Aleksanteri Institute, 2013), pp. 6–17.
35. Author's calculations from the International Monetary Fund's CDIS database.
36. For details of these agreements see Emil Danielyan, 'Russia Tightens Grip on Debt-Burdened Armenia', *Azatutyun.am*, 17 September 2001, <https://www.azatutyun.am/a/1567028.html> (last accessed 11 July 2018); Vladimir Socor, 'Armenia's Giveaways to Russia: From Property-for-Debt to Property-for-Gas', *Eurasia Daily Monitor* 3: 76, 19 April 2006, <https://jamestown.org/program/armenias-giveaways-to-russia-from-property-for-debt-to-property-for-gas/> (last accessed 11 July 2018).
37. Lower figure from United Nations Population Fund (UNPF), *Report on Sample Survey on Internal and External Migration in RA* (Yerevan: UNPF, 2008), p. 58; higher figure from Garik Hayrapetyan, 'The Transition of Demographics and the Demographics of Transition', presentation to the conference 'Armenia: End of Transition – Shifting Focus', Institute of Armenian Studies at the University of Southern California, 10 April 2017, <http://www.youtube.com/watch?v=2omhcOJ8haY> (last accessed 11 July 2018).
38. International Monetary Fund (IMF), *Republic of Armenia: Selected Issues*, IMF Country Report No. 06/434 (Washington DC: IMF, December 2006), p. 5. More recent figures in the region of 60–65 per cent can be found in the World Bank's Migration and Remittances Data, <http://www.worldbank.org/en/topic/migrationremittancesdiasporaissues/brief/migration-remittances-data> (last accessed 11 July 2018).
39. IMF, *Republic of Armenia*, p. 5.
40. Emil Danielyan, 'Migrant Remittances to Armenia Rebound in 2017', *Azatutyun.am*, 9 May 2017, <https://www.azatutyun.am/a/28476831.html> (last accessed 11 July 2018).
41. Vahram Ter-Matevosyan, Hamazasp Danielyan, Serge-Varak Sisserian, Nina Kankanyan and Nayiri Shorjian, 'Institutions and Identity Politics in the Armenian Diaspora: The Cases of Russia and Lebanon', *Diaspora Studies* 10: 1, 2017, pp. 64–80, p. 65. In

the Russian census of 2010, 1.13 million Armenians were recorded as citizens of Russia.

42. Kristin Cavoukian, '"Soviet Mentality?" The Role of Shared Political Culture in Relations between the Armenian State and Russia's Armenian Diaspora', *Nationalities Papers* 41: 5, 2013, pp. 709–29, p. 718; Ter-Matevosyan et al., 'Institutions and Identity Politics', pp. 75–6.
43. Kristin Cavoukian, 'Identity Gerrymandering: How the Armenian State Constructs and Controls "its" Diaspora' (PhD dissertation, University of Toronto, 2016).
44. Armen Grigoryan, 'Armenia and the Iran Deal', *Central Asia-Caucasus Analyst*, 31 August 2015, <https://www.cacianalyst.org/publications/analytical-articles/item/13263-armenia-and-the-iran-deal.html> (last accessed 11 July 2018).
45. Laure Delcour, 'Faithful but Constrained? Armenia's Half-Hearted Support for Russia's Regional Integration Policies in the Post-Soviet Space', London School of Economics Ideas: Geopolitics of Eurasian Integration, June 28, 2014, <https://ssrn.com/abstract=2460335> (last accessed 11 July 2018).
46. Author's interview with EU official, Yerevan, 7 April 2015.
47. Ibid.
48. Personal conversation, Western diplomat, Yerevan, June 2016.
49. Vahram Ter-Matevosyan, Anna Drnoian, Narek Mkrtchyan and Tigran Yepremyan, 'Armenia in the Eurasian Economic Union: Reasons for Joining and its Consequences', *Eurasian Geography and Economics* 58: 3, 2017, pp. 340–60, pp. 349–50.
50. See, for example, the 2012–16 polls of the Eurasian Development Bank (EDB), EDB Integration Barometer, <https://eabr.org/en/analytics/integration-research/>, and the Caucasus Barometer, <http://caucasusbarometer.org/en/datasets/> (both last accessed 18 March 2019).
51. In the 2015 Caucasus Barometer, support for membership of the EAEU at 55 per cent was higher than for membership of the EU at 39 per cent. In the 2016 OPEN Neighbourhood 'EU Neighbours East' poll, trust in the EU at 54 per cent was higher than for the EAEU at 47 per cent. Caucasus Barometer Armenia 2015, <http://caucasusbarometer.org/en/datasets/> (last accessed 18 March 2019); ECORYS, *OPEN Neighbourhood – Communicating for a Stronger Partnership: Connecting with Citizens across the Eastern Neighbourhood*, Annual Survey Report: Regional Overview

– Eastern Partnership Countries (Birmingham and Brussels: ECORYS, 2016).
52. David M. Herszenhorn, 'Russia to Close Radar Station in Azerbaijan', *The New York Times*, 11 December 2012, <http://www.nytimes.com/2012/12/12/world/europe/russia-to-shut-down-radar-station-in-azerbaijan.html> (last accessed 11 July 2018).
53. Valery Dzutsati, 'Moscow Shows Renewed Interest in the Fate of Minorities in Azerbaijan', *Eurasia Daily Monitor* 9: 125, 2 July 2012, <https://jamestown.org/program/moscow-shows-renewed-interest-in-the-fate-of-ethnic-minorities-in-azerbaijan-2/> (last accessed 11 July 2018).
54. Mariam Seidbeyli, *Azerbaydzhanskaya diaspora v Rossii: Osobennosti i tendentsii formirovaniya i razvitiya* (Baku: Serq-Qerb, 2011), pp. 194–5; Arif Yunusov, *Migration Processes in Azerbaijan* (Baku: Adiloglu, 2009), p. 113.
55. Bradley Jardine, 'Russia Closes Azerbaijani Diaspora Organization', *Eurasianet*, 22 September 2017, <http://www.eurasianet.org/node/85246> (last accessed 11 July 2018); Rahim Rahimov, 'Moscow Pressing Azerbaijani Diaspora to Send a Loud Signal to Baku', *Eurasia Daily Monitor* 14: 69, 22 May 2017, <https://jamestown.org/program/moscow-pressing-azerbaijani-diaspora-send-loud-signal-baku/> (last accessed 11 July 2018).
56. Examples include the first president of Azerbaijan, Ayaz Mutalibov; former Minister of Defence Rahim Gaziyev; and former Minister of National Security Namik Abasov. The analogy of the touchline comes from Hugh Roberts's discussion of political émigrés and interested outsiders 'on the touchline' of Algerian politics. See Hugh Roberts, *The Battlefield: Algeria 1988–2002* (London and New York: Verso, 2003), pp. 223–5.
57. Svante E. Cornell, 'Azerbaijan: Going it Alone', in S. Frederick Starr and Svante E. Cornell (eds), *Putin's Grand Strategy: The Eurasian Union and its Discontents* (Washington DC and Stockholm: Central Asia and Caucasus Institute, 2014), pp. 145–56, pp. 152–3.
58. Zaur Shiriyev, *Betwixt and Between: The Reality of Russian Soft Power in Azerbaijan*, Heinrich Böll Stiftung, 16 October 2017, <https://ge.boell.org/en/2017/10/16/betwixt-and-between-reality-russian-soft-power-azerbaijan> (last accessed 11 July 2018).
59. Laure Delcour and Kataryna Wolczuk, 'The EU's Unexpected "Ideal Neighbour"? The Perplexing Case of Armenia's Europeanisation', *Journal of European Integration* 37: 4, 2015, pp. 491–507.
60. Author's interview with EU official, Yerevan, 7 April 2015.

61. Author's interview with Gevorg Ter-Gabrielyan, Director, Eurasian Partnership Foundation, Yerevan, 8 April 2014.
62. Heghine Buniatian, 'EU to Provide Armenia with Fresh Aid', Radio Free Europe/Radio Liberty, 4 November 2014, <https://www.rferl.org/a/european-union-armenia/26673213.html> (last accessed 11 July 2018).
63. Rilka Dragneva, Laure Delcour and Laurynas Jonavicius, *Assessing Legal and Political Compatibility between the European Union Engagement Strategies and Membership of the Eurasian Economic Union*, EU-STRAT, Working Paper No. 7, November 2017.
64. Iskandaryan, 'Armenia's Foreign Policy', p. 6.
65. Thomas de Waal, *Great Catastrophe: Armenians and Turks in the Shadow of Genocide* (Oxford: Oxford University Press, 2015), pp. 200–3.
66. Zaur Shiriyev, 'Azerbaijan Building Up Forces in Nakhchivan', *Eurasianet*, 10 August 2017, <http://www.eurasianet.org/node/84691> (last accessed 11 July 2018).
67. Murad Ismayilov and Norman A. Graham (eds), *Turkish–Azerbaijani Relations: One Nation – Two States?* (London and New York: Routledge, 2016).
68. Aynur Karimova, 'SOCAR Turkey Enerji to become largest industrial company in Turkey by 2023', *Azernews*, 31 August 2015, <https://www.azernews.az/oil_and_gas/87405.html> (last accessed 11 July 2018).
69. IMF, CDIS database, data for 2009–15.
70. Burcu Gultekin Punsmann, *The Caucasus Stability and Cooperation Platform: An Attempt to Foster Regional Accountability*, International Centre for Black Sea Studies Policy Brief No. 13, April 2009.
71. Svante E. Cornell, 'Turkey's Role: Balancing the Armenia–Azerbaijan Conflict and Turkish–Armenian Relations', in Svante E. Cornell (ed.), *The International Politics of the Armenian–Azerbaijani Conflict: The Original 'Frozen Conflict' and European Security* (New York: Palgrave Macmillan, 2017), pp. 89–105, p. 90.
72. For contrasting views on this initiative see Tatul Hakobyan, *Armenians and Turks: From War to Cold War to Diplomacy* (Yerevan: Lusakn, 2013), pp. 333–81; Cornell, 'Turkey's Role', pp. 95–100; de Waal, *Great Catastrophe*, pp. 214–34.
73. Rasmus Christian Elling provides an overview of commonly

cited figures in the range of 9–23 million in *Minorities in Iran: Nationalism and Ethnicity after Khomeini* (New York: Palgrave Macmillan, 2013), p. 28.
74. For a recent overview see Brenda Shaffer, 'The Islamic Republic of Iran's Policy toward the Nagorno-Karabakh Conflict', in Cornell (ed.), *International Politics of the Armenian–Azerbaijani Conflict*, pp. 107–24.
75. Elling, *Minorities in Iran*, pp. 9–10.
76. The trigger for the violence in Iranian Azerbaijan was a caricature of Azerbaijanis as cockroaches in a state-run newspaper. This is symptomatic of a tradition depicting Azerbaijanis negatively as *tork-e khar* ('Turkish donkeys'), i.e. rural and backward. Elling, *Minorities in Iran*, pp. 65, 78–9, 176–9.
77. Svante E. Cornell, *Azerbaijan since Independence* (Armonk, NY and London: M.E. Sharpe, 2011), p. 327. The Güney Azərbaycan Milli Uyanış Hareketi (Southern Azerbaijan National Awakening Movement, <http://www.gamoh.org>) is banned in Iran but informally based in Azerbaijan.
78. Shaffer, 'Islamic Republic of Iran's Policy', pp. 111–12.
79. Razmik Panossian, *The Armenians: From Kings and Priests to Merchants and Commissars* (London: Hurst, 2006), p. 309.
80. Author's interview with Richard Giragosian, Director, Regional Studies Center, Yerevan, 22 April 2015.
81. Raffi Hamparian, 'Why the ANCA Works Relentlessly for U.S. Aid to Artsakh', *The Armenian Weekly*, 29 July 2016, <https://armenianweekly.com/2016/07/29/anca-us-aid-to-artsakh/> (last accessed 11 July 2018).
82. 'Za poslednye godi SShA predostavili Nagornomu Karabakhu i ego narodu na $45 mln: Dzhon Kheffern', *Aravot*, 27 July 2017, <http://www.aravot-ru.am/2017/07/27/246726/> (last accessed 11 July 2018).
83. Personal conversation, US policy-maker, Washington DC, 16 December 2014.
84. State of Rhode Island, House Resolution 2012 H-8180 Supporting the Nagorno-Karabakh Republic's Efforts to Develop as a Free and Independent Nation, 17 May 2012.
85. See <http://www.justiceforkhojaly.org> and Murad Ismayilov, 'Power, Knowledge and Pipelines: Understanding the Politics of Azerbaijan's Foreign Policy', *Caucasus Survey* 2: 1–2, 2014, pp. 79–129, pp. 96, 100.
86. On the background and emergence of a Turkish–Israeli–Azerbaijani

strategic triangle see Alexander Murinson, *Turkey's Entente with Israel and Azerbaijan* (London and New York: Routledge, 2010).
87. Eduard Abrahamyan, 'Pakistan–Armenia Friction Has Intensified', *Eurasia Daily Monitor* 13: 197, 15 December 2016, <https://jamestown.org/program/pakistan-armenia-friction-intensified/> (last accessed 11 July 2018).
88. 'Armenia Blocks Pakistani Presence in Ex-Soviet Body', *Azatutyun.am*, 24 November 2016, <https://www.azatutyun.am/a/28137853.html> (last accessed 11 July 2018); Eduard Abrahamyan, 'Armenia and India Build Strategic Relationship', *Eurasia Daily Monitor* 14: 70, 23 May 2017, <https://jamestown.org/program/armenia-india-build-strategic-relationship/> (last accessed 11 July 2018).
89. On these two narratives and the problems they pose see Gerard Toal, *Near Abroad: Putin, the West and the Contest over Ukraine and the Caucasus* (Oxford: Oxford University Press, 2017), pp. 20–33.
90. Ibid., p. 284.
91. Vadim Romashov and Helena Rytövuori-Apunen, 'Russia's Karabakh Policy: New Momentum in Regional Perspective', *Caucasus Survey* 5: 2, 2017, pp. 160–76, p. 161.
92. The following analysis builds on an unpublished paper generously shared with me in January 2016 by Cory Welt, to whom I give thanks.
93. The concept originates in John Mearsheimer's discussion of how great powers gain power. John J. Mearsheimer, *The Tragedy of Great Power Politics* (New York and London: W.W. Norton, 2001), pp. 153–4.
94. Author's interview with Zardusht Alizade, author and political analyst, Baku, 18 June 2014.
95. Mearsheimer, *Tragedy of Great Power Politics*, p. 154.
96. Satenik Tovmasyan, 'Russian Arms Deliveries Are Not Disturbing Parity, Says CSTO Chief', *ArmeniaNow.com*, 18 June 2015, <https://www.armenianow.com/karabakh/64504/armenia_csto_bordyuzha_weapons_russia_azerbaijan_sale> (last accessed 11 July 2018).
97. See, for example, Azad Isazade, 'Armeniagate', *WarReport* 51, May 1997, pp. 16–17.
98. Romashov and Rytövuori-Apunen, 'Russia's Karabakh Policy', pp. 167–72.
99. Bobo Lo, *Russia and the New World Disorder* (London: Royal Institute for International Affairs, 2015), pp. 49–50.

100. Timothy W. Crawford, *Pivotal Deterrence: Third-Party Statecraft and the Pursuit of Peace* (Ithaca and London: Cornell University Press, 2003), pp. 29–37.
101. Ani Mshetsyan, 'Anatoliy Sidorov: Nagornyy Karabakh ne yavlyaetsya chlenom ODKB i organizatsiya ne okazhet Artsakhu podderzhku v sluchae voyny', Arminfo, 6 March 2018, <http://arminfo.info/full_news.php?id=29813&lang=2> (last accessed 4 December 2018).
102. Yu. Belousov, 'Yuzhnyy forpost Rossii', *Krasnaya Zvezda*, 10 October 2013, <http://www.redstar.ru/index.php/pavlyutkina/item/12045-yuzhnyj-forpost-rossii> (last accessed 3 August 2017).
103. 'Foreign Minister Sergey Lavrov's Remarks and Answers to Media Questions at a News Conference on the Results of Russian Diplomacy in 2016', 17 January 2017, Ministry of Foreign Affairs of the Russian Federation, <http://www.mid.ru/en/press_service/minister_speeches/-/asset_publisher/7OvQR5KJWVmR/content/id/2599609> (last accessed 11 July 2018).
104. On uncertainty and ingratiation effects see Crawford, *Pivotal Deterrence*, pp. 20–1.
105. Ibid., pp. 37–43.

Chapter 8

1. Dov Lynch, *Engaging Eurasia's Separatist States* (Washington DC: United States Institute of Peace, 2004); Donnacha Ó Beacháin, Giorgio Comai and Ann Tsurtsumia-Zurabashvili, 'The Secret Lives of Unrecognised States: Internal Dynamics, External Relations, and Counter-Recognition Strategies', *Small Wars and Insurgencies* 27: 3, 2016, pp. 440–66; Laurence Broers, Alexander Iskandaryan and Sergey Minasyan (eds), *The Unrecognised Politics of De Facto States in the Post-Soviet Space* (Yerevan: Caucasus Institute, 2015).
2. Nina Caspersen, *Unrecognised States* (Cambridge: Polity, 2012), pp. 54–9.
3. Ibid., pp. 108–9.
4. Author's interview with Arkady Ghukasian, former de facto president of the Nagorno-Karabakh Republic, 1997–2007, Stepanakert, 19 September 2014.
5. Author's interview with Artak Beglaryan, Spokesman to de facto

Prime Minister Araik Harutyunyan, Stepanakert, 18 September 2014.
6. Author's interview with Hratchya Arzumanyan, political analyst, de facto Ministry of Foreign Affairs, Stepanakert, 13 September 2014.
7. Author's interview with Ararat Danielyan, de facto Minister of Justice, Stepanakert, 10 September 2014.
8. Author's notes, meeting with senior de facto official, Stepanakert, March 2005.
9. Stepanakert Press Club, *Mountainous Karabakh in the Mirror of Public Opinion* (Stepanakert: Stepanakert Press Club, Berlin: Friedrich Ebert Foundation and Yerevan: Center of Social Technologies, 2004), p. 151. Within the same project the corresponding figures for 2003 were 44.9 per cent and 48.3 per cent respectively (p. 203).
10. Hrant Mikaelian, *Societal Perceptions of the Conflict in Armenia and Nagorno-Karabakh* (Yerevan: Caucasus Institute, 2017), pp. 24–5.
11. Ibid., p. 25.
12. Author's interview with Hayk Khanumyan, political activist and chairman of the Revival party, Stepanakert, September, 11 September 2014.
13. This means, inter alia, that Nagorny Karabakh's attitude towards other post-Soviet de facto states is correspondingly polite but distant. Author's interview with Masis Mayilian, Director, Foreign and Security Policy Council, Stepanakert, 8 September 2014.
14. Author's interview with Edgar Khachatryan, Director, Peace Dialogue, Vanadzor, 5 March 2015.
15. Ibid.
16. *The Armenian Weekly*, 'Violence Against Opposition Group in Berdzor Draws Condemnation', 2 February 2015, <https://armenianweekly.com/2015/02/02/berdzor/> (last accessed 12 July 2018).
17. Gegham Baghdasaryan, 'Kogda politicheskaya sistema prebyvaet vne politicheskogo prostranstva', *Analitikon*, February 2015, <http://theanalyticon.com/?p=5991&lang=ru> (last accessed 12 July 2018).
18. International Crisis Group, *Nagorno-Karabakh: Viewing the Conflict from the Ground*, Europe Report No. 166, 14 September 2005, p. 12.
19. Author's interview with Spartak Tevosyan, Stepanakert, de facto Minister of Finance and Economics, Stepanakert, 10 September

2014. An alternative accounting of the loan is that the loan is in part repayment of Armenia's levying of customs duties on goods that pass through Armenia on the way to Nagorny Karabakh. Here a border that has to all intents and purposes disappeared in the real world reappears in financial accounting and provides a logic for the interstate credit. Author's interview with Ashot Gulyan, de facto Speaker of Parliament, Stepanakert, 22 September 2014.
20. Interview Gulyan.
21. Author's interview with David Harutyunyan, Minister-Chief of Government Staff and Chairman of the Standing Committee on State and Legal Affairs at the National Assembly, Yerevan, 7 April 2015.
22. Interview Tevosyan.
23. Ibid.
24. Author's interview with Ashot Baghshyan, Director, Village and Agricultural Fund of the Nagorno-Karabakh Republic, Stepanakert, 17 September 2014.
25. Author's interview with Mher Mkhitaryan, Deputy Director, Artsakh Development Fund, Stepanakert, 15 September 2014.
26. Author's interview with Artak Balyan, Director, State Tax Inspectorate, Stepanakert, 19 September 2014.
27. Interview Gulyan.
28. Author's interview with Araik Harutyunyan, de facto prime minister, Stepanakert, 24 September 2014.
29. The term 'monopoly mediator' originates in Abram de Swaan's historical work on statebuilding in Europe. De Swaan argued that bilingual local elites in the periphery held quasi-monopolies mediating between their monolingual 'clientele' in the hinterland, and the central state network operating in the standard metropolitan language. Abram de Swaan, *In Care of the State* (Oxford: Oxford University Press, 1988), p. 59.
30. Author's interview with civil society activist, Stepanakert, 22 September 2014.
31. Giorgio Comai, 'Conceptualizing Post-Soviet De Facto States as Small Dependent Jurisdictions', *Ethnopolitics* 17: 2, 2018, pp. 181–200.
32. For a factual record of the process of demilitarisation and the struggle between Ghukasian and Babayan see Kimitaka Matsuzato, 'Demilitarizatsiya i demokratizatsiya Nagorno-Karabakhskoy Respubliki (1988–2005 gg.)', *Demo* 22, 15 December 2005, pp. 8–9.

33. Interview Ghukasian.
34. Caspersen, *Unrecognised States*, p. 52.
35. Interview Mayilian.
36. Interview Arzumanyan.
37. Stepanakert Press Club, *Mountainous Karabakh in the Mirror of Public Opinion*, p. 149.
38. On this see Caspersen, *Unrecognised States*, ch. 4.
39. Personal conversation, activist, Stepanakert, 12 March 2005.
40. Author's interview with Eduard Agabekyan, former mayor, Stepanakert, 11 September 2014.
41. Steven Levitsky and Lucan A. Way, *Competitive Authoritarianism: Hybrid Regimes after the Cold War* (Cambridge: Cambridge University Press, 2010).
42. Donnacha Ó Beacháin, 'Elections without Recognition: Presidential and Parliamentary Contests in Abkhazia and Nagorny Karabakh', *Caucasus Survey* 3: 3, 2015, pp. 239–57.
43. Ibid., p. 248.
44. Interview Mayilian.
45. Ibid.
46. Ibid.
47. Ibid.
48. Author's interview with Vitaliy Balasanyan, 2012 presidential candidate, Stepanakert, 12 September 2014.
49. I argue this point in Laurence Broers, 'Recognising Politics in Unrecognised States: 20 Years of Enquiry into the De Facto States of the South Caucasus', *Caucasus Survey*, 1: 1, 2013, pp. 59–74.
50. Author's interview with David Ishkhanyan, ARF party representative, Stepanakert, 22 September 2014.
51. Karine Ohanyan, 'Vybory v Karabakhe: "match-revansh" so storony vlastey', *Demo* 12, 30 June 2005, p. 8.
52. Personal conversation, opposition activist, Stepanakert, 18 March 2012.
53. Masis Mayilian, *Elections During Armistice: 2015 Parliamentary Elections in the Nagorno-Karabakh Republic*, Caucasus Institute Policy Brief, May 2015.
54. Author's interview with Alexander Iskandaryan, Director, Caucasus Institute, Yerevan, 6 March 2015.
55. Interview Beglaryan.
56. Personal conversation, journalist, Stepanakert, September 2015.
57. Karen Israelov, 'Tretiy srok: Stoit li radi nego narushat' moral'?',

Demo 16, 30 September 2006, p. 7; Arsen Markaryan, 'Imidzh ili tretiy srok?', *Demo* 17, 15 October 2006, p. 7.
58. 'Obrashchenie Prezidenta NKR Arkadiya Gukasyana k Narodu Nagorno-Karabakhskoy Respubliki', *Demo* 3, 28 February 2007, p. 9; Ghukasian today upholds that he never considered a third term. Interview Ghukasian.
59. Personal conversation, Martuni, Nagorny Karabakh, June 2013.
60. Emil Sanamyan, 'With New Constitution, Is Karabakh Following in Azerbaijan's Footsteps?', *Eurasianet*, 18 February 2017, <https://eurasianet.org/node/82466> (last accessed 12 July 2018).
61. 'Protests Hit Nagorno-Karabakh after Security Forces "Beat Up Two"', OC Media, 4 June 2018, <http://oc-media.org/protests-hit-nagorno-karabakh-after-security-forces-beat-up-two/> (last accessed 12 July 2018); 'Karabakh Premier, Security Chiefs Resign after Protests', *Massispost*, 6 June 2018, <https://massispost.com/2018/06/karabakh-premier-security-chiefs-resign-after-protests/> (last accessed 12 July 2018).
62. The constitutions of 2006 and 2017 both refer to the territorial boundaries of the republic in their final chapters on 'Final and transitional provisions' (Articles 142 and 175 respectively). See Chapter 3, note 29. These articles appear to concede the negotiability of territories acquired in 1992–4, but make their negotiation contingent on the fulfilment of the NKR's claim to the former Shahumyan district to the north.
63. Personal conversation, de facto foreign ministry official, Stepanakert, 13 September 2014; see Radio Free Europe/Radio Liberty, 'From the Turmoil of Aleppo to the Conflict in Nagorno-Karabakh', 5 September 2016, <https://www.rferl.org/a/nagorno-karabakh-syrian-armenians/27967773.html> (last accessed 12 July 2018).
64. Developments in these territories are challenging to research. The following is based on the fact-finding missions of the OSCE, local media and on around half a dozen day trips to the regions of Lachin, Kelbajar and Agdam by the author in 2005–15. Inevitably, these provide only snapshots of complex, long-term processes.
65. OSCE, *Report of the OSCE Fact-Finding Mission (FFM) to the Occupied Territories of Azerbaijan Surrounding Nagorno-Karabakh (NK)* (Vienna: OSCE, 2005).
66. Ibid., p. 5.
67. Ibid., p. 24.
68. Author's conversations with local residents, Lachin, September

2014. Investigative journalist Onnik Krikorian heard similar complaints in 2006. Onnik Krikorian, 'Lachin: Pusteyushchie zemli', *Demo* 17, 15 October 2006, p. 8.
69. OSCE, Executive Summary of the 'Report of the OSCE Minsk Group Co-Chairs' Field Assessment Mission to the Occupied Territories of Azerbaijan Surrounding Nagorno-Karabakh', October 2010.
70. National Statistical Service of the NKR, *Rayony Nagorno-Karabakhskoy Respubliki v Tsifrakh* (Stepanakert: National Statistical Service of the NKR, 2011), pp. 15–17.
71. National Statistical Service of the NKR, *Statistical Yearbook of Nagorno-Karabakh Republic 2009–2015* (Stepanakert: National Statistical Service of the NKR, 2016), p. 24.
72. Interview Iskandaryan.
73. Author's conversation with a settler, Lachin, September 2014.
74. Author's conversation with a settler, Kelbajar, June 2013.
75. Author's conversation with a settler, Lachin, September 2014.
76. Interview Mayilian.
77. Gerard Toal and John O'Loughlin, 'Land for Peace in Nagorny Karabakh? Political Geographies and Public Attitudes Inside a Contested De Facto State', *Territory, Politics, Governance* 1: 2, 2013, pp. 158–82, pp. 173–4.
78. Mikaelian, *Societal Perceptions*, p. 28.
79. Ibid.

Chapter 9

1. Author's interview with Araz Azimov, Deputy Foreign Minister, Baku, 20 February 2015.
2. Personal communication, Carey Cavanaugh, former US Minsk Group co-Chair 1999–2001, March 2018.
3. Michael W. Doyle, *Liberal Peace: Selected Essays* (London and New York: Routledge, 2012).
4. Carey Cavanaugh, 'OSCE and the Nagorno-Karabakh Peace Process', *Security and Human Rights* 27: 3–4, 2016, pp. 422–41.
5. John J. Maresca, 'Lost Opportunities in Negotiating the Conflict over Nagorno Karabakh', *International Negotiation* 1, 1996, pp. 471–99, p. 476.
6. Anders Bjurner, 'The Minsk Peace Process' (unpublished m.s., 1996), p. 8.

Notes

7. Maresca, 'Lost Opportunities'; on this period see also John J. Maresca, *Helsinki Revisited: A Key U.S. Negotiator's Memoirs on the Development of the CSCE into the OSCE* (Stuttgart: Ibidem-Verlag, 2016), pp. 166–72.
8. Author's interview with John J. Maresca, former US ambassador to the CSCE, Baku, 10 June 2014.
9. In addition to Armenia and Azerbaijan, the following states volunteered to attend the Minsk Conference: Belarus, Finland, France, Germany, Italy, Netherlands, Portugal, Russia, Sweden, Turkey and the United States. With the loss of Portugal and the Netherlands, these states form the permanent Minsk Group to this day. Maresca, *Helsinki Revisited*, p. 145.
10. CSCE, CSCE Budapest Document 1994 – Budapest Decisions II (Intensification of CSCE action in relation to the Nagorno-Karabakh Conflict), p. 6.
11. Confusingly, in this early period these states designated co-Chairmen of both the pending Minsk Conference *and* the Minsk Group tasked with preparing for it.
12. Bjurner, 'The Minsk Peace Process', p. 10.
13. In May 2016 the parties agreed to increase the number of PRCiO field assistants to thirteen, although more than two years later this had still not been implemented.
14. Philip Remler, *Chained to the Caucasus: Peacemaking in Karabakh, 1987–2012* (New York: International Peace Institute, 2016), p. 64.
15. The Minsk *Group* co-Chairs definitively replaced the Minsk *Conference* co-Chairs, although one still finds reference to this earlier role in the literature on the early 1990s.
16. Author's interview with Carey Cavanaugh, former Minsk Group US co-Chair 1999–2001, Tbilisi, 3 September 2014.
17. Interview Maresca.
18. UN Security Council resolutions 822, 853, 874 and 884 all affirm the principles of territorial integrity and the inadmissibility of the use of force to change borders. The resolutions can be accessed at <http://www.un.org/Docs/scres/1993/scres93.htm> (last accessed 12 July 2018).
19. Helsinki Additional Meeting of the CSCE Council, 24 March 1992, Summary of Conclusions, Article 9.
20. OSCE, Lisbon Summit Declaration, Articles 20 and 21.
21. Armenia's objections to these formulas were registered in a separate annex.

22. Moorad Mooradian, 'The OSCE: Neutral and Impartial in the Karabakh Conflict?', *Helsinki Monitor* 2, 1998, pp. 5–17, p. 14.
23. On this distinction see Gerard J. Libaridian, *The Challenge of Statehood: Armenian Political Thinking since Independence* (Watertown, MA: Blue Crane Books, 1999), pp. 55–7.
24. This discussion draws on P. Terrence Hopmann, 'Minsk Group Mediation of the Nagorno-Karabakh Conflict: Confronting an "Intractable Conflict"', Institut für Friedenforschung und Sicherheitspolitik an der Universität Hamburg (IFSH), *OSCE Yearbook 2014* (Baden-Baden: IFSH, 2015), pp. 167–79.
25. Remler, *Chained to the Caucasus*, pp. 70–1.
26. Ali Abasov and Haroutiun Khachatrian, *Karabakh Conflict. Variants of Settlement: Concepts and Reality* (Baku: Areat and Yerevan: Noyan Tapan, 2006), p. 155.
27. 'Land for a liberal peace' similarly underpinned other plans put forward by practitioners and academics in the 1990s. Two examples are the peace plan devised by John Maresca in 1994, and a thirteen-point framework for a solution put proposed by scholars David Laitin and Ronald Grigor Suny in an article published in 1999. Both envisaged the formation of a Republic of Nagorno-Karabakh within the preserved boundaries of Azerbaijan, compensated by wide powers of self-government. John J. Maresca, *War in the Caucasus: A Proposal for Settlement of the Conflict over Nagorno-Karabakh* (Washington DC: United States Institute of Peace, 1994); David D. Laitin and Ronald Grigor Suny, 'Armenia and Azerbaijan: Thinking a Way Out of Karabakh', *Middle East Policy* 7: 1, 1999, pp. 145–76.
28. Yevgeny Primakov, *Russian Crossroads: Toward the New Millennium*, trans. Felix Rosenthal (New Haven and London: Yale University Press, 2004), p. 201.
29. Interview Azimov.
30. See Carey Cavanaugh's comments in Carey Cavanaugh, Hamlet Isaxanli, Ronald Suny and Brenda Shaffer, *Negotiations on Nagorno-Karabagh: Where Do We Go from Here? (Event Summary)* (Cambridge, MA: Caspian Studies Program, Harvard University, 2001), p. 10.
31. Tatul Hakobyan, *Karabakh Diary: Green and Black* (Antelias: n.p., 2010), pp. 257–8.
32. Personal conversation, Vafa Guluzade, Baku, February 2005.
33. See Hakobyan, *Karabakh Diary*, pp. 260–1; Thomas de Waal,

Black Garden: Armenia and Azerbaijan through Peace and War, 2nd edn (New York: New York University Press, 2013), p. 276.
34. Author's interview with Vartan Oskanian, former Foreign Minister of Armenia 1998–2008, Yerevan, 10 March 2015.
35. Author's notes, meeting with former Azerbaijani official, Baku, February 2005.
36. Levon Ter-Petrossian, 'War or Peace? Time for Reflection', *Respublika Armenii*, 1 November 1997.
37. Interview with Arkady Ghukasian, *Parts of a Circle*, Film Three: The Search for Peace (London: Conciliation Resources, 2015).
38. See Tabib Huseynov, 'Mountainous Karabakh: New Paradigms for Peace and Development in the 21st Century', *International Negotiation* 15 (2010), p. 16.
39. The full text of the Madrid document is available on the website of the ANI Armenian Research Center, <http://www.aniarc.am/2016/04/11/madrid-principles-full-text/> (last accessed 12 July 2018).
40. Interview Oskanian.
41. Interview Azimov.
42. Ibid.
43. For competing Armenian and Azerbaijani readings of five of the key Madrid Principles see the series of briefs produced by the Karabakh Contact Group, a civil society and expert-level format supported by peacebuilding NGO Conciliation Resources, <http://www.c-r.org/where-we-work/caucasus/karabakh-contact-group-0> (last accessed 12 July 2018).
44. Interview Oskanian.
45. For details see Remler, *Chained to the Caucasus*, pp. 99–111.
46. Ambassador James Warlick, 'Nagorno-Karabakh: The Keys to a Settlement', 7 May 2014, <http://carnegieendowment.org/2014/05/07/nagorny-karabakh-keys-to-settlement-event-4429> (last accessed 12 July 2018).
47. For an overview of these debates see Susanna Campbell, David Chandler and Meera Sabaratnam (eds), *A Liberal Peace? The Problems and Practices of Peacebuilding* (London and New York: Zed Books, 2011).
48. See 'Special Issue – OSCE Mediation and Conflict Management: Unraveling Complexities in OSCE Mediation', *Security and Human Rights* 27: 3–4, 2016.
49. See the statement by the United States Mission to the OSCE,

'Closure of the OSCE Office in Yerevan', PC.DEL/579/17, 4 May 2017.
50. Oliver P. Richmond and Jason Franks (eds), *Liberal Peace Transitions* (Edinburgh: Edinburgh University Press, 2009); Oliver P. Richmond, *A Post-Liberal Peace* (London and New York: Routledge, 2011); Roger Mac Ginty, *International Peacebuilding and Local Resistance* (New York: Palgrave Macmillan, 2011); Oliver P. Richmond and Audra Mitchell (eds), *Hybrid Forms of Peace Resistance* (New York: Palgrave Macmillan, 2012).
51. David Lewis, John Heathershaw and Nick Megoran, '"Illiberal Peace?" Authoritarian Approaches to Conflict Management', *Cooperation and Conflict*, 23 April 2018, DOI: 10.1177/0010 836718765902.
52. For perspectives on authoritarianism that look beyond regime classification see Marlies Glasius, 'What Authoritarianism Is . . . and Is Not: A Practice Perspective', *International Affairs* 94: 3, 2018, pp. 515–33.
53. Christina Stenner, 'Understanding the Mediator: Taking Stock of the OSCE's Mechanisms and Instruments for Conflict Resolution', *Security and Human Rights* 27: 3–4, 2016, pp. 256–72, pp. 265–9.
54. I draw here on arguments presented by Lewis, Heathershaw and Megoran in their discussion of discursive practices as a component of authoritarian conflict management. Lewis et al., '"Illiberal Peace?"'.
55. Interview Azimov.
56. Maresca, *Helsinki Revisited*, p. 156.
57. Personal conversation, Western diplomat, May 2011.
58. Personal conversation, Azerbaijani official, 2014.
59. Author's notes, senior Azerbaijani official, Baku, 8 May 2012.
60. Ilham Aliyev, 'Threats to international peace and security caused by terrorist acts: Strengthening international cooperation in the implementation of counter-terrorism obligations', Statement to the United Nations Security Council, 4 May 2012. Reproduced in Agshin Mehdiyev and Tofig F. Musayev, *The Republic of Azerbaijan in the United Nations Security Council 2012/2013*, pp. 40–5, p. 40 (New York: Liberty Publishing House, 2014).
61. Author's notes, meeting with senior de facto official, Stepanakert, 19 March 2012.
62. Author's interview with senior de facto official, Stepanakert, 12 March 2015.
63. Ibid.

64. See 'List of Foreign Citizens [Who] Illegally Visited Occupied Territories of the Republic of Azerbaijan' on the website of the Azerbaijani Ministry of Foreign Affairs, <http://www.mfa.gov.az/en/content/915> (last accessed 26 April 2018). There is no agreed or advertised procedure for visitors to the territory to notify the Azerbaijani authorities in advance.
65. For background see Shahin Rzayev, 'Lapshin's Case: What, How and Why?', JAMnews, 10 February 2017, <https://jam-news.net/?p=18176> (last accessed 12 July 2018); for an interview in Russian with Aleksandr Lapshin after his release see BBC Azeri, 'Aleksandr Lapşin: "Özümü asmamışam . . . maskalı adamlar məni kamerada boğub"', <http://www.bbc.com/azeri/region-42455241> (last accessed 12 July 2018).
66. Radio Free Europe/Radio Liberty, 'U.S. Envoy Barred from Armenian Cemetery in Azerbaijan', 22 April 2011, <https://www.rferl.org/a/us_envoy_bryza_barred_from_ancient_armenian_cemetery_in_azerbaijan/9502346.html> (last accessed 5 December 2018).
67. Author's notes, meeting with Leila Alieva, director of the Centre for International and Regional Studies, Baku, 22 February 2005.
68. International Crisis Group, *Nagorno-Karabakh's Gathering War Clouds*, Europe Report No. 244, 1 June 2017, p. 15.
69. 'New Defense Minister Wants Bigger Role for Armenian Army', *Azatutyun.am*, 5 October 2016, <https://www.azatutyun.am/a/28034239.html> (last accessed 12 July 2018).
70. Maria Titizian, 'Is This What You Wanted?', *EVN Report*, 3 April 2018, <https://www.evnreport.com/raw-unfiltered/is-this-what-you-wanted> (last accessed 12 July 2018).
71. BBC News, 'Azeri Killer Ramil Safarov: Concern over Armenian Anger', 3 September 2012, <http://www.bbc.co.uk/news/world-europe-19463968> (last accessed 12 July 2018).
72. For a collection of articles about the *Stone Dreams* scandal and an interview with Akram Aylisli in which he discusses his motives in releasing the novella see the special section 'Dreams in the Black Garden: Literature and the Nagorny Karabakh Conflict', *Caucasus Survey* 2: 1–2, 2014, pp. 41–78.
73. BBC News, 'Azeri Writer Akram Aylisli Hounded for "Pro-Armenian" Book', 15 February 2013, <http://www.bbc.co.uk/news/world-europe-21459091> (last accessed 12 July 2018).
74. Hratch Tchilingirian, 'New Structures, Old Foundations: State Capacities for Peace', in Laurence Broers (ed.), *The Limits of*

Leadership: Elites and Societies in the Nagorny Karabakh Peace Process, *Accord* 17 (London: Conciliation Resources, 2005), p. 66.
75. 'Deported Pianist Burak Bedikyan Thanked Turkish MFA for Immediate Reaction', *Today.Az*, 27 December 2006, <http://www.today.az/view.php?id=34405> (last accessed 5 December 2018); 'Grazhdanku Estonii s armyanskoy familiey deportirovali iz Baku', Turan, 28 March 2018, <http://www.turan.az/ext/news/2018/3/free/politics%20news/ru/70129.htm> (last accessed 12 July 2018).
76. Sergey Minasyan, 'Coercion in Action: Deterrence and Compellence in the Nagorno-Karabakh Conflict', *PONARS Eurasia Policy Memo* 242, George Washington University, September 2012, p. 1.
77. V. P. Gagnon Jr., *The Myth of Ethnic War: Serbia and Croatia in the 1990s* (Ithaca and London: Cornell University Press, 2004), p. 8.
78. Zaur Shiriyev, 'Azerbaijan's New Law on Status of Armed Forces: Changes and Implications', Eurasia Democratic Security Network, 23 January 2018, <https://eurasiademocraticsecuritynetwork.wordpress.com/2018/01/23/azerbaijans-new-law-on-status-of-armed-forces-changes-and-implications/> (last accessed 12 July 2018).

Afterword

1. Bruno Coppieters, Michael Emerson, Michel Huysseune, Tamara Kovziridze, Gergana Noutcheva, Nathalie Tocci and Marius Vahl, *Europeanization and Conflict Resolution* (Gent: Academia Press, 2004).
2. This dynamic echoes preponderant India's veto power over Pakistan's future development, as argued by Walter Russell Mead in an interview with Nasir Jamal, 'India Enjoys Veto Power over Pakistan's Progress', *The Dawn*, 15 August 2010.
3. Stephen M. Saideman, 'At the Heart of the Conflict: Irredentism and Kashmir', in T. V. Paul (ed.), *The India–Pakistan Conflict: An Enduring Rivalry* (Cambridge: Cambridge University Press, 2005), pp. 202–24, p. 224.
4. Gerard Toal, *Near Abroad: Putin, the West and the Contest over Ukraine and the Caucasus* (Oxford: Oxford University Press, 2017), p. 300.
5. Warren Zimmermann, *Origins of a Catastrophe: Yugoslavia and its Destroyers*, rev. edn (New York: Times Books, 1999), p. vii.

Index

Abiyev, Safar, 192
Abkhazia, 4, 7, 19, 28, 124, 203, 204, 280
Abrahamyan, Ara, 224
'affair of the seven', 73
affective dispositions, 130–41
  conceptualisation of, 126
  effects of, 129
  sources of, 126–9
Agabekyan, Eduard, 265, 268
Agaev, Rasim, 104
Agdam, 29, 37, 38, 98, 146, 198, 283
Aghayev, Ahmad bey, 51
Albania (Caucasian), 87, 107–9, 109n, 117
  Caucasian Albanian school in Azerbaijan, 106–11, 114
Albanians (Caucasian), 58
Aliyev, Abulfaz see Elchibey, Abulfaz
Aliyev, Heydar, 36, 231, 285, 288
  association with Azerbaijanism, 64, 113–14, 115
  claims regarding Soviet-era policy towards NKAO, 138–9,
  discusses territorial swap plan with Robert Kocharian, 288–90, 292
  dismissal from Politburo, 36, 132
  interactions with patronage networks, 36–7, 145, 169, 171–2, 173
  returns to power, 38, 63
  subordinates resign in 1999, 159
  Western-oriented foreign policy of, 216
Aliyev, Igrar, 57

Aliyev, Ilham, 1, 114, 115, 159, 188, 216, 218, 219, 220–1, 299, 300
  extends rule through referendums, 171, 178
  increases military spending, 185, 189
  interactions with patronage networks, 170–3, 220
  references to Armenia, 115, 117
Aliyeva, Mehriban, 172
All-Armenia Fund, 234, 258
Alma-Ata, 33
Amasiya, 135, 137
Amnesty International, 14, 143
Arab states, 11
Ararat
  mountain, 73, 75, 118
  plain, 20, 21, 74
  Republic, 69
Aras (river), 20, 50, 52, 53, 54, 58, 59, 64, 82, 85, 111, 116
Ardabil, 115
Ardahan, 66, 69, 71, 73
Armavir, 74
Armenakans, 68
Armenia
  1 March 2008 violence, 159, 164–5, 180, 229
  'Armenian cause', 233
  Armenian oblast, 67, 82
  Armenian Soviet Socialist Republic see Armenian Soviet Socialist Republic
  'asset-for-debt' arrangements with Russia, 223

Armenia (*cont.*)
  attitudes towards territorial withdrawals, 274
  balancing with Russia strategy, 202–7, 211, 222
  borders, 20, 65, 74–5, 77, 82, 102
  conditions in the Armenian army, 201
  declares independence, 31, 96
  Democratic Republic of Armenia *see* Democratic Republic of Armenia
  demography, 193–5, 195n
  economic decline and recovery in 1990s–2000s, 188
  Eastern Armenia, 67, 69
  elections in, 156–7, 164
  foreign policy of 'complementarity', 222, 230
  gas pipeline with Iran, 223, 225
  geopolitical culture of, 49, 74, 76–7, 80, 89, 99, 101, 118–19, 146, 261, 275, 312–13
    vision of 'augmented Armenia' in, 98–104, 146, 313
    vision of 'compliant Armenia' in, 94–8, 104, 312
    vision of 'integral-reformist Armenia' in, 90–4
  'Greater Armenia', 74, 88, 108
  joins Eurasian Economic Union, 225
  labour migration to Russia, 223–4
  nationalism, 43, 67, 72–4, 90, 233, 274
  popular attitudes towards army, 176
  post-electoral protest in, 164
  regime type, 155–6
  relations with European Union, 225, 229
  repatriation initiatives, 195
  sovietisation of, 25, 27, 46
  strategy of deterrence, 199–201, 204–5, 207, 211
  'total mobilisation posture', 210
  trade patterns, 222
  transition to parliamentary system, 166, 177
  Velvet Revolution in, 153, 167, 183, 226, 230, 268, 306
  Western Armenia, 65–7, 69, 74
  'Wilsonian Armenia', 69–70, 69n
Armenian Communist Party, 27, 131
  fracturing of, 162–3
  under-representation of Azerbaijanis, 135
Armenian diaspora, 43, 71, 96, 233–6
  as vehicle of soft power, 236
  attitudes toward Soviet Armenia, 75–6
  community in Russia, 224
  fundraising activities, 234, 258
  lobbying activities, 217, 234–5
Armenian genocide, 3, 68, 68n, 82, 89, 235
  1965 protests related to, 75
  commemoration of, 137
  popular narratives about, 42, 73, 137–8
Armenian language, 65
  division into Western and Eastern dialects, 65, 76
Armenian National Constitution, 66
Armenian National Council of America, 234
Armenian Revolutionary Federation (Dashnaktsutyun), 22, 23, 25, 43, 68–9, 76, 162, 253, 264, 265–7
Armenian Secret Army for the Liberation of Armenia, 69, 304
Armenian Soviet Socialist Republic
  Armenia after World War II
  Azerbaijani minority in, 24, 24n
  displacement of Azerbaijanis from, 122
  dissidence in, 73–4
  elite politics of, 36
  ethno-demography in, 134–7
  first multiparty elections in, 35
  founding of, 24
  nationalism in, 72–4
  politics of commemoration in, 42
  post-World War II reception of repatriated Armenians, 71

Index

resettlement of Azerbaijanis after World War II *see* Azerbaijanis: resettlement from territory and population of, 70
Armenian–Azerbaijani conflict
  affective dispositions driving, 41–2, 128–30
  as an enduring rivalry, 11–14, 308–16; *see also* enduring rivalry
  casualties, 38, 38n
  ceasefire, 38
  communal violence *see* communal violence
  conspiracy theories on, 17, 43
  distinctiveness from other post-Soviet conflicts, 5–7, 213–14, 238
  early chronology of, 6, 29, 33
  geography of, 20
  non-combat related deaths, 192, 201
  popular narratives of, 3–4
  strategic inconclusiveness of, 174–5, 176
  structure, 6
  territorial scope, 6
Armenians
  affective dispositions towards Azerbaijanis, 131–2, 134–40
  affective dispositions towards Turks, 42, 137–8, 176, 315
  concerns about assimilation of, 80–2
  demography of in Ottoman Empire, 66, 68
  demography of in Russian Empire, 67–8
  displacement of, from and within Azerbaijan, 122, 138, 140
  internally displaced, 123
  narrative of Armenian–Azerbaijani conflict, 3–4
  population movements in seventeenth to nineteenth centuries, 21
  post-World War II repatriation of, 71
  stereotypes about Azerbaijanis, 44
  Syrian, 271

'Armeno-Tatar war', 21
ArmRosGazprom, 223
Artashat, 74
Artsakh, 147
  medieval principality, 87, 108
  research on 'Northern Artsakh', 101–2, 120
  revival as a term for Nagorny Karabakh, 4, 86, 93–4, 99, 249, 269
Artsakhfrukt, 260
Artsakhpress, 260
Arutyunov, Grigor, 75
ASALA *see* Armenian Secret Army for the Liberation of Armenia
ASAN public service centres, 170, 170n
Askeran, 29, 99, 141
asymmetric conflict, 186, 207–10
Ataturk, 62
authoritarian conflict management, 297
authoritarian conflict strategies, 297–306
Avars, 227
Aylisli, Akram, 303
Azerbaijan
  Assembly of Friends of Azerbaijan, 221
  Azerbaijan American Alliance, 220
  'Azerbaijan Democracy Act', 219
  Azerbaijan Democratic Republic *see* Azerbaijan Democratic Republic
  'Azerbaijani laundromat', 220
  Azerbaijani Soviet Socialist Republic *see* Azerbaijani Soviet Socialist Republic
  Azerbaijanism *see* Azerbaijanism
  'blacklist' of visitors to Nagorny Karabakh, 301–2
  borders, 20, 50
  civil society restrictions, 218–19
  compellence strategy, 304
  composition of defence spending, 191
  conditions in Azerbaijani army, 191–2

387

Azerbaijan (*cont.*)
  constitutional referendums in, 171, 178
  Council of State Support to NGOs in, 219
  declares independence, 32, 96
  demography, 193–5
  elections in, 156, 169, 171, 219
  elite stability, 172
  geopolitical culture of, 49, 64, 80, 104–5, 115, 118–19, 312, 313–14
  'Greater Azerbaijan' tradition, 58, 60–3
  informal elite factions in, 171–2
  labour migration to Russia, 228
  limited aims strategy, 206–7, 211
  lobbying, 219–20, 235
  military expenditures in, 185, 189–93
  multilateralist diplomacy of, 236–7
  nationalism, 58, 59, 111, 113, 114–15, 119
  oil and gas reserves, 188
  oil revenues effects, 188, 216–17
  opposition in, 170–1, 178
  pipeline and transportation infrastructure, 216
  policy towards internal displacement, 145–6
  political economy of, 170
  preponderance over Armenia, 185, 187, 195–6, 200, 208–10
  relations with Russia, 227–9
  relations with West, 215–22
  restrictions on Armenians visiting Azerbaijan, 304
  sovietisation of, 25, 27, 46, 54
  'sultanistic' regime type, 171, 171n, 172
  territorial integrity claim, 3, 64, 95, 96, 112, 116, 145, 213, 222, 263, 278, 282, 283, 285, 288, 290, 293
  'Western Azerbaijan', 117
  see also Iranian Azerbaijan
Azerbaijan Democratic Republic (1918–20), 22, 23, 55, 106
  demography of, 53
  territorialisation of, 53–4, 55, 55n
Azerbaijani Communist Party, 27, 28, 31–2, 36–7, 63, 131, 134
  dissolution of, 169
  over-representation of Armenians in, 130–1
Azerbaijani International Operating Company, 215, 215n
Azerbaijani language, 56
  name change, 63–4
  script changes, 57
Azerbaijani Popular Front, 31, 36, 37, 38, 60, 63, 109–10, 111, 134, 169, 217
Azerbaijani Soviet Socialist Republic
  Armenian minority in, 24, 24n
  displacement of Armenians from, 122, 133–4
  elite politics of, 36, 130
  founding of, 24
  indigenisation of, 130–1
  post-World War II reception of resettled Azerbaijanis, 72
  role of Armenian population in, 130
  statute on NKAO, 27
  struggle to define position on Karabakh, 109–10
  territorialisation of, 55, 55n, 62
  titular identity of, 54–5
  wider Armenian population in, 24n, 28
Azerbaijani Turks *see* Azerbaijanis
Azerbaijanis
  affective dispositions towards Armenians, 130–4
  affective disposition towards Russia, 42
  Azerbaijani Turk identity, 52–6, 52n, 59, 106
  concerns about Armenian encroachment on, 82–3
  debates over identity of, 51–3, 56
  displacement of from Armenia, 122, 138
  internally displaced, 123
  narrative of Armenian–Azerbaijani conflict, 3

resettlement from Armenia after World War II, 72, 72n
role in Safavid Iran, 50
situation of in Soviet Armenia, 135–7
stereotypes about Armenians, 44
Azerbaijanism, 64, 112–15, 114n, 232, 236
'proto-Azerbaijanism', 57–8, 59, 62, 64, 106–7
'wide Azerbaijanism', 114–19, 182, 313
Azimov, Araz, 48, 277, 292, 294

Babak (Khorramdin), 115
Babayan, Samvel, 262–3
Baghirov, Mir Jafar, 59
Bagirov, Kyamran, 169
Baku, 3, 22, 28, 29, 32, 37, 38, 43, 53, 54, 56, 68, 81, 115, 121, 132, 143–4, 152, 169, 189, 192, 220, 225, 228, 236, 304
communal violence in, 36, 126, 133–4, 303
cosmopolitan identity of, 131, 134
guberniya in Russian Empire, 53, 127
nineteenth century ethnic tensions in, 21, 52, 127, 130
massacres in 1918, 23, 23n
oil industry, 21, 127
Baku Commune, 22, 53
Baku–Tbilisi–Ceyhan pipeline, 185, 189, 215
Baku–Tbilisi–Erzurum pipeline, 188, 216
Baku–Tbilisi–Kars railway, 216
Balasanyan, Vitaliy, 266
Balayan, Zori, 41
Balkans, 17, 33, 39–40
Bangladesh, 94
Base Metals, 260
Bashirli, Ruslan, 179
Basque Country, 235
Batumi, 66
Beirut, 253
Belarus, 152, 190, 205, 217, 279, 280n, 301
Berdzor, 84, 100, 147

Berlin, 253
Birthright Armenia, 102, 195, 195n
Bishkek Protocol, 38, 276, 280
'Black January', 36, 169
Bolsheviks, 22, 23, 24–5, 26, 53
Bordyuzha, Nikolay, 239
Bosnia, 150, 280
Bosniaks, 111
Brexit, 2
Brezhnev, Leonid, 59, 161
Britain, 53, 71, 152, 215n
British Petroleum, 215
Bryza, Matthew, 302
Budapest, 280, 303
Buniyatov, Ziya, 41, 57, 108
Byzantium, 65

California, 234
Caplan, Robert, 40
cartography *see* maps
Caspian (sea), 5, 20, 88, 118, 188, 232, 233
Caucasus mountains, 20, 60
'caviar diplomacy', 219, 221
CEPA (Comprehensive and Enhanced Partnership Agreement) *see* European Union
'Charter of Four' *see* Karabakh Charter
Chechnya, 2, 4
China, 222, 227, 296
Clinton, Hillary, 180
Cold War, 11, 12, 59, 62, 278
Collective Security Treaty Organisation, 190, 203, 206, 239, 244
Colombia, 235
Commonwealth of Independent States, 227, 236, 280
communal violence, 29–30, 32–3, 44, 46, 123, 144
against Armenians in Azerbaijan, 133–4
against Azerbaijanis in Armenia, 136–8
evidence of organisation of, 34
effects on identities, 45
in Nagorny Karabakh, 138–41
need for micro-theory of, 47

389

Communist Party of the Soviet Union, 27, 29, 30
competitive authoritarianism, 157, 265
Conciliation Resources, 14
Conference for Security and Co-operation in Europe, 279–80
  mandates the Minsk Conference, 279
conflicts in the former USSR, 4–5, 18
Constantinople, 65
'Contract of the Century', 185, 215
Corsica, 2
Council of Europe, 6, 178, 219–20, 236
Crimea, 5, 19, 51, 204, 296
CSTO *see* Collective Security Treaty Organisation
Cyprus, 222, 254
Czech Republic, 235

Dadivank, 87, 272
Dagestan, 227
Dashkesan, 142
Dashnaktsutyun *see* Armenian Revolutionary Federation
Davutoğlu, Ahmet, 232
de facto state, 249–50
Demirchian, Karen, 159, 289
demobilisation, 175, 175n, 177, 180, 268, 305, 316
Democratic Party of Artsakh, 267
democratic peace theory, 152–3
Democratic Republic of Armenia (1918–20), 22, 23, 25, 68, 70, 71, 76
  territorialisation of, 68–9
Department for International Development, 217
Derbent, 50
deterrence, 187, 196, 199–202, 304
  Armenia's deterrent, 199–201, 204–5, 207, 211
  pivotal deterrence, 205–6, 243–8
  Russia's extended deterrence to Armenia, 203–4
  serial deterrence, 207
displacement, 10, 44, 120, 121, 141, 143–4, 148, 150–1, 198, 284
  disputed definition of refugee and internally displaced person, 122, 122n
  during Operation Ring, 31, 97n, 142
  mass movements in seventeenth century, 21
  nineteenth century population exchanges after Russian conquest, 21
  phases of, 122–3
  problems with quantification of, 122
  resettlement campaigns after World War II, 71–2, 72n
  scope and timing of, 123–4, 124n
Drmbon, 260

Elchibey, Abulfaz, 36, 38, 48, 60–2, 64, 111–12, 115, 169, 227, 232
enclaves, 24
enduring rivalry, 10–14
  democratization and, 152–4
  resolution of, 13
  role of leadership in, 315
Erebuni, 203, 204
ethnic cleansing, 33, 44, 102, 104, 124
  communal ethnic cleansing, 124, 125–6
  strategic ethnic cleansing, 124–5, 141–3
Eurasian Economic Union, 176, 204, 222, 225–6, 229, 243, 310
European Azerbaijani Society, 220, 220n
European Court of Human Rights, 149–50, 249
  Chiragov and Others v. Armenia case, 149–50, 249
  Sargsyan v. Azerbaijan case, 149–50
European Friends of Armenia, 234
European Stability Initiative, 219, 221
European Union, 6, 8, 15, 216–9, 222, 225, 238, 245, 310
  aid to Armenia, 229
  aid to Azerbaijan, 217

Index

CEPA negotiation with Armenia, 229–30
Eastern Partnership, 217, 229
European Neighbourhood Policy, 216
relations with Azerbaijan in 2014–15, 218–19, 218n
Extractive Industries Transparency Initiative (EITI), 216, 218

fedayi (Armenian guerrillas), 42, 42n, 43, 71, 84
Finland, 56, 197, 280n, 281
Fizuli, 38, 98, 139, 146, 198, 283
'four-day war' (2–5 April 2016), 1, 176, 185, 191, 198, 199, 211, 237, 268, 281, 302, 304, 308, 311, 315
  as limited aims operation, 207
  casualties, 1, 1n, 192
  illiberal domestic outcomes following, 210, 268, 303, 305
  impacts on Armenian domestic politics, 167, 177, 181, 201, 303
  international responses to, 205, 239
France, 7, 197, 222, 277, 280n, 281
Free Motherland (party), 267
Freedom House, 155–6, 263, 265
'frozen conflict', 2, 5, 11–13, 242, 308–9
  as prevailing script of Eurasian geopolitics, 213, 237, 245
Füle, Stefan, 225

Gali, 124
Gandzasar, 87, 108, 109
Ganja, 3, 38, 44, 53, 101, 116
Garni, 74
Gazprom, 223
Gellner, Ernest, 48
Geneva, 279
geo-body, 83, 314
  Armenian, 64–77, 81, 82, 89–90, 92, 95, 274
  Azerbaijani, 50–64, 80, 82, 118, 313
  definition of, 49

geopolitics, 4–5
  critical geopolitics, 8–9
  geopolitical culture, 9, 10, 13, 49–50, 312
  see also Armenia; Azerbaijan
Georgia, 7, 22, 23, 28, 56, 73, 86, 101, 118, 188, 194, 214, 2 , 221–2, 225, 228–9, 236, 263, 283
  conflicts in, 2, 4, 5, 238, 243, 280
Georgia (US state), 234
Georgian Dream, 228
Germany, 101, 174, 197, 222, 280n
Ghukasian, Arkady, 174, 262–3, 264, 268
Goble, Paul, 288
Gorbachev, Mikhail, 26, 29, 35, 36, 77, 90, 92, 168–9
Gorbacheva, Raisa, 43
Goris, 100, 258
Grachev, Pavel, 279
Greek–Turkish rivalry, 12
Grigorian, Manvel, 164, 167, 176
GUAM organisation, 236
Gugark, 137
Gulistan (treaty), 20, 21, 67
Gulistan (village), 149–50
Guluzade, Vafa, 281, 289
Gulyan, Ashot, 260, 267
Gyumri, 203, 244
  Russian military base *see* Russia: Gyumri military base

Hadrut, 99, 139
Hamadan, 60
Harutyunyan, Araik, 260–2, 268
Hasanov, Zakir, 185, 192
Hawaii, 234
Hay Tad, 233
Hayasa, 74
Heffern, John, 234
Helsinki Final Act, 295
Heydarov, Kamaleddin, 220
Heydarov, Tale, 220
High-Level Planning Group, 280
Hnchaks, 68, 76
Holbrooke, Richard, 280
Honduras, 235
Hrazdan thermal plant, 223

391

Human Rights House Network, 218
Hunanyan, Nairi, 289
Huseynov, Suret, 38
Huseynzade, Ali bey, 51
hybrid regimes, 154–5, 159, 160–1, 182, 276, 314, 316

Igdir, 118
illiberal peace, 297, 306
India, 11, 237
  rivalry with Pakistan *see* India–Pakistan rivalry
India–Pakistan rivalry, 11, 153, 186, 195, 199, 308
informal politics, 161, 165
  networked regimes/power, 162, 165, 169, 171, 175, 182–4, 316
interim status, 293
internal displacement, 141, 284
  of Armenians, 123
  of Azerbaijanis, 123
  resettlement of internally displaced persons, 143, 145
  within Nagorny Karabakh, 140, 142
International Research and Exchanges Board (IREX), 218
Internews Azerbaijan, 15
Iran, 8, 20, 21, 48, 51, 56, 58–9, 62, 64, 86, 215, 222, 230, 243, 257, 288, 290
  Azerbaijani population of, 50, 51, 54, 58, 62–4, 194, 232
  border with Azerbaijan, 54, 60, 64, 236
  diffusion of Armenian–Azerbaijani rivalry across, 232–3
  gas pipeline with Armenia, 223, 225
  mediation initiative, 279
  nationalism, 57–8, 232
  relations with Armenia, 233, 236
  relations with Azerbaijan Democratic Republic, 54
  role of Azerbaijanis in Safavid Iran, 50
  Safavid Iran, 50, 87, 127
  see also Iranian Azerbaijan

Iranian Azerbaijan, 50, 57–9, 106, 215, 232–3
  regional movements in, 59, 63, 232
  modernisation and incorporation of, 63
  World War II-era Soviet presence in, 58–9
Irevan *see* khanates: Erivan khanate
irredentism, 312
  Armenian irredentism, 73, 312–13
  Azerbaijani irredentism, 59–64, 312
Isfahan, 21
Iskander missiles, 200, 200n, 206, 211
Ismayilova, Khadija, 219
Israel, 11, 193, 233, 297
  relations with Azerbaijan, 236–7
  rivalry with Arab states, 153, 174, 186, 308
Istanbul, 68
Italy, 280n, 281
Ivanishvili, Bidzina, 228

Japan, 174
Javakheti, 71, 73, 73n
Jebrayil, 38, 98, 146, 283, 303
Julfa, 21, 302
Justice Commandos of the Armenian Genocide, 69

Kapan, 43, 124n, 126n, 137
Karabakh Armenians, 3, 86, 238, 250, 267, 283, 291, 300
  affective dispositions of, 138–40
  exclusion from peace process, 7, 28, 299
  proposed rights in 'package' peace plan, 285, 287
  representation in Nagorno-Karabakh Defence Army and Armenian military, 198, 255
  self-determination claim, 97 *see also* Nagorno-Karabakh Republic: self-determination claim
  'total mobilisation posture', 209
Karabakh Azerbaijanis, 3, 86, 95, 96, 283, 294, 300

affective dispositions of, 138, 140
displacement, 142, 147
Karabakh Charter, 159, 159n, 178
Karabakh Committee, 35, 92, 95, 104, 162–3
Karabakh conflict *see* Armenian–Azerbaijani conflict
Karabakh khanate *see* khanates
Karabakh Liberation Organisation, 114–15, 114n
Karapetyan, Samvel, 101, 117
Karelia, 56
Kars, 66, 69, 71, 73
Kars (treaty), 231
Karvajar, 100, 272
Kashatagh, 100, 271–3
Kashmir, 2, 237
Kasprzyk, Andrzej, 281
kasraviyya, 58
Kasum-Ismayilli, 97n, 142
Kavburo (Caucasus Bureau), 24–5
Kazakhstan, 33, 227
Kazan, 295
Kazimirov, Vladimir, 280
Kelbajar, 38, 98, 100, 112, 146, 147, 231, 258, 283, 293
  settler activity in, 271–3
Kevork VI, Catholicos, 75
Key West, 289–90
Khachen (medieval principality), 87, 108
Khachen (river), 85
khanates, 20, 50, 67, 116–17
  Erivan khanate, 82, 117
  Karabakh khanate, 87, 106, 116–17
Khankendi, 112
Khanlar, 141–2
Khojaly, 37, 140, 141, 147
  district, 112
  massacre, 37, 142, 220, 235
Khojavend, 112
Khrimian, Mkrtich, 67
Kirovabad, 3, 34, 44, 45
Kocharian, Robert, 164, 165–6, 223, 285, 291, 292, 299
  becomes president of Armenia, 158–9, 255, 287
  claims incompatibility of Armenians and Azerbaijanis, 304
  discusses territorial swap plan with Heydar Aliyev, 288–90
  heads State Defence Committee in Nagorny Karabakh, 264
  interactions with patronage networks, 166
Korea, South, 2
  rivalry with North Korea, 153
Kosovo, 264, 296
Kura (river), 85, 116
Kura-Aras basin, 72

Lachin, 37, 38, 84, 98, 100, 143, 147, 149, 258, 283
  Lachin corridor, 100, 287, 289, 291
  settler activity in, 271–3
Lapshin, Aleksandr, 301
Lausanne (treaty), 70
Lavrov, Sergey, 242, 245
Lebed', Aleksandr, 33, 133
Lenin, Vladimir, 74, 94
Lezgins, 227
Libaridian, Gerard, 76, 165, 281
liberal peace, 278, 285n, 298, 306, 309–10
  challenges to, 296–7
Libya, 296
Line of Contact, 2, 100, 114, 149, 180, 200, 201, 257, 268, 274, 306
  as a strategic factor, 196–8
  civilian populations in close proximity to, 143, 198
  fighting in April 2016, 1, 191, 197, 302, 304
'literature of longing', 59
London, 14, 221
Lori, 71
Los Angeles, 234
Louisiana, 234
Lukoil, 216

MacArthur, Gen., 174–5
Macedonia, 48
Madrid Principles, 293–5, 297, 306
Maine, 234

393

Mamedova, Farida, 108, 114
Mammadov, Anar, 220
Mammadov, Ziya, 220
Mammadyarov, Elmar, 189, 292
Manukyan, Vazgen, 163, 164
maps, 9, 49, 118–20
   of Armenia, 82, 99, 102
   of Azerbaijan, 82–3, 109, 111, 112, 114–15, 118, 313
Maragha, 37, 99, 142
'March Days', 23, 23n
Mardakert, 99, 100, 143, 180, 198, 258, 260, 273
Maresca, John, 279–80, 282, 299
Markaryan, Gurgen, 303
Markaryan, Tatul, 292
Martuni, 99
Massachusetts, 234
Mayilian, Masis, 265–6, 274
Media Initiatives Center, 15
Medians, 58
Medvedev, Dmitriy, 173, 242–3, 295
Meghri, 288, 290
Mehtiyev, Ramiz, 219
melikdoms, 87, 89, 99
meliks, 87
Melkonian, Monte, 69, 76
Meskhetian Turks, 122
Metsamor nuclear plant, 223
Mexico, 235
Michigan, 234
Middle East, 2, 7, 20, 55–6, 59, 128, 243, 271, 273, 309
Milošević, Slobodan, 33
Minsk Conference, 279, 280, 281, 283, 298, 300
Minsk Group, 7, 242–3, 277, 310
   'common state' plan, 287
   development of co-Chair structure, 280–2
   elaboration of Basic ('Madrid') Principles, 292–3
   narrowing of format, 298–9
   'package' and 'step-by-step' approaches, 284–5, 291–2
   'territorial swap' plan, 288–90
Mirkadirov, Rauf, 179
Mnatsakanyan, Zohrab, 226

Moldova, 4, 56, 58, 216, 221, 225, 236, 238, 283, 287
Moldovans, 58
monopoly mediator, 261, 261n
Montenegro, 254
Moscow, 8, 20, 28, 32, 35, 65, 92, 110, 168, 218, 225, 228, 253
Moscow (declaration), 276
Moscow (treaty), 24, 231
Movement-88, 265
Muradyan, Igor, 92
Musavat party, 22, 52, 169
Mutalibov, Ayaz, 36, 37–8, 110, 169

Nadir Shah, 87
Nagi, Akif, 114–15
Nagorny Karabakh, 2, 3, 10, 19, 71, 73, 165, 187, 189, 248
   ambiguous status within Russia's extended deterrence, 244–5
   as defined in 1997 'package plan', 285–6
   attitudes towards return of displaced Azerbaijanis, 147–8, 300–1
   attitudes towards territorial withdrawals, 274
   borders, 9
   Christian and Muslim populations of, 85
   competing geographies defining, 269
   demography, 269, 271–2
   disputed status after World War I, 22, 53
   fighting in April 2016, 1
   geography and terrain of, 85, 196
   in Armenian geopolitical culture, 88–104
   in Azerbaijani geopolitical culture, 104–118
   in territorial swap peace plan, 288–90
   internally displaced population, 123, 142–3, 144
   names for, 86
   reserve mobilisation estimates, 200
   settler populations in, 271–4
   war breaks out in 1991–2, 37

Index

Nagorno-Karabakh Autonomous Oblast, 31, 36, 43, 46, 55, 82–3, 88–9, 99, 101, 102, 109, 111–12, 252, 257
- abolition of, 32, 96, 112, 313
- affective dispositions within, 138–41
- allocation to Azerbaijan by Soviet state, 24–5
- ambiguity of autonomy in, 27–8, 96, 138
- area of, 97–8, 269
- borders, 26, 142, 274
- campaign for unification with Armenia, 90, 92–3
- contestation of under Soviet rule, 26
- cultural production in, 28
- debate over upgrade of, 93
- demography of, 26, 138–40
- displacement within, 140–1
- economy, 258
- enclave geography of, 49, 90, 98, 100, 258, 271
- founding of, 24–6
- resolution to join Soviet Armenia, 29, 35, 77, 132
- under direct rule from Moscow, 30

Nagorno-Karabakh Defence Army, 197–8, 255
- role of citizens of Armenia in, 255

Nagorno-Karabakh Republic, 4, 6, 12, 159, 197, 249, 282, 312
- anthem of, 196
- area of, 99, 99n, 269, 269n
- as a small dependent jurisdiction, 262
- attitudes towards independence or unification of, 254
- borders with Armenia, 251, 253, 255–7
- bureaucratic structure, 253
- citizenship and currency arrangements, 253
- civil society in, 267
- competitive democratisation with Azerbaijan, 264
- constitutional referendums in, 268
- declares independence, 97
- development of regime type in, 262–9
- elections in, 265–6
- exclusion from peace process, 7, 283, 299
- flag, 253
- founding of, 32, 96, 252, 264
- informal incorporation into Armenia, 165, 255
- 'interstate credit' allocated to, 165, 257–8, 258n, 260
- perceptions of the territorial extent of, 102, 274–5
- polarised narratives about, 249–50
- political economy of, 257–62
- political parties in, 266–7
- problems researching, 251
- recognition campaign, 234–5
- redistricting within, 99–100, 269
- renaming of former Azerbaijani settlements in, 99
- self-determination claim, 3, 6, 80, 88, 94–5, 97, 102, 235, 252, 263, 293, 301
- territorial integrity claim, 100

Nairi, 74
Nairit chemical plant, 223
Nakhichevan, 25, 38, 53–5, 60, 71, 73, 81, 116, 171, 231, 302
- founding of autonomous republic in, 24, 27
- in territorial swap peace plan, 288–90
- 'Nakhichevanisation' narrative, 81–2, 138

Naxçivan Autonomous Republic, 173
World War I era violence, 22
Namazov, Eldar, 289
Nation-Army concept, 210, 302–3, 305
National Democratic Institute, 218
National Unity Party, 73–4
nationalism, 21, 36, 39, 48, 80, 88, 94, 102, 183, 275, 302, 314
- Armenian nationalism *see* Armenia
- Azerbaijani nationalism *see* Azerbaijan
- emotion-centred study of, 126

395

nationalism (*cont.*)
  eventful study of, 44–5
  depictions of minority identities in majority nationalisms, 111
  in Soviet Union, 19, 34–5, 40, 59
  Iranian nationalism *see* Iran
NATO, 6, 215, 231, 238, 281, 303
Naxçivan *see* Nakhichevan
Nazarbayev, Nursultan, 279
Netherlands, 179, 280n
New Azerbaijan Party, 118, 169
New South Wales, 235
Non-Aligned Movement, 236
Northern Route Export Pipeline, 215
Norway, 215n, 216
Novorossiysk, 216
Nuri, Said, 179

occupied territories, 99, 102, 143–4, 165, 269–74, 277, 291, 292–3, 301
  Armenian attitudes towards return of, 273–4
  settlement of, 271–3
Oganezov, Grisha, 44
Operation Ring, 31, 32, 97n, 142, 143, 202
Organization for Security and Co-operation in Europe, 6, 7, 219, 276, 295–6
  arms sales embargo, 190n
  closes office in Armenia, 296
  closes office in Azerbaijan, 218
  election monitoring reports, 156
  fact-finding missions, 271–2
  liberal principles of, 298
  Lisbon summit of, 283, 299
  mediation structures for Armenian–Azerbaijani conflict, 280–1
  Office for Democratic Institutions and Human Rights, 156
Organization of Islamic Cooperation, 236
Organized Crime and Corruption Reporting Project (OCCRP), 220
orientalism, 127

Orwell, George, 180
Oskanian, Vartan, 289–90, 292–3
Ottoman Empire, 3, 20–1, 22–3, 42, 51–2, 66, 68–9, 71, 89
  Armenian population of, 65–6; *see also* Armenians
  massacres of Armenians in, 66–7
  millet system in, 66
Özal, Turgut, 288

Pakistan, 153, 190, 199, 235
  relations with Azerbaijan, 237
  rivalry with India *see* India–Pakistan rivalry
Palestine, 2
Pan-Armenian National Movement, 30, 35, 95–6, 97, 104, 177, 292
  fracturing of, 163
Pan-Azerbaijanism *see* Azerbaijan: 'Greater Azerbaijan'
Pan-Turkism, 56, 57, 62, 111
Panah Ali, 117
Panahabad, 117
Paris, 253
Paris Peace Conference, 54, 81
Parthia, 64
Pashayev network, 172
Pashinyan, Nikol, 167–8, 183, 226, 315
'patriot-businessmen', 31, 39
Peace Dialogue (NGO), 176
peacebuilding, 157, 179, 267, 297
Persia, 21, 52, 65
'Piedmont principle', 56
Pishevari, Mir Jafar, 58
Poland, 48
Polyanichko, Viktor, 32, 36
Portugal, 280n
Portukalian, Mkrtich, 67
Prague Process, 292
Pridnestrovie, 287; *see also* Transdniester
Primakov, Yevgeny, 242, 281, 287
Provisional Government of Azerbaijan (Iran), 58–9, 59n
Putin, Vladimir, 2, 5, 173, 224–5

Qabala, 227
Qalleh Bazz, 115
Qubatly, 38, 98, 146, 283

Raffi, 89, 99, 101
Ramkavar party, 76
Rasulzade, Mamed Emin, 52, 57
'refuchess', 141, 143, 144
refugees, 3, 37, 43, 69, 109, 117, 122–3, 131, 133–4, 140–1
  attitudes towards return of, 144–5, 147, 174, 301
  beliefs about compensated departure of, 125–6, 149
  resettlement of, 143
remittances, 195, 223–5, 228
Repat Armenia, 195, 195n
Republican Party of Armenia, 166–7, 176
Research on Armenian Architecture (NGO), 101
restitution, 148
Revival (party), 267
Rhode Island, 234
rivalry *see* enduring rivalry
Romania, 56
Rome, 64, 279
Russia, 4, 7, 71, 140, 213, 215, 215n, 277, 280n
  Armenian community in, 224
  arms supplies to Armenia and Azerbaijan, 190–1, 202
  as entrepreneur of authoritarian conflict management, 296
  'asset-for-debt' arrangements with Armenia, 223
  assumes permanent co-chairmanship of Minsk Group, 281
  attitudes towards in Armenia, 176, 226
  Azerbaijani community in, 228
  balancing with by Armenia and Azerbaijan, 202
  conquest of Caucasus, 20, 50
  Gyumri military base, 203, 203n, 244
  linkages in Armenia, 222–5
  linkages in Azerbaijan, 227–9
  pivotal deterrence strategy, 205–6, 243–7
  relations with Azerbaijan, 227–9
  roles in Armenian–Azerbaijani conflict, 6–7, 237–47, 309
  roles in 'near abroad', 5, 5n, 8, 238
Russian Empire, 20, 21, 51–2, 87, 127
Russian–Georgian war, 188, 229

Saakashvili, Mikheil, 214
Safarov, Ramil, 303
Safavid Iran *see* Iran: Safavid Iran
Sahakyan, Bako, 147, 265, 268
St Petersburg, 65
Sakharov, Andrey, 288
Sargsyan, Serzh, 1, 48, 159, 164, 165, 268, 299
  announces accession to EAEU, 225
  attempts to extend power, 166–7, 177, 305
  diaspora policy, 224
  low legitimacy, 167
  resignation, 167
Sargsyan, Vazgen, 159, 289
Sargsyan, Vigen, 210, 302
Sasna Tsrer, 167
Saudi Arabia, 215n
Savalan, Mount, 115
Schiltberger, Johann, 85
security dilemma, 32–3, 46
Sefilian, Jirair, 167, 256
Seljuks, 127
Serbia, 48, 254
Sevan (lake), 114, 118, 135
Sèvres (treaty), 69–70
Shah Abbas, 21
Shahumyan (region), 32, 97, 97n, 99, 102, 141–2, 147, 149, 252, 271–2, 291
Shahumyan, Stepan, 23
Shanghai Cooperation Organization, 236
Sharur-Daralagaz, 54
Shevardnadze, Eduard, 214
Shiraz, Hovhannes, 73
Shusha, 23, 30, 37, 53, 112, 117, 138, 140, 142, 144, 146, 291

Sino-Indian rivalry, 12
Siradeghian, Vano, 163
Smith, Chris, 219
Smyrna, 65, 68
SOCAR (State Oil Company of the Azerbaijan Republic), 188, 191, 231
SOFAZ (State Oil Fund of Azerbaijan), 188
South Africa, 190
South Ossetia, 4, 7, 19, 28, 124, 203, 204, 241, 287
Soviet Union, 2, 3, 4, 6–7, 17–18, 26–7, 36–7, 48, 69, 71, 76, 91–2, 95, 202
   attribution of advanced and backward qualities to constituent peoples, 127–8
   failed liberalisation of, 29–33
   incorporation of Armenia and Azerbaijan, 23, 54–6
   internationalism, 28, 29, 88, 144, 145
   nationalities policy, 18–19, 24, 40–1, 56–7, 94
   occupation of Iranian Azerbaijan in World War II, 58–9
   repatriation of Armenians after World War II, 71
   resettlement of Azerbaijanis after World War II, 72
   territorial autonomy in, 19, 23
Special Administration Committee (*Komitet Osobogo Upravleniya*), 30–1
Sri Lanka, 296–7
Stalin, Joseph, 25, 71, 72, 75, 94
Stalinism, 92
Stepanakert, 30, 37, 84, 85, 88, 100, 112, 140, 146, 165, 183, 258, 265–6, 273
Stepanakert Press Club, 15, 256
Stockholm, 279
Stone Dreams, 303
Sudan, 296
Sultanov, Shahin, 192
Sumgait, 3, 29, 30, 32, 33, 43, 44, 124, 125, 137, 144
Surmalinsk, 54

Sweden, 217, 280n, 281
Swedish International Development Cooperation Agency, 217
Switzerland, 180, 232
Sydney, 253
symbolic politics, 30, 41–2, 43, 44, 133, 133n, 314
Syria, 2, 239, 273, 296
Syunik, 87, 100

Tabriz, 50, 54, 62, 112, 115
Taghiyev, Ramin, 179
Talibov, Vasif, 173
Tartu, 65
'Tatars', 21, 51, 52
Tbilisi, 81, 179
Tehran, 8, 54, 58–9, 63
   Tehran Communiqué, 279
Ter-Petrossian, Levon, 104, 163, 164, 165, 167
   advocacy of phased negotiation, 174, 207, 291–2
   becomes leader of Armenia, 35
   contested re-election in 1996, 164
   recruitment under, 163
   resignation, 158, 291
Ter-Petrossian, Telman, 163
territory
   as cause of conflict, 12–13
   in enduring rivalries, 12
Terter, 112
Terter (river), 196
Thomson, Gen. William, 22
Tiflis, 68
Topchibashev, Ali Mardan-bey, 51
Trans-Adriatic Pipeline, 216
Trans-Anatolian Natural Gas Pipeline, 216
Transcaucasia, 20, 20n, 22, 53, 71, 115
   Armenian population of, 21, 65, 67, 127
   demography of, 21
   growth of nationalism in, 41
   Muslim population of, 51–2, 54, 127
   separation from Russia, 22
Transcaucasian Democratic Federative Republic, 22

Index

Transcaucasian Socialist Federal Soviet Republic, 24, 56
Transdniester, 4, 7
'truncated asymmetry', 187, 210–12, 311
Tsitsernakaberd, 75
Turkey, 3, 8, 44, 52, 63, 71, 95, 101, 185, 190, 202, 243, 280n, 284
  and Armenian genocide, 82, 89
  border with Armenia, 203, 231
  control over Kars and Ardahan, 69, 71
  diffusion of Armenian–Azerbaijani rivalry across, 230–1
  domestic politics and the Caucasus, 232
  economic relations with Azerbaijan, 188, 216, 231
  in Armenian narratives *see* Armenians: affective dispositions towards Turks
  nation-building in 1920–30s, 56–7
  pipeline infrastructure involving, 188–9, 215n, 216
  policy towards South Caucasus, 231–2
  trade with Armenia, 233
  treaties with Soviet Union, 24
  World War I era, 22–3, 53
Turkmanchay (treaty), 20, 21, 67
Turkmens, 87, 127
Turks, 57
  in relation to Azerbaijani Turks, 44, 52
Turquoise Council of Americans and Eurasians, 221

Ukraine, 2, 5, 7, 19, 190, 221–2, 236, 238, 239, 241, 243, 263, 296
UNHCR *see* United Nations High Commissioner for Refugees
Union of Armenians of Russia, 224
Union of Azerbaijani Organizations in Russia, 228
United Kingdom, 216, 220
United Nations High Commissioner for Refugees, 123
United Nations Security Council, 7, 282, 296, 300
  resolutions on Armenian–Azerbaijani conflict, 3, 282
United States, 7, 71, 202, 215, 215n, 222, 232, 233, 234, 277, 280n
  aid to Armenia and Azerbaijan, 217–18
  Section 907 effects, 217, 235
Urartu, 74
Urmia, 50
USAID, 218, 234
uti possidetis juris, 95, 112, 263

Van, 66
Vardenis, 100, 136, 273
Venice Commission, 178
Vezirov, Abdurahman, 36, 104, 168–9, 168n
victimhood, 42–3
Volsky, Arkady, 30

'war on terror', 221, 300, 309
Warlick, James, 295
Washington, 1, 8, 253, 263, 276
World Bank, 157
World War I, 20, 21
World War II, 56, 58–9, 73, 94, 130, 138

Yelizavetpol' (*guberniya* in Russian Empire), 53, 68, 127
Yelq, 166
Yeltsin, Boris, 62, 279
Yeni Fikir, 179
Yerazi ('Yerevan Azerbaijanis'), 145, 172
yerbazlik, 171
Yerevan, 21, 22, 25, 28, 54, 70, 73, 74, 75, 84, 137, 165, 167, 180, 211, 229, 253, 258, 264, 265, 267, 291
  'Azerbaijani palimpsest' beneath, 115, 118
  guberniya in the Russian Empire, 53, 67–8, 127
  Republic, 69
Yerkir, 65, 66, 71
Yerkrapah, 164, 167, 176

399

Yugoslavia, 19, 32, 97, 283
  International Criminal Tribunal for the former, 17
Yunus, Leyla, 179–80
Yunusov, Arif, 122, 179–80

Zangelan, 38, 98, 99, 146, 283
Zangezur, 22, 25, 43, 53, 55, 71, 82, 117
Zheleznovodsk Communiqué, 279
Zulfuqarov, Tofik, 289

EU representative:
Easy Access System Europe
Mustamäe tee 50, 10621 Tallinn, Estonia
Gpsr.requests@easproject.com

www.ingramcontent.com/pod-product-compliance
Lightning Source LLC
Chambersburg PA
CBHW052054300426
44117CB00013B/2123